NINETEEN STARS

A Study in Military Character and Leadership

Edgar F. Puryear, Jr.

D1468413

PRESIDIO

Copyright © 1971 by Edgar F. Puryear, Jr.

First edition, first printing. Published 1971
by Green Publishers, Orange, Virginia.

First Presidio edition printed 1981,
this edition printed 1992.

Published by Presidio Press
505 B San Marin Dr., Suite 300
Novato, CA 94945-1340

Library of Congress Cataloging in Publication Data

Puryear, Edgar F., 1930-
    Nineteen stars.

    Includes bibliographical references and index.
    1. Leadership. 2. United States. Army—Biography.
3. Generals—United States—Biography. I. Title.
UB210.P8   1982   355.3'3041'0922 [B]   81-14365
ISBN 0-89141-148-8 (pbk.)

Printed in the United States of America

To

Brigadier General Robert F. McDermott, USAF Retired

whose vision and confidence

made this work possible

Books by EDGAR F. PURYEAR, Jr.
From Presidio Press

NINETEEN STARS
STARS IN FLIGHT
GEORGE S. BROWN

FOREWORD

More than ten years ago, I was visited by a persuasive Air Force captain, an able young instructor at the Air Force Academy, Edgar F. Puryear, Jr., who asked my assistance in interviewing a number of Army officers concerning leadership qualities exhibited by certain key leaders of the Second World War. His evident enthusiasm gained my interest and support and I agreed to do what I could do to advance his enterprise.

Puryear, a Ph.D. in political science from Princeton and an active flyer, who had developed several lectures on leadership for cadets at the Air Academy, desired to expand his studies into a book which might be used for teaching future military leaders. In attempting to capture the elusive qualities that make some men succeed in persuading officers and men to do even more than they believe they can perform, he proposed to choose four great leaders in the Second World War and to ask hundreds of their former associates what had made these men excel in a field where many of their fellows failed to make their mark.

Before talking to me, Puryear had decided on four officers who had exercised leadership in different ways. He asked me not only for general suggestions on how to proceed in regard to the three Generals of the Army George C. Marshall, Douglas MacArthur, and Dwight D. Eisenhower, and General George S. Patton, Jr., but also for specific information on Generals Marshall and Eisenhower many of whose friends and associates I had interviewed since 1946. At his request, I supplied names and addresses of some 204 officers and civilians who should be able to assess the leadership qualities of General Marshall.

In the years that have passed since that first visit, I have watched this project progress. I have talked with the author on numerous occasions before he conducted his interviews and have later benefitted enormously from material which he was good enough to share with me. In several cases, he arranged for individuals with whom he talked to turn over to the Marshall Library documents and photographs which they had collected. I watched with great interest the development of his lectures and shared with him the delight he felt in the enthusiastic responses he received from the cadets who heard him and from other audiences to whom he spoke.

In later years, Captain Puryear left the Air Force and turned to the study and practice of law. However, he has kept his interest in the training of officers and has continued his connection with military training by conducting a class at the Judge Advocate General School at Charlottesville and as a consultant to the Reserve Officer Training Corps section at the Pentagon. In his years of legal study and practice, he has kept his interest in the study of leadership and has continued to hold that an examination of the qualities which made Marshall, MacArthur, Eisenhower, and Patton succeed as commanders would greatly inspire students and cadets who plan to become officers either in the Reserve Corps or the Regular services. Acting on that conviction, he has found time in an extremely busy schedule to put his lectures into book form and to offer it as a study aid for future officers.

The author has been aware that a broader study of commanders might have placed greater focus on some qualities which may have been played down in the careers of the four men he has studied. However, he believed that the emphasizing of the work of four men who are particularly well known to civilians and members of the military service would serve better the aim that he had in mind.

Born out of a series of lectures, the chapters of the volume have the virtues and the defects of such exercises in teaching— there is a tendency to popularize, to repeat, to categorize, and to oversimplify. Sometimes there is a tendency to search overzealously for similarities in leaders or to assume that all four men measured up to most of the tests set for successful leaders. At the same time, this approach is particularly useful for students unfamiliar with the overall background of the four men in question and unaware of the way in which their common training and experiences as officers counted heavily in their careers despite their differences in temperament and style. Thus, the flamboyant Patton, the imperious MacArthur, the genial Eisenhower, and the austere Marshall are alike in their devotion to duty and their reactions to reversals.

More detailed study by later biographers of the papers of the officers in question will undoubtedly change specific judgments on some of the generals. However, this study will bring to the student the testimony of hundreds of old friends, classmates, subordinates, and superiors of the four great World War II leaders; the author's extensive interviews and correspondence has revealed many anecdotes and experiences which are published here for the first time.

The student who has faced difficulties in some of his studies can draw consolation from the realization that three of the four had some setbacks in their courses at the undergraduate level. The important thing was that all of them did well when they came to their professional training. Despite initial low grades, all of them saw their grade curves move upward as their work continued. Marshall, toward the bottom of his class in his first year; Eisenhower, well down the list in his years at West Point; Patton, forced to take a fifth year to graduate—all stood at the top or near the top of their classes at the service schools.

Many young officers, facing years of slow promotions and tours of duty in unpleasant assignments, can find some assurances about their futures in comparing their lots with that of all four officers who met many disappointments and frustrations before they reached high command. They may even conclude that the testing which comes of adjustment to difficulties may provide the inner strength for their roles in time of crisis. The author has dug deeply into these experiences in the lives of his four subjects.

Some readers may disagree with the precise qualities of a great commander listed by the author. Some will doubt that all four men measure up to half or more of the tests. But they will agree that all four are great commanders and that certain basic qualities—such as inner strength, call it integrity or character or what you will, a knowledge of one's craft, an ability to inspire confidence in one's men, the power to bring out the best in those who follow a commander—are common to all. The many anecdotes depicting these qualities and the testimony of those who served under them provide a valuable source book for future officers.

The chapters preserve much of the spirit and enthusiasm which undoubtedly marked the lectures when they were given. Although the written word seldom can catch all the fire that a good teacher can impart to an interested group of students, these chapters should impress young officers or prospective officers with the woes and rewards associated with the military career. The chapters will provide no special formula by which one can attain four or five star rank or gifted leadership but will help them understand a little better than they have before something of what is required to make men follow a leader into conflict. He will see what General Marshall was talking about when he told the House Military Affairs Committee in 1940:

> You have to lead men in war by bringing them along to endure and display qualities of fortitude that are beyond the average man's thought of what he should be expected to do. You have to inspire them when they are hungry and exhausted and desperately uncomfortable and in great danger; and only a man of positive characteristics of leadership, with the physical stamina that goes with it, can function under those conditions.

And he will realize what Marshall was trying to tell the first graduating class of the Officer Candidate School at Fort Benning in 1941:

> Remember this: the truly great leader overcomes all difficulties, and campaigns and battles are nothing but a long series of difficulties to be overcome. The lack of equipment, the lack of food, the lack of this or that are only excuses; the real leader displays his qualities in his triumph over adversity, however great it may be.

FORREST C. POGUE
Director, George C. Marshall Foundation

INTRODUCTION

World War II offered the greatest challenge for American military leadership in the history of the United States. Upon the quality of this leadership rested the freedom of the United States and the entire world. Winston Churchill, after the war was over, spoke informally in a Pentagon office in 1946 to a group of thirty of the most outstanding U.S. Army and Army Air Corps leaders of World War II. With the chair tilted back, his feet propped up on a desk, and smoking a big, black cigar, he told this group that he knew the United States had the materiel with which to swing the fate of the war to the side of the Allies, but that he was truly amazed that we produced such superior military leadership.

Indeed, the United States had a wealth of military leaders, and one of the purposes of this volume is to determine *how* these leaders were produced. The comment is often made that "leaders are born, not made." The statement, if taken literally, would mean that at birth one's ability to be a leader is already decided—that environment has no role in the development of an individual. If the quotation is interpreted less strictly, it might mean that a person is born with certain qualities that offer the potential, if developed through environment, for successful leadership. Whether interpreted strictly or liberally, the quotation that leaders are born, not made, implies that one must be born with certain qualities to be a leader.

One of the members of this group to whom Churchill spoke was General of the Army Dwight D. Eisenhower, commander of the largest armada of military forces in the history of warfare. General Eisenhower, during a discussion of leadership with the author, was asked to comment on the statement, leaders are born, not made. "I think," he said, "that there is something to the expression 'born to command' or 'born to lead'. But there are many people who have the potential for leadership, just as there are probably many people born with the potential to be great artists that never have the opportunity or the training for the full development of their talents. I think leadership is a product of native ability plus environment. By environment, I mean training and the opportunity to exercise leadership."

Also in this group of thirty officers was General Eisenhower's American Army field commander, General of the Army Omar N. Bradley. His answer to the born leader question was, "I would say some are born. A person can be born with certain qualities of leadership: good physique, good mental capacity, curiosity, the desire to know. When you go to pick out the best pup in a litter of bird dogs, you pick out the pup even though he is only six weeks old. He is curious, going around looking into things, and that kind of dog usually turns out to be the best dog.

"But there are qualities one can improve on," he continued. "A thorough knowledge of your profession is the first requirement of leadership and that certainly has to be acquired. Observing others is important—trying to determine what makes them stand out. That's why I think we can learn a lot by studying past leaders. Studying Lee, other Civil War leaders, Jackson, Lincoln. Trying to see what made them great."

The question was put somewhat differently to General Anthony C. McAuliffe: "Do you think the ability to handle masses of men is something a young man can train himself to do?" McAuliffe, author of the most famous one word speech of World War II ("Nuts," in reply to a German order to surrender when his men were surrounded at Bastogne), said, "I think that's a God given gift you are born with. People like General MacArthur, General Patton, Field Marshal Montgomery were actors in addition to being leaders. They had a sort of flair that had a great effect on masses of men." The decisiveness of leadership was a quality a man could develop, in his opinion, but "I think," he added, "you can improve it only to an extent; but you have to be born with a large measure of it." Even General McAuliffe gave a qualification which supports the "made" leader when he stated that "After character, knowledge is most important. Knowledge builds confidence and decisiveness. When you know your business thoroughly, I think you are encouraged to be bold and decisive in action. That has been typical of General MacArthur and General Patton. I think their broad knowledge of the military profession contributed greatly to their boldness in decision and their success as leaders."

One of the strongest supporters of the born leader thesis was General J. Lawton Collins, Commander of the VII Corps in the Army in World War II, and Chief of Staff of the U.S. Army from 1949-1953, who believes that "only a limited number of people combine the necessary qualities of character, integrity, intelligence and a willingness to work, which leads to a knowledge of their profession, to become successful leaders. These are God-given talents we inherit from our forebears." Still, he does not believe one is limited at birth for he added, "There are, however, techniques of leadership that anybody can learn if given a modicum of intelligence and a willingness to work."

Another very successful Corps Commander of World War II, General Wade H. Haislip, reflected that "One thing that disturbed me when I started out in this business (the military profession) was the old theory that leaders are born, not made. When I started studying, I tried to break down that theory; and I developed what I consider the basic elements with which anybody can be successful if they stuck to it."

General Eisenhower was reported to have said of his World War II Air Commander, General Carl "Tooey" Spaatz, that "He was the only general I had who never made a mistake." General Spaatz was also asked about the "why" of successful leadership. "I think leaders just happen to grow up," he said. "I think you must be born with certain characteristics, but it's more a case of what takes place after you are born that decides whether or not you are going to be a leader."

General Mark W. Clark, Commander of the Fifth Army in Italy in World War II, concluded, "I would say that most leaders are made. A fellow that comes from a long line of ancestors with determination and courage has no doubt inherited some leadership qualities. I have seen many times in combat where somebody who is small and meek was given the opportunity and had leadership you never before realized he had, and he becomes a Medal of Honor winner. There are some qualities you inherit that make you a good leader; but many who have not these qualities develop them, or just seem to come up with them when opportunity knocks."

General Lucian K. Truscott, respectively a division, corps and an army commander in World War II, said, "I suppose men are born with traits that can be cultivated in the direction of leadership. But there is also no doubt that leadership can be cultivated. The idea of any man being born an army commander or being born to be a theatre commander, such as General Eisenhower, just isn't so. The characteristics of leadership, any leadership, necessarily has to have certain decisiveness, a certain confidence. In most cases you will find that decisiveness and confidence come from knowledge based on studies and training. The fundamental thing is your basic knowledge, the development of your mind, and your ability to apply this knowledge as you go along your military career." General William H. Simpson, who led the Ninth Army in World War II, believes, "Everyone is not a born leader. Leadership can be learned. I wish somebody had told me that when I was young. The successful handling of men requires the application of certain qualities of leadership. There are few natural leaders, very few."

General Albert C. Wedemeyer, senior American commander in China during the latter part of World War II, replied to the comment leaders are born, not made, "No, I don't agree with that. I think there are some men who have a better chance of developing into leaders. This is primarily because of their interest in the activities that lead to leadership. I think most genius is the result of hard work; and any young man, if he has guts and stick-to-itiveness, can make good in life, if given an average body and mind. It's up to the individual; but there must be a spark, a continuing curiosity."

The comments of the above officers, all of whom achieved great distinction as successful wartime commanders, offer a sample of the thinking of American military leaders. The strongest supporters of the born leader thesis believe there are certain qualities you must be born with, but that even these character-istics must be developed. There are others who have concluded that anyone can be a leader if they want to work at it. But *none* of them concluded that anyone is born a leader.

If leaders are made, how are they made? NINETEEN STARS is a comparative study of the leadership of four of the most out-standing American generals of World War II—of how they were made and how they led. The author has selected for this com-parative study: General of the Army George C. Marshall, Chief of Staff, United States Army, from 1939 to 1945; General of the Army Douglas MacArthur, Commander in Chief in the Far East from 1939 to 1945; General of the Army Dwight D. Eisenhower, Supreme Commander of Allied Forces for the in-vasions of North Africa, Sicily and of Europe, the greatest inva-sion in the history of warfare; and General George S. Patton, Jr., Commander of the I and II U.S. Army Corps in North Africa, of the U.S. Seventh Army in Sicily and the U.S. Third Army in Europe. The reasons for the selection of these four personalities is too obvious to deserve more than a cursory men-tion—Generals Marshall, MacArthur and Eisenhower held the three most responsible military positions of World War II; General Patton was the best known combat general of the war. The title of the manuscript is the total number of stars of these four military leaders.

The study of great captains and the classical writers on war will always be necessary in the development of military leaders for wars will always be won by men. Weapons may change, but not human nature. The United States will always need trained military leaders for "Only the dead," said Plato, "have seen the end of war." Is war the normal condition of mankind? History will prove or disprove this thesis; but until wars are no more, we need the study of military leadership. We have been fortunate in past wars. We have had time to prepare, but no longer does warfare permit time. A great nation, such as ours, which is responsible for the world's freedom, must be prepared for instant war. No longer can we depend upon nations such as Great Britain and France to hold off the enemy while we spend several years deciding whether we shall enter the conflict, having the luxury of leisurely preparation for war. In the future, we will be hit first.

During the course of the research on this book, the author received comments to the effect that the subject of his inquiry was not leadership but generalship, or that a particular personality was not a leader but was a staff officer. Others commented that the topic being researched was not leadership but was command. Still others said it was administration or management. There is no need to argue semantics. This book is a discussion of four generals, why they became top generals and how they ran the show after achieving their high positions of military responsibility in time of war. No one can deny that they held top positions of responsibility. The word used here to encompass how they ran the show will be leadership.

In discussions of leadership it is often maintained that there is no pattern to successful leadership. The author believes there is a pattern—that never before has there been a scholarly study in depth of a few of the most outstanding generals during a war. In the research for the comparative study, the author has studied the military memoirs and biographies of the prominent World War II personalities; conducted personal interviews with World War II leading figures such as General of the Army Dwight D. Eisenhower, Supreme Commander of Allied Forces in Europe during World War II; General of the Army Omar N. Bradley, Commander of the 12th Army Group consisting of four American armies; Generals Mark W. Clark, Commander of the Fifth Army and Fifteenth Army Group in Italy; Courtney Hodges, First Army Commander; William H. Simpson, Ninth Army Commander; Lucian K. Truscott, Commander, 3rd Division, VI Corps and Third Army; Walter Krueger, Sixth Army Commander of the Southwest Pacific; Jacob L. Devers, Sixth Army Group Commander in France; John E. Hull, War Plans Division, General Staff (1942-1944); Charles L. Bolte, 34th Infantry Division Commander; Joseph T. McNarney, Deputy Chief of Staff to General Marshall during World War II and Deputy Supreme Allied Commander; Carl "Tooey" Spaatz, Air

Introduction

Chief to General Eisenhower in Europe during World War II and first Chief of Staff for separate Air Force (1947-1948); Albert Weydemeyer, senior American Commander in China during the latter part of World War II; Thomas T. Handy, War Plans Division, Deputy Chief of Staff (1944); Wade "Ham" Haislip, XV Corps Commander of Third Army; Anthony "Nuts" McAuliffe, 101st Airborne Division; Nathan F. Twining, Chief of Staff, USAF (1953-1957); Thomas D. White, Chief of Staff, USAF (1957-1961); J. Lawton Collins, VII Corps of First Army and Chief of Staff, U.S. Army (1949-1953); and over one hundred other key World War II American officers ranging in rank from brigadier general through general and comprising the "who's who" of World War II. The documents consulted included the diary of Henry L. Stimson, Secretary of War (1939-1945), other personal diaries, the hundreds of military memoirs and biographies, the personal correspondence of some of the key figures, speeches, war reports, and authors, such as Forrest Pogue, biographer of George C. Marshall. The author has also had significant correspondence on leadership with over three thousand officers who served as subordinates, contemporaries and senior officers of the four personalities being compared. In all of the interviews and in the letters of correspondence, the author asked these men why the officers they served under were successful leaders and why were they themselves successful as military leaders.

In comparing the leadership of these officers, it became clear that there are certain qualities that were essential elements of their success. The author does not contend that a study of these qualities will guarantee to the reader the same greatness achieved by these four generals; however, it will certainly, at a minimum, make the average man better. It is a great mistake to make no conscious effort at leadership training. It should not be the by-product of other forms of training. Services of all nations publish material listing rules of thumb on how to lead men, but listing rules is not enough. The qualities for successful leadership need to be given life and meaning.

The literature on military leadership is in agreement that there are some qualities absolutely necessary for successful leadership, such as professional knowledge, decision, equity, humanity, and courage. But what is decision? How do you become a good decision maker? Are these born qualities of leadership; or can these qualities be developed? How does an officer lead with equity? Does courage mean one is never afraid? Is courage limited to the battlefield?

The qualities of leadership need to be given meaning—to be made alive through the personalities of well-known and proven leaders. If this were not true, it should be enough to list all the necessary qualities and expect anyone reading them to become a great leader. The qualities necessary for success require more than just listing. What is necessary is a description of leadership and the qualities for success. That is the objective of NINETEEN STARS; and as such, it does not claim to have *the answer* to success as a military leader, but it does have *an answer*.

ACKNOWLEDGEMENTS

The inspiration for this book came from a desire to find out how one gets to the top of the military profession, how one leads on the way up, and the leadership role after achieving high positions of great responsibility.

I have been aided greatly by others and I want to make acknowledgement here of that assistance.

Dr. Forrest C. Pogue, author of the definitive biography of General of the Army George C. Marshall, was truly vital to this manuscript in his guidance and inspiration along the lonely path of scholarship.

The editorial assistance of Ruth Davis Kaufman was invaluable for her technical assistance and the confidence she inspired in the writing. The Reverend Kenneth J. Sharp was also helpful with his editorial advice. During the process of publishing the manuscript Mayo L. Coiner made many sound suggestions for improving the book for which I am most appreciative.

Myrna Whitmore Richards was marvelous for her patience in transcribing the tapes of the interviews and the typing of the first draft of the book.

I want to especially express my gratitude to Colonel Philip J. Erdle of the United States Air Force Academy for the opportunity of sharing ideas, for his friendship, and for his contagious enthusiasm and belief in this endeavor. Others at the Air Force Academy who gave assistance were Lieutenant Colonel James E. Banks, Colonel Bernard W. Marschner, Major Paul L. Briand, Jr., Dr. Mancur L. Olson, and Lieutenant Colonel Roy E. Feaga.

I owe much to the cadets and young officers who, after hearing the lectures which were the nucleus of this work, made comments and offered ideas which helped to mature and define the concepts that unfolded in this leadership study.

Ambassador John S. D. Eisenhower was wonderful in assisting me with arranging an interview with his father, Dwight D.

Eisenhower, as was Colonel Charles W. Sampson, an interview that meant a great deal to the success of this project.

The interview with General of the Army Omar N. Bradley was most meaningful because of his personal relationship during World War II with the personalities in this comparative study.

General Robert W. Porter, Jr., USA Retired, who after 44 years in the U.S. Army is still serving his country in retirement, was instrumental in the completion of the manuscript through his encouragement and insistence that the collective ideas and years of experience of so many dedicated American military leaders be imparted to the new generation of young officers.

The vision of Colonel John Jay Douglass, USA, Commandant of the Judge Advocate General School, Charlottesville, Virginia, was important to this work. Other Staff members of the JAG School were also helpful: Colonel Albert S. Rakas, Major Malcolm J. Howard, Major James R. Coker, and Captain Thomas E. Workman.

In the process of researching this book, I have been much aided by others too numerous to mention, particularly the hundreds of officers I interviewed and corresponded with, who gave of their time and wisdom gained through years of experience.

For her infinite patience during the extensive traveling and the long hours of researching and writing of the manuscript, I want to express a special gratitude to my wife, Agnes, and to my sons, Beverly Spotswood Parrish (Chug), Edgar F. (Chip), Scott Braxton (Colt), and Alfred Anderson (Cotton).

E.F.P., Jr.

TABLE OF CONTENTS

Foreword   v
Introduction   ix
Acknowledgements   xvii

I. THE EARLY YEARS—Leadership as Cadets   1

George S. Patton, Jr.   1
Dwight D. Eisenhower   10
Douglas MacArthur   21
George C. Marshall   35
Cadet Careers Compared   39

II. ALTRUISM—PATIENCE—DEDICATION—The Leadership of
General of the Army George C. Marshall   43

World War I   44
China   48
Fort Benning: 1927-1932   53
Fort Screven   58
Chicago: 1933-1936   59
Vancouver, Washington   66
Washington, D. C.   68

III. DUTY—HONOR—COUNTRY—The Leadership of
General of the Army Douglas MacArthur   103

General Arthur MacArthur   104
Early Career   107
World War I   109
Chief of Staff   112
The Philippine Army   123
World War II   124
Showmanship   141
MacArthur and the Press   143
Oratory   144
Relationship with Subordinates   147

IV. SOLDIER—STATESMAN—DIPLOMAT—The Leadership of
    General of the Army Dwight D. Eisenhower   153

    Pre-World War II Career   153
    Ike as an Allied Leader   170
    General Eisenhower and His Commanders   179
    The Political Leadership of the Supreme Commander   198
    Command Responsibility   210

V. BLOOD AND GUTS—The Leadership of
   George S. Patton, Jr.   233

    Early Career   234
    Patton's World War II Leadership   243
    Relations with Subordinates   269
    Forward, action at any cost   274

VI. THE MILITARY CHARACTER   289

    Humility   297
    Religion   308
    Politics   320
    Attitude Toward War   325
    Selflessness   336
    The Role of Character   345

VII. DECISION AND COURAGE   351

    The Role of Decision   351
    The Role of Courage   367

VIII. PREPARATION AND LUCK   377
    The Role of Preparation   377
    The Role of Luck   388

IX. THE PATTERN   393
    Command   393
    The Pattern of Successful Military Leadership   395
Footnotes   403
Index   429

THE EARLY YEARS

Leadership as Cadets

George S. Patton, Jr.

"When the West Shore local from Weehawken pulled up at the dingy old railroad station at West Point one warm day in June, 1904, among the motley group of candidates to detrain was a tall, well-built lad with blond hair and a determined look in his gray eyes."[1] Thus did one of his classmates describe the arrival of Cadet George S. Patton, Jr.

The arrival of Patton at West Point was the fulfillment of his childhood ambition. In his early youth he played with toy soldiers as many children do; but his fascination for soldiering did not fade away as it does for most. There was a spinster aunt in the Patton home who devoted many hours reading to "Georgie". Her selection of books included the finest adventure stories ever written: the works of Sir Walter Scott—*Rob Roy*, the *Legend of Montrose, Kenilworth, The Pirate, The Talisman, The Tales of Crusaders*, and the immortal *Ivanhoe*; the books and poems of Rudyard Kipling—*Soldiers Three, Captains Courageous, Kim, The Seven Seas, The Jungle Book; The Three Musketeers, The Count of Monte Cristo*, and other books by Alexandre Dumas; the stories of early American pioneer days by James Fenimore Cooper—*The Spy, The Last of the Mohicans, The Prairie, The Pathfinder*, and *Deerslayer*. In the extensive library of his boyhood home were other books with which he became very familiar: *The Arabian Nights, The Corsican*, Ferror's *Greatness and Decline of Rome, Robinson Crusoe*,

1

Sayers' *The Man Born to be King*, *Westward Ho,* and *King Arthur and the Knights of the Round Table*. Exposure to these classics developed a spirit of imagination and chivalry in young Patton that was part of his personality throughout his adult life.

Whenever his aunt was interrupted as she read to George and his sister, Nita, he became impatient. Georgie, snuggled up close to his beloved aunt, would look up into her eyes and say, "Read; damnit, Auntie, read." His Aunt Annie would act shocked and say to the boy she loved so much, "Now Georgie, you shouldn't say that." Such language was learned naturally by the young boy, raised on an 1800-acre ranch near San Gabriel, California, that his mother had inherited from her father. In the rugged atmosphere of ranch life, profanity was part of the cowboy's language. Ranch life also served as an outlet for expressing his imagination. From Scott's *Lady of the Lake* he named his first boat "Elaine". He always called his favorite horse "Galahad" and had a dog named "Lancelot". He scouted enemy soldiers from a tall palm tree overlooking the ranch, fought duels with homemade, child-size rapiers and rode down enemy knights on his own stallion. He had ample opportunity to learn how to shoot, and he was an expert rifleman and pistol shot as a soldier.

In addition to his exposure to the finest adventure classics and an outdoor life of ranching, he had a family with a rich civilian-military heritage. His great-grandfather was Hugh Mercer, a brigadier general in the Continental Army during the American Revolution, who at the time of his death from a British bullet in the battle of Trenton had established an outstanding military record. His grandfather, a graduate of Virginia Military Institute, was a colonel in the Confederate Army during the Civil War. The saddle his grandfather used in battle was always in the Patton home, bearing a plaque inscribed:

Colonel George S. Patton, C.S.A. on which he was killed at the second battle of Winchester—brought through the union line together with his horse and sabre by his faithful orderly.

Colonel Patton had organized and trained a group (in Charleston) called "The Kanawha Rifles." He fought with his men under historic Confederate leaders such as Jackson, Floyd, and Early in many Virginia campaigns until he was killed in the battle of Winchester.

Patton's mother was described by a lifelong friend as "completely selfless—a saint on earth." His father, George S. Patton, Sr., like his father before him, was a graduate of V.M.I. There were many other close relatives who served in the military forces during times of crises. During his childhood, George Junior heard many first hand accounts of war from these relatives. He was always an eager listener to stories involving soldiering.

The natural ambition of any American soldier aspirant was to go to West Point. George Patton was no exception. While he waited for an appointment to that historic institution he followed the tradition of his grandfather and father by enrolling as a "Rat" [first year] at V.M.I. In February of his first year at V.M.I. he returned to compete for and win an appointment to West Point as a member of the Class of 1908. George Goethals of the Class of 1908 commented:

In our plebe year I stood next to George Patton in ranks till he was turned back and lived across the hall from him in the barracks. He was very neat in appearance and so prided himself. In those days, we would go to drill at 3:30 P.M. followed by a dress parade. On returning to the barracks area the command "at ease" would be given while the orders were read out. This took an average of fifteen minutes. During this time, the upper classmen would leave the plebes strictly alone as regarded bracing: but George would remain strictly at attention, bracing as hard as he could. He was 'Boning chevrons'.

Drill regulations were recited once a week. Saturdays. He would begin to bone the next lesson Sunday afternoons, and by the time Saturday came around again he would have the lesson "specked blind". I would tell him, "See here, George, your drill regs count only 15 points on graduation whereas plebe math, where you are already shaky, count 200. Put 80% of your drill reg time on math, you'll pass the drill regs easily anyhow, and will be almost sure to conquer math too if you do." But he would have nothing divert him from his time on drill regs.[2]

As it turned out he finished second in the class in drill regs and math was the subject on which he was turned back. Patton was preoccupied with the study of drill regs because performance in this area was related to one's standing as a soldier and, therefore, had meaning in the selection of cadets for higher rank.

A greater determination to be a soldier could not be displayed than was shown by Patton; for after a year as a "Rat" at V.M.I., and despite flunking his first plebe year, he decided to repeat plebe year at West Point. It was indeed unique for a man to go through the difficult first year at a military school three times, but Patton did not let this initial failure deter him. After repeating his first year at West Point, he went on to obtain the rank of first cadet corporal in his third class year [sophomore year] and sergeant major as a second classman [junior year]. Each of these ranks was the highest a cadet could obtain during those respective years and signified that he was considered by the Tactical Department at West Point to be the best soldier in his class. He was not, however, spending all of his study time on drill regulations. In 1904 Cadet Classmate Fletcher suggested to Patton that "if he were not such an avid reader of military history, strategy and tactics, he would have more time to study the subjects on which his class standing depended."[3]

Patton was very close to George Goethals. They would often confide in each other and Goethals was thus able to gain insight into Patton's ambition and character. In a letter he related:

Saturday mornings we would have recitations in drill regulations. George and I went to an early section and would have the hour before dinner to ourselves. I would often go over to his room and we would clean rifles together to get ready for inspection and review right after dinner. He confided to me a lot about things during these sessions, both official and personal. He said he wanted to make three goals at the Academy: Stand number one in drill regulations; become Cadet Adjutant his first class

year; and get his "A" [his athletic letter] through breaking
an Academy record in track.[4]

Another classmate revealed that Patton also aspired to make
his letter in football. He failed in this; but his determination and
guts were clearly illustrated by the fact that though he broke his
arm two successive years and dislocated his shoulder in another
in the attempt, he stuck with the team the full four years. He
did graduate number one in drill regulations, broke several
Academy track records, and was cadet adjutant in his first class
year. Since the top cadet rank was first captain, one might
wonder why someone as ambitious as Patton did not aspire to
the highest rank. Apparently it was a result of his devotion to
his father. One of his classmates wrote that "Patton told me his
father had been cadet adjutant at VMI and he was going to be
adjutant at West Point. He was."[5] It might also have been
because of the nature of the job of cadet adjutant. The
adjutant, not the first captain, was the "star" of the parade and
generally all eyes were centered upon him. It was the adjutant
who barked out the orders of the day and relayed in a loud
voice the quiet commands of the first captain to the corps. He
would make many facing movements and strut around like a
proud rooster. Patton, who was tall, erect, and soldierly, was by
all accounts a magnificent specimen of an adjutant.

There is another aspect of George Patton's decision to stay at
West Point and repeat his first year that might cause wonder.
During his first plebe year, one of his classmates said that
Patton "told me he had just inherited a million dollars. I think
that most of the plebes under similar circumstances would have
resigned immediately." [6] But Patton was not the normal plebe.
He obviously possessed a unique and burning desire to be a
soldier, staying in the military profession although he possessed
wealth that would have made a civilian life infinitely attractive.
A fellow Californian who was at West Point with him said
"Never as a cadet or later as an officer did he ever hint in my
presence that his income was larger than that of most other
army men." [7]

His roommate recollected:

> George lived and breathed, ate and slept, yes—I will go
> so far as to say, even loved as a soldier. The profession of
> arms was, in his opinion, the highest calling to which a
> man could devote his life. Nothing could approach it. He
> had money by inheritance and by marriage which ran into
> the millions but I never once heard him express the idea
> that he might like to forsake a military career, with all its
> hardships, for one of ease and affluence even though it
> could have been his at the snap of a finger. How rare it was
> to find one that devoted to the life of a soldier.[8]

Patton's soldierly qualities as a cadet left an indelible
impression upon his classmates. Colonel Robert H. Fletcher, in
a letter dated November 28, 1962, remarked, "I can see him in
my mind's eye now—tall, straight, with his perfectly fitting uniform and accessories immaculate. He looked and was every inch
a soldier."[9] Another said, "His general appearance, actions, remarks and seemingly intense interest in what he was doing, particularly in military matters, attracted attention in his cadet
days."[10] Numerous other classmates bore out Patton's soldierly
qualities with such statements as, "In the Class of 1909 he was
everything he ought to be, and we all recognized that he would
be 'top-hole' if and when the bands began to play";[11] "A blond
Nordic, he was tall, slender, but well proportioned. In appearance and manner he was the beau ideal of the youthful
leader";[12] "I thought that Patton, as a cadet, was outstanding.
He was thoroughly imbued with the military spirit, was enthusiastic, energetic, and a very strong character"[13] "He was a firm
believer in the spit and polish method of leadership";[14] "Patton
impressed me as a man dedicated to the army and to becoming
an important personage";[15] "By general repute the No. 1
'soldier' in his class . . . always military in bearing and
speech . . . He put his heart and soul into everything he undertook . . . he succeeded by diligent application";[16] "His burning
desire to become a great general was paramount. Nothing else

mattered . . . Regardless of what his cadet mates thought he sought to have his superiors recognize his ambition and his efforts in that direction."[17]

Patton took an unusually high interest in his military appearance. Several classmates thought he had his uniforms made by an expensive tailor in New York City. Major General Thomas A. Terry heard Patton say, "I think I shall put some small tucks over my shoulder so my shoulder will completely fill my coat."[18] Cadet William H. Simpson, later to be an Army Commander in World War II, pointed out that cadets in his day kept their trousers pressed by putting them between two boards, placing them under the mattress and then sleeping on them during the night. This was not good enough for Patton. He purchased an iron and pressed his own trousers daily.[19]

As a cadet Patton was friendly with others but maintained some reserve. He was not popular among his fellow cadets for reasons easy to understand. Classmate Robert Sears wrote of Cadet Patton:

> With the exception of his roommate, Philip S. Gage, I doubt if George Patton had any really intimate friends while a cadet at West Point. He was generally recognized as the outstanding soldier in the class and as such was highly respected, but as he was a rigid disciplinarian and lived up to the letter of his military duties, one could hardly expect him to be popular. Cadet Officer of the Day had a much greater responsibility for reporting breaches of military discipline and dereliction of duty than the Officer of the Guard. I well remember one occasion when I was Officer of the Day and George Patton was Officer of the Guard, I turned in 4 skins and George turned in two sheets of skins. You can well imagine that George would never have succeeded in politics.[20]

Because of this strictness in military matters Patton earned the nickname among his classmates of "Quill", meaning a cadet excessively interested in making rank, even at the expense of his fellow cadets. His lack of popularity was not a result of Patton's being overbearing or rough in carrying out his duties but of his insistence upon strict attention to duty. To the less single-minded person he probably seemed somewhat overzealous. Those reported by Patton did not, as a rule, think kind thoughts of him as they walked off hours or spent hours of confinement in their room. Normally, in the system, fellow classmates were easier on each other; Patton did not choose to conform to this "tradition"; so he was not as well liked as he might have been. He obviously did not care whether he was liked or not. He was concerned only with his duty and recognition as a soldier; and as such, he certainly earned the respect of his classmates.

In carrying out his cadet rank responsibilities there was never any doubt that when Patton gave an order his instructions were to be carried out with dispatch and efficiency. He was strictly military and official at all times. As a first classman he never hazed a plebe or any other underclassman. He was concerned only with the military and character development of his juniors and was all business in the performance of this mission.

A study of the "Skin book" [a record of cadet offenses] for each of Patton's years at West Point reveals something very rare; on occasion he turned himself in for the violation of cadet regulations! While some of his classmates concluded that he did this as part of his "showmanship", others thought it indicative of his intense dedication. But, in situations where he shared responsibility, he took care that no action of his reflected adversely on a colleague, or on himself. His roommate reflected:

> Patton was what I would call "an ideal room-mate"—always doing his share of the necessary "chores" in caring for our rooms. [We had a suite of two, a study room and a bedroom off from it. This was because Patton was the Adjutant of the Corps of Cadets.] Every other week one of us was "room orderly" and if one was careless about anything where the room was concerned, the room orderly was the one to get "skinned." I cannot recall one instance where I got demerits for anything improper that George had done or failed to do when I was room orderly. This,

by way of showing he was meticulous, always, about his duty and responsibility even in those youthful days.[21]

Patton was always on the go. He did not enjoy many of the courses at West Point and, therefore, did not study them any more than necessary. He concentrated on the courses and the outside reading which had the most relevance, in his opinion, to becoming a great soldier. However, he did work as hard at athletics as at being a soldier. One classmate commented:

> I think that his outstanding characteristic during his cadet days was to be first in everything he undertook, whether it was skill in sports such as tennis, football, or track, or complete success in things military. He despised and was intolerant of weakness or inefficiency. He "boned" perfection in everything—even in his strength which he maintained at a very high level by calisthenics, by working in the gym, by hours of roadwork, by football, by horseback riding, long walks, swimming, etc.—all in addition to the strenuous athletic and other programs at the Academy.[22]

Patton concentrated on any sport that would further his military proficiency (particularly fencing and horsemanship) and keep his body strong and in tip-top shape. In athletics and in all of his other endeavors at West Point, "George was a poor loser. He couldn't stand to be defeated in anything he earnestly attempted. His 'will to win' was paramount in his nature no matter what it cost."[23] One cadet who opposed Patton in a broadsword match wryly reflected upon an experience which illustrated his drive and will to win even against an ill-matched competitor; "My most vivid recollection of him as a cadet was at one of the classes in broadsword, when I, a frail little mouse, was unfortunate enough to be opposite him. I was sore for a week."[24] Swords and horses were still contemporary weapons in Patton's cadet days and he strove for perfection in their use as in every aspect of his profession. He was determined to stay in top physical condition since physical endurance was vital to effective command leadership.

When Patton was turned back from the Class of 1908 to 1909, one member of his new class was told by a member of 1908 that it was Patton's ambition to become a great general. The new classmate's reaction was that becoming a general "received no consideration by many of us, especially those in the bottom of the class . . . Our ambition was to get passing marks at each recitation to avoid being 'turned out' for the next examination and remain at the Academy."[25] However Patton, even though he was having academic difficulty, looked ahead to what he saw as the inevitability of high command.

Cadet Patton was a doer and "was frequently noticed favorably by those looking for someone to take charge of an activity."[26] He sought responsibility and was a person to whom one could assign a task and consider it done. There was no need to check on him. It is clear that Patton decided early in his life that he wanted to be a soldier. Nothing deterred him from that goal. He was a cadet who set his sights high and followed through from the beginning to the end.

Dwight D. Eisenhower

Probably no sharper contrast to the Patton image could be drawn than that seen in the early background and motivation of Dwight D. Eisenhower. Eisenhower grew up with no knowledge of or interest in West Point or even in a military career. He became interested in going to a service academy through a close friend named "Swede" Hazlett, who had a consuming ambition to attend the Naval Academy. Hazlett spent many hours discussing his goal and gave much of his time to studying for a competitive appointment. He found in his friend, Ike, a patient listener.

After graduating from high school Eisenhower could not afford to go immediately to college so he began working to save for his education. The outlook for completing his education under such circumstances made the idea of the free education and career offered by the service academies increasingly attractive. Spurred on by his friend he decided to compete for the Naval Academy. He finished first in the state in the competitive exam but found that at nineteen he was too old for entrance into Annapolis. West Point had a higher entering age, and when his Senator offered him the chance to go to West Point he accepted.

In contrast to Cadet Patton, Eisenhower failed to take the military side of his West Point career very seriously. One of the yardsticks for evaluating military performance as a cadet was the rank a man obtained. Cadet Eisenhower made cadet rank on several occasions, but had difficulty keeping it. As a yearling [sophomore year] he made the rank of corporal but was "busted" for a prank and walked the area for one month. Apparently he retained some confidence on the part of the Tactical Department, which evaluated and had responsibility for rank, for he later became a cadet sergeant. He rebounded from his demotion from corporal to an appointment as his company's supply sergeant. The promotion was announced at the end of his third class year and was to become effective after summer leave. But the honor was short-lived; he was again busted to private, this time for dancing. While attending a cadet dance the night before his two months' furlough, the girl Eisenhower was dancing with asked him to do the turkey trot and he obliged. In those days, unfortunately, regulations prescribed only two-steps and waltzes, and there was a "tac" officer present who observed this violation. Eisenhower found that he was a private again and that he would have to spend another month walking the area upon his return from furlough. But he rebounded a third time in his first class year by becoming the senior color sergeant.

When he did hold cadet rank, he regarded it with something less than the fervor of George Patton. Classmate Harold W. James wrote, "He and I were the two color sergeants during our first class year. We used to mutter under our breath while we stood at parades, but I guess nothing important was discussed or I would have remembered." Colonel James added humorously, "Had I known he was to be a future president my attitude would have been different."[2 7] But when it came to performance of duty, Eisenhower showed another side to his personality. At a review before the Army's Chief of Staff, Cadet James was carrying the colors with Eisenhower. He remembered that "As we passed the stand I was supposed to dip my flag, but I forgot. Ike, the senior sergeant, really chewed me out."[28]

Eisenhower was far from being a model cadet. Holding the cadet regulations and cadet regimentation rather lightly, he was willing to take his chances with the system. Fond of eating, he made many forbidden excursions for food. "One of the worst offenses at the Point," said classmate Charles C. Herrick, "was to get caught off the reservation. But somehow it never worried Ike and some of the others. They'd sneak out the lavatory window, and past the sentry post and off they'd go up the Hudson in a rented boat to Newburgh for coffee and sandwiches. Imagine, they'd travel 30 miles—15 there and 15 back—just for chow. If any of those guys had been caught they'd have been thrown right out of the Academy."[29]

The primary reason for Eisenhower's failure to achieve officer rank as a cadet was that he just didn't care, "while a cadet he made little effort to excel in purely military activities, although he could no doubt have reached high rating had he done so."[30]

Eisenhower was as carefree in his attitude towards academics as he was towards the military, a fact reflected in his rank of 61st out of 164 in the graduating class. Clifford R. Jones said Eisenhower "had no difficulty with classwork. My room was across the hall and while the rest of us were cramming like mad I'd see Ike with his feet on the desk, reading a magazine."[31] Another classmate wrote that Eisenhower "never had any difficulties with the academic department or the tactical department but he was too busy making friends with everybody to 'bone tenths' or 'files' " (i.e. to care about academic or class standing). There was general agreement among his classmates that he could have finished much higher in the class had he wanted to; but, as they said in his yearbook biography "poor Dwight merely consents to exist until graduation shall set him free." His casual attitude was portrayed in his *Yearling Book* by reference to a history recitation in the slang for which he was famous as a cadet:

"Well, sir, 'bout that time Napoleon he runs across old Archduke Charles 'round Vienna somewheres, and there was a big scrap. They called it 'Waggem' or some such funny name like that. Charles he stayed with it for a while, but he couldn't do much 'cause things was gettin' too hot for him, so he beat it to keep from gettin' mauled proper."

In reading an anecdote cited by Cadet Frank E. Emery, Jr., one can picture Eisenhower's infectious grin:

I remember Ike picking up five fast demerits during our military engineering course. The instructor was a martinet who insisted upon complete accuracy down to the last detail. He asked Ike to explain a detailed problem on the blackboard. We had all worked on the problem before and we knew the answer was "one yard." Ike went through the problem—and then as he neared the answer, turned and said waggishly to the instructor, "Is three feet all right, sir?" Cadet Eisenhower walked the area for that one.[32]

Eisenhower himself recalled another instance of indifference to classwork. "They had a course," he said, "called Military History. One of the things we had to study was the battle of Gettysburg. We were required to remember the name of every general officer or acting general officer in the entire opposing forces. You also had to learn what the officer commanded—the exact character of the command. Then you had to remember the situation or the position of each of these commands at such and such an hour on such and such a day. I always did hate memory tests, although I have a pretty good memory; but this wasn't the kind of thing that interested me, so I didn't pay any attention and I almost got 'found' [flunked] in military history."[33]

Actually, he was very articulate and "could express himself better," said classmate James A. Van Fleet, "than almost any member of the class. Consequently, he was in the top section in English all the time. Some of the boys kidded him about it, claimed he was bookworming his way to the top. They kept it up until one day Ike pledged that he wouldn't open a book on English out of class for the rest of the term. I don't know why he did it. Anyhow, he finally hit the bottom of the class. But he wouldn't crack a book until the class members released him from his pledge."[34] Finally they did release him, and he must have made a remarkable recovery since his academic record shows he finished 10th out of 212 in first year English. Had he put his mind to studying all his courses in a similar manner, he would have finished many files higher. One member of 1915 thought Eisenhower's indifference to class standing was influenced by his decision to "go infantry" upon graduation. Since it was not one of the coveted branches (branch selection was based on class standing), he did not bother to "bone" for another branch.[35]

Cadet Eisenhower was extremely popular. He was an extrovert—a good mixer, a hail-fellow well-met. He liked people and they liked him. He was handsome, with an infectious grin and a pleasing personality. He was always pleasant and considerate in his dealings. Colonel Clifford R. Jones recalled, "unless an individual happened to be an 'odd-ball,' or did something quite unusual, memories of him do not stand out. Eisenhower was not an 'odd-ball', and I don't remember him doing anything unusual. All that I can say about him is that all who knew him liked him a lot. I certainly did."[36] Colonel Jones was not completely correct, for Eisenhower did stand out as a most promising football player in his early years. This was one of the reasons for his popularity.

He participated in everything with gusto and enjoyment. His classmates remembered that he would sing the old ballad "Darling Clementine" in the shower at the top of his voice. He was always ready to join any activity that promised fun, be it a boodle fight or a drag (date) of some classmate. One colleague commented that "at lunch one day I got hit on the back of the head with a piece of beef. I looked around for the culprit and all I could see was a crew of stern-faced cadets, but there was just the suspicion of a smile on Ike's face, and I figured he was my man. I heaved a potato in Ike's direction—but a poor plebe picked that moment to stand up. He got it right in the eye."[37]

Cadet Eisenhower was frequently doing things to help his classmates. The cadets had developed a routine called "bugling" to carry them through some academic assignments. If a cadet was called upon to recite (as they all were almost daily in every course) and was not prepared, he would "bugle," i.e. stay at the board, stalling and praying that the bugle would sound recall from class before his turn. One day cadet Hume Peabody was at the board—

> I was supposed to recite last. I hadn't the foggiest notion about my topic—as I had previously confided to Ike—and my only hope was to "bugle." I covered part of the board with meaningless figures and listened with a sinking heart to recitation after recitation. When the man before me finished reciting, there must have been at least five minutes left—but the ax never fell. Ike stood up and asked a question, then another and still another. The instructor was completely taken in, and answered each question thoroughly. Then that blessed bugle blew and I was off the hook. No "bugler" was ever more expertly rescued from his plight than I was by Ike that day so long ago.[38]

In another instance he was helpful to a classmate when he was hospitalized for a knee injury from football. A classmate who was seriously ill began calling the wardmaster. The wardmaster, who was "a surly so-and-so," ignored the sick cadet's call until Eisenhower finally got out of bed and yelled, "Give him what he wants or I'll knock the living hell out of you!" The wardmaster complied.[39]

While some cadets were preoccupied with academics and military conduct, Eisenhower was devoting his spare time to sports.

During his day cadets did not have intramural athletics, but they engaged in sports as their individual choices dictated. Ike chose football, playing in his plebe year on the Cullum Hall or "Scrub" football team. The plebes, as well as cadets, who played on the Cullum Hall team were those who could not make the varsity. There was no plebe team as such in those days, and a plebe could play varsity ball his first year if he was good enough. Eisenhower showed great promise as a player, making first string varsity at left halfback as a yearling (sophomore). Describing a 19 to 0 Army victory over Rutgers, *The New York Times* reported that Eisenhower was "one of the most promising backs in Eastern football." One classmate wrote, "We thought we had an All-American halfback in the making."[40] Another writer reported that "Eisenhower in the fourth quarter could not be stopped" in Army's 18 to 7 win over Colgate.

Nonetheless in the Tufts game on the following Saturday, November 13, 1912, he was stopped. He sustained a knee injury that was to end his football career and nearly cause his discharge from the Academy. When he was dismissed from the hospital a month after the injury, Dr. Charles Keller, the attending physician, warned Eisenhower that complete recovery was possible "provided you don't do anything foolish. That knee has been badly hurt, and joint injuries take a long time to heal."[41]

Classmate Hyde wrote, "I have a recollection of him appearing in the riding hall with his leg in a cast. He said he was excused from marching formations but nothing had been said about riding."[42] Dr. Keller had particularly cautioned Eisenhower not to go through the dismounting drills when he took part in horseback riding. He was to stay put on the horse, a challenge to his pride caused him to ignore that warning. The riding master was a rigid disciplinarian, and one afternoon "flatly, in cold, angry tones, . . . charged Dwight with malingering and ordered (him) . . . from that time forth to take part in all the movements of the drill." He did not fall back on the doctor's orders and make an excuse to the drill master. All afternoon he mounted and dismounted as "pain stabbed through his injured knee, increasing with each maneuver until his vision darkened and his teeth clenched to keep back cries of agony."[43] When the afternoon was over, Eisenhower was back in the hospital, his knee red and swollen and his football career definitely at an end. The injury was so bad he was still limping in his second class year.[44]

He was terribly disappointed. He loved his challenging game of stamina, skill and courage and he was a fierce competitor. But rather than give up his contact with the game he rejoined the Cullum Hall team as a coach. A former varsity football teammate said, "Due in great part to his ability as a coach and as a teacher the team went undefeated."[45] He continued coaching throughout his West Point career. Another former teammate attested that:

> Cadet Eisenhower never lost his enthusiasm about the game. In my last year I borrowed an officer's horse for a midnight ride—without the officer's knowledge. They slapped me under arrest and I walked the area for weeks— and couldn't play on the team. But my release was effective three weeks before the game with Navy and Ike was determined that I wouldn't get any more demerits which might keep me from playing.
>
> Then our class was invited to a dance—and I decided to break arrest and attend the affair via the back door. Ike heard of my plan and one afternoon while I was playing Kelly pool in the club he came stalking in and told me that he'd smash a billiard cue over my head if I tried to break confinement. I stayed in quarters.[46]

That having to give up football was a heavy blow to Eisenhower is revealed in his own words many years later: "When I was broken up in 1915 I was not able to play actively in athletics again at West Point, so I started to resign a couple of times, but my classmates talked me out of it. Once I put in my papers and my classmates held them up. They got the company captain to hold them up while they talked me out of it. I stayed."[47]

Although he was extremely disappointed by the termination
of his football career, he never complained and found another
outlet in addition to coaching. "There were practically no extracurricular activities at West Point," said classmate Joseph C.
Haw, "other than athletics; so there was little opportunity to
exhibit leadership qualities and there were practically no offices
to which a cadet could be elected by his fellows as concrete
evidence of leadership."[48] There was, however, one elective post
which in those days was indicative of popularity and leadership—cheerleader. Cadet Gibson pointed out that "the corps
had only one cheerleader. This man had to be a real leader and
the most popular cadet in the first class. We elected Ike."[49]

What opportunity did he have to exhibit leadership as a
cheerleader? For one thing "he wrought a complete change in
the attitude of the corps about the Navy games. He preached
the doctrine of,

> "Not the goal, but the race,
> Not the quarry, but the chase"

and if in running a good race and making a good chase we
defeated Navy, well and good; but the most important thing
was to play the best game we could. And that doctrine was
adopted by the Corps."[50] One must also understand that in
those days *all* cadets turned out for football practice every day
of the week and cheered the team on under the leadership of
the cheerleader. Ike was therefore, out at practice every afternoon spurring on team and corps alike.[51]

In this capacity, he also influenced the sportsmanlike conduct of the Corps. Classmate Robert L. Williams remembered
one incident typical of his fairmindedness: "One Saturday afternoon the opposing team was penalized for some infraction or
other and a spontaneous cheer went up from the plebes. Ike
frowned, turned to the stands, and yelled: 'We don't cheer for a
gain like that.' Suddenly everybody became silent."[52]

"I can almost remember the hour one evening," recalled
Hugh P. Avent of the Class of 1915, "during a rally before the
Navy game when as I watched him lead the rally, I said to
myself, 'Here is a cadet who is a real leader, one head above the

rest in the quality of leading.' I have since tried to evaluate the qualities which seemed to make him stand out. Of course he had energy, a native intelligence, ability, and a charming cheerfulness to an unusual degree. Several in the class, however, had these traits too and did not go to the height that Ike did. The Eisenhower of our cadet days seemed to present a manly quality or an 'animality' not possessed by all. He was full of confidence and knew how to impart it into the atmosphere. His cheerfulness was imparted to others, too. He carried about him an 'air of intrepidity'."[53]

The role of Eisenhower's personality in his leadership and in his success is pinpointed in this statement by a classmate:

> I knew Ike quite well, observing him frequently at drills and exercises and often listening to his conversation at rest periods. The one outstanding characteristic notable at all times was his cheerfulness, friendliness, and good humor. Everyone liked him and apparently he liked everyone in turn. If there is such a thing as a "magnetic personality," he had it and has continued to have it. It has been his greatest asset. He had the priceless ability to make anyone that he met for the first time feel that he had a genuine interest in him and in his ideas. In Ike's case it was *not* that type of personality one might think of as "boot licking" or fulsome praise of others. Nor is it "being a jolly good fellow" type, although Ike always has been pleasantly good natured. It is rather that he looked you straight in the eye and listened very intently to everything that you had to say. To my mind it was this quality of appearing to be completely absorbed in what one was saying that formed the basis of Ike's engaging personality. And it was "engaging," for he made people like him. [54]

At graduation Eisenhower received two distinctions, AB and BA connoting something different than their usual meaning. AB meant "Area Bird," and referred to the time he spent walking the area for violating regulations. BA was an abbreviation for "Busted Aristocrat," meaning a cadet who achieved rank and was busted. Obviously these titles were not indicative of the "model" cadet. In military conduct he bordered on the reckless; in academic pursuits he was almost indifferent, enjoying a good time too well to study very hard.

What conclusions can be drawn concerning Eisenhower as a cadet and his leadership potential at graduation? His performance in football showed the initiative and drive necessary for successful leadership. His conduct at riding drill, which ended any hopes of playing football, illustrated other qualities necessary for successful leadership—guts, this coupled with the refusal to make excuses and the refusal to quit. Instead of being bitter about his injury, he channeled his drive into cheerleading, where he displayed a high degree of leadership ability. He had a strong impact on the morale and sportsmanship of the Corps of over 600 and was, so to speak, their field leader in this respect. When he wasn't cheering on the Corps, he displayed that leadership as a coach since he could no longer be a player.

In reflecting upon Eisenhower's exploits as a cadet on the dance floor, in the classroom, and in rowing 30 miles for food, one can understand why the closing sentence of his graduation yearbook biography branded him, "Dare-Devil Dwight, the Dauntless Don." In summing up his cadet days, one must conclude that he displayed a latent leadership ability, which if awakened and directed into military channels, would take him very far.

The insight gained from studying Eisenhower's personality in those early years of his military life is important to understanding his leadership success. He was popular with his classmates but not because he tried to get along by agreeing with everybody. This is hardly the way to popularity within the military establishment. Numerous interviews with classmates and extensive correspondence reveal Eisenhower as positive and assertive, but not argumentative. He could see both sides of the question. "He held firm convictions and was a strong adherent to principles. He never sought to force his convictions on others . . . In my opinion, the central motivating force of his character can be epitomized in the single word, 'integrity'." [55] He expressed his opinions very forcefully on whatever subject was under discussion and defended them with equal force. In short, he had character, and it was this quality, along with his outgoing and pleasant personality, that made him so popular.

Douglas MacArthur

Douglas MacArthur's father, Arthur MacArthur, was a career Army officer who received considerable recognition for his heroism and leadership during the Civil War and the Spanish American War. When it was time to select a college, both father and son were pleased when, in 1899, Douglas won an appointment to West Point. Cadet MacArthur was much more mature than his contemporaries when plebe summer started for the Class of 1903. At 19 years and 4 months, he was older than the majority of his classmates, and since he had been reared in the Army, was considerably more experienced and knowledgeable about the military. Many years after his graduation from West Point in June 1903, Douglas MacArthur was to say that "as an Army 'brat' it was the fulfillment of all my boyish dreams." As a boy, however, he did more than dream about it; he studied and prepared for West Point from the age of five. He had the tutelage and image of a father who was a brilliant military leader in combat, and who devoted his waking hours to the serious study of the military profession. It was not easy to be the plebe son of a famous fighting major general, and Douglas MacArthur, whose father was receiving national acclaim in American newspapers for his exploits in the Philippines in 1899, suffered for it. Some of the more immature upper classmen took his father's fame as a license to put Douglas through some severe hazing. His plebe tentmate, Frederick H. Cunningham, became so disgusted with what happened to MacArthur that he resigned. It was suspected that Cunningham was the source of an anonymous letter to the editor of the *New York Sun,* which appeared shortly after he left, denouncing hazing at West Point. An investigation into hazing was conducted during the summer of 1899, but no evidence was found which resulted in the dismissal of any upperclassmen. However, on December 11, 1900, President McKinley, following the death of a cadet, supposedly the result of hazing, ordered an investigation of the treatment of plebe cadets at West Point. Although the investigation was supposed to center around the deceased cadet, Oscar L. Booz, it soon switched to an investigation of the hazing of Douglas MacArthur during his plebe summer. MacArthur's plebe summer occurred a full year after Cadet Booz had left, but his first year was intensively investigated anyway.

The Congressional Committee investigation offers an insight into the personality and character of Cadet MacArthur. The following is a partial transcript of that investigation:

Q. Mr. MacArthur, we have received a great deal of evidence that you were severely hazed. The committee is desirous of having you tell your own story in your own way, giving to us the names of the cadets by whom you were hazed, the date as near as you can, the time, the place, and the physical effect on you personally of the hazing at that time.

A. I cannot tell exactly the time; it was after I had been a plebe about a month, I should say.

Q. And the year, please?

A. 1899. The hazing I underwent I have seen something about; I have heard accounts of it in the newspapers, and elsewhere, and, like all such matters that start out as a comparatively small thing, it has grown to very large proportions. The hazing that I underwent was in no way more severe or more calculated to place me in a serious physical condition than has ordinarily taken place. I was not in any physical condition that would tend to injure me at all. I have heard it stated, in fact I have seen it in the newspapers, that I was at one time hazed until I

suffered severe convulsions. No such affair took place. I
was hazed at the time in question until I was quite tired; I
might say more than that. As far as my physical muscles
were concerned I did not have complete control of them,
but as far as being in convulsions, or in any way delirious,
or anything of that kind, or out of my head, I most
emphatically deny it . . . I was not obliged to attend
hospital for any cause during plebe camp. On the night in
question I think I was suffering with a case of exaggerated cramps. That is the only thing I could call it. The
place of exercising was over in camp in one of the 'A'
company tents. I did not exercise, I do not think, longer
than men frequently have and suffer no consequences at
all. I was not in a condition of nausea that would cause
any bad effects.

Q. What did your exercising consist of?

A. It consisted of eagling. (Going from a standing to a squat-
ting position and rising with arms extended.)

Q. How many, please?

A. I don't know; I would say, at a rough estimate—well, I
could not even make a rough estimate. I did not keep
track.

Q. Have you any recollection?

A. Eagling was interspersed with other exercising; I would
do one and then the other.

Q. How many, should you say, in all?

A. I should say, perhaps, 250 would be a good estimate.

Q. And what else, please?

A. Hanging from a stretcher. (To hang by one's hands from a tent pole.)

Q. How long did you have to hang from a stretcher?

A. I should say two minutes at a time.

Q. In all, how many minutes?

A. I don't know. The whole performance, I should say, took an hour and was equally divided between the different exercises.

Q. What were the others?

A. Eagling, hanging from stretcher, what is known as dipping, and I think that was all. (push-ups)

Q. You say you were suffering from cramps at the time you exercised?

A. Afterwards.

It was a trying experience for the general's son but MacArthur obviously had the guts to take any of the strenuous exercising they could give him. He was not a quitter, he did not seek sympathy, nor did he desire to be in the limelight. He resented the exaggerated stories printed in the newspapers of the hazing he had supposedly been subjected to. The story given to the Committee, however, by his former classmate and tent mate, Frederick H. Cunningham, presented a much grimmer picture of what Plebe MacArthur went through:

Q. Do you remember an occasion when MacArthur had been in a tent being exercised and on returning to your tent was overcome?

A. I do.

Q. What time in the evening was it?

A. We returned from mess and I went to the sink; I knew he had been summoned to report to some tent on the company street—Company A. When I returned from the sink he was gone; it was probably about half past 7 or 8 o'clock.

Q. And when did you see him?

A. I saw him reel into the tent about an hour later.

Q. Then what took place?

A. I got up and caught him as he fell.

Q. And what did you do to him?

A. I laid him gently on the floor of the tent.

Q. In what condition was he then?

A. He was lucid.

Q. Was he in violent convulsions?

A. He classified them as cramps.

Q. I am asking you to tell what you thought.

A. I think if you saw him in the same condition on the street you would call them convulsions.

Q. Was his body writhing?

A. Yes, sir; he showed the most activity, however, in his limbs.

Q. To what extent were his limbs in motion?

A. To such an extent I had to hold them to keep them still, and finally he asked me to throw a blanket under them in order that the company officers could not hear his feet striking the floor. He had no control over them.

Q. Did you put a blanket under them?

A. I did.

Q. Was there anything put in his mouth?

A. There was nothing.

Q. Did he ask for anything to put in his mouth?

A. He suggested that if he cried out, to prevent his cries being heard, that we put a blanket in his mouth. There was no suggestion of cotton at all.

Q. Was there anybody else in the tent besides yourself and MacArthur?

A. I cannot distinctly remember now; I am not sure; but I think Smith, M., was on guard that night; I am not sure; but I know as soon as MacArthur returned his inquisitors came around back of the tent and were much concerned over what they had done.

Q. What did they do?

A. As near as I can remember they did almost everything in the exercising line.

Q. I mean, what did they do back of the tent?

A. I believe Barry (who was the yearling who had done most of the hazing and was later sent home) ordered someone —a fourth- classman—

Q. Do you mean Barry?

A. Yes, sir, Barry. He ordered someone to go to the tank and get water for him, and when it was brought he used it so far as he could bathing his head.

Q. Do you remember his condition in the morning?

A. He got all up feeling very—well, he felt, to use a slang expression, very "all in."

Q. What is the meaning of that?

A. He did not feel like doing anything. He was urged by some—I do not know the names of them—to go on sick report, but he would not do it.

Q. He turned out for drill and other duties as if nothing had happened, did he not?

A. Yes, sir.

Q. You think that MacArthur was let alone after that?

A. Yes; I know he was, because I heard—I do not know what was told me, but I heard it — the next morning that by his plucky work the night before in the soiree that he had got a bootlick on the whole corps.

Q. Do you know who it was?

A. I am under the impression it was Barry.

Q. The exerciser?

A. Yes; he came around with the statement that he was making no apologies or did not apologize for things of that sort, and then he followed it with that remark.

Q. Is it fair to say that they indicated a deep concern over the severe hazing that MacArthur had had the night before?

A. It would indicate a slight worry on the part of those who had indulged in it.

Q. What was meant by bootlick; you said that Barry had told MacArthur that he had received a bootlick from the whole corps?

A. That he had got a bootlick on the whole corps.

Q. What did that mean?

A. It means admiration of his plucky resistance of the night before and that they were proud of him and they would practically give him the glad hand after that, and I believe that the effect of it after that was that he was not hazed.

A more eloquent testimony to strength of will and determination would scarcely be possible. No normal individual enjoys hazing, and MacArthur was very normal in this respect. But "Cadet MacArthur," said one classmate, "accepted the hazing activities as just part of the course in the training of a plebe." Another classmate wrote:

MacArthur and his fellow new-cadets had been thrown together willy nilly upon their metamorphoses from town, city and farm into a uniformed, organized Class of cadets. None had known the other, and in their new uniforms confusion compounded confusion in our efforts to identify each other. It was MacArthur's character which drew us to him early that summer—his sense of honor, his self assurance, his courage, his determination—the qualities we all like and admire brought him ever-increasingly to our attention. He was a man to be watched, a man for whom destiny held high promise.[56]

When MacArthur started academics in the Fall of 1899, the cadet who stood next to him in the company ranks was a young midwesterner named Clark Lynn. Cadet Lynn reflected:

Before the general transfer of cadets to their appropriate positions in the class, I served in a section then forming. MacArthur and I were in the same section since his name began with an "M" and mine with an "L". I can remember one day in class during the first semester of academics that he was assigned a rather difficult problem for solution. With no notes of any kind he recited on the subject. It was done so perfectly and without hesitation that it astonished the cadets present and the instructor as well. That was my first exposure to his marvelous ability to express himself. When he became the cadet commander in our first class year he fulfilled the expectations we had all had of him since the fall of 1899.[57]

Initially the cadets were sectioned for classes alphabetically, but after enough recitations upon which to base a distinction the cadets were sectioned according to academic performance. Cadet Max C. Tyler, who graduated fourth in the Class of 1903 and was sectioned in almost every subject with MacArthur for the four year period, said that "In the classroom he put on a wonderful show. Whenever he had a recitation to make it was a finished product. He had a commanding presence. He talked well and he usually knew his stuff. Whenever he didn't know his stuff it was pretty hard to tell if he did or didn't, and he usually got away with it."[58] The number seven man in the graduating

class was Cadet Julian L. Schley. Like Tyler he was sectioned
with MacArthur throughout the four years. "MacArthur's recitations," he said, "were a show. I remember in a physics class
how he illustrated a problem on infinity with two parallel mir-
rors. The instructor did not understand the problem much
better than the cadets, but after MacArthur's presentation we
all did."[59]

"MacArthur studied harder than any other member of the
Class," Schley continued. "He was a brilliant man, but he didn't
lean on it."[60] Schley remembered how MacArthur as a cadet
would study by candle light after taps when the gas lights were
required to be out. He would lie on his stomach and read with
his elbows under his chin while mastering his assignments. To
prevent detection he placed blankets on all four sides of the
bed. In his plebe year MacArthur had the decided advantage, for
his studies, of rooming with a first classman, an uncommon
arrangement. Since first classmen were permitted to stay up an
hour later than the plebes, MacArthur had additional study
time. He took full advantage of the opportunity.

Much has been made of a rivalry between Douglas MacArthur
and the grandson of another general, Cadet Ulysses S. Grant,
III. If there was any such competition, Grant didn't know anything about it. He was to write in later years, "At West Point
MacArthur was, of course, outstanding in his studies and in the
performance of his military duties, probably the most outstanding cadet who ever graduated from there. There was no
doubt that he was the most promising cadet in the Corps. . ."[61]

Actually the rivalry was between their mothers. Both Mrs.
MacArthur and Mrs. Grant were keenly ambitious for their sons
whom they idolized. But no one seriously challenged
MacArthur. He was number one in a class of 134 at the end of
fourth class year, and number one in a class of 104 at the end of
third class year. During his second class year he dropped to
number four out of 97. He was again number one in his class of
93 members in June 1903, graduating with an academic average
that went unchallenged for decades.

He did not, however, study at the sacrifice of other activities. Classmate Jacob W. S. Wuest said:

> He worked at whatever he undertook, vigorously and rapidly, but with the precision of a well-regulated and well-oiled machine, and he found time from his arduous studies for numerous extra-curricular activities. He played baseball and part-time football; he managed football and other athletic teams; he worked on class committees; he always seemed to be where he was needed. He did these extra jobs well, apparently without great effort and with little concern for the valuable time he was giving them while his close competitors for academic honors were extending themselves to keep up his pace.[62]

Cadet MacArthur was as outstanding militarily as he was academically. As a yearling, he was the ranking corporal, in his second class year, the ranking sergeant; and in his first class year he held the highest rank in the Cadet Corps, first captain.

The skin book shows that MacArthur's offenses as a cadet were trivial. ("Not wearing belt in gymnasium," "Wrong number of section on paper at recitation," "Tent walls not down at retreat," and there were three occasions during his four years when he was late.) There was one exception to this trivia —in his first class year he was written up for an unauthorized visit to a professor's home. The story behind this infraction reveals the pride that was characteristic of MacArthur throughout his career, a pride that in this instance almost cut short that career. As a result of a short period of hospitalization, MacArthur's name had been listed with the "goats" to take a special examination in mathematics. He rebelled at being placed on this list and went to the professor's home to protest although such action was against regulations, without prior permission. Even at the risk of his rank as first captain he even pushed further, informing the professor that "he had no right to put his name on the goat list, and that if it were not withdrawn before classes the next morning, he would submit his resignation from West Point."[63] The instructor said he was not familiar with the case but that he would investigate. The next morning MacArthur's name was removed from the goat list. This act may be viewed as egoistic, perhaps it was the pride of a man who wants to be first in everything he does.

Never an outstanding athlete at West Point, he was varsity material in baseball. His team captain said of him, "He was far from brilliant, but somehow he could manage to get on first. He'd out-fox the pitcher, draw a base on balls, or get a single, or outrun a bunt, and there he'd be on first."[64] Not good enough or big enough to play varsity football, which he deeply enjoyed, he settled for the job of team manager.

"There was something about MacArthur that made you understand that when he gave an order you had better follow it," said his roommate George Cocheu. "Once there was a strike of the waiters in the dining hall during our first class year. There was more than a little confusion among the Corps, and it was about to reach the point of rebellion. During the chaos of the first meal affected by the strike, First Captain MacArthur stood up before the Corps and issued some crisp orders instructing the cadets on how to perform in the difficult time. Immediately we all settled down and followed his orders."[65]

As first captain, MacArthur had to cope with another type of rebellion—the occasional silent treatment by cadets of "tac" officers (commissioned officers responsible for cadet discipline). "It disturbed him," a member of his cadet staff remarked, "because it was rebellious. To MacArthur it showed lack of proper respect to a superior. Stooping to silencing was wrong. If a cadet believed a 'tac' to be overly harsh, he could hate him if he wanted, but no more than that should be done."[66]

One of MacArthur's biographers attributed an amazing act of defiance to his subject:

General Arthur MacArthur was at West Point on this historic day. He had come home to see his son graduate from the United States Military Academy. Here is a story never before whispered to anyone. It comes from an "Old Grad."

When Douglas' father left the Philippines he was having a feud with Judge Taft (later President Taft) who had been sent out to the Philippines to take over as soon as fighting had ceased. There arose a sharp difference of official opinion. General Arthur MacArthur could not certify that the fighting had ceased when in fact there were active operations in many provinces. The feud apparently was not forgotten, and when Judge Taft became Secretary of War, General MacArthur was ordered back home.

Douglas MacArthur never forgot this; he considered it an injustice to his father. And Secretary of War Taft never forgot it—for Douglas MacArthur got his revenge. It came quickly on the day of his graduation from West Point (1903). Here is the authentic story: It was the custom to invite the cadet's father to sit on the platform and hand the diploma to his own son. General Arthur MacArthur sat proudly with the dignitaries waiting for the biggest moment in his life.

When Douglas stepped forward as Number One man and Cadet First Captain, Secretary Taft extended the diploma and his hand. Douglas accepted the diploma—ignored the hand—saluted as a soldier--faced about—and walked straight to his father, placed the diploma in his father's hand and then sat down at his feet. Douglas MacArthur left West Point that day never to return until 1919 when Secretary of War Baker sent him back to take command—to save the old Academy.[6 7]

As interesting as this story is, it is, nevertheless, part of an account notable for errors. A very cursory study quickly reveals that "Judge" Taft was not Secretary of War in 1903, Elihu Root was, that the diplomas were handed out by Root for the graduation of the Class of 1903 on the 11th of June, and that Taft was in the Philippines on that day.

Comments from MacArthur's classmates etch a portrait of his character, personality and leadership as a cadet: "You never caught him in an informal manner." "He was generally popular, but not one of the boys—too serious." "MacArthur was friendly and on good terms with the class, but intimate with very few." "He was a good mixer, but not a back slapper." "In large groups he stood aloof." "He was always well disciplined." "He was the finest drill master I have ever seen." "Anything he was connected with he just seemed to drift to the head." "Not overzealous, but you knew he was going to do his duty." "You always knew exactly where you stood with MacArthur." "He had an air of distinction about him." "He had a dignity of position." "Many of us were in awe of him." "He had style. There was never another cadet quite like him." "MacArthur as a cadet had a dual personality. When performing his official duties he was all business, but when off duty he had a personal warmth that was not surpassed by anyone I have ever known."

Perhaps the best portrayal was that given by his roommate George Cocheu who said of Cadet MacArthur, "Think of the sort of man he is today and you have the picture of what he was like as a cadet."

MacArthur's career as a cadet can be simply and briefly described: it was brilliant. He graduated number one in his class. He established an academic record which went unbroken for decades, and there was never a first captain—a list which includes Lee and Pershing—who was a more outstanding cadet than MacArthur. Only three other cadets in the then 100-year history of West Point had achieved the dual honor of graduating number one and holding the rank of first captain.

MacArthur's success at West Point was attributable to intelligence, willingness to accept responsibility, determination, hard work, and a desire to excel. Conscientiously applying himself to academics, he was nonetheless not branded a bookworm. He excelled in everything military and participated in athletics. Although his manner was reserved when on duty, he was personally warm and friendly. Clearly it was no gamble to predict, as many did, that MacArthur would gain great future success if he continued to capitalize on his ability, balance, and drive.

George C. Marshall

When it was time for George C. Marshall to enter college he decided to follow his older brother to the Virginia Military Institute. Life for a cadet at the Institute when Marshall entered in 1897 was a Spartan existence. Living conditions by today's standards were primitive: there was no running water, no central heating, and outside toilets. When there was no heat in the winter, the cadets had to break the ice in the basin to wash themselves. The food was bad, and one cadet in the Class of 1901 commented that the "bread was so tough we couldn't eat it, so we threw it."[68] Smoking and drinking were prohibited. Discipline was rigid, and there was no deviation from the rules. It was truly an austere existence, and of the over one hundred students who entered VMI in 1897, only thirty-four were around to graduate in June 1901.

Added to these hardships were the miserable experiences inflicted by the upper classmen upon first-year students, affectionately called "Rats".Rats had the opportunity to shine shoes for upperclassmen; to go through a line of cadets fortified with wooden paddles for spanking purposes, making sitting down very difficult for several hours. They were assigned to sleep in the beds of senior cadets who risked going to town in the evening in violation of regulations and wanted to minimize the danger of "bed checks." The seniors amused themselves by putting new cadets into the wardrobes and turning them over. Along with several other irritating exercises classified as hazing, one of the favorite hazing formations for rats was the bayonet squatter. A bayonet was placed on the floor, point up, and the rat was ordered to squat over it in such a manner that the bayonet remained upright, exerting just enough body pressure to keep the bayonet erect, while straining hard to avoid any undue pain to his buttocks in the process. One day early in his first year when Marshall was still weak from an attack of typhoid fever from which he had recovered just before entering school, he was put through this hazing exercise. Sitting on the bayonet, his legs started to tighten as he refused to give his tormentor the pleasure of watching him whine. His limbs began to burn as he concentrated all of his will to remain just on top of the bayonet. Eventually the strain of this excruciating position got the best of him. As he fell over from exhaustion the bayonet shot into his rear. The upperclassman, seeing the blood, became frightened fearing he might have caused serious injury. Should Rat Marshall report him, expulsion from VMI was certain. Marshall got up and silently left the room. He never mentioned to the authorities who had inflicted the injury upon him. The only official indication of the event was an entry showing that Marshall was excused from duty for three days in September 1897. In deference to Marshall's courage and silence, from that day on it was declared that the spunky "northerner" was not to be hazed again.

"The routine of cadet life," Marshall said in later years, "I became accustomed to and accepted. I think I was more philosophical about this sort of thing than a great many boys. . . It was part of the business and the only thing to do was to accept it as best you could and as easily as you could." He went on to say that "This I tried to do and I think I was fairly successful in doing."[69]

What bothered Marshall most was the early morning rising. "In the early morning," he said, "we generally got up at dark. We took pride in sleeping with these very wide double windows open—in fact the older cadets made us do it when you were a new cadet and the snow would fly in on us. We had to strap around the blankets in the bunk to keep the corners from coming off. So we just slept like dead men which meant we were in very good health."[70]

When the youthful Marshall entered VMI he was described as a "long, a lean and a gawky cadet, sensitive and shy; a Pennsylvania Yankee in a Southern School at a time when the Blue and Gray had not yet been welded in the fires of the Spanish war . . . He landed in the awkward squad, and he stayed there, on and on. He could not drill. He could not march. All he could do was sweat, look uncomfortable, and be embarrassed whenever he was spoken to."[71]

The awkwardness was soon outgrown, however, and by his second year at VMI Marshall was the top cadet in his class militarily—the highest ranking corporal in his second year, the ranking first sergeant in his third year, and in the final year he was selected for the most coveted cadet rank of all, first captain.

When Forrest Pogue, one of Marshall's biographers, asked Marshall why he achieved the rank of cadet captain he replied, "In the first place I tried very hard. In all the military affairs I was very exacting and very exact in all my military duties; and I was gradually developing an authority from the very mild authority, almost none, shown by the corporal, to the much stronger, very profound authority of the first sergeant. Because [in the latter post] I fell the company in, I called the roll and all things of that sort. I kept tabs on it entirely, and marched the detail to guard mount every morning. . . I suppose they judged me in making me 1st sergeant and in estimating what my development would probably be by the time I would be first captain. . ."[72]

It was clear very early in his cadet career that he sought to achieve military distinction. Once on the parade field his shoes were shined with such a mirrorlike finish he was accused by a "tac" of wearing patent leather shoes. His rifle was typical of a cadet on the make; he paid a sergeant two dollars to put a lustrous polish on its stock. His record in military discipline was unequaled—in four years as a cadet he did not receive a single demerit! Some of the credit for this remarkable distinction can be attributed to a deal made with his two roommates, a New Orleans boy named Leonard K. Nicholson and a Virginian, Philip B. Peyton. "Buster" Peyton, like Marshall, aspired to achieve cadet rank and realized it would require work. Nicholson, however, due to inherit his father's newspaper, was lazy, unimpressed and aspired to nothing. The deal among the three young men stipulated that Marshall and Peyton would assume all responsibility for sweeping and dusting the room—including Nicholson's part—making up and folding the cots, properly placing the beds, chairs, tables, guns, clothing, and other items. Nicholson would not lift a hand to help, but his name would be posted every day as room orderly. As such, he would receive any demerits which were awarded to the room. With two such responsible roommates, this did not happen very often.[73] The system worked during all three of their upper class years and Marshall's demerit record was a contributing factor in his cadet success.

But Marshall was not all business as a cadet in spite of his ambition. As first captain, he would frequently leave his room after call to quarters or taps without authorization to visit a girl he was courting. At VMI, this was called "running the block." If caught, he would have been busted from the highest ranking captain to the lowest ranking private. "It was decided," said classmate Banks Hudson, "that someone would have to tell him he might get caught and thrown out. We drew lots and I got the job. He just said 'Let me handle that'."[74] In later life, when Marshall was asked about running the block, he replied, "I was very much in love."[75]

Marshall excelled militarily as a cadet, but in academics his performance was only average. Marshall himself said of his academics at VMI that "I was a very poor student and . . . I did very badly my first year. I think I was 35th in a class of a hundred and something. But I ended up, I believe, my last year, 5th in my class . . . I started rather late."[76] There was little emphasis given to academics at VMI in Marshall's days. "The program," said one of Marshall's classmates, "concentrated on military training. They didn't let education interfere with military things."[77]

In his second class year Marshall decided to play football. Although light compared to linemen of his day, his determination and guts made up for his lack of size. To play football at VMI was an ordeal. Practice was held during the cadets' one free period of the day, from 3:00 until 4:00, allowing only one hour for getting into football attire, practicing, bathing and redressing before going off for an hour of drill with the rest of the cadet corps. Even with his late start, he was an outstanding football player. One account of a VMI football game noted that "The tackling of G. Marshall in breaking up the interference was of the highest order, and a prominent University of Virginia athletic man said he was the best tackle in the South . . ."[7 8]

Cadet Careers Compared

In comparing the cadet careers of these four young men who were later to achieve great distinction as military leaders, one can see some similarities and a few differences. All four exhibited leadership as cadets. Marshall and MacArthur received the highest possible cadet rank each successive year, as did Patton until his final year, when he was awarded the rank he most coveted, that of Cadet Adjutant. Cadet Eisenhower achieved rank on three occasions, lost it twice, but was elected by his classmates to the sole elective post. His lack of seriousness towards military discipline cannot take away the fact that he was looked upon by supervisors and contemporaries alike as a leader.

The aspiration to be a soldier was an early one for Marshall, MacArthur and Patton, and their determination never faltered. They excelled militarily because they worked hard at it, even the brilliant and gifted MacArthur. In contrast, Eisenhower, whose first choice was the Naval Academy, went to West Point because of the opportunity it offered for an education. With this opportunity went an obligation to serve as a commissioned officer in the United States Army; but it was not an obligation that was based on a legal commitment alone. It went much deeper than that. The members of the Corps of Cadets at the Military Academy consisted of men who devoted themselves to a career of service and who, with the threat of war, showed not a lust for combat but a willingness to pay the supreme sacrifice to defend what we in America hold dear.

The surrounding hills, the rugged beauty of the countryside and the gothic-like structure of West Point overlooking the Hudson River are an impressive sight to the visitor. Its beauty goes much deeper than that to the man who spends four years there. It is an institution rich with historic traditions and legends. It has a mystic something, invisible, indescribable, yet something potent and real. As one cadet described it, "It may be the men of the Corps long dead who are keeping bright the watchfires of the Academy, kindled long ago. It may be the Spirit of the Post, bringing home the fame of the men who have made that spirit so glorious, keeping alive in the memory an appreciation of their deeds, of the solemn duty they left to those who follow after, of the priceless privilege it is to follow where they have pointed the way. Whatever it may be, it is undoubtedly the most valued heritage that the Alma Mater of the Army can transmit to her sons."

Historically, the motto of West Point has been Duty, Honor, Country. A cadet's life at the Academy revolves around these three words. A sense of honor had great value—that a man's word was truly his bond. Love of country was a burning fire that grew brighter and brighter. And again in the words of someone who experienced this revered life, the words, Duty, Honor, Country, "are more closely linked in the mind of a soldier than in any other professional man. He cannot escape from them if he would. When the last sad note of 'Taps' has passed into silence, wistfully as if it were loath to die, whether the stars above look down on him in garrison or in the crowded camp, if he stops to think of the day's work and to judge fairly, he will know if his honor has been kept unsullied and his duty well done. If these things be true, then it must follow that he has served his country with the best he had."

These are the words of an idealistic senior cadet about to leave his Alma Mater to pursue a career of selflessness. But it is an idealism that sticks with the graduate of West Point, and the values of duty to one's country as a man of honor have become the vital part of his character. The proud tradition of this great institution follows her graduates, "reaping honor and glory from his deeds or being wounded to the heart at his forgetfulness of her care." The later comments of graduates are no less idealistic than those of the young man in his senior year. "The inspiration you will find," General Eisenhower said in making the graduation address at West Point on June 3, 1947, "on revisiting this place is even more stirring than that of a son returning home. The pulse quickens to the feeling that here is enshrined something of the selflessness of all of the men who have fought and died for our country. Their spirit charges that our own work be no less devoted. It fires our purpose that this nation shall ever remain secure as it steadfastly pursues its far-reaching efforts toward man's betterment."

Douglas MacArthur showed equally strong feeling when he said:

Fifty years have passed since I participated in West Point's Centennial exercises. These fifty years of war and peace have seen emerge from West Point's classes a succession of graduates who have given the country an indomitable leadership which has never failed the Academy's great tradition. As I look beyond those fifty years to the day I joined the long grey line, I recall I then felt that as an Army "brat" the occasion was the fulfillment of all my boyish dreams. The world has turned over many times since then and the dreams have long vanished with the passing of the years, but through the grim murk of it all, the pride and thrill of being a West Pointer has never dimmed. And as I near the end of the road, what I felt when I was sworn in on the Plain so long ago, I can still feel and say—that is my greatest honor. I have no doubt but that those who now compose the Corps will find the same satisfaction I do now in reflecting upon this day of theirs fifty more years hence.

A man does not have to go to West Point to have the concept of Duty, Honor, Country become the heart and soul of his endeavor. General Marshall reflected when he gave the commencement address at Virginia Military Institute on June 12, 1940:

I have been attempting to recall this morning just when I first became conscious of the direct influence of my cadet days on my career. In dealing with the men of

my first company I did have the super-confidence of a
recent cadet officer. . . At retreat formation in some
isolated company garrison in the Philippines, I would find
my thoughts going back to evening parade with the background of the Brushy Hills and the sunset over House
Mountain. These would revive in me the thought of what
the Corps, what the Institute expected of a cadet officer in
the performance of his duty; also the influence of the
reveille ceremony of Newmarket Day had its effect on my
course of action. This institution gave me not only a
standard for my daily conduct among men, but it endowed
me with a military heritage of honor and self-sacrifice.

It is doubtful that there will ever be a greater virtue than
honor, or a word that can bring a greater thrill than country or
a more noble feeling than that of duty well done. It was an ideal
that did not die with graduation, but instead grew stronger as
they served and as this concept served them in their careers as
leaders in the service of their country.

ALTRUISM-PATIENCE-DEDICATION

The Leadership of
General of the Army
George C. Marshall

Within the United States Army there is a conviction that some officers are fit for command and others possess only the qualifications of staff officers. The command position carries the prestige. To the commander goes the credit when his unit performs well—as well as the blame and any unpleasant consequences if things go poorly. The detailed and often routine administrative work required to run a military unit, and the digging for information which enables the commander to make decisions, is done by the staff officer. There is no glory and little recognition for the staff officer's accomplishments, only hard work and drudgery.

General of the Army George C. Marshall received his greatest military recognition as a staff officer—Chief of Staff of the United States Army from 1939 to 1945. Few people, other than military historians, can remember who was the Army Chief of Staff during the Civil War, the Commanding General of the Spanish-American War or Chief of Staff during World War I. The names hallowed in history are those of the field generals: Robert E. Lee, U. S. Grant, J. E. B. Stuart, Joe Johnston, Stonewall Jackson, Phil Sheridan and John J. Pershing. But Marshall never held a significant field command in war. One officer said of him several years after his death, "Any study of General Marshall should emphasize one important point; he was a staff officer and, as such, great among the greatest, but he was

not a Grant or a Bradley in the field. He didn't even look right
in a field uniform."

The office of Chief of Staff of the United States Army, exalted though it is, is still considered a staff position. There is no
doubt that as a staff officer Marshall was "great among the
greatest". President Harry S. Truman said of Marshall's role as
Chief of Staff during World War II: "Millions of Americans gave
their country outstanding service. General of the Army George
C. Marshall gave it victory." For his personal stature and the
challenge of the office at the period he held it, General Marshall
will not be forgotten in history as have been previous Chiefs of
Staff. It would be unfair, however, for the image of this soldier
to be solely that of a staff officer; and it would be equally unjust to have less than a multidimensional picture of the leadership required in the role of a staff officer.

It was General Marshall's opinion "that leadership in conference, even with subordinates, is as important as on the battlefield". It is the writer's opinion that General Marshall was right;
but to do him justice, to determine why he achieved greatness
as a military officer, requires exploration of his total career in
the United States Army.

World War I

In the spring of 1917, when the first American unit was preparing for action overseas against Germany, Marshall was stationed at Governors Island as aide-de-camp to General J.
Franklin Bell. He wanted badly to go over with the initial American expeditionary force to fight in Europe, so badly he told a
friend, "I'll do anything. I'll even be an orderly." The unit first
called was the 1st Division commanded by Major General
William L. Sibert, to whose staff Marshall was assigned in June
1917. On June 26, he was aboard the first American convoy for
Europe embarking from Hoboken, New Jersey.

On December 14, 1917 General Sibert was relieved as com-
mander of the 1st Division and replaced by Major General
Robert L. Bullard, an event of some significance for Marshall.
General Bullard had known Marshall for many years and re-

spected him as one of the brightest young officers in the Army. Marshall rose quickly under General Bullard, going in January 1918 from an inconsequential staff assignment to the key staff position of G-3 (operations) for the Division.

Although the staff officer is not normally looked upon as a leader, leadership in a staff capacity is just as necessary as it is for the field commander. When Lieutenant Colonel Marshall took over as G-3 of the 1st Division he found a disturbing situation. The system for disseminating orders was so cumbersome that often field or operational orders were received so late that the movements of lower commanders (particularly battalion, company, and platoon commanders) were severely handicapped by lack of sufficient time to make a reconnaissance study before launching an attack.

Marshall decided to do something about it. Leaving the office one day to take the next day's orders to the staff conference for final approval before they were published, he gave a copy of the orders to one of his subordinate officers, E. J. Dawley, telling him not to leave the telephone. Marshall told Dawley he would call him immediately after the orders were approved. Dawley was then to call each Corps in turn, talking only to the Corps Commander, his Chief of Staff, or his G-3, and announce the orders for the next day. "I told Colonel Marshall," said Dawley, "that I understood his directions, but that such a use of the telephone was a direct violation of security. He replied, 'Thank you for calling it to my attention. Do as I say. I will accept all responsibility'."[1]

The procedure was carried out as Colonel Marshall ordered. When Dawley transmitted the orders to I Corps the Chief of Staff, Brigadier General Malin Craig, said to him, "Look here young man, do you know what you are doing?" Expecting a reprimand for violating security, Dawley answered "Yes sir, but I am carrying out Colonel Marshall's instructions." General Craig replied "Oh, I do not mean that. I mean that you are saving about two hours for this Corps in the transmission of orders to lower echelons, and it is going to give our lower commanders a decent chance."[2] (This was the same Malin Craig who was Army Chief of Staff in 1938. Marshall was then his deputy and replaced Craig as Army Chief of Staff in 1939.)

Marshall's initiative in this instance was used after World War I at Command and Staff, Fort Leavenworth, as a classic example of staff leadership.

In May 1918, a young captain, Paul L. Ransom, was commanding Company B of a machine gun battalion of the First Division during the Battle of Cantigny; it was one of many companies supporting the infantry attacks by barrage fires. When the Cantigny attack was over Company B was relieved of its support duty and returned to the rear for rest and refitting. Shortly after his company reached the rear area, Captain Ransom was angered to receive orders from Division Headquarters to move to the front with a battalion of the 16th Infantry to relieve the 28th Infantry then holding Cantigny. He knew that A Company of the machine gun battalion, which had not participated in the attack and was completely rested, was stationed nearby and was in much better condition to do the job. Eight of his machine guns had fired over 100,000 rounds and had to have new barrels, and four of his guns had been destroyed by artillery fire.

Captain Ransom put his officers to work to prepare the company for the move back to Cantigny that night in compliance with the order he had received. He then marched down to Division Headquarters for First Division, determined to see General Bullard and request that A Company be used for the mission rather than B Company.

The Division Chief of Staff at that time was Marshall. Captain Ransom stamped into his office and "told him," Ransom said, "in a belligerent tone, I fear, that I wanted to see the General and why I wished to see him." In reply Colonel Marshall spoke very quietly. He told Captain Ransom that his company had been especially selected because of the vital importance of holding Cantigny, that he was sure his officers and men were equal to the task, and that action was being taken to re-equip his company immediately.

"From a staff officer of a different type," said Ransom, "a young captain might have received a curt and abrupt dismissal and left with a feeling of resentment. I left with a feeling of added pride in my outfit, which I transmitted to my company when I returned. The morale of the officers and men was restored and we went into fighting that night a better unit than we had ever been before."[3]

Seldom does a staff officer achieve any recognition for his work in time of war. Colonel Marshall, as a result of his work on the St. Mihiel drive in August 1918, was an exception. In conjunction with another colonel, Marshall planned the St. Mihiel attack, a significant victory since it was the first major offensive by the newly formed American First Army, under Pershing's command and direction. With a minimum loss of Allied lives and material, it further added to the destruction of German morale since it followed Amiens, the German's Black Day.

After his St. Mihiel achievement, Colonel Marshall was assigned to prepare the plans and troop movement schedules for the transfer of troops, guns and other materiel from the St. Mihiel front to the Meuse-Argonne front, a movement of some 500,000 soldiers, 2700 guns and thousands of tons of supplies. The planning for St. Mihiel and the Meuse-Argonne went on simultaneously, but Marshall was to have a major role in the latter offensive. To insure secrecy, the men and materiel were transferred at night in the remarkably short time of two weeks. The Germans were caught completely by surprise and the attack was successful. Marshall was solely responsible for directing the operations of this attack and was given full credit for its success.

Marshall had entered action in World War I as a relatively new captain and within a year held the rank of full colonel, his promotions resulting from brilliant staff work. General Bullard, in recommending Marshall for promotion to Colonel, said, "He had had, of all officers of the General Staff up to the present, the widest experience in actual staff work in G-3."

Ironically, General Marshall's excellence as a staff officer during World War I prevented him from getting what he most wanted. Shortly after the war, at a dinner paying tribute to officers who had made a significant contribution to the Allied victory, Marshall sat next to his roommate from Virginia Military Institute, Major Buster Peyton. Major Peyton, who had not

seen Marshall for some time, complimented him on the laudatory remarks he had heard about his outstanding staff work.
Marshall replied "I would rather have commanded a regiment
than anything they could have given me."

Throughout the war, he tried his best to get command. On
June 18, 1918, he put in a memorandum requesting he be relieved from duty on the General Staff and assigned to duty with
troops. His division commander, General Bullard replied "I cannot approve because I know that Lieutenant Colonel Marshall's
special fitness is for staff work and because I doubt that in this,
whether it be teaching or practice, he has an equal in the Army
today."[4] General Bullard did, however, recommend that Lieutenant Colonel Marshall be moved up to the Operations Staff of
General Headquarters.

During the Meuse-Argonne campaign, Marshall was requested
by Brigadier General Frank E. Bamford, then commanding the
1st Division, to command the 28th Infantry Regiment. The
request was turned down, again on the basis that he could not
be spared from the staff work he was doing. Before the war
ended, General Pershing made Marshall Chief of Operations for
the First Army and put in his name for promotion to brigadier
general. But the war ended a month later before the promotion
could be acted upon. Marshall had to wait 18 years to become a
brigadier general, in 1936. By comparison General MacArthur,
who graduated from West Point two years after Marshall finished VMI, made the rank of brigadier general in 1918 and by
the end of the war was commanding the 42nd Division.

China

Before World War I was over, Colonel Marshall was selected
by General John J. Pershing as his aide-de-camp—a position he
retained until 1924—an unprecedented six years. For four of
those years, 1920-24, Pershing was Chief of Staff. In July 1924,
at the close of General Pershing's tour as Chief of Staff of the
Army, Lieutenant Colonel Marshall was assigned to the 15th

Infantry at Tientsin, China. The mission of that unit was to keep the Peking-Mukden Railroad open from Peking to Chingwandeo, under the Protocol of 1901, and to safeguard the lives and property of foreign nationals.

For the first three months Marshall acted as the commanding officer of the 15th Infantry. Upon the arrival of Colonel William K. Naylor, Marshall became the Executive Officer, the number two position in the chain of command. After so many years in staff work he enjoyed being with the troops again, and found that his years away from command were not a handicap.

His initial reaction to his new assignment was one of concern. "I find the officers," Marshall wrote to Pershing in 1924, "are highly developed in the technical handling or functioning of weapons, in target practice, and bayonet combat, and in the special and intricate details of paper work or administration generally; but that when it comes to simple tactical problems, the actual details of troop leading, they all fall far below the standards they set in other matters."[5]

Marshall decided to do something about leadership in the 15th Infantry. Every year the unit went to Nan T'ia Ssu on the seashore for camp and weapons practice. One of the training events held at this time was competition for the Chief of Infantry's Rifle squad. Each eight-man squad of infantry was required to fire a tactical course involving an advance of 300 yards up a corridor 200 yards wide, firing at a group of targets. This test, in theory, determined the best rifle squad in the 15th.

An observer of this maneuver in 1927, watching it for the first time, noted, "When I went out on the range, there was Lieutenant Colonel George C. Marshall. A squad started out and fired its course in about fifteen minutes. It then assembled and made its way back to the starting line. Then Colonel Marshall made a general critique of the performance before the whole squad. He drew the squad leader aside and pointed out the mistakes he had made, such as erroneous sight settings, inadequate use of cover, etc. All this took about fifteen minutes more. Then another squad started out and the whole performance was repeated."[6]

This operation took ten days. Colonel Marshall was there every day, watched every squad, and his remarks to the last squad were just as comprehensive, alert, and to the point as they had been with the first. Nine years prior to this time, Colonel Marshall had been handling operations involving millions of men, and he might have considered working with squads quite a step down; but apparently he never did. Although he could have turned this phase of the training over to a qualified company grade officer after a day of personal observation, this was not the way Marshall led. His specific mission was to train the regiment and he carried it out with single-minded attention, to the point of personally watching how every soldier in the 15th could perform in combat exercises. The mission at hand deserved and got his full effort.

When Marshall arrived at Tientsin, the regiment was wearing the summer uniform of left-over wartime khaki. Shades ranged from dark olive to light beige, and the American soldiers looked an indifferent secondbest compared with the smartly uniformed British contingent in Tientsin. "Not long after Colonel Marshall's arrival," one of the officers said, "the morale of the regiment had been raised to such an extent that every man in it bought with his own money a smart, tailor-made uniform of Hongkong Khaki for parades and dress occasions. This was entirely voluntary; and if any pressure was exerted, it was by the men themselves, not from higher up."[7]

Colonel Marshall also improved the appearance of the barracks by instituting a competitive inspection every .Saturday morning in which the winning company was awarded a trophy known as the "Banner Blue". He extended his concern to the spiritual condition of the Post, helping Chaplain Luther Miller improve the chapel. The men contributed spare time to painting and fixing the buildings; and through voluntary contributions from the officers, new pews were put in and new altar pieces were purchased. Chapel attendance picked up when Colonel and Mrs. Marshall attended services every Sunday.

Marshall's characteristic solicitude for both the officers and enlisted men under his command—particularly for the latter—

was evident during his tour with the 15th Regiment. He would personally review every charge that was preferred against any member of the regiment; and an officer had better be well prepared with the facts of the charge when he appeared before Marshall.

"One example of General Marshall's attitude toward the enlisted man," said Captain Frank B. Hayne, commander of "G" Company in the 15th Infantry, "stands out very clearly in my memory!" It was during the annual contest for the Chief of Infantry's Squad Problem, a keenly competitive situation. Captain Hayne was acting as umpire for the practice run of a squad from a rival company. The problem was to keep enough hits on a group of silhouette targets to permit the squad to advance over 600 yards. As soon as the corporal in charge got fire superiority at 600 yards, he sent his automatic rifleman down range 500 yards to keep the hits up at 100 yards, a maneuver which was impossible under combat conditions besides being very dangerous for the man advancing. Captain Hayne called the corporal and told him to start the problem over and make normal advances of not more than 50 yards at a time. The corporal was very much put out, knowing that the umpire was a captain of a rival company; and he turned away sullenly without saluting, a breach of discipline very rare in the 15th Infantry. "I called him back," said Captain Hayne, "and gave him a rather severe dressing down which Colonel Marshall overheard."

Colonel Marshall went over to Captain Hayne, and the two of them walked back to the firing point. When they were out of hearing of the men, Marshall said, "Hayne, you were perfectly right in reprimanding that man; but you weakened your position by losing your temper. You must also remember that the man is an American citizen just the same as you are."[8]

The junior officers of the 15th Infantry Regiment soon learned the value of personal leadership. They discovered that Marshall was exacting in his demands for proper military dress and discipline. That the troops were thousands of miles from home was no excuse for laxity. On the contrary, as representatives of the United States abroad, Americans should make a greater effort to maintain high standards than would be required at home in the States.

Marshall made a conscious effort to fill the vacuum of leisure time at this foreign outpost. To avoid boredom and improve professionalism he encouraged his officers to learn Chinese, and himself achieved a degree of proficiency in the language. Other professional courses were taught and even riding instructions were given to the infantry officers. But it was not all work. He had a skating rink built, arranged hunts, and had keen competition going on among the various companies of the regiment to see who could put on the best amateur theatrical production.

Ordinarily the executive officer of a military unit, prior to World War II, had little authority, no precise duties, and was left much to his own devices. One of the junior officers with the 15th Infantry in Tientsin commented, however, that "Our Colonel was a very fine gentleman who allowed Colonel Marshall to run the regiment."[9] Another officer assigned at Tientsin observed that "Lieutenant Colonel Marshall was assigned to the regiment as executive officer and second in command, though it was not long before it became clear to everyone that he was running the show—not through any undue assumption of authority, but because his ideas were sound and when put into effect at once began to improve the command in appearance, discipline, and particularly in training."[10]

Upon completing his tour at Tientsin, Lieutenant Colonel Marshall was assigned to the Army War College as an instructor. He had been requested for this assignment on five different occasions; and in the summer of 1927, he had no choice but to again leave the work he most loved, duty with troops.

Soon after returning to Washington, Mrs. Marshall was operated on for goiter trouble. While she was recovering from the operation, Colonel Marshall was decorating their new quarters and unpacking and arranging the furniture. Then on September 15, 1927, the day before Mrs. Marshall was scheduled to leave the hospital, her heart failed, and she died suddenly while writing a letter.

The adjutant at the War College at that time was Captain Frank B. Hayne. When he heard the news, he attempted to call Marshall at Walter Reed Hospital, but was unable to contact him. "Quite unexpectedly," Hayne said, "Marshall called me at my office and asked me to meet him at his quarters. Colonel Hjalmar Erickson, who was also a close friend of the general's, joined me; and we went together to his quarters. While we were waiting in his sitting room, he came in, obviously under great emotional strain and as white as a sheet; he sat down at his desk and wrote on a piece of paper, 'Make all arrangements for the funeral. Don't ask me any questions'."[11] Marshall went to his room and remained there the rest of the day.

Fort Benning: 1927-1932

Shortly after Mrs. Marshall's death, Colonel Marshall received orders assigning him as deputy commandant to the Infantry School at Fort Benning, Georgia. Lieutenant Colonel Marshall's tour at Fort Benning from 1927 to 1932 covered some of the worst years of the depression. A married Army private found it very difficult to live on the twenty-one dollars a month take-home pay. To help the married enlisted personnel, Marshall arranged a system whereby a man could buy a steaming dinner pail of food at a modest price from the company mess to take home to his wife and children. This saved money for the family, and it saved the wife the trouble of preparing one meal a day. Since regulations did not permit such action, Marshall took some risk in instituting it. As one of the officers on the Post said, "A little thing perhaps, but what a heart."[12] Colonel Marshall also assisted family feeding by personally supervising the building of chicken yards and hog pens and the planting of vegetable gardens.

There were insufficient funds for badly needed construction at the Infantry School; more than anything else, there was a pressing need for new lecture halls. While there was no money, there was lumber if some of the old World War I buildings were torn down. The head carpenter on the post was an enlisted man affectionately called "Jiggs" by everyone, and the head janitor was a Sergeant Kriz. These two men were in daily contact with Marshall during the planning and construction of the assembly halls; and the completion of the buildings was attributable in large measure to the dedication and ingenuity of Jiggs and Kriz. When the first lecture hall was finished, Colonel Marshall called an assembly of the instructors, staff, and student officers of the advanced class of the Infantry School at the new hall. When the men were all gathered, Colonel Marshall walked from the stage down into the audience, took the hand of the carpenter Jiggs and walked with him back up to the stage. There he expressed appreciation for the work done by everyone, particularly by Jiggs. He closed by saying, "This is Jiggs Hall in honor of your work."

A similar ceremony was held when the second assembly hall was finished. After his talk expressing appreciation to Sergeant Kriz, Marshall proclaimed, "This is now Kriz Hall in honor of the janitors of the Infantry School." These two assembly halls remained Jiggs and Kriz Halls until the Infantry School's permanent buildings were constructed at a new site.

At Fort Benning, as at Tientsin, Marshall had the welfare of his men always in mind. "One instance," wrote Lieutenant General Frank E. Fraser, "where General Marshall came to my aid will never be forgotten. It was at the Infantry School in 1932, in either April or May." He had been selected to carry out a machine gun problem involving firing over troops. Captain Fraser and his company were assigned to defend his position as long as possible against an enemy three times his strength in numbers. Unfortunately for Captain Fraser, he had never commanded a machine gun company. At 0700 on the day he was to work his problem, things started off fine. Only his classmates and rating officers were scheduled to be present. The rating officers for the performance were to be the Commandant, Major General Campbell King, Lieutenant Colonel George C. Marshall, and the Tactics and Weapons Section faculty.

Just as they were to begin someone yelled, "Attention". Two staff cars pulled up, and several officers got out, coming over to watch the firing. Hand salutes were being snapped, frequently. Captain Fraser soon learned why. The party included General Douglas MacArthur, Chief of Staff; Major General Stephen O. Fuqua, Chief of Infantry; and Major General Elbert King, 4th Corps Area Commander. A more awe-inspiring assemblage of Army personalities could not possibly have been present.

"I was frozen," said Fraser, "mentally and physically, and I had no place to hide. Colonel Marshall sensed this because he came over and said, 'Well, Fraser, shall we go over this problem? First of all we will forget the new arrivals. Now, where are we on the map? You and I will check this, and then we will tell our machine gun people what we want them to do and what to expect.' After some more quiet-voiced conversation to me, Colonel Marshall said, 'Now for the gun check.' This was necessary in order to insure that each man firing would be aware of what he was to do, and to insure safety in the overhead firing of live bullets."

"It was my lucky day," said Fraser. "Every phase of firing was on target. General MacArthur complimented the faculty for the instruction given, and we (sic) as students for absorbing it."[13]

Marshall taught a great deal about leadership through example. One of his instructors during this tour was Major Omar N. Bradley, assigned to Fort Benning in 1929. "After once having assigned an officer to his job," Bradley wrote, "General Marshall seldom intervened. During the two years I served him as chief of the weapons section in the Infantry School, he sent for me only once to discuss the work of my section. And during that same two-year period, he visited me in my office but twice. From General Marshall, I learned the rudiments of effective command. Throughout the war I deliberately avoided intervening in a subordinate's duties. When an officer performed as I expected him to, I gave him a free hand. When he hesitated, I tried to help him. And when he failed, I relieved him."[14]

"During the period that I knew General Marshall best," wrote one of the junior officers at Fort Benning, "he was a widower. Nevertheless he always maintained a most hospitable home. He had a spacious set of quarters and shared them most generously by inviting in groups of his acquaintances at every opportunity. He was very considerate of the younger folks. I remember well a Sunday morning horseback ride that he organized for a company of young people in honor of my fiancée. After a brisk ride along some of the horseback trails on the reservation, we assembled at General Marshall's quarters and had refreshments and played mentally stimulating games. He was always exercising young people's minds as well as their bodies. I remember that he gave a present to his honored guest at that time, my fiancée. It was a much prized whale-bone-centered riding crop that was greatly treasured by the recipient."[1 5]

On October 16, 1930 Marshall remarried. His second wife was a widow, the former Katherine Tupper Brown. The best man was General Pershing.

In the days prior to World War II, Army personnel generally stayed on the post both on and off duty, and provided their own off duty entertainment. Colonel Marshall, who was a fine horseman himself, encouraged young officers to play polo, jump ride, hunt on horseback, and take part regularly in vigorous sports. There was, of course, a large supply of horses, since the weapons of that time were a long way from mechanization. He also encouraged the use of other post facilities for tennis, golf, gardening, swimming, and hunting. These sports promoted physical fitness, and, even more importantly, contributed to comradeship, teamwork, and high morale.

Marshall encouraged visits from the civilians in town. In addition, since Fort Benning was one of the most important Army posts in the South, it frequently had important outside visitors. Rather than the usual military parade for honored guests, Colonel Marshall conceived a new idea—a parade of post activities. On the grounds, there was a natural amphitheater in the woods which was selected as the site for these parades. Teams representing the various activities of the post were selected and placed in a nearby concealed position in the woods. Each team wore the costume and carried the equipment of the sport or activity it represented. On a signal from a loud speaker and with a few explanatory remarks from the announcer, a team would parade in front of the reviewing stand, stop, address the distinguished visitor, and make a short comment about its activity. The hunt team rode by in pink coats and, with the Infantry School Club hounds, would pass in review. Then came a team from the Garden Club, dressed in old clothes with hoes and rakes on their shoulders, and so on with the dozens of other activities.[16]

Colonel Marshall's idea was unique. It brought to the attention of the reviewing officer the high morale of the post and the Infantry School more effectively than any military review or other ceremony with all its spit and polish. It was indicative of Marshall's imagination and his ability to communicate the esprit of his men to visitors.

His tour as Deputy Commandant at Benning was one of the most important of Marshall's career. It was equally important for the United States Army. The contribution he made in the training of officers was to have a long-range impact on the military fortunes of the country. He taught professionalism, inspired hard work, and encouraged the brilliant, promising officers to be patient. Lieutenant J. Lawton Collins, who had been with Marshall at Benning, wrote a very discouraging letter to General Marshall in August of 1936. Collins had spent seventeen years as a lieutenant and was beginning to have doubts about his future in the Army. Marshall replied that the Army would be "showing signs of real modernization when they reach down and pick you and several others of your stripe, which I imagine will be done, and shortly."[17]

When Marshall became Chief of Staff he did just that. Collins became a Corps Commander in First Army under General Courtney Hodges and in 1949 became Chief of Staff of the Army. Other men who were on Marshall's staff, or who were outstanding students at Benning from 1927-1932 as captains and majors and who later achieved distinction in World War II were: General of the Army Omar N. Bradley; General Courtney H. Hodges, Commander of the First U.S. Army in Europe; Lieutenant General Joseph W. Stilwell, Commander of American and Chinese Armies in the Far East; Lieutenant Generals Willard S. Paul and Harold R. Bull; Major Generals Thomas G. Hearn, Norman D. Cota, Lowell W. Rooks, William W. Eagles, Edwin F. Harding, Matthew Ridgway, and Richard G. Tindall. A total of 160 members of the Benning faculty and Infantry School students who caught Marshall's eye at the time became general officers in World War II. Of course, only the best of the officer corps were selected for Benning; but having come to Marshall's favorable attention there certainly did them no harm.

Fort Screven

From Fort Benning, Lieutenant Colonel Marshall was assigned as commander of a Battalion to Fort Screven, Georgia, a small post, hence a step down in responsibility. Marshall had no difficulty, however, in adjusting; he went immediately from an extremely hard, demanding schedule to a pace suitable to his new position.

He concentrated during his tour at Fort Screven on the same things he had at previous posts: the training and development of officers and men, not just the routine functions of keeping a post operating. One of the most pressing problems at Fort Screven was the low morale of the officers and men, reflecting —as in civilian life—results of the economic depression. He rode his horse each morning around the small reservation, noting things that needed correction or which could be improved, stopping frequently to talk with soldiers and members of their families to learn about individual and family problems. Before long, he had the confidence and respect of the post personnel of all ranks and had even learned the name of every individual on the post.

During this tour he was especially concerned with the morale of his non-commissioned officers. He had found, during his duty in China from 1924 to 1927, that the British Army NCO's bore much greater responsibility than their American counterparts. Believing that the NCO's should be the backbone of the Army, Marshall worked hard to improve their prestige. At Fort Screven, he organized a committee of the senior NCO's to make suggestions for improving the post, and he gave them an opportunity to carry out their suggestions.

When the Civilian Conservation Corps was established in 1933, Fort Screven became the headquarters of District F, which included South Carolina, eastern Georgia, and Florida. It was charged with assisting in the location, building, supplying, and administration of the CCC Camps scattered over these three states. This responsibility required a heavy drain of the officers stationed at Fort Screven. Senior officers were assigned to command CCC Camps; others from the Fort were assigned to administrative duties; young lieutenants, with little or no experience, found themselves building camps in such isolated areas that they were forced to make many decisions unaided. They soon found that even though mistakes were made, they were supported in full by Colonel Marshall. He was tolerant of honest mistakes, because he was aware a man learned from them; but as his officers gained experience he expected fewer errors. If they were based on negligence, laziness, or indifference, the officer was reassigned.

With comparatively few officers left on the post, Colonel Marshall was pleased at the increased opportunity for his officers to get excellent command and staff experience. The NCO's also carried new responsibilities. Some of the companies were in effect commanded by the First Sergeants, and an NCO even acted occasionally as officer of the day.[18]

Chicago: 1933-1936

Marshall had been very pleased to be assigned to the 8th Battalion at Fort Screven, duty that brought him back to work with troops, and expected the normal three-year tour there. But

in 1933, his duty with regular Army troops came to an abrupt
end. To his complete surprise, shock, and disappointment, he
received orders to report to Chicago as Senior Instructor for the
Illinois National Guard. He was so disappointed when he received his orders that "he wrote," Mrs. Marshall said, "to
General MacArthur, then Chief of Staff, that he was making his
first request for special consideration that he had ever made
while in the Army." Mrs. Marshall wrote that "after four years
as an instructor at Fort Benning, he felt it would be fatal to his
future if he were taken away from troops and placed on
detached service instructing again. He asked that he might remain with his Regiment. . ."[19] The request was denied.

Colonel Marshall was human. Leaving his troops was a great
disappointment; in fact, he thought it might be the end of his
Army career. Mrs. Marshall said of him during the first months
in Chicago that "George had a grey, drawn look which I had
never seen before, and have seldom seen since." After they had
been there for a year someone said to Mrs. Marshall at a reception, "Where is your husband? I want to meet him for I hear
Colonel Marshall is the cream of the Army." Mrs. Marshall said
to herself, "I felt like saying, 'Maybe so, but the cream was a bit
sour a year ago'."[20] Marshall did not sulk; he did not become
bitter and quit. Showing a characteristic resilience he immediately threw himself into his work. He saw much that needed to
be done and went about doing it.

Prior to the assignment of Marshall, the Senior Instructor of
the Illinois National Guard was Colonel Emory S. McAdams,
whose policy was to allow the Guard units to handle their own
training. Very little attention was given to attempts by the junior regular Army officers assigned to the Guard to improve the
quality of the training. "If an instructor," wrote Colonel Arthur
Pickens, an officer who served with the Illinois Guard from
1930 to 1934, "became insistent for more advanced training, he
was reported and toned down by Colonel McAdams."[21]

In 1933, Roy D. Keehn was appointed commander of the
33rd Division and promoted to the rank of major general. In
civilian life, Keehn was a very successful lawyer among whose

clients was the Hearst Syndicate, and a man with a great deal of political influence. Prior to his appointment as commander of the 33rd Division he had been a Guard major, serving as Division Judge Advocate.

When Keehn took office, he and Colonel McAdams had a very amicable relationship. The Division continued to drift along, practicing close order drill at weekly meetings. Summer camp was devoted to more drill and shooting up the allotted ammunition on the firing range. Lethargy was rampant; no one cared about changing the situation. But several months after Keehn took command things did change. Labor unrest was becoming unmanageable; and, though the Guard had the responsibility for keeping order, it became clear to Keehn that the present Guard organization and level of proficiency could not handle the situation. He called the War Department in Washington and asked for "the top colonel in the Army." He was told that Colonel George C. Marshall was the best. "Would you take him?" He said yes.

General Keehn knew almost nothing about military training. He had long and actively participated in the Guard; but his role of Division Judge Advocate General did little to educate him militarily. With Colonel Marshall as senior instructor, all this changed. Marshall asked Keehn to join him on many of his visits to the Guard units, and what Keehn found appalled him—poor attendance, inadequate training, incompetent officers, and general indifference. General Keehn, after becoming aware of the status of his Division, gave Marshall *carte blanche* authority to improve the training. Regular Army officers who opposed the changes made by Marshall were reassigned. Guard officers who failed to rise to the task at hand were dropped from the organization.

After General Keehn had observed Colonel Marshall for several months, he went to see Chief of Staff Douglas MacArthur on one of his trips to Washington and told him that Marshall was too good to be wasted in a Guard position. He should be promoted to brigadier general, General Keehn insisted, and given a challenge worthy of his talents. General MacArthur

informed Keehn that he had Marshall under consideration for
the position of Chief of Infantry, a position that would have
made Marshall a general. Unfortunately, the post would not be
vacant for another three years.

Actually the period with the Illinois National Guard was a
challenging assignment, and it played an important role in
Marshall's future. It was a period of labor disorders, when
strikes of employed and unemployed workers were frequent
and always troublesome. On many occasions Marshall had to be
called out to prevent or quell strife between management's
army of strike-breakers and the workers. He was the first Army
officer to train Guard troops in the technique of suppressing
civil disorders.

The assignment was also a political baptism; then, as now,
Guard units were political organizations. The officers were
political appointees, and the Guard was under the Illinois Governor's command. A regular Army officer is normally sheltered
from politics; but the tour with the Illinois Guard was a political education for Colonel Marshall which would assist him
greatly in Washington, D. C., in the years ahead.

Marshall worked hard for high standards in the training of the
Illinois National Guard. During the two-week summer camp
when he had the Guard units full time, he organized a number
of schools, stressed the importance of the instructors being
thoroughly qualified and prepared to present their subject to
the troops in small groups, and insisted that demonstrations be
given to show the men a correct picture of what they were to
do. He always insisted that training aids be used; and if they
were not available, the instructors had to use their own ingenuity to get them built.

In working with the junior officers of the Guard, he told
them what needed to be done and turned them loose to do it. If
an officer made a mistake, but was doing his best, he could
count on a hearing and another chance. Colonel Marshall would
not, however, keep anyone long who failed to produce. "If you
did not do the thing that you were sent to do," said one of his
junior officers of that time, "well, you suddenly were gone—to

another station—so quietly that the official record of the officer did not bear a scar."[22]

The high point of Guard training came during the two-week summer camp when units from all over the state practiced working together as a team. This was usually the only such opportunity they had, and confusion was a normal state during summer camp. It was no different during Colonel Marshall's first summer camp as senior instructor. It was the custom for advance parties from each regiment or separate detachment to arrive at least a day before the whole unit was due. The regular Army instructors who were assigned to each Guard unit also came with the advance party. Colonel Marshall arrived the day before the advance parties, secured a saddle horse, and watched each unit arrive, deploy, and set up. At no time during the day did he make himself known. To the advance parties he was just a horseman riding around while everyone was busy setting up tents, digging latrines, fixing food, piling up supplies, posting signs, building headquarters, and performing other necessary activities for establishing a camp.

That afternoon Colonel Marshall passed the word that he wanted to see all the regular Army instructors at 1900. At the meeting, he asked each regular Army officer to identify himself and the unit to which he was assigned. He then talked to each officer and his unit. Some of the units had performed poorly, running around in confused circles trying to get settled; some had performed in an average manner; and the 130th Infantry had done a superb job. While the other units were still working hard to get established, the 130th officers and men were sitting quietly talking, singing, and smoking. They had set up their tents, stored their baggage, dug their latrines and accomplished everything else as quickly as a regular unit would have. Colonel Marshall asked the R.A. instructor for the 130th, Captain Walter S. Wood, to stand up. "Why," he asked, "had his outfit done things so quickly and efficiently?" Captain Wood replied that it was a proud group, an old regiment drawn from country towns. It had sent troops to the Black Hawk War, the Mexican War, the Civil War, to the Mexican border in 1915 and 1916,

and to World War I. Its members took their soldiering seriously.
Colonel Marshall did not pursue the point further. He thought
Captain Wood's answer would suffice to get across the point of
discipline, order, and team work among even part-time soldiers.
He then outlined for each unit what was expected of them and
closed with a, "Thank you, gentlemen."[2 3]

In the summer of 1933, the 33rd Division of the Illinois
National Guard had their annual field training exercise at Camp
Grant near Rockford, Illinois, 90 miles west of Chicago. Toward
the end of the 15-day encampment, Colonel Marshall planned a
trip for the 33rd Division to the World's Fair then in progress in
Chicago. He thought the men would enjoy it; and, in addition,
moving the Division 90 miles would provide marvelous training.
On the last day of the summer camp, the 33rd marched 15
miles to a train station, bivouacked overnight, and boarded a
train for Chicago the next day. One of the officers present,
Harry L. Bolen, remembered that "Marshall's frequent inspections of the troops along the march route and his personal
inspection of the bivouac area was the incentive needed to strive
for perfection in this particular exercise."[2 4]

The same officer also recalled that Colonel Marshall personally commended their senior regular Army officer, Captain
Wood, "which made all of us feel that our extra efforts had
been worthwhile."[2 5]

The movement of an inexperienced group of part-time
soldiers a distance of 90 miles was a difficult task. Mistakes
were made, men and materiel got confused, tempers occasionally flared up. There were two regiments in the 33rd division,
the 129th from northern Illinois and the 130th from the southern part of the state. The operations order for the movement of
the Division directed that only pup-tents would be taken for the
bivouac rather than large wall tents and folding cots. On his way
to a meeting at Division Headquarters on the first day of the
bivouac, the regimental commander of the 130th, Colonel
Robert W. Davis, had to pass through the bivouac area of the
129th Infantry. What he saw made him furious. The 129th, in
violation of the movement orders, had brought along wall tents

and cots. The 130th, in compliance with orders, had not brought along such luxuries. The purpose of the meeting was assignment of materiel to the regiments. The first items to be issued were one-ton trucks. Colonel Davis blurted out "I want tents and cots for our officers before I want any trucks." This angered the Division Commander, but Colonel Davis held his ground. During the argument, Colonel Marshall eased through the group of officers to where Colonel Davis was standing. He came up beside Davis and said, "Bob, you're talking too much, better cool down before the Old Man gets any hotter and I'll take the matter up with the Division Inspector. He's the officer whose responsibility it is. Just leave it to me." Colonel Davis said of Colonel Marshall's intervention, "This kept me from a reprimand from the Division Commander, cooled me off, and everything worked out all right."[26]

As the senior military instructor to the Guard, Marshall did not have authority to command, only to advise and influence, an indirect leadership harder to carry off successfully than direct command. But he was successful. "We all had," wrote one of the regimental commanders of the Guard, "a great fondness for him and a strong desire to please him with the excellence of our training." One of his senior commanders in the Illinois Guard said of Colonel Marshall's tour, "He never seemed to tire year in and year out in his efforts to further the training of the Illinois National Guard, and I can honestly say that at no period during the 37 years that I was connected with the Illinois National Guard did we make as much progress in our training as the period from 1933 to 1936 when General Marshall served as the Senior Instructor. . ."[27]

All the Guard career and part-time officers and men who served with and under him concurred in that opinion. Patient and even-tempered regardless of provocations, he was always available for counsel with any person who had a problem. His professional knowledge of everything pertaining to soldiering won for him the confidence and respect of all officers and men. He often told his officers that the most important thing was to learn their assignment, use the judgment derived from knowledge and experience, make a decision, then stick to it.

Vancouver, Washington

In 1936, Colonel Marshall was promoted to the rank of brigadier general and given a new assignment. Within a few days after his promotion, he received orders to take command of the 5th Infantry Brigade. This brigade was part of the 3rd Division stationed at Vancouver Barracks, Washington, located immediately across the Columbia River from Portland, Oregon.

Soon after his arrival at Vancouver Barracks, his unit was scheduled to go to Fort Lewis for summer training. At the time the guard house was filled with about seventy prisoners—a lazy, troublesome group of runaways, deserters, and poor soldiers. Since the majority of the men on the post were going to Fort Lewis, Marshall asked the adjutant to draw up a list of the men he would need to run the post for the summer. The adjutant listed, among other things, a requirement of twenty guards for the prisoners. General Marshall deleted the whole twenty and left the adjutant only two old sergeants awaiting retirement to care for the seventy prisoners.

The adjutant was disturbed. He thought the two sergeants inadequate to meet the challenge of guarding such a recalcitrant group. General Marshall assured him that the prisoners would not cause any more trouble. The day before the troops left, Marshall went to the guard house and spoke to the men. "He didn't say much," said the adjutant, "just explained what was to happen and that he trusted them. The results were amazing. During the summer not one man ran away. All did their jobs under the planning and supervision of the two sergeants, and there was no trouble at all. I consider his leadership in the situation to have been remarkable."[28]

In addition to having command of the 5th Infantry Brigade, Marshall was the District Commander of the CCC Camps for the Northwest. One day a group of Negro enrollees rebelled against

their officers; they were immediately assembled in the camp for
Brigadier General Marshall to speak to them:

> You are deeply concerned, he said, even wrought up to
> violence, because you feel you have been discriminated
> against on account of your color. As your district com-
> mander, let me tell you how very wrong you were to take
> matters into your own hands. I will have none of this type
> of action. As I stand before you here I do not see the
> pigmentation of your flesh. I try to see the men and their
> hearts underneath the flesh. It matters not to me if you are
> white, black, red, yellow, or even blue. You have the right
> and privilege of appealing to me when you are disturbed
> and feel you cannot carry on in a normal, disciplined man-
> ner. You will be dealt with as men, not as members of any
> particular race. My decision on your appeal will rest only
> on the merits of your case—not otherwise, I can assure
> you.[29]

When he had finished, the enrollees, to a man, rose and cheered.

At Vancouver Barracks, as throughout his career, part of
Marshall's success as a leader was a result of his ability to listen
when subordinates reported to him. He quickly grasped the
basic points and had a remarkable memory for details. One
officer remembers of Marshall at Vancouver, "I can see him
now as I sat in his office. His was an innate thoughtfulness—his
desk uncluttered as always, his arms folded across his chest and
his chair turned so that his eyes seemed lost in the soft green-
ness of our Northwest Spring. He hated wordiness, long orders
and explanations."[30]

Marshall was always reserved in his dealings with the men in
his command, but there was no fear in him. His officers and
men did not find the reserve to be a barrier, nor were they in
awe of him. Brigadier General Talley wrote:

> I first met General Marshall in 1938 at Vancouver Bar-
> racks. I was at the officers club bar with a group of others.
> Unknowingly, we were blocking the path to the exit, until

I noticed several officers in our group step aside to allow
someone to pass. Looking over my shoulder I saw it was a
general officer whom I did not recognize. One of the other
officers said, 'It's General Marshall.' He joined our group,
chatted for a few minutes and went on. I noticed at the
time that all of the officers remained completely relaxed,
were glad to have him greet us and to stay if only for a few
minutes. All were pleasantly at ease, and when the General
had gone, the conversation picked up where it had been
broken and no one made any remark of any sort about the
General. It was apparent that he was easy to talk to.

The same officer commented, "When I saw him in later years
(during World War II), he was equally approachable."[3][1]

But again a three-year tour of duty was to come to an abrupt
end. On February 27, 1938 a short article in the *New York
Times* reported:

GENERAL MARSHALL CALLED TO CAPITAL

Vancouver, Wash., Feb. 26 (AP). Brig. General George C.
Marshall, commandant at Vancouver Barracks, left here for
Washington, D. C., by plane today following an order received by radio from General Malin Craig, Chief of Staff,
to report for special duty. . .[3][2]

This call to Washington marked the end of troop duty for Brigadier General George C. Marshall.

Washington

Shortly after his arrival in Washington in February 1938,
Marshall became Assistant Chief of Staff, War Plans Division of
the General Staff, and special assistant to General Craig. In
October 1938 came the announcement of Marshall's appointment as Deputy Chief of Staff. It was, therefore, no surprise
within Army circles when on April 28, 1939, President

Roosevelt informed the American people that General Malin Craig's successor as Chief of Staff, upon the latter's retirement on August 31, would be Brigadier General George C. Marshall. Marshall thus went from brigadier to four star general, jumping the ranks of major and lieutenant general, as well as twenty major generals and four brigadiers who were senior to him. He was the second non-West Pointer to achieve the position of Chief of Staff. The first had been Leonard Wood, "the doctor from Harvard."

Personnel

General Marshall's selection as Chief of Staff was to have a marked impact upon the many able officers he had encountered during his career. There was always a list of names in the upper right hand drawer of General Marshall's desk—a list of officers who had impressed him throughout his career. As already noted, during World War II, 160 officers who had been at Benning from 1927 to 1932 during Marshall's hegemony became general officers.

One of these 160 officers was General of the Army Omar H. Bradley. In November 1940, Brigadier General Robert Eichelberger, then superintendent at West Point, asked Bradley, who was then on General Marshall's staff, if he would like to be his commandant of cadets. Bradley, who after two years in Washington longed to get away from paper work and back to command of any sort, said yes. Upon securing General Marshall's approval, Eichelberger went to Bradley and said, "Congratulations, Omar, you've got it. General Marshall just approved the request."[33]

But Marshall was bothered by this assignment. A week later he called Bradley into his office and asked him, "Are you certain that you want to go to West Point as commandant of cadets?" Bradley answered "Yes, sir. It's a command job and it will give me a chance to help develop officers there." Then Marshall offered him an alternative. "I was thinking," Marshall

replied, "of bringing Hodges up from Fort Benning to become
Chief of Infantry. How would you like to go down there and
take his place?" Bradley caught his breath and said, "That, sir,
changes the entire picture." Commandant of the Infantry
School was one of the choicest "soldiering" jobs in the Army.
"General Marshall, his decision already made," said Bradley,
"then informed me, 'Very well. I'll send you down just as soon
as I can bring Hodges to Washington'."[34] In 1941, the assignment came through and, with it, a promotion from the rank of
lieutenant colonel to brigadier general.

Another of the officers brought along the career ladder was
Dwight D. Eisenhower. "One thing that General Marshall
despised more than anything else," according to General Eisenhower, "was anyone thinking rank—looking out for himself.
One day we were talking [in Marshall's Pentagon office in 1942]
about something, and he told me about a man who came in to
see him and towards whom he had been favorably disposed.
This man came in and told General Marshall all the reasons why
he needed to be promoted. It was just absolutely necessary, and
Marshall said he was almost livid. 'I told the man,' Marshall said,
'now look, the men that get promoted in this war are going to
be the people that are in command and carry the burdens.' He
went on to say, 'the staff isn't going to get promoted at all'."

"Suddenly he turned to me and said, 'Now you are a case. I
happen to know General Joyce tried to get you as a division
commander. General Kreuger told me that he would be glad to
give you a Corps at any time. Well, that's just too bad. You are
a brigadier, and you are going to stay a brigadier and that's
that'." General Marshall talked to General Eisenhower like that
for about five minutes. Then General Eisenhower said to him,
"General, you are making a mistake. I don't give a damn about
your promotion and your power to promote me. You brought
me in here for a job. I didn't ask you whether I liked it or didn't
like it. I'm trying to do my duty." Eisenhower continued, "I
got up to leave his office (he had a large office). Something just
happened to make me look around and I saw a faint smile on
General Marshall's face. I had the grace to smile myself. I knew
I had made an ass of myself."

"You know," General Eisenhower said, "from that day on he started promoting me. Well, not that day, within ten days. He had written the request for the promotion to major general to the Senate himself. He said the operations division as he had set it up in the United States Army was not truly a staff position. He said I was a commander since I was making deployments, etc. This was his rationalization. It wasn't too long after that that he decided to send me to England, and when he sent me there he gave me another star and then another, etc."[35]

A later conversation between Marshall and Eisenhower sheds some light on significant characteristics of both. On June 12, six days after the invasion of Europe, General Marshall, along with General Arnold and Admiral King, came over to see General Eisenhower. Marshall remarked, "Eisenhower, you've chosen all these commanders or accepted those we sent from Washington. What's the principal quality you look for?" General Eisenhower later noted, "Without even thinking I said 'selflessness.' After I thought of it I realized that that man himself gave me that idea. This was the greatest quality of all. Going back to that commotion in his office and my reactions, General Marshall made up his mind that here was a guy that was not thinking about his own possibilities of promotion in the work he was trying to do. I think that the selflessness quality was one of those thoughts that was not really an original thought but my subconscious brought it out." General Eisenhower said of that event in the Pentagon in 1942, "I probably would have finished the war as the Operations Officer of the War Department if it hadn't been for that conversation with General Marshall."[36]

An amusing incident came out of General J. Lawton Collins' tutelage under Marshall at Fort Benning. "Down at Benning during those early years," said General Collins, "General Marshall had often said to me, 'Now look, if war comes along or is in the offing, don't let them stick you on a staff job like they did me. You insist on getting out in the field and getting with troops'." Just prior to World War II, Captain Collins was an instructor at the Army War College. Because of the impending war the College was closed and the faculty and staff reassigned,

Captain Collins being ordered to the office of the Secretary of the General Staff for temporary duty. "I stayed there for some months," he reflected, "and then as we got closer and closer to war, the Secretary to the General Staff was insisting that I take a permanent assignment. I steadfastly refused, and finally he said, 'General Marshall wants you here.' I said, well, let me see General Marshall. I went in to see the Chief of Staff and I reminded him of this incident. General Marshall replied, 'All right Collins, I will let you go'."[37]

Naturally, not all of the officers who achieved high positions in World War II were at Benning with Marshall. One officer came to Marshall's attention when he was Brigade Commander at Vancouver Barracks—General Mark W. Clark. General Clark, after graduation from the War College in 1936, was ordered to Fort Lewis, Washington, where he was assigned to the General Staff of the Third Division and made the Division G-2 and G-3. The Division Commander, Chief of Staff, and many of the other senior officers were about ready for retirement and had not attempted to become well versed in the recent developments of tactics and techniques and maneuvers. But Major Clark, fresh out of the War College, was anxious to try out the theories he had been taught; and, fortunately, most of the senior officers of the division supported him.

There were two brigade commanders for the division, one at Vancouver Barracks about 65 miles away, and one at Salt Lake, Utah. Marshall was the brigade commander at Vancouver, and Major Clark's responsibilities on the General Staff of the Division put him in constant contact with Marshall. General Clark reflected:

I would say my association with George Marshall in 1936 to 1940 at Fort Lewis probably was one of the greatest breaks I ever had. He had a little airfield at Fort Lewis and I would get one of the pilots to fly me down to Vancouver to see Marshall, landing on the parade ground there. I would phone Marshall I was coming. I would work up a series of problems and wanted somebody to go over them with me who had more experience than I did. Marshall was the fellow, so we struck up quite a friendship during the time Marshall was at Vancouver. He loved it. I saw quite a lot of him and he had some very original ideas for maneuvering the troops, some that were not in the book at all. Some officers would say "Oh, that's wrong because it wasn't taught at Leavenworth." Marshall demonstrated in some of the problems things that surprised the dickens out of us.[38]

General Marshall became Chief of Staff in 1939 and shortly thereafter Lieutenant Colonel Clark was called to Washington for a very responsible role, G-3 for the chief of staff of the commander of the Army ground forces, Major General Lesley J. McNair. This opportunity was the beginning of an extremely rapid rise in rank and responsibility for Mark Clark. He was jumped in rank from lieutenant colonel to brigadier general; and by the end of the war, he had his fourth star and the command of an Army.

According to Clark, "They could have picked one of fifty fellows that I know for the job I got, who would have done it at least as good, maybe better; but I happened to be there at the time, in the proper grade and age, and Marshall was looking."[39]

It would, however, have been impossible for Marshall to select all the general officers needed for World War II on a personal basis. When necessary he relied on the judgment of others whom he respected. During an inspection trip at Pearl Harbor with Admiral Nimitz in 1943, he called aside Major General Charles H. Corlett, the Commander of the 7th Division which was in training to go to the Marshall Islands. As the two men walked out of Admiral Nimitz's office, General Marshall took General Corlett by the arm and said to him, "Corlett, would you like to know how you happened to be made a general officer? I did not know you. I was aware that you were in command of the 30th Infantry, but little else. I came down to my office one morning and going through my mail, I found five requests for you by senior officers. I immediately called G-1 [Personnel] and told him to make Corlett a general officer."[40]

In December 1940, General Marshall was presented with one of his first major personnel problems. The officer in charge of construction in the quartermaster corps was not keeping up with the increasing demands upon his department. "He apparently," Stimson said, "lacks the gift of organization." General Marshall recommended replacing the officer. The post included the difficult and delicate task of selecting contracts on the ever-increasing war production and procurement projects, a job which that officer had handled without a taint of scandal. "His release," said Secretary Stimson, "made another problem to be handled at the coming press conference," although Stimson agreed with Marshall's request, and recognized that "Marshall had given careful and fair consideration to it and felt just as kindly towards [that officer] as I did."[41] But preparation of one's country for a possible war did not call primarily for kindness. Aggressive and intelligent leadership was needed.

Pearl Harbor

On December 7, 1941 the United States suffered the most disastrous surprise attack in her history when the Japanese bombed Pearl Harbor. As a result there were 3,963 casualties—896 wounded and 3,067 either killed, dead of wounds, or missing and declared dead. The battleships Arizona, California, Oklahoma, and West Virginia were sunk; and the Nevada was beached to avoid its sinking. The auxiliary vessels Utah and Oglala were also sunk. The other battleships in the harbor, Pennsylvania, Maryland and Tennessee, the cruisers Helena, Honolulu and Raleigh, the destroyers Shaw, Cassin and Downes, and the auxiliaries Curtis and Vestal were seriously damaged. A total of 249 airplanes (patrol, fighter, scout bombers, torpedo bombers, battleship and cruiser planes, and utility and transport planes) were destroyed.[42]

Colonel Trevor N. Dupuy in an article entitled, "Pearl Harbor: Who Blundered?," concluded that "no disaster of the magnitude of Pearl Harbor could have occurred without the failure—somewhere and somehow—of leadership."[43] This question poses a challenge: what was General Marshall's role in the Pearl Harbor disaster and how much of it was a failure in the Army Chief of Staff's leadership? There were eight detailed and separate investigations of the Pearl Harbor Attack, the longest of which was that conducted by the U.S. Congress—39 volumes of testimony, evidence, conclusions, and recommendations. The discussion and the attempt to place blame has obviously been extensive and needs only brief mention at this time. The exhaustive Congressional study concluded:

> Virtually everyone was surprised that Japan struck the Fleet at Pearl Harbor at the time that she did. Yet officers, both in Washington and Hawaii, were fully conscious of the danger from air attack; they realized this form of attack on Pearl Harbor by Japan was at least a possibility; and they were adequately informed of the imminence of war.[44]

The report went on to state that the authorities in Washington had warned the command in Hawaii and that the commanders there had failed to discharge their responsibilities in light of these warnings. On November 24, 1941, General Marshall informed Lieutenant General Walter C. Short, the Army Commander in Hawaii, that the deterioration in American-Japanese diplomatic relations was such that there was a definite threat of war with Japan; and he, therefore, ordered him to report what steps he planned to take to meet the threat. Unfortunately the only concrete step taken by General Short was to be more careful of Japanese sabotage.

One can criticize General Marshall for one aspect of his leadership in this event—he failed to follow up on the measures General Short had taken to cope with the possible danger of war with Japan. However, the responsibilities of a Chief of Staff in 1941 were overwhelming. The officer in that position had to delegate to his subordinates; otherwise, since he was human, he could not possibly accomplish the job. No one man can do everything when he leads hundreds of thousands, even millions, and must concern himself with global strategy.

Then, there was the famous message of December 7, 1941. The United States had broken the Japanese code and her diplomatic messages were clearly and immediately knowledgeable to us. Colonel Rufus Bratton received two messages early Sunday morning that disturbed him greatly. One was an order to the Japanese Ambassador in Washington, D.C. to destroy the Japanese Embassy code machine and all classified documents. The other message was even more foreboding; it stated, "Will the Ambassador please submit to the United States Government (if possible to the Secretary of State) our reply to the United States at 1 P.M. on the 7th, our time." Marshall was out horseback riding at Fort Myer when this message was decoded. When he returned to his home, he was told there was an important message awaiting him. When he read it he was alarmed. He drafted a message of warning to General Short in Hawaii and all other commanders in the Pacific area including the Western Coast of the United States, but it was not received in time to do any good at Pearl Harbor. It was impossible, of course, to know the complete significance of the time of one P.M.

The accusation has been made that, on President Roosevelt's order, Marshall was not to inform the Army and Navy Commanders in Hawaii of the threat of an attack on Pearl Harbor. The supposed reason was that Roosevelt wanted the Japanese to attack Pearl Harbor to bring us into the war. Such a preposterous and irresponsible accusation against President Roosevelt and his Army Chief of Staff need not be discussed any further since none of the numerous official investigations corroborate it.

In concluding this point, there was no doubt that General Short received at least enough information to justify security measures as a precaution to an attack. He did not do so, and the worst blame one could place upon General Marshall and his leadership was his trusting that a senior commander would follow-up on an order in an appropriate manner.

Personnel Selection

In January 1942 one of the most difficult problems facing Secretary Stimson and General Marshall was the selection of an American general for assignment to China. It would be an extremely challenging job since the Chinese were in rapid retreat from the Japanese onslaught. The American general would be even more taxed because his command would include Chinese troops as well as American, and he would have to deal with a corrupt political system in China. One of the first officers considered was Lieutenant General Hugh Drum. General Drum, however, "took the position" Stimson wrote, "that he did not think the role in China which I had offered him was big enough for his capabilities."[45]

Secretary Stimson discussed General Drum's position that evening with General Marshall. The next day, the situation came to a head. "The afternoon," wrote Stimson, "was taken up with the wretched Drum affair. . . I received a letter from Drum who had evidently been scared at the effects of his recalcitrancy with reference to his going to China and had written in this letter to me that he would do anything I wanted him to do." Stimson showed the letter to General Marshall who saw it as additional evidence of General Drum's "unfitness and thought that it indicated mainly that he was trying to protect himself against criticism for having virtually declined to go."[46]

Any officer who seemed to Marshall to be anxious to select an assignment to suit his own personal preference was in trouble. "General William N. Haskell came in to see me," Secretary of War Stimson wrote in his diary early in 1941, "in regard to his detail in the next eight months before he finally retires. I am fond of Haskell . . . but when I spoke to Marshall about it I found that Haskell had very much irritated Marshall by his choosiness in regard to his future."[47] General Marshall had excellent rapport with Secretary of War Stimson; but he refused to give General Haskell special consideration for the simple reason he had asked for it.

One of the officers who served with Lieutenant Colonel Marshall in China commented, "Someone in the Army in 1929 named the officers who were with George C. Marshall in China from 1924 to 1927 as the 'China Gang'. This charge implied that we were fair-haired buds and received favored treatment from G. C. M. This charge had no basis. General Marshall could be your friend but you never asked him for favors because we were all fully aware of his integrity."[48] His attitude toward assisting young officers was summed up by an officer who said that General Marshall had "great loyalty to those subordinates he considered good officers, and little patience with those he thought were not."[49]

If Marshall supported a man and he failed, that ended the sponsorship. General Patton in September 1942 suggested to Secretary Stimson an officer named Smith, for a position in the Advanced Armored Force. Secretary Stimson brought the matter up with General Marshall; but, Stimson reported, "Marshall was strongly adverse. He said he had always been a friend of Smith and had brought him forward last year in maneuvers in the hope of giving him a chance, but he failed lamentably and his only question was whether Smith was fit for his present position. . ."[50]

General Marshall's selection of men played a vitally important role in the success of the American armies. After the successful invasion of North Africa, Secretary Stimson said in General Marshall's presence that he "felt the chief credit for this belonged to him." General Marshall modestly replied that "the main thing had been the choice of men to do it." Stimson agreed, but went on to say that the credit for the selection of the best men belonged to General Marshall. "He had been hard-boiled and severe," wrote Stimson, "in his release of men who did not measure up when the time came, and he had picked out very good men to carry it out."[51]

There was at least one dissenting opinion regarding Marshall's treatment of his officers. The wife of one of his senior generals wrote that the Chief of Staff "was my child's godfather and spent the night my son was born walking the corridors of the hospital. I thought he was wonderful, but about his leadership I cannot speak very highly. He later treated my husband terribly and unforgiveably. . . . He let his tried and true friends down. . . . he wrecked my husband's career, broke his heart and took the rank of major general away from him. . ." Actually this officer's wife could not have paid General Marshall a greater compliment. Her husband had made an unforgiveable error in judgment during World War II. Though he was one of General Marshall's closest friends, Marshall showed no favoritism. The officer was busted to the rank of colonel.

"I cannot afford the luxury of sentiment." General Marshall told Mrs. Marshall one evening while they were walking, "mine must be cold logic. Sentiment is for others."[52] Yet, the officers sponsored by Marshall never forgot him and Secretary Stimson remarked that "they were all as loyal to him as their leader as if they were here in the Pentagon."[53]

Relationship With Eisenhower

Since General Marshall had been aide-de-camp to General Pershing during the last part of World War I, he was aware of the animosity that had existed between his boss and Army Chief of Staff General Peyton March. General Marshall saw to it that such friction never occurred between himself and General Eisenhower.

"You do not need," General Marshall told General Eisenhower when he went to Europe in 1942, "to take or keep any commander in whom you do not have full confidence. So long as he holds a command in your theater it is evidence to me of your satisfaction with him. The lives of many are at stake; I will not have you operating under any misunderstanding as to your authority, and your duty, to reject or remove any that fails to satisfy you completely."[54] Not once during World War II did General Marshall violate this rule; and there was never any doubt that all officers in the European Command were under General Eisenhower, and in the Far East under General MacArthur.

Throughout World War II, General Marshall also insisted that the Combined Chiefs (composed of American and British officers) not interfere with General Eisenhower's conduct of operations in North Africa, Sicily, Italy, France, and Germany. He objected strenuously whenever the Combined Chiefs attempted to issue orders or advice to any field commander.

In January 1945, just prior to the Yalta Conference, top Allied generals met at Malta. One of the most important items on the agenda for this meeting was the selection of a strategic plan for concluding the war against Germany. The British presented one plan; General Eisenhower, represented by Chief of Staff General Walter B. Smith, argued for another. General Marshall, who was present, felt so strongly about General Eisenhower's authority as Supreme Commander that he insisted Ike's plan be adopted and presented an ultimatum to the British members of the Combined Staff. He informed them that if the British plan was submitted to the Prime Minister and President Roosevelt, and approved, he would have no choice but to ask for General Eisenhower's release as Supreme Commander. Such an attitude by the usually restrained and quiet Marshall won the day. General Eisenhower's plan was approved.

The harmony between General Marshall and General Eisenhower was unblemished. General Eisenhower had heard about the brilliant George Marshall for over twenty years, first from his earliest and most influential teacher, Major General Fox Conner, who had considered Marshall a genius. "I was predisposed towards Marshall," Ike said, "because I had heard all my life from Fox Conner that Marshall was the ideal soldier."[5 5] For his part, Marshall respected Eisenhower for his honest frankness, intelligence, capacity for work, and most of all for his selflessness.

Once Eisenhower had taken over command in Europe, General Marshall attempted to relieve him of things which would distract him and wear him down. He instructed Ike not to get involved in politics and above all not to waste his precious time and energy defending past actions; he had the future to worry about. When very important persons came to visit him, General Marshall instructed General Eisenhower to refrain from arguing or debating with them and to "merely listen politely, yes them if necessary; but, above all," he was not to "waste his brain power."[5 6]

In December 1943, after General Eisenhower had been selected as Supreme Commander for the Allied invasion of Europe, he was trying to decide if he should come home for a few days. He had been under a terrific strain and needed a break to restore mental freshness; but how could he leave with the mammoth undertaking before him? General Marshall finally decided for him. On December 30, 1943, Marshall sent a message saying, "Now, come on home and see your wife and trust somebody else for twenty minutes in England."[5 7]

Marshall saw that Eisenhower received his third star by sending him to the European command and selecting him to command the invasion of North Africa. Harry Hopkins wrote one day in 1943, that the President had been lunching with Marshall and "I came in on the tail end of that. Marshall was talking about the difficulties of not having Eisenhower a full General." President Roosevelt said no to promoting Ike at that time because the American Army in North Africa was mired in the mud, going very slowly and that he would not promote Eisenhower "until there was some damn good reason for doing it."[5 8] When the Germans were knocked out of Tunisia, Ike got his fourth star.

Marshall's relationship with Eisenhower was typical of his mode of leadership. As Chief of Staff, he followed a similar approach with all the officers under him. "Army officers are intelligent," General Marshall would say. "Give them the bare tree, let them supply the leaves."

One former staff officer under Marshall said, not necessarily correctly, that the Chief of Staff "sacrificed toleration for perfection, the spirit for the letter, the trivia for the immediate end; in other words, it was either 'white' or 'black'; ruling out completely any shade of grey . . . he expected his subordinates to be right *ALL* the time; the subordinate might be *RIGHT* many times and then err; he was then 'finished'."[5 9]

This was a harsh appraisal, and perhaps a little unfair. General Marshall was a perfectionist, but in a special sense. He perceived perfection, he sought perfection personally, he tacitly urged his subordinates to be satisfied with nothing less than perfection; yet he did not really expect perfection to be attained either by himself or others. Almost everyone came away from his presence wishing sincerely that he had done a little better toward satisfying the General.[60]

In 1943 Brigadier General Thomas J. Betts was in the Office of the Secretary of the General Staff waiting to see General Marshall. The secretary at that time was Colonel Stanley Mickelson, who was with General Marshall when General Betts arrived. Waiting in the outside office was Major General Orlando Ward, who had been Secretary to the General Staff from 1938 to 1941. The Secretary's position was important, for he was the officer who monitored papers and callers for the Chief of Staff. After a few minutes Colonel Mickelson came out of General Marshall's office with a rueful smile on his face.

"Did you give the old man what he wanted?" asked 'Pink' Ward.

"No," answered Colonel Mickelson, "I never have."

"Neither did I," said General Ward. Then he too smiled, ruefully, yet a little proudly. "You never will. Nobody ever will."[61]

General Walter B. Smith, who was Secretary to General Marshall during 1941 and 1942, believed that some officers who worked for General Marshall failed because they were incapable of expressing themselves lucidly and succinctly when they presented a proposal or problem to him. "Those who speak slowly and haltingly and seem to fumble," he commented in September 1942, "are soon passed by in the rush to get things done."[62] The officers on Marshall's staff quickly learned that they went into his office with their work well prepared. If they did not, they could count on quick reassignment.

General Marshall wanted men who could and would make decisions. He delegated a great amount of his work. Bearing a crushing load, he expected his subordinates to relieve him of some of the burden of his office and to give careful deliberation and diligent application to their work.

General Eisenhower said that something that annoyed Marshall "was any effort to 'pass the buck', especially to him. Often he remarked that he could get a thousand men to do detailed work, but too many were useless in responsible posts because they left to him the necessity of making every decision. He insisted that his principal assistants should think and act on their own conclusions in their own spheres of responsibility, a doctrine emphasized in our army schools but too little practiced in peacetime."[63]

In 1940 Omar Bradley was assigned by General Marshall to Washington as Assistant Secretary of the General Staff, a job that included responsibility for briefing General Marshall on papers that came to the Chief of Staff for decisions. After a few weeks in the job Marshall called Bradley and his assistants into his office. "Gentlemen," he said, "I'm disappointed in you. You haven't yet disagreed with a single decision I've made." Bradley replied, "General, that's only because there has been no cause for disagreement. When we differ with you on a decision, sir, we'll tell you so."[64]

It was standard procedure during World War II for division commanders, after their divisions completed stateside training, to receive a briefing before sailing with their units for combat in Europe or the Far East. This briefing included a talk from General Marshall. "I had expected," one division commander wrote about his briefing, "to be counseled and advised as to his standards for combat readiness. Instead, he devoted the entire time to excoriating the type of officer who gives answers he thinks the chief wants to hear rather than the hard facts. He was in a bad mood because of some specific incident, and he strongly impressed us who were present with the importance of an officer having the moral courage to report facts, unpleasant as they may be, to the ears of the commander, rather than trying to keep bad news from him."[65]

When General Marshall was visiting in Europe in 1944, he stopped at Heerlen, Holland, which at that time was

Headquarters of the 30th Division, commanded by Major
General Charles H. Corlett. General Marshall was concerned because some parts of the divisions were prepared and others were
not. Since replacements for the divisions then in action presented a major problem to the Army commanders, General
Marshall asked Corlett if it would help to send replacements
over by regiments to be incorporated into divisions already in
Europe. General Corlett immediately answered "Yes." Marshall
gave him a stern look and said, "Corlett, you are not giving me
this answer just because I am Chief of Staff, are you?" General
Corlett blew up at the implication that he was a yes-man, and
left little doubt in General Marshall's mind that he had been
given a straight answer.[66]

Almost a fanatic in his antipathy towards yes men, Marshall
usually insisted that the officer repsonsible attend the briefing
when a paper or staff report was presented, and he admonished
all who were present to speak out regardless of the presence of
their immediate superiors.

Relationship With Secretary Stimson

When Marshall was appointed Army Chief of Staff in 1939,
the Secretary of War was Harry H. Woodring, and the Assistant
Secretary was Louis Johnson. Woodring and Johnson did not
get along; in fact, often the friction between them was so bad
they were not on speaking terms. Mr. Woodring was a pleasant,
easy-going gentleman; Mr. Johnson was ambitious, aggressive,
and dynamic. It was a challenging atmosphere for General
Marshall, who had to work with both men, guarding against
involvement in any disputes between his two civilian bosses.
The difficult situation, fortunately, lasted only a short time.

On June 25, 1940, President Roosevelt offered Henry L.
Stimson the position of Secretary of War. He accepted, and on
July 9 was confirmed by the Senate. When Stimson received his
first briefing as Secretary of War from Army Chief of Staff
George C. Marshall, it was the renewal of an old acquaintance.

In 1916, Stimson had been asked by former President Theodore Roosevelt, on the strength of his experience as Secretary of War from 1910-1911, to draw up a list of officers for a division Roosevelt wanted to raise. Stimson had found Marshall's name mentioned for this division by many officers whom he had greatly respected. The formation of the division never materialized; but it was an indirect beginning of the association between Marshall and Stimson. During World War I, Stimson went on active duty as an Army lieutenant colonel; and in 1918, he met Marshall personally for the first time at the Staff College in Langres, France. After the war, the two had no close contact; but in 1928, when Stimson became governor of the Philippines, he asked Marshall to go with him as his aide.[67] Marshall turned down the request because he wished to break away from further staff duty.

After Stimson had been in office less than a month, he commented on a conversation with Marshall on July 22, 1940, ". . . on the whole it was a very interesting and helpful talk with Marshall, who is always anxious to help and is very loyal and faithful."[68] As World War II progressed, a warm and close relationship developed between the two men, and Stimson's dependence upon Marshall increased markedly. In March 1941, President Roosevelt discussed with Stimson a plan to send some senior officers to observe the war in Europe. "I think," Stimson wrote, "it probably would be a good thing to send General Arnold. I do not like to spare Marshall at this time. He is too important here."[69]

As the war crisis worsened, Stimson's concern became even more evident. On May 5, 1941 he noted, "Marshall was intending to leave for a trip to Alaska today, but I felt so clearly that very ominous trouble was in the offing, I told him not to go. It is not time for him to be away with the critical things that are coming up . . ."[70] As a matter of fact, he did not like to have Marshall away at any time. A November 1941 entry revealed that "Marshall is down at the maneuvers today and I feel his absence very much."[71] Stimson "soon understood," said his biographer, McGeorge Bundy, "that the greatest problem [i.e. a competent Chief of Staff] a Secretary of War can have would never happen while Marshall was alive and well."[72]

When the United States entered the war on December 7, 1941, Stimson realized more sharply than ever how indispensable was General Marshall. A few days after Pearl Harbor, Stimson recorded in his diary: "I had a long talk with General Marshall about his own position and the need of giving him better help for the tremendous task that he is carrying on ... I told him that it was more important that his life and brain should be kept going, than anything else that I could see on the horizon."[73]

In January 1942, Winston Churchill came to the United States for talks with President Roosevelt. The Prime Minister, who had been carrying great responsibilities for almost two years before the United States entered the war, was tired. After his conference with Roosevelt, he decided to travel to the southern part of the United States for some warm weather and rest. Stimson was disturbed by his choice of traveling companion. He said:

> I have no quarrel with Churchill's decision to get rest, but I am troubled and distressed that he has taken with him for the journey General Marshall, simply to have a talk with him in the plane as they went down. Marshall is very busy, very much overworked, and should not be taken from his work. He will have to come back on a night train and will lose twenty-four hours out of his precious time without getting any rest from it. It was only due to the President's urging him that he did not decline Churchill's invitation, and I think it was one of the thoughtless things which the President ought not to do.[74]

A similar and even more aggravating incident occurred in May of 1943 when President Roosevelt and Prime Minister Winston Churchill met in Washington to discuss war strategy. There were points upon which the two differed vigorously. Churchill was adamant to the end, finally saying to the President, "Well, I will give up on my part if you will let me have George Marshall to go

on a trip to Africa." The President traded on the spot and
agreed to let Marshall go. Churchill's objective was obvious: he
wanted to use his eloquent persuasiveness on General Marshall
to secure his agreement to excursions in the Eastern Mediterranean. Secretary Stimson, when he heard of this, said
indignantly, "To think of picking out the strongest man in
America, and Marshall is surely that, the one on whom the fate
of the war depends, and then to deprive him in a gamble of a
much needed opportunity to recoup his strength with about
three days rest and send him off on a difficult and rather
dangerous trip across the Atlantic Ocean where he is not needed
except for Churchill's purposes, is, I think, going pretty far."[7 5]

Prime Minister Churchill's purpose in wanting General
Marshall to join him was as suspected. Captain Butcher, General
Eisenhower's naval aide, wrote in his diary on May 29, 1943,
"General Marshall is accompanying the Prime Minister this far
[Algiers], at the PM's request to the President, because the PM
openly and avowedly is seeking to influence Ike to pursue the
campaign in the Mediterranean . . . Presumably, he then wants
the Allied effort to continue in the Mediterranean area rather
than across the Channel as already agreed . . . the PM has shown
every courtesy to General Marshall, making certain that he was
accorded all honors meant for the PM . . . The PM recited his
story three different times in three different ways last night. He
talks persistently until he has worn down the last shred of opposition."[7 6] But the Prime Minister failed in his mission. He did
not alter General Marshall's belief that the Allies should concentrate on invading Europe across the Channel. In the Army
Chief of Staff, the stubborn Prime Minister met his match.

The rapport between Secretary of War Stimson and Chief of
Staff General Marshall was superb. Seldom during the war was
there a difference of opinion between the two. But there was a
slight rift when in May 1942 Stimson effected a reorganization
that had the result of removing the "commander" connotation
from the Chief of Staff office. Marshall felt badly about the
change. "Secretly," Stimson wrote, "at the bottom of his heart,
Marshall had evidently felt that that deprived him of a position

that he had before. He was very nice about it," Stimson continued, "and we talked with utmost friendship, but it made me feel very badly."[77] Stimson was so bothered about Marshall's reaction he brought the matter up at lunch with President Roosevelt the next day, though he had no intention of changing his mind. He told the President how loyally Marshall had accepted the decision, even though it appeared to be a demotion and had caused General Marshall embarrassment because of the questions which were asked regarding speculation over a loss of confidence in the Chief of Staff.

There was a historic reason for Stimson's refusal to grant the Chief of Staff the title of Commander. After the Civil War, Army generals, particularly the Chief of Staff, started to assume an alarming role of independence from the authority of the President, who was constitutional Commander-in-Chief of all armed forces. The senior generals believed they should not be subject to unknowledgeable whims of presidents and secretaries of war on military matters. An example was General Sherman's decision to move Army Headquarters from Washington to St. Louis, because he didn't care for the politically corrupt atmosphere in the nation's capital.

When Elihu Root became Secretary of War, he put a decisive halt to the Army's assertion of hegemony. He selected the title of Chief of Staff to emphasize the top Army officers' subordinate role to the President of the United States. Secretary Stimson was an ardent supporter of Root's reform; in 1942, therefore, he refused permission to grant the Chief of Staff the title of commander. While Stimson had no concern over General Marshall's understanding of the subordinate role of the soldier, he was concerned with precedent and with the unknown factor of what the next Chief of Staff might be like. But he left no doubt in the mind of all Army commanders that General Marshall had unconditional authority over every officer in the entire United States Army.

Relations With the President

General Marshall was so highly respected by President Roosevelt that he bore complete responsibility for military strategy, and reported directly to the President on such matters. Since Stimson wholeheartedly shared this respect, he never felt jealousy or resentment towards Marshall over this close relationship. Part of Marshall's success with President Roosevelt resulted from his unwavering formality. FDR never called General Marshall, George. He never went to see the President for informal chats as did Chief of Naval Operations Stark. Marshall was strictly business, and because of this his opinions carried great weight with the Chief Executive. His reserve and dignity played a significant role in the effectiveness of his leadership. But still it bothered President Roosevelt that General Marshall would not drop his formality occasionally, and he went so far as to ask Harry Hopkins to speak to Marshall about the matter. Marshall replied to Hopkins that to do so would be completely out of character and he would not acquiesce.

One afternoon, shortly after he had become Chief of Staff, Marshall returned from a meeting in the White House and told a member of his staff, "I probably will not be Chief of Staff tomorrow." It seems that he had just crossed the President by insisting that the heads of the aircraft industry must be made aware of the fact that the international situation was extremely serious and that they had to give first priority to the defense of the country. The uncooperative attitude of many aircraft industry executives had reached the point where something had to be done. "The President," said General Marshall, "was quite perturbed at my forthright stand." However, General Marshall was not fired. After a day to think about it, the President concluded that his Chief of Staff was correct and supported his recommendations. No more than Marshall himself did Roosevelt want to be served by yes men.

President Roosevelt was a nautical man. He had been Assistant Secretary of the Navy in 1917, and from childhood on
he was an avid sailing enthusiast. Using this interest, General
Marshall would often explain to the President various new army
organization plans in nautical terms. On one occasion, for example, he drew a large diagram on a piece of cardboard cut in
the shape of a ship. Comprising the forward section, or bow, of
the ship was a newly designed regular army triangular division.
Back of that were two or three square National Guard Divisions,
and at the stern were the service elements to support the
forward divisions. Thus an imaginative Army Chief of Staff
educated a naval President in terms he understood.[7][8]

Marshall had the complete confidence of the President, and
seldom during World War II did the President ever go against the
advice of his Army Chief of Staff.

Relations With Congress

The Chief of Staff of the Army even in time of war has many
bosses. For Marshall, there was, first, the Commander- in-Chief,
the President of the United States; his immediate senior in the
chain of command was Secretary of War Stimson; and always
ready to add their voices were the gentlemen of the Congress.
Secretary Stimson, upon General Marshall's recommendation,
requested in 1941 that Congress extend the Selective Service
Act, initially passed for only one year. If it was not extended,
the Army would again be limited to volunteers at a time when
war was clearly impending. The Secretary of War had discussions with Congressional leaders, who were almost unanimous in
their agreement that the extension would never pass. But it did
pass—by one vote. The responsibility for getting this bill
through Congress had rested with General George C. Marshall.
This was the Army Chief of Staff's first battle with Congress
and his first significant victory.

Not long after that battle was won, General Marshall had a
particularly difficult fight in Congress getting legislation to

permit the draft of eighteen-year-olds. After the bill had finally passed, President Roosevelt sent a longhand note to General Marshall:[79]

THE WHITE HOUSE, WASHINGTON

Dear George:

  You win again

               F. D. R.

There were other run-ins with Congress, one occurring in the fall of 1941 when General Marshall took steps to purge the Army of incompetent officers. He briefed Secretary Stimson on his action at a war council meeting on September 15, 1941. Stimson's reaction to the proposal was, "I anticipate trouble." It was not long in coming. "We had scarcely finished our meeting," he said, "when Senator Tom Connally of Texas . . . bounded in with his hair standing up on end and full of anger and resentment because two Texas Generals of the National Guard had been retired and sent back from active duty."[80] General Marshall had retired one general because of age and the other because of incompetence. He refused to reconsider bringing either general back to active duty. He had given careful consideration to his action before executing it and his decision was firm. It was this kind of strength, courage, and honesty which progressively won for him the confidence of the members of Congress.

Only once during the war was General Marshall's rapport with Congress threatened. At the urging of the United States Navy, President Roosevelt was considering promoting Marshall to Field Marshal and King to the position of Admiral of the Fleet. The first Stimson had heard of this maneuver was on February 16, 1943, when Navy Secretary Knox mentioned the proposal to him. "When I got back to the Department," Stimson said, "I told Marshall of this because it contained a request from the President that I should go to the hill and talk with the Chairmen of the two committees on Military Affairs. Marshall was dead against any such promotion."

"He said," Stimson continued, "that it really came from the lower admirals in the Navy Department forcing this upon King and Knox and upon the President." General Marshall had a reason for his opposition to the promotion. He was afraid it would destroy all his influence both with Congress and with the people because he would appear to be self-seeking. His selflessness was part of his character and vital to his leadership. This promotion would present an obstacle to accomplishing his primary mission of winning the war. Stimson remarked of Marshall's position on the promotion, "It was a wonderfully unselfish thing for Marshall to do . . ."[81]

Because of Marshall's opposition Stimson sent a memorandum that same day to President Roosevelt stating, "I have talked the matter over with Marshall and he feels, so far as he is concerned, his promotion would be harmful rather than helpful, particularly with reference to his relations with Congress and the reaction of the American people. He feels very strongly on the subject, and I am inclined to agree with him."[82] Several days later Stimson discussed the matter with President Roosevelt and they decided to drop it.[83] The issue was later reopened, however, and eventually President Roosevelt and Congress decided to award the five-star rank over General Marshall's opposition.

In the fall of 1943, rumors started circulating in Washington that General Marshall would be leaving Washington to become D-Day Commander for the invasion of Europe. On September 15, 1943, Secretary Stimson was visited at his home by Senators Warren R. Austin, Styles Bridges, and John Gurney, ranking Republican members of the Military Affairs Committee. Each of them had been very helpful in the work of that committee concerning issues in which the Army was involved. Austin stated their case: They were extremely worried about the possibility that General Marshall was to be taken away from the position of Army Chief of Staff to take a field command.

"They told me," Secretary Stimson wrote, "how much they relied on him, not only individually, but how they were able to carry controversial matters through with their colleagues if they could say that the measure in question had the approval of Marshall."[84]

Marshall was a good judge of when and how much to tell the Congress, and on at least one occasion effectively used the carrot rather than the stick by convincing members that they had in-group status. In mid-April 1944, Marshall ordered General Mark Clark, Army Commander in Italy, to come to Washington for consultations before the May offensive in Italy. The trip was to be completely secret. For security reasons, General Marshall would not let the Clarks go home; instead they were taken to General Marshall's quarters at Fort Myer, and the next day were flown to the Greenbrier Hotel in West Virginia to give the general a much needed rest. A few days later, General Clark returned to Washington for conferences. Just before he was to leave for Italy, General Marshall told him to be at a certain private club in Washington at seven o'clock, and to be punctual. "When I arrived," General Clark said, "I discovered that he had taken over the entire place for the evening and that it was filled with specially invited guests, most of whom were Congressmen. We ate oysters and threw the shells in a bowl in the center of the table. Finally, Marshall said for me to tell everything. I did, explaining exactly how we were going to capture Rome."[85] A better way of flattering Congressmen has yet to be found.

Marshall took the Congressmen and Senators into his confidence by telling them the Army's problems candidly, and they knew that he never asked for anything the Army didn't need. Genral Marshall spent considerable time getting ready for his Congressional sessions; and when he appeared before a committee, he was prepared with the facts pertaining to the Army's plans and operations which enabled him to argue his point persuasively. He was patient, modest, intelligent, and lucid in answering questions. He never demanded, he asked; consequently, he always got what he asked for.

Relations With Press and Public

The President, the Secretary of War, and the Congress were all forces influencing the Chief of Staff's conduct of the war; but in the American democracy the final authority is the people—though its voice was somewhat muted by unusual wartime controls. The pulse of American public opinion was gauged in part by the press; questions a citizen could not ask directly, the reporter sometimes could. After the invasion of the Philippines by the Japanese, things went very badly for the American forces there, as General MacArthur and his men were driven back to Corregidor. An underground feeling of doubt began to develop in some quarters towards General Marshall. "One of my friends," wrote a member of the Army's public relations staff in 1942, "who was head of the Washington Bureau of a large midwest newspaper came to my home one evening and told me of the dissatisfaction which was spreading with regard to General Marshall's fitness for leadership."[86] Reporters asked that General Marshall hold a press conference; but at the time, the policy of the War Department was for Secretary of War Stimson to hold all press conferences—an arrangement more than satisfactory to Marshall.

A few days after the suggestion of a Marshall press conference, Secretary Stimson had to leave Washington on an inspection of the Panama Canal and its defenses. Instead of canceling the scheduled War Department press conference, however, General Marshall was persuaded by Stimson and others to conduct it. The Washington correspondents crowded into the room where the press conference was to be held; General Marshall came in, told the correspondents that he realized they had many questions to ask concerning the conduct of the war, and requested that they individually state all their questions at the beginning. Then he would attempt to answer them together. One by one a large number of representatives of the press arose and stated their questions. General Marshall listened attentively, and when there were no more questions he began to talk. He told them he was going to be quite frank and tell them just as much as he could so they could carry the information back to their papers. An observer said:

> He spoke for more than thirty minutes, giving an account of practically everything that happened up to that time, telling of the various efforts that had been made to send supplies to our forces on Bataan. He told of the purchase of ships and the provision in advance of insurance funds of families of the ships' crews engaged in the attempts. He told, as much as he could safely disclose, the extent of the disasters we had suffered which had prevented the carrying out of plans long ago drawn up to meet such an eventuality.[87]

General Marshall's conduct of the press conference was masterful. His honest and frank statements, taking the press into his confidence, completely won the doubters to his support. The rumbling comments of dissatisfaction with his ability ceased entirely. A member of the Army public relations staff said that General Marshall "exhibited a magnetism I had never seen before."[88] Throughout the rest of the war Marshall held press conferences once or twice a week. He habitually asked for all questions first, then would answer each question in turn, giving his reply directly to the correspondent who had asked the question. His memory for facts and names was phenomenal. He was not only frank, but trusting. He indicated which facts were classified secret, trusting the reporters not to violate his confidence; they never did.

In another aspect of publicity, General Marshall's influence caused the United States Army to follow an entirely different practice than the British, who were strongly opposed to the release of names and identifications of units and commanders who achieved meritorious records in combat. General Marshall believed that publicity for American fighting forces should be distributed, as earned, among the various commanders, units, and individual soldiers—in contrast to the British method of concentrating on a small number of senior generals. It was also Marshall's belief that quick recognition should be given to units for outstanding service in combat. He directed that citations could be made immediately, announced to the press, and the paper work could follow later. The time lag occasioned by filling in the forms first would have minimized the value of making the award.

Relations With Subordinates

Secretary of War Stimson commented in his *Diary* on December 31, 1943, that "the unique feature of Marshall's leadership was that no matter where an American officer was stationed, even those who are winning individual distinctions on the battle front, they were all as loyal to him as their leader as if they were here in the Pentagon." One reason certainly was that almost all of the senior officers in these positions were personally selected by Marshall and had a strong desire to live up to his expectations in performing their duty. But he also inspired a more personal kind of allegiance. General J. Lawton Collins said:

General Marshall had great human qualities. He was a gregarious person. He got around. He took a personal interest in the people under him. Here is an example of the thing he did that made people terribly loyal to him. I was ordered out to the West Coast right after the declaration of war. I was Chief of Staff of the VII Corps at the time and we were ordered to the West Coast. The Japs fired a single shell on southern California and everyone got excited. I went out with the Corps Commander, General Richardson, and a handful of our staff. Mrs. Collins and my family were down in Birmingham, Alabama. I kissed her goodbye and said, 'Honey, I will find a house on the West Coast and you can bring the children out.' I saw her two years later. [Just before Colonel Collins left for the Pacific.] General Marshall had had Beetle Smith, who was the Secretary to the General Staff, arrange that at a certain time there would be a line from Washington to San Francisco open so that I could talk to Mrs. Collins. That's the kind of thing that only the fellow who has great human qualities would do.[89]

Marshall showed this type of thoughtfulness for the senior commanders and their families throughout the entire war. Lieutenant General Willis D. Crittenberger, a Corps Commander in Fifth Army in Italy in 1944, remembered that General Marshall paid him a visit while on an inspection tour in Europe. When the Chief of Staff returned to the States, he personally called Mrs. Crittenberger in San Antonio and said to her, "Mrs. Crittenberger, this is General Marshall. I just called to let you know I saw your husband in Italy. He is in fine health and getting along very nicely."[90] He did this for all of the senior commanders he visited and for many junior officers and enlisted men.

On a trip to North Africa in 1943, General Marshall was surprised to see in Algiers Major General Lucian Truscott, who had been in command of an Army Corps at Anzio. The two had a long talk and General Marshall asked Truscott if he knew Ike had asked for him for the invasion of Europe. General Truscott replied that he had not heard of the request. It would have meant an Army command for Truscott, but he couldn't be spared from the Italian battle. "He felt," said Truscott, "I should know Eisenhower had asked for me, and be aware that my services at Anzio had been well understood and were fully appreciated." General Truscott had a reputation for being a "soldier's soldier;" but tough as he was, he records of his reaction to Marshall's compliment, "I was deeply touched, for there was no call upon General Marshall to tell me this. It was one of those generous and thoughtful things that always distinguished him in his dealings with his subordinates."[91]

"I met General Marshall in person only once," one World War II veteran of the Bataan Death March wrote. "This was the time when he sent his personal plane to San Francisco to transport me wherever the spirit moved, in order to reunite me with the widely scattered members of my immediate family, right after I returned from my prolonged incarceration in a Japanese prison

camp. After I had accomplished this mission, I reported to the
General at the Pentagon to thank him for his consideration.
General Marshall put everything aside, delayed very important
appointments, made me feel at home, and devoted a lengthy
period of time in a most human approach to my personal
situation."[9][2]

But his thoughtfulness was not just for senior officers. A
member of his staff during the twenties said that General
Marshall had "an innate humanness toward all who served under
him. He did not believe in wasting time, yet he always was
ready to go out of his way to show sincerity, respect, consideration, interest, and kindness to those under him, regardless of
how low the rank. I have many wonderful memories of such
thoughtfulness to me. I was a junior lieutenant. There was
nothing he could have possibly gained by it [if he had an
ulterior motive, which he didn't]. It was just part of his
nature."[9][3]

Marshall was equally thoughtful to his personal staff. One
day in 1933, while in Chicago with the National Guard, General
of the Armies Pershing paid an unexpected visit to Marshall's
office. General Pershing was sensitive about being "stared at";
so Colonel Marshall, realizing this was an exciting event to his
staff, made up reasons requiring each member of his staff to
come into the office. As they did so, each had the opportunity
to personally see the exalted World War I leader without making
Pershing feel as though he were on exhibit.

As a junior officer and company commander Marshall knew
every enlisted man in his command by name. He spent long
hours interviewing every man, acquainting himself with their
backgrounds and personal problems, and stood quickly between
his men and anyone bringing complaints against them. While he
might take the hide off a man deserving it, woe to anyone else
who sought to do the same. Naturally his men loved him and
respected him for that kind of loyalty. It was an attribute that
he displayed equally as a five-star general and Chief of Staff of
the Army, never feeling too exalted to be interested in the
enlisted man. He was called by many "a champion of the common soldier."

As Chief of Staff during World War II he made frequent inspection trips. "Although he made his inspections," Mrs. Marshall said, "at such a pace that officers found difficulty in keeping up with him, he missed little, very little indeed." Once, while watching him inspect troops at Fort Knox, she noticed that he went quickly through two lines of men and then paused to talk for several minutes with a soldier in the rear line.

"I asked why he had picked out that particular soldier," Mrs. Marshall wrote, "and he replied, 'I caught the man's eye and I knew something was wrong. I wanted to find out what'."

"Did you find out?" she asked.

"Yes," he answered, "everything was wrong. The man ought never to have been drafted. He was over-age, had a large family, and was in no physical condition for active service. He was a good soldier too, wanted to do his part, and I had to question him for some time before I could get at his trouble. The Draft Board made a slip-up on that fellow."[94] Arrangements were made that very day to send the soldier back to his family.

General Marshall was always an active thinker and it was a sore point with him that many of his fellow officers were not. He often said, "Give me an officer who can and will think for himself. Deliver me from the lazy thinker." He was patient with officers and enlisted men with limited capabilities for thinking and reasoning, but very tough on those who had ability but failed to use it. He had a thorough knowledge of every command to which he was assigned, and this gave him the opportunity to assist subordinates with difficult problems. His understanding and tolerance of genuine shortcomings of other men generated a desire in these men to increase their knowledge in order to perform better. With his talent for analyzing the capacities of his men, he could quickly recognize the "dead beat" and was equally quick in dealing with him. He knew the capacity of each of his men and was not satisfied with anything other than their best. He loved to see initiative in both officers and enlisted men; he encouraged them to "Step out and do something. What if you do make a mistake."

An incident in Marshall's early career gave promise of the leadership capabilities that later came to full flower. When

Marshall was stationed in the Philippines, there was a group of ten young officers who were approaching the end of their three-year tour. They were fed up with their "colonial army" existence, with units that were undermanned and were really only skeleton organizations, with a shortage of money. It was a low ebb for the Army.

To occupy the time of these disgruntled officers, a voluntary officers school was established, scheduled for 11:00 a.m. daily, and instructed by First Lieutenant George C. Marshall. One of these ten officers wrote later that because of "the fine impression he had made on our garrison, the response was 100% and our interest and attention never failed. None of us who participated ever forgot it. This is just a small incident in the life of a great man, but it shows his flair for real leadership in an instance when his students really 'had to be shown'."[9][5]

This interest in teaching younger officers was typical of General Marshall thoughout his career. "I first met General Marshall," reminisced one officer, "in 1924 as a newly-made Lieutenant Colonel. He was executive officer of the Fifteenth U.S. Infantry. I was a second lieutenant in the 15th Infantry when he arrived. We came home in 1927 on the good ship *Thomas*, a converted cattleboat used as a transport in those days. Every night on board the transport Colonel Marshall talked informally to all the officers of the 15th aboard. Attendance on our part was voluntary. His talks concerned people, incidents, and leadership of World War I. Nowhere that I know could a junior officer get a teacher like General Marshall."[9][6]

Throughout the twenties and thirties, when he was of senior rank and had command responsibility, Marshall devoted a great deal of his time to the professional growth of the officers junior to him. He gathered new lieutenants early in their tour and urged them to study their military specialty—infantry, cavalry, artillery, or whatever it might be—and often held seminars on military subjects at his home in the evenings and on weekends.

General Marshall's contacts with these young officers he thought highly of continued over the years. He always remembered the dedicated, hard working, professional officers from all his assignments, engaging in extensive correspondence with them all over the world and following closely the careers of the men who showed promise.

Certainly one of the reasons for Marshall's success as a leader was not only his personal determination to learn but also his desire to share the knowledge he gained with his associates and subordinates, regardless of rank. He did this eagerly and willingly, without thought of personal glory, for the benefit of a common cause.

Marshall's leadership was outstanding throughout his military career, and it undoubtedly reached the high point when he was Chief of Staff of the Army during World War II. He was a leader with his military officers and men, with the press, Congress, the American people, the President, and with our Allies. He was known as a selfless, dedicated man serving his country—a man who was honorable in his dealings with everyone. His success as a leader was the culmination of over forty years of study and preparation, and no higher tribute can be paid to his leadership than the words of President Truman, "Millions of Americans gave their country outstanding service. General of the Army George C. Marshall gave it victory."

DUTY-HONOR-COUNTRY

The Leadership of General of the Army Douglas MacArthur

On April 5, 1964, General of the Army Douglas MacArthur died, after a stubborn fight for life at Walter Reed Army Medical Center, from acute kidney and liver failure. He was 84 years old. The tributes paid to him were impressive: Former President Harry S. Truman said, "I am deeply sorry at the passing of General Douglas MacArthur, who has given of himself with exceptional strength and valor and will be remembered as one of the great military men in our history." Former President Herbert Hoover commented, "He was one of the world's outstanding military commanders. He was also a statesman for peace. The world is a finer place for his having lived in it and for the standards of courage and character he set. Truly his watchword was: duty, honor, country. He was a great man, a great general, and a great patriot." General of the Army Dwight D. Eisenhower stated, "The entire nation will stand in sad salute to one of the outstanding military leaders of American history. He earned the admiration and respect of his fellow citizens and the personal devotion of those he led in battle. As one of those privileged to serve for some years under his direct supervision, I share with all his friends a feeling of special loss and sorrow." Secretary of Defense Robert McNamara called him, ". . . a great captain whose qualities and courageous leadership were legendary in his own time." Fleet Admiral Chester Nimitz reflected, "Our country has lost one of its greatest military leaders, who from his earliest adult days exhibited those qualities of courage, military character, leadership and administrative skill that have marked his entire career." Foreign military leaders were equally magnanimous in their eulogies. Field Marshal Viscount Montgomery said, "He was the best soldier the United States produced during World War II." General DeGaulle called him "the great victorious leader of the Pacific," and Generalissimo Chiang Kai-shek said, "His brilliant leadership,. . . is a shining symbol and serves as an inspiration to free men everywhere."

Every leader of stature in the world had some statement to make, and in summary one only needs to quote adjectives used by them to describe the man and his leadership: "brilliant", "exceptional", "great", "greatest", "last of the great figures", "an inspiration", "gallant", "heroic", and on and on.

Time may prove MacArthur to be the greatest general in the history of the United States. His life and career were filled with bests, firsts, mosts, and onlys. He was first in his graduating class at West Point, establishing a new high for academic performance at that institution. He was the youngest brigadier general in World War I, the youngest Superintendent in the history of the Military Academy, the youngest major general, the youngest peacetime Chief of Staff in U.S. history, the first American to become a field marshal of a foreign nation, and the only American officer to be a general in three wars.

General Arthur MacArthur

The preparation of Douglas MacArthur for the military profession truly started from the cradle. His father, Arthur MacArthur, whose military career began during the Civil War, was one of the most outstanding and dedicated officers our country has ever known. When the 24th Wisconsin Infantry Regiment was organized in 1862, Arthur MacArthur was selected as adjutant and received a commission as first lieutenant in August of that year. His youth—he was 17—was no drawback when the test of battle came; he quickly won the respect of all for his courage. During the battle of Missionary Ridge, on November

25, 1863, his regiment started to break up under heavy fire while charging a steep hill. MacArthur seized the colors from the wounded colorbearer's hand, led another charge, and planted the flag on the crest of Missionary Ridge. As the official record has it:

> For this particular critically timed act of heroism he was, at the age of eighteen, awarded the Congressional Medal of Honor.

This episode is even more dramatic as described by Douglas MacArthur in his memoirs:

> On the day of the battle—November 25, 1863—the Confederate Army under General Braxton Bragg is deployed in defense of Missionary Ridge. At the foot of the ridge is a first line of rifle pits, with successive lines up its rugged face. It is a broken, ragged slope, difficult to ascend even under the most peaceful condition.
>
> Sheridan, now a major general, is ordered to take the rifle pits at the foot of the ridge. The troops carry the line at the point of the bayonet. But their position is desperate, exposed to concentrated fire from the slopes and crest. Should they go forward or back?
>
> No one seems to know just what orders may have been given, but suddenly the flag of the 24th Wisconsin starts forward, With it is the color sergeant, the color guard of two corporals and the adjutant.
>
> Up they go, step by step. The enemy's fire is intense. Down goes the color bearer. One of the corporals seizes the colors as they fall but is bayoneted before he can move. A shell takes off the head of the other corporal. But the adjutant seizes the flag and keeps on. He seems to be surrounded by nothing but gray coats. A burly sergeant fires point blank in his face and off whirls his hat. A Confederate colonel thrusts viciously at the bared throat but even as he lunges a bullet strikes and the blade just rips a shoulder strap. No movement yet from our lines. And then above the roar of battle, that well-known adjutant's voice: "On, Wisconsin."

They came then, they came with a rush and a roar; a blue tide of courage, a whole division of them. Shouting, cursing, foot by foot they struggle forward. And then, suddenly, on the crest, the flag! Once again that hoarse cry: "On, Wisconsin!" As he stands silhouetted against the sky, every Confederate seems to be firing at him. Through the ragged blue line, from one end of the division to the other, comes an ugly growl, like that of a wounded bear. They race those last few steps, eyes blazing, lips snarling, bayonets plunging. And Missionary Ridge is won.

The adjutant falls on the ground, exhausted and retching. He is a terrible sight, covered with blood and mud and filth, hatless, his smoke-blackened face barely recognizable, his clothes torn to tatters. Sheridan just stares at him and then, blood and filth and all, takes him in his arms. And his voice breaks a little as he says, "Take care of him. He has just won the Medal of Honor."

Afterward Arthur MacArthur took command of the regiment and led it for the rest of the war. He was subsequently appointed lieutenant colonel, and then colonel —at 19 the youngest officer of his rank in the Union Army.[1]

Not long after the battle of Missionary Ridge, MacArthur became regimental commander, receiving his majority ahead of division captains senior to him. He went on to lead the regiment in numerous battles, performing with consistent bravery, and was a full colonel before the end of the war. As far as can be ascertained he was the youngest man in either the Northern or Southern forces to command a regiment. Before his 21st birthday he had led his regiment for a year and a half, through nine significant battles.

In his final battle of the war, on November 30, 1864, his exploits, as described by the adjutant Captain Edwin Parsons, read like a story book tale:

I saw the colonel sabering his way toward the leading Confederate flag. His horse was shot from under him, a bullet ripped open his right shoulder, but on foot he fought his way forward. A Confederate major now had the flag and shot him through the breast. I thought he was done for, but he staggered up, drove his sword through his adversary's body, but even as the Confederate fell, he shot our colonel down for good with a bullet through the knee.[2]

After the war Arthur MacArthur decided to make the Army his career. He lost his wartime rank of colonel and enlisted in the regular army as a second lieutenant. By 1896, he was a lieutenant colonel. With the outbreak of the Spanish-American War in 1898, he was made a brigadier general of volunteers and sent to the Philippines where he fought with distinction, participating in the capture of Manila.

During his tour as division commander in the Philippines in 1899, there were three members of Arthur MacArthur's staff who were to receive considerable recognition as soldiers. One was Captain Peyton C. March, his senior aide. A second was Captain J. Franklin Bell, his scout. Both were regular army officers. The third officer of note was Colonel Frederick Funston of the 21st Kansas Volunteers. Bell became a general of volunteers within a year. March was to rise to the rank of colonel of volunteers and Funston to brigadier general. All three had the greatest admiration and respect for Arthur MacArthur. They had reason to be grateful to him, and they would all later play a role in the career of Douglas MacArthur.

With the cessation of war, Arthur MacArthur was appointed commanding general and military governor of the Philippine Islands. When in 1906 he was promoted to the rank of lieutenant general, he was only the twelfth officer in the history of the United States Army to hold that rank. After MacArthur's retirement in 1909, the rank was discontinued until World War I.

Early Career

Douglas MacArthur was born and raised in the Army, the son of a dedicated officer with a brilliant career. The senior

MacArthur was an example for any young man to follow, and
to Douglas, who naturally had a uniquely intimate association
with the great soldier, it was inevitable that the army would be
his life. In the summer of 1899 the lifetime ambition of father
and son was achieved when Douglas became a member of the
Class of 1903 at West Point. He entered with a proud military
heritage, a knowledge of the army, and a maturity which few of
his classmates could equal.

From graduation on MacArthur's assignments groomed him
for future high command. His first assignment was to the Philippines, where there still were insurgent warring elements among
the natives, and which was therefore the only part of the world
where an American could see action at that time. Douglas got
his share of it for a year; and shortly after his return to the
United States, he and his father were appointed military observers of the Russo-Japanese War by President Theodore
Roosevelt. On one occasion during this tour, he "watched the
Japanese charge a Russian-held hill; six times they were driven
off. MacArthur couldn't stand it. He dashed across country,
spurred on the Japanese troops, and took them up the hill to
victory."[3]

On his return from this mission he became military aide to
President Roosevelt, later carried out a number of civil engineer-
ing assignments, and was assigned to the General Staff between
1913 and 1917, with time out for a brief excursion to Vera
Cruz on the staff of General Funston, who had served under
Arthur MacArthur in the Philippines in 1901.

An example of his mastery of any situation was his year's
assignment as military censor for the War Department. Certainly, dealing with independent and freespeaking American
journalists offers a challenge that most military men would seek
to avoid. When he took over the position, the first thing he did
was to call the reporters together and say to them: "Gentlemen,
I know nothing about this job or your jobs. I'm going to throw
myself at the mercy of the court. I'm going to take you around
and show you everything. There will be no bars. You will know

what to print and not to print for the best interests of the country. I am a lamb. I beg of you to protect me from myself."[4]

The exceptional caliber of MacArthur's performance was recognized by a rare tribute. The twenty-nine newspaper correspondents permanently on duty at the War Department handed Secretary of War Baker, at the end of MacArthur's duty, a signed statement of their appreciation for his services.

No man can ever know to what extent the cordial relations the Major [MacArthur] has maintained with the press may have influenced national thought on military matters. It is unquestionable that his hours given to our conferences have not been wasted. They have borne fruit in what we in our turn have written, and if wise decisions are reached eventually as to the military policy of the country, we cannot but feel that the Major has helped, through us, to shape the public mind.[5]

World War I

During his tour on the General Staff, MacArthur became associated with one of his most potent admirers, Newton D. Baker, Secretary of War for President Wilson during World War I. MacArthur was on Baker's staff when the U.S. entered the war. A potential problem faced the Secretary involving the National Guard divisions which had been called up. Each thought it should be the first Guard division to go overseas. On one occasion Baker described the situation to MacArthur:

The problem was really sentimental and nobody knew what turn public sentiment would take about it. There were two states, New York and Pennsylvania, which each had a full division in its National Guard. All the other National Guard divisions were made up from contingents from combinations of States. If we sent overseas the New

York division, the rest of the country might be jealous at the preference given to New York, while in New York on the other hand, there might be resentment at sending their boys first all from one State.

I said to Major MacArthur that I wished we had a division in which there were components from every State so that each State could take pride in the fact that some of its own boys were among the first to go. Major MacArthur suggested that in the formation of the National Guard division, there were frequently minor elements left over which were in a sense unattached to any divisional organization, and that these might be grouped together. I sent for General Mann, the Chief of the Militia Bureau, and asked him whether there were enough of the surplus organizations to form a division, and explained to him that I wanted them when brought together, to represent as many States and as widespread geographical distribution as possible—if possible to practically cover the United States. Major MacArthur said: "Like a rainbow."

General Mann went back to his office and in some hours reported the proposed constitution of the Rainbow Division, and I told him that I wanted him to command the division and Major MacArthur to be its chief of staff. Both were full of enthusiasm about the project. General Mann was so enthusiastic that after leaving my office, he returned in about two hours dressed in a trench coat and various overseas equipment to show how rapidly he had gotten ready to take his place in the division.[6]

MacArthur was promoted to the rank of colonel, (skipping the rank of Lieutenant colonel) and arrived in France on October 29, 1917, as Chief of Staff of the 42nd (Rainbow) Division. It was apparent that he did not confine himself to paperwork.

He has many exploits to his credit, but one which had the most inspiring effect on the men was no doubt when he decided to go over the top with the doughboys. He was then Chief of Staff, though later placed in command of one of the brigades. He went to Company B of the 167th Infantry, took off his uniform and put on that of an enlisted man, asked for a rifle with fixed bayonet, and, taking his place in the ranks of the company, led the boys over the top. This he kept up all day.[7]

Colonel Albert Gilmore, a classmate of MacArthur's, heard of the exploit and when he saw him the next day Gilmore said to MacArthur, "They told me up front this morning that you went over last night in a trench raid." MacArthur replied, "I knew that my staff was able to handle any difficulty that might arise and I thought the men would be glad to see a high ranking officer among them."[8]

On August 6, 1918, he left his staff position to become commander of the 84th Infantry Brigade; and in November, he was the 42nd Division commander as a brigadier general. His combat record is best portrayed by the citation for the Distinguished Service Cross:

> When Company D, 168th Infantry, was under severe attack in the salient du Feys, France, he voluntarily joined it, upon finding that he could do so without interfering with his normal duties, and by his coolness and conspicuous courage aided materially in its success.
>
> An oak-leaf cluster is awarded General MacArthur for the following acts of distinguished service: As brigade commander General MacArthur personally led his men and by the skillful maneuvering of his brigade made possible the capture of Hills 288, 242 and the Cote-de-Chatillon, France, October 14, 15, and 16, 1918. He displayed indomitable resolution and great courage in rallying broken lines and in reforming attacks, thereby making victory possible. On a field where courage was the rule, his courage was the dominant feature.[9]

He also won the Distinguished Service Medal for his "exceptionally meritorious and distinguished service."

In 1920 most career officers who had obtained high rank during the war were reduced in permanent rank. (Patton and Marshall were reduced from full colonel to major, Eisenhower from lieutenant colonel to major.) There was one conspicuous exception—even though he was only a permanent major and was very junior in age compared to the regular corps, it was announced by President Wilson that MacArthur, who was serving at that time as the youngest Superintendent in West Point history, had been nominated for the permanent rank of brigadier general. Newton Baker, who had deep respect for MacArthur, was Secretary of War at the time of this appointment, which also required the concurrence of the Chief of Staff. The position of Army Chief was filled at that time by General Peyton C. March, former aide to Arthur MacArthur in the Philippines in 1899. March himself was no stranger to success, for under Arthur MacArthur he rose in rank from captain to brigadier general.

Chief of Staff

In 1930, Douglas MacArthur was selected as Chief of Staff of the Army. This position is usually the highest ambition of an Army officer. In this role an officer can make the greatest contribution since it makes him a four star general and military adviser to the Secretary of War, and through him, to the President. As Chief of Staff, MacArthur was charged with the planning, development and execution of the army program designed for the present and long range defense of the United States.

When President Herbert Hoover announced the appointment he stated, according to the newspapers, that "he is the only one of the Major Generals having a sufficient period to serve in the Army before retirement to serve the full four years as Chief of Staff." This statement attributed to the President was unfortunate because it was not true. There were ten other major generals in 1930 who could have served the full term: Dennis E.

Nolan, Johnson Hagood, William D. Connor, Fox Conner, Preston Brown, Malin Craig, B. H. Wells, Paul B. Malone, Frank Parker, and Frank R. McCoy. There were nine major generals on active duty at that time who would reach the mandatory retirement age before the expiration of the four-year tour as Chief of Staff.

The protest against MacArthur's selection was partially based on the erroneous statement by the President, since many had concluded that the records and qualifications of the ten officers named above ought to have received consideration. The *New York Times*, for example, commented in an editorial:

> If they were ruled out because it was thought that they could not serve a full term, the mistake is to be deplored ... Their merits should have been brought to the attention of President Hoover. It is not conducive to morale in the commissioned ranks when the claims of capable officers are overlooked. In this case the failure seems to have been due to a blunder about the period of service remaining to eligible Major Generals.[10]

A better understanding of his reason for selecting MacArthur is furnished by Hoover's memoirs. "I had long held," he wrote, "that the choice of Chief of Staff by seniority led only to dead ends. I therefore searched the Army for younger blood and finally determined upon General Douglas MacArthur. His brilliant abilities and his sterling character needs no exposition from me."[11]

Never in the discussion, however, did anyone question the qualifications of MacArthur. Undoubtedly there was disappointment on the part of the other major generals, and their friends, who were not selected. But the heartaches of the older officers were soon gone, and the esprit and discipline that are so much a part of the true soldier replaced disappointment with loyalty. Since MacArthur throughout his career had always been one of the youngest this or that, having older men as subordinates was not a new challenge to him.

For the more than 100 years since the American Revolution, preparation for war by the United States had always been attempted in a haphazard way by separate and uncoordinated departments within the Army. When war came, there were inefficient staff work, inadequate hospital facilities, inadequate supplies, incompetence in the movement of troops, and many other problems. To overcome this, Congress passed legislation for the creation of a modern general staff. The duties of the general staff included coordination between military branches, and the development and execution of plans. But the creation of the general staff did not solve the problem, for the general staffs prior to 1930 clung too long to the antiquated and inadequate systems that had guided the conduct of previous wars. It was the classic case of entering the next war with the plans and weapons of the last.

Under the leadership of MacArthur all this changed. Never before had there been a Chief of Staff so able to obtain from the President, the Congress, and the American people what was vital for the army. Soon after he took office as Chief of Staff, MacArthur settled a long-standing controversy between the air services of the army and navy over coast defenses. The agreement was to entrust the mission to the army.

It was during MacArthur's administration that the horse was replaced with mechanized equipment for greater mobility and speed, against the opposition of those who nostalgically wanted to keep the horse. He formed a "cavalry" regiment consisting of armored cars, the Christie tank, and machine gun squadrons transported by motor vehicles. In doing this General MacArthur said he wanted "to preserve the cavalry spirit, an asset which, while intangible, is nonetheless a vital factor in combat." This spirit was very obvious in World War II in such units as the Third Army under General George S. Patton, Jr.

MacArthur established a general mobilization plan (i.e. a selective service system) of six field armies of approximately 4,000,000 men, a modified plan of price control, a plan for the transition of industry into the production of war items. The latter resulted from surveys of factories vital to defense to determine the wartime duties that would be assigned to them. He also got a start on a unified procurement system for the services to curtail waste, and established a general headquarters air force to promote greater efficiency in the coordination of the air-ground forces.

He resisted all attempts by Congress to reduce the number of army posts as a measure of economy. Supposedly the reduction would also offer an opportunity for concentration of troops for better training. This was thwarted because MacArthur and the General Staff felt that the Army had already been cut to the very bone and further cutting would dangerously reduce its efficiency.

MacArthur prevented another great threat to the Army during the early years of the depression, when there was an attempt by Congress to cut the size of the officer corps from 12,000 to 10,000. "An army," MacArthur said in protesting this action, "can live on short rations, it can be insufficiently clothed and housed, it can even be poorly armed and equipped, but in action it is doomed to destruction without the trained and adequate leadership of officers. An efficient and sufficient corps of officers means the difference between victory and defeat." He went on to impress upon Congress that this small professional force of officers would act as a cadre for the mobilization of civilian soldiers. "The regular Army is the bulwark and basis of the whole structure. It is the instructor, the model, and, in the emergency, the leader of the whole... Through schools, research, study and practical training the regulars devote their lives to keeping abreast of the time of complicated and rapidly changing arts and sciences..." The Army was already short 6,000 officers according to the number proposed by the National Defense Act of 1920. To carry on the responsibilities required of the Army by that act a reduction from the present level of 12,000 would severely endanger the country's defense.

Each year MacArthur was successful in preventing a reduction in Army personnel, and in 1935 he even got an increase. Legislation passed in that year authorized increasing the size of the Army from 126,875 officers and men to 165,000. During his five-year tour the Army Air Corps was boosted in size from 1500 airplanes of every character (many of which were obsolescent, some ready for salvage, and over half unfit for combat) to 2,320 up-to-date aircraft.

The successive war reports of General MacArthur constantly argued for preparedness. In his December 1931 report, he outlined his plan to mechanize every part of the Army possible to increase mobility, security, and striking power. In 1932, he pointed out that the United States was seventeenth in military strength among the nations of the world. (The ranking in order of size of regular and trained reserves in 1932 was: Russia, France, Italy, Spain, Japan, Poland, China, Rumania, Czechoslovakia, Yugoslavia, the British Empire, Sweden, Turkey, Switzerland, Belgium, Greece, Great Britain, and finally the United States!) A *New York Times* editorial said in reply to this alarming contrast of U. S. weakness:

> MacArthur's comparison of the present regular Army, National Guard and Reserves of the United States with mobilizable European armies is not pertinent. The Chief of Staff can hardly hope that in these times of difficulty in balancing the budget an increase of the army can be authorized.[12]

How absurd this seems with the benefit of hindsight.

In 1933, he warned that "the Army's strength and its readiness for employment are below the danger line." In 1934, he frankly listed our deficiencies in materiel and strength of personnel: "We now have in the regular Army 118,750 enlisted men; in the National Guard, 175,000 enlisted men; the enlisted reserve is practically non-existent. We need a regular army of 165,000 men; a National Guard of 210,000 men; a well-trained enlisted reserve of not less than 120,000 men; an Officers Reserve Corps of 120,000 . . ." He charged that the U.S. Army tanks were "hopelessly out-of-date, hundreds dating from the World War, with only twelve modern ones on hand." The artillery weapons were inferior, semi-automatic rifles were needed to replace the 1905 Springfields. Only in airpower were we on a par with other nations.

As he argued for preparedness his critics called him "an insatiable pillager of the public purse", "thief", and "warmonger". During his tour as Chief of Staff he was called at one time or another, "Kid General", "arrogant MacArthur", "Three musketeers-all-in-one", "polished popinjay", and "bellicose swashbuckler".

But MacArthur could hold his own with his critics. In 1931, the now extinct *The World Tomorrow* magazine circulated a questionnaire among 19,372 clergymen asking their view toward bearing arms for their country in time of war. The majority of the clergymen polled replied, according to the magazine, that they would not bear arms to defend the United States. This was a disturbing commentary to General MacArthur, who was asked by the editor of *The World Tomorrow*, Kirby Page, to present his opinion on the question. His reply was directed not only to the clergymen, but to all who refuse to take up arms in defense of their country. He answered that he was surprised "that so many of the clergymen of our country have placed themselves on record as repudiating in advance the constitutional obligations that will fall upon them equally with all other elements of our citizenship. . ." and he chastized them for exercising ". . . privilege without assuming attendant responsibility and obligation. . . to avail themselves of the privileges conferred by democracy upon its citizens, but who, in effect, proclaim their willingness to see the nation perish rather than participate in its defense." In his conclusion he cited the twenty-first verse of the eleventh chapter of St. Luke: "When a strong man armed, keepeth his palace, his goods are in peace."[13]

On June 8, 1932, to a crowd of thousands who had gathered to hear him give the commencement address to the graduating class of 1,362 members of the University of Pittsburgh, he argued for preparedness and criticized pacifists:

Pacifism and its bedfellow, communism, are all about us.

In the theatre, newspapers and magazines, pulpits and lecture halls, schools and colleges, it hangs like a mist before the face of America. . .

Day by day this cancer eats deeper into the body politic.

For the sentimentalism and emotionalism which have infected our country, we should substitute hard common sense. Pacifist habits do not insure peace or immunity. . .

We should at all times be prepared to defend ourselves. . . It is the undefended riches which provoke war. The wealth of the United States presents a tempting spectacle which may ultimately lead to another World War. . .

When speaking to a reunion of the Rainbow Division in 1935, he said in answer to the pacifist criticism: "They who preach by word or deed, 'peace at any price,' are not possessed of anything worth having. Every nation," he went on to say, "that would preserve its tranquility, its riches, its independence and its self respect, must keep alive its martial ardor and be at all times prepared to defend itself."

On December 12, 1934, President Roosevelt announced that General MacArthur would be continued in the office of Chief of Staff indefinitely. He did so because he wanted MacArthur there until more complete military legislation was in Congress. The extension was not met with wholehearted enthusiasm in some circles. A *New York Times* article commented, "Considerable pressure has been brought to bear upon the President from veteran's organizations against General MacArthur's reappointment. Protests were predicated chiefly on the rout of the 'Bonus Army,' which General MacArthur carried out under orders from President Hoover. . ."[14]

The Bonus March

The bonus March of 1932 provided a unique test of MacArthur's leadership. After many wars in the history of the

United States there has been a march of veterans on the nation's capital, usually during a period of depression. With the severe depression of the 1930s there was again a veterans' march. They hoped to persuade Congress to pay a $2,500,000,000 bonus to veterans of World War I. To give emphasis to their plight, a movement was started to encourage veterans from all over the United States to march to Washington. The first group of 300 reached Washington on May 30, 1932, and quartered themselves in vacant building on Pennsylvania Avenue. Out of sympathy for former comrades-in-arms, Douglas MacArthur set up mobile kitchens to feed them. Soon the numbers became too large to support. The wrecked buildings were inadequate; so makeshift shacks were erected on vacant lots out of pick-up lumber. Wives and children were brought in, and there was soon a town of veterans within the city of Washington, called affectionately, "Hooverville".

As the group grew in size, it grew in boldness. Soon the Washington police were unable to control the riots of the recalcitrant elements of the bonus marchers. There was also grave concern that an epidemic could spread from the shacks where there was inadequate sanitation, food, and shelter.

Finally President Hoover was forced to take action. He instructed his Secretary of War, Patrick J. Hurley, to remove the veterans. Hurley in turn ordered the Chief of Staff Douglas MacArthur as follows:

> You will have the United States troops proceed immediately to the scene of disorder. Co-operate fully with the District of Columbia police force which is now in charge. Surround the affected area and clear it without delay. Turn over all prisoners to the civil authorities. In your orders insist that any women and children who may be in the affected area be accorded every consideration and kindness. Use all humanity consistent with the due execution of this order.

With tear gas, the back end of sabers, and the threat of bayonets, the bonus marchers were driven from the city by 700 army troops. Those with cars were given gas and oil to head them on their way. As they left the city, the shacks of Anacostia, along the Potomac River and anywhere else were burned to the ground. The Army troops suffered casualties from the rocks and sticks thrown at them; but, with a minimum of strife, the area was cleared.

The important aspect of MacArthur's role in the eviction of the bonus marchers was that he personally took command. Any intelligent man knew that the American public would resent chasing veterans away from their nation's capital, regardless of the provocation. MacArthur, knowing the certainty of criticism, could easily have avoided it by giving the assignment to the commander of the military district of the Washington, D. C. area, or to the Corps commander. It was typical of the career of General MacArthur that he never gave orders for others to do what he would not do himself. As he told a fellow officer, "If the President gives me orders to act, I would not give this distasteful and disagreeable job to any other officer of the United States Army."[15]

And indeed criticism was forthcoming. The *Baltimore Sun* commented: ". . . may we suggest that somebody, somewhere in Washington, clap an official hand over the mouth of . . . MacArthur. That gentleman who sent all the way to Fort Myer for a uniform so that he could be properly garbed for a military operation which could have been carried out by a colonel and a few men armed with tear bombs, is unburdening himself of military romanticism undefiled, bare of the tiniest alloy of common sense. . ."

At that time, the Chief of Staff wore civilian clothes at his office in the War Department. MacArthur sent home for his uniform, believing that since this was an Army operation he should dress accordingly. On his shoulders were the four stars of a full general, on his chest eight rows of campaign ribbons and decorations.

One newspaper related that "Along with his right hand man, Major Dwight D. Eisenhower, MacArthur mounted a horse to lead his men on their mission." The *New York Times* printed a special story on a Major George S. Patton, who was "compelled by duty last night to evict from the main camp. . . a man who saved his life on the field of battle fourteen years ago. . ."[16]

Pershing had supposedly opposed MacArthur's selection as Chief of Staff, favoring his former operations officer, Major General Fox Conner, for the position. But when the tour was almost over Pershing stated, "I have only praise for General MacArthur as Chief of Staff. He thoroughly comprehends the requirements to develop a unified fighting force for the national defense. He is progressive without being radical. His courageous presentation to high authority of his sound views has been admirable. By wise administration of his office, he has won the entire confidence of the Army and the country."

Survival in Washington is not easy for a military man. Perhaps MacArthur's ability to remain effective in the seat of our nation's government was partially based on his philosophy as expressed to a close friend a few years after he had stepped down as Chief of Staff:

> The more you become acquainted with the bureaucracy of our governmental departments the more pessimistic you will become. "Red tape," "Bureaucracy," "Routine," "Laissez faire"—whatever you wish to call it—its deadening effect is felt by everyone who comes within the scope of its influence. The great figures that we produce are those who pay little attention to such matters and retain their freedom of initiative when an emergency arises. I recall my complete disagreement with the Orange Plan when I became Chief of Staff but I realized at once that I would be wasting my time in trying to educate others to my own point of view. I, therefore, short-circuited by seeing the President personally. . . The President agreed with me [on a change in the plan] entirely.[17]

The best summation of his performance as Chief of Staff is furnished by the citation accompanying the oak leaf cluster for his Distinguished Service Medal, awarded to MacArthur in 1935:

Douglas MacArthur, general, chief of staff, United States Army, for exceptionally meritorious and distinguished services in a position of great responsibility. As chief of staff of the army of the United States since Nov. 21, 1930, he has performed his many important and exacting duties with signal success.

He devised and developed the four-army organization of our land forces; he conceived and established the General Headquarters Air Force, thus immeasurably increasing the effectiveness of our air defenses; he initiated a comprehensive program of modernization in the army's tactics, equipment, training and organization.

In addition, the professional counsel and assignment he has continuously rendered to the President, to the Secretary of War and to the Congress have been distinguished by such logic, vision and accuracy as to contribute markedly to the formulation of sound defense policies and the enactment of progressive laws for promoting the nation's security.

One officer reflected on MacArthur's tour as Chief of Staff:

He worked long hours at his office and seemed content to spend most of his evenings at his quarters at Fort Myer across the Potomac. Always a prodigious reader and student of history, he would relax with a book in his library, or spend the evening chatting with old friends on his staff who would drop in and stay for hours discussing the problems of the War Department and the national and international situations in general.

MacArthur devoted every day of his tour as Chief of Staff to keeping our defenses above the danger line. Because of his leadership, his preparation for Congressional sessions on the Army budget, his speeches, his writings, the universal high regard of the President of the United States for his professional competence, and his image with the American people, he accomplished wonders. However, it was not easy. He said to a friend in the early 1930's, "I have humiliated myself seeking allotments to replace leaking, slumlike barracks housing our soldiers. I have almost licked the boots of certain gentlemen to get funds for motorization and mechanization of the Army." But it was his patience, dedication, and determination during this period that gave us a better prepared force, as inadequate as it was, at the outset of World War II.

The Philippine Army

When his tour as Chief of Staff was over, MacArthur undertook a new responsibility—Field Marshal of the Philippine Army. When General MacArthur accepted the Philippine position, he was 57 years old. He had won all that his profession had to offer. He might easily have gone gracefully into retirement, secure in his brilliant record, wrapped comfortably in his honors. But this was where he showed the stuff he was made of. When he decided to build an army from scratch, he was not chasing personal glory. He had little to gain, but much to lose. He did not do things for the approval of others; he did a job that needed to be done.

Again he had to fight the politicians who advocated economy at the expense of preparation. It was a tough job trying to build an army in a foreign country with nationals of that country resisting a conscript army, politicians clamoring for more of the budget for public works rather than military defense, and left wing elements demanding the pacifist position. He worked hard to train his small army, studying the terrain they would fight in, the equipment and tactics that would be necessary to meet situations that most others said would never arise. He gave this effort all of the drive, experience, and genius he had. When the Battle of Bataan occurred, its defense was no "miracle," as the press acclaimed; it was the result of years of preparation and study.

As he worked on the defense of the Philippines, someone asked him one day, "Well, what do you care if the Philippines fall to Japan? You have personally done the best you can."

MacArthur replied to him, "Personally, I must not fail! Too much of the world's future depends on success here. These Islands may not be the door to the control of the Pacific; they may not be even the lock to the door. But they are surely the key to the lock that opens the door, for America. I dare not allow that key to be lost!"

World War II

It was his position in the Philippines, during the crisis of 1941, that made him the obviously qualified officer to be the senior American Army Commander in the Pacific. The brilliant defense of the Philippines by a destitute group of American and Filipino fighting men will always be remembered as a magnificent defeat. Only by order of the President of the United States did MacArthur leave the men on Bataan. After he left the besieged island of Bataan, he remarked, "I was the leader of that lost cause, and from the bottom of my stricken heart I pray that a merciful God may not delay too long their redemption." The defeat and the subsequent treatment of the captured Americans and Filipinos made MacArthur a leader driven by hatred for his enemy. Bataan became an obsession with him, a cult. He lived for the day he would return. The dead of Bataan lived in his heart, and he had a constant lust for vengeance.

When he set up his headquarters in Australia, his staff was instructed to answer all telephone calls with, "Bataan speaking." As the Allies moved closer to the Philippines and General MacArthur's headquarters moved forward with the troops, each time he named his headquarters, "Bataan". His personal aircraft, instead of being named, "Jean", was called, "Bataan". His only comment after the remarkable victory at Buna was, "The dead of Bataan will rest easier tonight." When MacArthur came upon the naked body of a dead Japanese soldier on the shell-torn shores of Los Negros, he commented to an officer standing beside him, "This is the way I like to see them." His desire to defeat the Japanese was so strong that he told General

Robert Eichelberger in one of the early Allied offensives, the attack on Buna, to "take Buna or die."[18] He wanted hatred for the enemy to filter down to all the men in his command, and reminded them on every possible occasion of the brutality of the enemy.

The bitterness he felt was not only for the enemy; he believed his own leaders had let him down in failing to send men and material to assist their valiant defense. During the difficult defense of Bataan, when Americans were fighting against overwhelming Japanese forces, when our soldiers were low on ammunition, food, medical supplies and other vitals, and when help looked hopeless, word was sent to Army Headquarters that California had been shelled. When MacArthur heard the news he told General Richard Sutherland, his Chief of Staff, "Wire them [the United States] that if they can hold out for thirty days, we'll send help."[19]

June 18, 1943, General MacArthur wrote to his good friend, Bonner Fellers:

It has been a desperate time for me ever since the war started, always the underdog, and always fighting with destruction around the corner. I could have held Bataan if I had not been so completely deserted. I have taken comfort from Stonewall Jackson's creed, that "if necessary we will fight them with sticks and stones." But I find that sticks break in our hands and stones can't go very far. A merciful God has miraculously brought me through so far, but I am sick at heart at the mistakes and lost opportunities that are so prevalent.

With my affections
/s/
Douglas MacArthur

Courtney Whitney, who was with MacArthur for over twenty years said, "I only saw him in tears twice—the first time was when the first men escaped from Japanese POW camps in 1942 and made their report to him of the Bataan Death March."[20]

The second time was when his son, Arthur, broke his arm ice-skating.

Brigadier General Bonner Fellers, who was constantly with MacArthur during World War II, said that "When we recaptured Bataan, General MacArthur got some fifteen miles ahead of his troops. There were snipers all around and I told him any minute someone might pick him off right through the heart, and he replied: 'That won't hurt any more than my heart has been hurting for the last three years'."

One of the first things General MacArthur did when he arrived in Manila in 1945, was to go to the army hospital where some of the rescued veterans of Bataan and Corregidor were being treated. "These are my own men," he said, "and I am one of them. I owe them a lot. I promised I would return, and I'm long overdue." As he went down the line of beds, he stopped at each bedside. Tears ran down the faces of these unfortunate men who had been subjected to beatings, malnutrition, and disease. "I tried to get here as soon as I could," he told them; "I am going to give you all the medical attention you need. Then you're going home."[2][1]

In all fairness to the decision makers in Washington at that time, it must be emphasized that everything possible was done to send assistance to Bataan. There was however, a war in Europe, only limited availability of men and supplies, and, because of the Pearl Harbor sneak attack, a temporary superiority of Japanese naval forces in the Pacific that made shipping to the Philippines almost an impossibility.

When the final victory came and MacArthur was preparing for his trip to Tokyo, he worked with men who had been with him at Corregidor as well as those who were with him on the long journey back. As one correspondent cabled back, "The old Bataan crowd is going to deal with the Emperor."

Soon after his arrival from Bataan, MacArthur was asked by the Australian Minister of War to attend the final defense conference that would settle a question which was a potential political bombshell—whether to hold the line between the coast and mountains at Townsville, Brisbane, Sydney, or, in the extreme south, Melbourne. Each region, of course, wanted to be within the defense zone and not abandoned to the Japanese. "After long hours of discussion, with MacArthur present but saying nothing," one of the observers remarked, "it was decided by the Council to hold the line at Brisbane. Turning to General MacArthur, the War Minister asked the General his opinion on the Brisbane decision: 'Gentlemen, since you ask me to comment, I would say that the defense of Australia lies in the Owen Stanley Range in New Guinea'."[22]

As a military leader who faced overwhelming odds at the beginning of World War II, he expressed his philosophy:

> It doesn't matter how much you have, so long as you fight with what you have. It doesn't matter where you fight, so long as you fight. Because where you fight, the enemy has to fight too, and even though it splits your force, it must split his force also. So fight, on whatever the scale, whenever and wherever you can. There is only one way to win victories. Attack, attack, attack!

When he became commander of all Allied army, navy, and air forces in the Southwest Pacific, that is exactly what he did. He did not personally exercise command over any of these forces. He developed the strategic plans, issued directives designating the operations, the commanders who would undertake these operations, and the forces and means to be used, and established the objectives. As any commander should, he left the tactical decisions up to his subordinate commanders, a strong factor in the success he had as a leader.

His Staff and Commanders

Ten hours after the Japanese attacked Pearl Harbor, they bombed the Philippines and were successful in destroying practically all the B-17's and most of the fighters at Clark Field on the ground. General MacArthur had ordered all the B-17's sent to Mindanao, but unfortunately the order could not be immediately carried out by the air commander.

The air commander was Major General Lewis H. Brereton. General Henry H. Arnold had called General Brereton right after the Pearl Harbor attack. "I then talked on the telephone with General Brereton out in the Philippines," General Arnold wrote, "to try to give him some idea of what happened at Pearl Harbor so that he would not be caught the same way and his entire air force destroyed. He explained to me what he was trying to do; but in spite of all the precautions taken, in spite of all the book-learning, in spite of all the experience we had accumulated during maneuvers, and in spite of all the techniques that had been taught at the Tactical School, within a few hours we also lost most of our airplanes in the Philippines. . . I could not help thinking that there must have been some mistake made somewhere in my Air Force command; and I took it upon myself to tell Brereton so."[2 3]

General Brereton wrote an account of his conversation with General Arnold in his diary on December 11, 1941:

> I had just returned from Clark Field when a long distance call came from General Arnold in Washington. He was excited and apparently under a great strain.
>
> "How in the hell could an experienced airman like you get caught with your planes on the ground?" General Arnold asked. "That's what we sent you there for, to avoid just what happened."
>
> I tried to explain what had happened, but halfway through the conversation the Japs came over strafing the field.
>
> "What in the hell is going on there?" General Arnold shouted.
>
> "We are having visitors," I replied.
>
> I asked General Arnold to withhold his judgment until he got a complete report on what happened at Clark Field... I immediately reported the conversation to General MacArthur and asked his assistance in setting facts straight. He was furious; it is the only time in my life I have ever seen him mad. He told me to go back and fight the war and not to worry. As I walked out of his office he asked Sutherland to get General Marshall on the 'phone.[2 4]

In reply to his criticism of Brereton, General Arnold received a wire from General MacArthur, stating that:

> Every possible precaution within the limited means and the time available was taken here with the Far East Air Force. Their losses were due entirely to the overwhelming superiority of the enemy force. They were hopelessly out-numbered from the start, but no unit could have done better. Their gallantry has been conspicuous, their ef-ficiency good. No item of loss can properly be attributed to neglect or lack of care. They fought from fields not yet developed and under improvised conditions of every sort which placed them under the severest handicap as com-pared to an enemy fully prepared in every way. You may take pride in their conduct. MacArthur. [25]

General Arnold's comment on the MacArthur cable was, "Loyalty-down is as essential in any command as loyalty-up, and General MacArthur always had loyalty-down. . ."[26]

Doubt was not, however, restricted to General Arnold. "But, when criticism of Brereton was brought to MacArthur's atten-tion in 1943," wrote one of General MacArthur's aides, "he quickly retorted with the true and extenuating circumstances of the situation: 'General Brereton had in the Philippines only a token force, which, excluding trainers and hopelessly obsolete planes, comprised but 35 bombers and 72 fighters. He was fur-ther greatly handicapped by the lack of airdromes, there being only one on Luzon, Clark Field, that was usable by heavy bombers and only five usable by fighters. Many airdromes were under construction in the Philippines, but they were not com-pleted and available by December 7 . . . A number of our air-planes were destroyed on the ground while landing for gas or while down for essential maintenance—but never as a result of negligence'."[27]

As the war progressed and times were difficult for the United States, there was much unhappiness among the men in the army and air corps. This was to be expected; but it reached a point among the air corps members of MacArthur's command that required action on his part. During General MacArthur's first briefing of General George C. Kenney, who replaced Lieutenant General Brereton, he made one point particularly clear: "Finally," General Kenney said of his conversation with General MacArthur, "he said that not only were the aviators antagonistic to his headquarters, but he was even beginning to doubt their loyalty. He would not stand for disloyalty. He demanded loyalty from me and everyone in the Air Force or he would get rid of them."[28]

MacArthur was intensely loyal to his staff. During World War II he never released a single member of his staff for making an error; he took the blame. If a commander, however, made a mistake, he was released immediately. One thing he could absolutely not tolerate was disloyalty. If an officer was disobedient, he was fired. If he displayed partiality for his own branch of the service at the jeopardy of the overall mission, he was reassigned.

Perhaps MacArthur was overly loyal—down. General Kenney remarked that "MacArthur's loyalty to those who are loyal to him and work for him is a wonderful trait. It marks the leader whose men trust him and follow him. In MacArthur's case it will even tolerate a degree of inefficiency. He cannot hurt a loyal friend. I believe that is why he kept some people around, in spite of the fact that they were largely responsible for the bad press that he had during World War II."[29]

It was his policy to see as few people as possible. He was always available to the senior members of his staff; the junior members worked through his Chief of Staff. In dealing with his staff he was positively brilliant in delegating responsibility. As one person put it, "It is by avoiding doing too much that General MacArthur gets so much done." He left his mind free of battle planning so he could concentrate on the long-range aspects of the war. Thus, he could instantly exploit each opportunity as it occurred. "I don't do much," he said, "except think a lot, scold a little, pat a man on the back now and then, and try to keep a perspective."

A former Chief of Staff, Lieutenant General Stephen J. Chamberlin, said he was a great leader because, "he could place responsibility in subordinates and let them go. Sometimes as a member of his staff I was scared, and I wondered if General MacArthur knew what I was doing. When I got to be Chief of Staff, I realized he always knew just what I was doing; but I don't know how he knew."[30]

One individual said of him, "MacArthur cannot stand to take advice. It is his greatest defect that he has to do everything alone." This was not true. Along this same line of criticism, the accusations were often made about General MacArthur that his staff during World War II was filled with "yes-men". This also was not true. He sought and received advice from his staff on all major decisions, and insisted upon honest opinions. He quickly got rid of anyone who appeared to him to insincerely or fawningly agree.

A story told by Admiral William F. Halsey indicates MacArthur's appreciation of officers with the backbone to disagree with him:

. . . I received a dispatch from my representative on MacArthur's staff, Capt. Felix L. Johnson, urgently requesting me to come to Brisbane at once. Mick, Bill Riley, Doug Moulton, and Ham Dow flew over with me. We went from the plane straight to MacArthur's office, where Felix met us. MacArthur was waiting for us, with his top staff officers and Vice Adm. Tom Kinkaid, commanding the Seventh Fleet. (Incidentally, there was an unusual bond between our two staffs: my Chief of Staff's son, Capt. Robert B. Carney, Jr., of the Marines, had married MacArthur's Chief of Staff's daughter, Miss Natalie Sutherland.)

Before even a word of greeting was spoken, I saw that MacArthur was fighting to keep his temper. What galled him, it soon appeared, was this: Nimitz, knowing that I not only had planned the layout for the base at Manus but had furnished naval forces to construct it, had sent a dispatch to COMINCH, with a copy to MacArthur, suggesting that the boundary of my area be extended to include Manus. I had had no hand in originating the dispatch; I did not even hear of it until after it had been sent; but MacArthur lumped me, Nimitz, King, and the whole Navy in a vicious conspiracy to pare away his authority.

Unlike myself, strong emotion did not make him profane. He did not need to be; profanity would have merely discolored his eloquence. It continued for about a quarter of an hour, illuminating two main themes: he had no intention of tamely submitting to such interference; and he had given orders that, until the jurisdiction of Manus was established, work should be restricted to facilities for ships under his direct command—the Seventh Fleet and British units.

When he had finished, he pointed his pipestem at me and demanded. "Am I not right, Bill?"

Tom Kinkaid, Mick, Felix, and I answered with one voice, "No, sir!"

MacArthur smiled and said pleasantly, "Well, if so many fine gentlemen disagree with me, we'd better examine the proposition once more. Bill, what's your opinion?"

"General," I said, "I disagree with you entirely. Not only that, but I'm going one step further and tell you that if you stick to this order of yours, you'll be hampering the war effort!"

His staff gasped. I imagine they never expected to hear anyone address him in those terms this side of the Judgment Throne, if then. I told him that the command of Manus didn't matter a whit to me. What did matter was the quick construction of the base. Kenney or an Australian or an enlisted cavalryman could boss it for all I cared, as long as it was ready to handle the fleet when we moved up New Guinea and on toward the Philippines.

The argument had begun at 1700. By 1800, when we broke up, I thought I had won him around, but next morning at 1000 he asked us to come back to his office. (He kept unusual hours from 1000 until 1400, and from 1600 until 2100 or later.) It seemed that during the night he had become mad all over again, and again was dead set on restricting the work. We went through the same arguments at the afternoon before, almost word for word, and at the end of an hour we reached the same conclusion: the work would proceed. I was about to tell him good-by and fly back to Noumea when he suddenly asked if we would return at 1700. I'll be damned if we didn't run the course a third time! This time, though, it was really final. He gave me a charming smile and said, "You win, Bill!" and to General Sutherland, "Dick, go ahead with the job."[3 1]

Once, General Kenney went into General MacArthur to request permission to fire anyone who was incompetent and to decorate the deserving. He got an immediate go ahead from General MacArthur. "You couldn't beat that for cooperation," General Kenney reacted. "If General MacArthur ever decides that he has confidence in you, he goes all the way. When anyone backs you up like that, it makes it easy to work your head off for him."[3 2]

General MacArthur was interested in results, and he wanted officers in the positions of responsibility who would get results. General Kenney decided shortly after his arrival in Australia to organize all his fighter groups into a single command. To head the new organization he selected a young colonel, whose new position would give him the rank of brigadier general. General MacArthur approved Kenney's request. When his staff heard of the proposal, an officer remarked, "That kid. Well, I hope he's twenty-one." MacArthur overheard the comment; he turned to his staff officer and said, "We promote them out here for efficiency, not for age."[3 3] The officer being promoted to brigadier was thirty-two years old.

A knowledge of his commanders was certainly a key factor in his military success in World War II. As a member of his staff put it, "One of the biggest jobs was knowing when to put Kreuger in and when Eichelberger. Some jobs Kreuger could do better than Eichelberger, and vice versa. This was again Mac's gift for leadership."[3 4] Kreuger was a Prussian type of general. He was exacting in detail and knew everything that was going on, a perfectionist. He took very few chances; he wanted things buttoned down before moving into action. General Eichel-berger, on the other hand, took chances and moved more rapidly.

The Pacific area is an oceanic hemisphere; and, as a conse-quence, the fighting there in World War II was amphibious. It was logically, according to the navy, a naval war. In addition, there was an emotional factor. The navy, smarting from the humiliation of the sneak attack on Pearl Harbor, wanted revenge. However, if they were to have the primary role, the army's position would be a secondary one; under the confident and strong MacArthur, this was never the case. Nor was his selection for this position, so ripe for conflict and strife, an accident. Secretary of War Stimson wrote in his diary on February 23, 1943, of MacArthur's position in the Pacific: "Marshall thinks that his [MacArthur's] dominating character is needed there to make the Navy keep up their job in spite of rows which we shall have between them."

The main disagreement between the army and navy was over the strategy for winning the war in the Pacific. The navy wanted to adopt a strategy of "island-hopping." MacArthur's approach was quite different:

> My strategic conception for the Pacific Theater con-templates massive strokes against only main objectives, utilizing surprise and air-ground striking power supported and assisted by the fleet. This is the very opposite of what is termed "island hopping," which is the gradual pushing back of the enemy by direct frontal pressure with the consequent heavy casualties which will certainly be in-volved. Key points must of course be taken, but a wise choice of such will obviate the need for storming the mass of islands now in enemy possession. "Island hopping" with extravagant losses and slow progress is not my idea of how to end the war as soon and as cheaply as possible. New conditions require for solution, and new weapons require for maximum application, new and imaginative methods. Wars are never won in the past.

One of MacArthur's key staff planners said of this:

The appeal of the MacArthur strategy was that it combined flexibility and economy at a time when these had to be substituted for strength. While its central feature was its military directness—"the principle of the objective," in bleak staff-school language—it allowed for all sorts of strategical and tactical deception in furthering the objective. What MacArthur proposed to do was to jump around strong points along the central axis of advance without throwing his forces out beyond his own air umbrella. Broadly speaking, he sought to split the Greater East Asia-South Sea Empire of the Japanese by penetration along interior lines. But, lacking the facilities to fight the Japanese head-on, he proposed no frontal strokes at Japanese strong points. What he sought for each individual battle was an opportunity to get around and behind the enemy, striking him obliquely on the flank and grappling for his supply lines. The whole MacArthur theory of maneuver was a hark-back past the man-devouring frontal assaults of World War I to the fluidity of Napoleonic times.[35]

The strongest single disagreement between MacArthur and the navy was over the final route to Japan. Admiral Nimitz wanted to bypass the Philippines and attack Formosa. MacArthur believed the Philippines should come first. In March 1944, Admiral Nimitz and General MacArthur met in the latter's office in Brisbane to discuss strategy. Nimitz in a letter to Chief of Naval Operations King wrote his impression of this meeting:

[MacArthur] seemed pleased to have the J.C.S. directive covering the entire calendar year of 1944 because it definitely provided for his entry into the Philippines via Mindanao—a plan which is very close to his heart. His cordiality and courtesy to me and my party throughout my visit was complete and genuine, and left nothing that could be desired. Everything was lovely and harmonious until the last day of our conference when I called attention to the last part of the J.C.S. directive which required him and me to prepare alternate plans for moving faster and along shorter routes towards the Luzon-Formosa-China triangle if deteriorating Japanese strength permitted. Then he blew up and made an oration of some length on the impossibility of bypassing the Philippines, his sacred obligations there—redemption of the 17 million people—blood on his soul—deserted by American people—etc., etc.—and then a criticism of "those gentlemen in Washington, who, far from the scene, and having never heard the whistle of pellets, etc., endeavor to set the strategy of the Pacific War"—etc. When I could break in I replied that, while I believed I understood his point of view, I could not go along with him and then—believe it or not—I launched forth in a defense of "those gentlemen in Washington" and told him that the J.C.S. were people like himself and myself, who, with more information, were trying to do their best for the country and, to my mind, were succeeding admirably.[36]

The difference of opinion over this strategy between the army and navy was finally resolved by President Roosevelt, who went to Honolulu to meet with his two senior commanders in the Pacific. Fleet Admiral William D. Leahy, Roosevelt's Chief of Staff, described this meeting:

That evening [July 27, 1944], the President had MacArthur, Nimitz, Halsey and me to dinner. After the meal, MacArthur and Nimitz met with the President and me to talk over the Pacific war situation. This discussion was not finished at midnight and was resumed the next morning (July 28), lasting until noon.

The spacious living room of the residence in which we were quartered was used as a conference room. Huge wall maps were hung and MacArthur and Nimitz from time to time would illustrate their discussions with the use of a long bamboo pointer. After so much loose talk in Washington, where the mention of the name MacArthur seemed to generate more heat than light, it was both pleasant and very informative to have these two men who had been pictured as antagonists calmly present their differing views to the Commander-in-Chief. For Roosevelt it was an excellent lesson in geography, one of his favorite subjects.

MacArthur was convinced that an occupation of the Philippines was essential before any major attack in force should be made on Japanese-held territory north of Luzon. The retaking of the Philippines seemed to be a matter of great interest to him. He said that he had sufficient ground and air forces for the operation and that his only additional needs were landing craft and naval support.

Nimitz developed the Navy's plan of by-passing the Philippines and attacking Formosa. He did not see that Luzon, including Manila Bay, had advantages that were not possessed by other areas in the Philippines that could be taken for a base at less cost in lives and material. As the discussions progressed, however, the Navy commander in the Pacific admitted that developments might indicate a necessity for occupation of the Manila area. Nimitz said that he had sufficient forces to carry out either operation. It was highly pleasing and unusual to find two commanders who were not demanding reinforcements.

Roosevelt was at his best as he tactfully steered the discussion from one point to another and narrowed down the area of disagreement between MacArthur and Nimitz. The discussion remained on a friendly basis the entire time, and in the end only a relatively minor difference remained—that of an operation to retake the Philippine capital, Manila. This was solved later when the idea of beginning our Philippine invasion at Leyte was suggested, studied, and adopted.

These two meetings were much more peaceful than I had expected after what I had been hearing in Washington. Here in Honolulu we were working with facts, not with the emotional reactions of politicians. MacArthur had shown exceptional ability early in his Army career and his rise had been rapid. It was no secret that in the Pentagon Building in Washington there were men who disliked him,

to state the matter mildly. The attitude of some of our
naval commanders has already been shown by the events
which led up to the conference at Honolulu. I personally
was convinced that MacArthur and Nimitz were, together,
the two best qualified officers in our service for this tremendous task. Nimitz promised that he would give the
Army commander the needed transportation and naval
support.[37]

General MacArthur followed up this decision with tenacity.
When President Roosevelt and Admiral King returned to the
United States they each found communiques from MacArthur
reiterating the importance of occupying the Philippines before
moving on to Japan, arguing that failure to take them would
permit complete blockade by Japan that would result in starv-
ing the Filipinos, and that "if we failed to liberate the Filipinos,
it would be a blot upon the honor of the United States."[38]

Under MacArthur's leadership, interservice rivalry was kept
to a minimum. Even Admiral "Bull" Halsey, so named because
of his tenacious and outspoken personality, was charmed by the
eloquence and logic of MacArthur:

> . . . the over-all strategy of the whole area was in
> MacArthur's hands, the Joint Chiefs of Staff had put tac-
> tical command of the Solomons subarea in mine. Although
> this arrangement was sensible and satisfactory, it had the
> curious effect of giving me two "hats" in the same
> echelon. My original hat was under Nimitz, who controlled
> my troops, ships, and supplies; now I had another hat
> under MacArthur, who controlled my strategy.
>
> To discuss plans for New Georgia with him, I requested
> an appointment at his headquarters, which were then in
> Brisbane, Australia, and I flew across from Noumea early
> in April. I had never met the General before, but we had
> one tenuous connection: my father had been a friend of
> his father's in the Philippines more than forty years back.
> Five minutes after I reported, I felt as if we were lifelong
> friends. I have seldom seen a man who makes a quicker,
> stronger, more favorable impression. He was then sixty-

three years old, but he could have passed as fifty. His hair was jet black; his eyes were clear; his carriage was erect. If he had been wearing civilian clothes, I still would have known at once that he was a soldier.

The respect that I conceived for him that afternoon grew steadily during the war and continues to grow as I watch his masterly administration of surrendered Japan. I can recall no flaw in our relationship. We had arguments, but they always ended pleasantly. Not once did he, my superior officer, ever force his decisions upon me. On the few occasions when I disagreed with him, I told him so, and we discussed the issue until one of us changed his mind. My mental picture poses him against the background of these discussions; he is pacing his office, almost wearing a groove between his large, bare desk and the portrait of George Washington that faced it; his corncob pipe in his hand (I rarely saw him smoke it); and he is making his points in a diction I have never heard surpassed.[39]

Admiral Nimitz and other prominent naval officers who had contact with MacArthur were favorably impressed. His professional knowledge, his ability to express his ideas, his consideration for his colleagues, his preparation, his drive were a winning combination.

Visiting Combat Areas

It is vital for a commander, if he wants to be successful as a leader, to visit the front. MacArthur's visits were infrequent, but he did so often enough to keep a feel for how things were going. On September 5, 1943, the most spectacular operation of the New Guinea campaign was held—the landing of Allied paratroopers in the Markham River Valley. On one of the Flying Fortresses, General MacArthur flew with the aircraft carrying the paratroopers. His air chief, General Kenney, tried without success to prevent MacArthur from going; but he said, "I just have to be with our paratroopers when they enter combat for the first time under such hazardous conditions."

When he went ashore at New Guinea, his landing boat had to pass through an entrance of the harbor that was shaped like a horseshoe. The two points were only 200 yards apart. The U.S. held one point and the Japanese the other. In spite of the danger of snipers, General MacArthur rode between the two points, standing erect, an easy target for a bullet. He went ashore and was warned by an Army officer concerned about the General's safety, "Excuse me, sir, but we just killed a Jap sniper here just a few minutes ago." General MacArthur's nonchalant reply was "Fine, that's the best thing to do with them," as he moved forward.

During the war, he flew to many of the combat areas in his B-17 Flying Fortress. He would drive along the dusty roads in his brown command car, unadorned except for four stars. Often he would stop and walk along some trail, always several steps in front of his aides. When he made his inspections, soldiers would drop what they were doing and rush over to get a glimpse of him.

Never did he show any concern for his personal safety. "I remember one incident," a member of his staff related after the war, "when we made a landing on Leyte Island. The area was heavily mined and boobytrapped by the Japs and moving around was rather dangerous. General MacArthur came ashore and started a ground reconnaissance of the area. He was immediately informed of the inherent danger and his reply, 'There never was a Japanese mine made that would kill me,' settled the matter. He then went on with his reconnaissance."[40] On other occasions, he made similar replies that the bullet, shell, or mortar had never been made that could kill him.

One member of his staff, Brigadier General Bonner Fellers, commented that during World War II, "I saw General MacArthur in combat and under fire dozens of times when he had no business being there. Over and over he made landings with the initial assault waves. Many times I have begged him, for God's sake to go back where it was not quite so hot. Usually his only retort was—'If you can't take it up here, you go back." He appeared to be illustrating a statement he had made when he received the baton of a Field Marshal in the Philippine Army in 1936, "Only those are fit to live who are not afraid to die."

Comments were made of MacArthur during the war that he "preserves an unapproachability," that he had a "chilly aloofness from the mob." To a degree these statements were true. One of the purposes of a leader's visiting his men, making landings on beachheads, and performing inspections is to let the men know their general is with them. But the MacArthur style in accomplishing this was different from that of most other generals. He was more aloof. Seldom did he have personal conversations with the soldiers as he walked around. He was not a really warm and compelling personality. He did not have the infectious grin of an Eisenhower or display the flamboyance of a Patton. Men were in awe of MacArthur as they would be of a king.

MacArthur did not believe in giving haranguing speeches to his men. He left that to his commanders. He did not believe that as Supreme Commander he needed to speak to his men and wave the flag. During his stay in Australia while preparing the Allied offensive, he kept very much to himself, appearing around town every now and then so people would be assured by his presence.

Showmanship

There was much about Douglas MacArthur that made others susceptible to hero worship. He was handsome, dashing, and oratorically brilliant. He had an incredible veneer of showmanship while he was at the same time a recluse. He was rarely seen by the troops, and his style of showmanship when he did visit surrounded him with a mystic aura.

The crux of his showmanship was a distinctive simplicity. Throughout all of World War II, he was always seen in a plain khaki uniform with an open-necked shirt and sharply pressed trousers. He wore no medals, only the rank of a four-star general, and his rakish hat with the gold braid on the bill. Other than this, his only accoutrements were a corn-cob pipe and a bamboo swagger stick. On other occasions, he smoked cigarettes in an uptilt position in a long black cigarette holder, swinging a brown, curve-handled cane.

There was a certain drama to his actions that made him stand out. His performance at the Japanese surrender on board the U.S.S. *Missouri* was characteristic. It occurred on Sunday morning, September 2, 1945. The Japanese delegation of diplomats and military officers arrived at 8:55. Awaiting them were the representatives from the United States (General "Vinegar Joe" Stilwell, George C. Kenney, Admiral "Bull" Halsey), Great Britain, China, Holland, France, and the Soviet Union. The eleven members of the Japanese delegation were dressed in morning coats or heavily-medaled dress military uniforms. A few minutes after everyone was in place, General MacArthur came out from his cabin. He was dressed in the type of khaki uniform he had worn throughout the war, with an open, tie-less collar, no medals, and his field marshal cap at the usual rakish angle. As he read his preliminary remarks, he stood erect; but his hands were shaky as he read from his prepared text. Then, there was complete silence as the surrender was signed. By 9:08, only fourteen minutes after the ceremony officially began, it was all over.

The signing by MacArthur was reminiscent of presidential practice. He used five pens, one of them his own. He signed, "Doug" with the first, "las" with the second, "MacArthur" with the third. For his second signature, he used two pens. Thus he could provide his friends with a pen that had played a significant role in history. One went to the archives at his beloved West Point.

When he went to Japan as conqueror in 1945 he traveled in a gleaming, silvery C-54. When he landed at the Atsugi airport, a band began to play as the ramp was let down. From the door of the aircraft, named *Bataan,* the first person to emerge was General MacArthur. He took several steps down the ramp as he puffed on his corncob pipe; then, he paused dramatically. He was the first Caucasian in Japan's history to take control of Japan. After he had gazed out for a few minutes, he continued down the ramp, warmly shaking hands with old friends who were in the advance party.

When the American delegation arrived at the U.S. Embassy, MacArthur commanded, "General Eichelberger, have our country's flag unfurled, and in Tokyo's sun let it wave in its full glory as a symbol of hope for the oppressed and as a harbinger of victory for the right." The American flag raised was the one that flew over the Capital in Washington, D. C. on December 7, 1941, and the same flag raised at Casablanca, Rome, and Berlin.

MacArthur and the Press

After his successful escape from Bataan and his arrival in Australia, MacArthur held a press conference. MacArthur sat in a chair facing the 51 reporters for the first few minutes, but then he quickly lapsed into his usual style. He got up and started pacing the floor, answering very frankly the questions that were asked. He had the group hypnotized. One reporter commented, "MacArthur was so much the center of attention that even the entrance of the American minister to New Zealand went unnoticed." He went on like that for an hour and 45 minutes and left. Certainly the most reassuring words MacArthur gave to the press were, "I am an old censor myself. My main purpose is not to suppress news from you, but to get news for you."

At this press conference he promised as full publicity as possible, emphasizing that in a democracy the people must know the truth and understand what we are fighting for. If the people are not informed, they are likely to believe half-truths; this could be prejudicial to the war effort. He also asked the press to be sure they had all the facts before they criticized. MacArthur has always had the ability to make friends with reporters. He was well aware of the value of good press relations; and in his days as Chief of Staff, he many times cut through red tape to promote cooperation between the Army and newspapermen.

Although he was personally eloquent in speeches and had an effective style, General MacArthur did not always have good publicity. His personal press conferences were rare occasions, and he had his staff act for him in handling the press. "His public-relations officers," General Kenney commented, "invariably adored MacArthur almost to the point of idolatry. To them unless a news release painted the General with a halo and seated him on the highest pedestal in the universe, it should be killed. No news, except favorable news, reflecting complete credit on an infallible MacArthur, had much chance of getting by the censors. They seemed to believe that they had a sacred mission, which was to 'sell' the General to the world, and they didn't trust the newspaper men to interpret MacArthur properly... Sometimes they [the censors] tended to be arrogant and almost insulting to the representatives of the press, of whom they did not have a high opinion."

"The General got the blame, especially back home, and the newspaper reaction too often was far from favorable. At one time he was criticized 'for applying dictatorial powers to the world's press' ... practically every one of the newspapermen who were accredited to the South West Pacific had no use for MacArthur's public-relations department during the war and have not changed their minds since."[41]

Oratory

Although he spoke to the press and his men very seldom, the occasions when he did so were classic. Such phrases as, "Only those are fit to live who are not afraid to die for their country"; and as he came upon a dead American soldier killed in battle during World War II: "I do not know the dignity of his birth, but I do know the glory of his death." Of Corregidor he said:

Through the bloody haze of its last reverberating shot I
shall always seem to see the vision of its grim, gaunt and
ghostly men, still unafraid;

and of Bataan he remarked:

The Bataan force went out as it would have wished,
fighting to the end of its flickering, forlorn hope. . . .
Nothing became it more than its last hour of trial and
glory.

Time, in describing his speaking ability, wrote of General
MacArthur in December 1941: "He would stride up and down
in his office, purpling the air with oratory, punctuated with
invocations of God, the flag, and patriotism, pounding his fist in
his palm, swinging his arms in sweeping gesture."

In conversation he was not much different: "Changing at will
from a mellifluous melodramatic whisper to a fiery snort, from
brutal fact to sheer rodomontade, he used phrases like, 'We
must foil the enemy'; 'We must stand on the eve of the great
battle'; 'We must not spill our precious blood on foreign soil in
vain, in vain." His speeches were almost theatrical but no
listener doubted their sincerity.

When MacArthur spoke to his men he seldom talked any
longer than fifteen minutes, and often as briefly as five minutes.
General Kenney, who was present for many of these talks, remarked, "He puts so much of himself into what he is saying
that many times he will be carried away by his own emotions;
but this only serves to further impress the listener with the deep
sincerity of the speaker. You feel that here is a man who really
believes what he is saying . . ."

At a banquet in Australia, in honor of the second anniversary
of MacArthur's arrival, Prime Minister John Curtin toasted the
General as the saviour of Australia. In reply MacArthur said of
Australia's fighting forces:

My thoughts go back to those men who went on their last crusade in the jungle thickness to the north, where they made the fight that saved this continent. Their yesterday makes possible our tomorrow. They came from the four quarters of the world, but whatever the land that gave them birth, under their stark white crosses, they belong now to Australia forever.

Prime Minister Curtin was so touched by this little speech he was stunned, and he appeared to be fighting off tears.

When he gave a speech, it was not an "off the cuff" presentation. He first wrote it out in longhand and then proceeded to edit and re-edit, and continued to do so until he was satisfied with it. He intended to impress his audience with his speech and in that attempt he never failed.

Even in conversation his eloquence was a moving force in his leading of men:

It was fascinating to listen to the General sitting there relaxed in his own home. You never go to sleep listening to MacArthur talking on any subject, but when he discourses on the art of war, he becomes fascinating. You soon realize that a master is at work. His analysis is so clear, so logical, and so simple that you wonder why you didn't come to the same conclusion by yourself.[42]

A similar reaction to MacArthur's conversational ability was noted by Lieutenant General Brereton on his first formal visit:

I noticed again one of General MacArthur's traits: he cannot talk sitting down. It seems to me that the more clearly he enunciates his ideas, the more vigorous his walking becomes. He is one of the most beautiful talkers I have ever heard and, while his manner might be considered a bit on the theatrical side, it is just part of his personality and an expression of his character. There is never any doubt as to what he means and what he wants.[43]

His oratorical ability reflects the serious reading he did throughout his life, particularly his study of the classics, especially military classics. One finds in his speeches and writings lines from the works of Napoleon, a line from some melodrama he saw on Broadway, an excerpt from a Lincoln speech, a statement by Plato, or perhaps a quote from the Bible.

That he considered communication vital to success as a leader was made clear in 1939 by General MacArthur in a letter he wrote to a former member of his staff in the Philippines. This officer at the time was teaching English at West Point:

> You were good enough to ask my opinion with reference to the objectives of the English Course at West Point. It is unquestionably so to train the cadet that he can clearly and lucidly present his basic thoughts and ideas. It is not the mission of the English Course to create or control those ideas, but it is its clear function to provide him with the medium through which he can present his views in an intelligent and even forcible manner. No man can hope to rise to distinction who cannot do this and no man, however humble his position, should fail to be able to do so. It is the very medium in which modern civilization lives. It is almost like the air you breathe. Without it a man may have the finest judgment in the world, he may be even wise as Solomon and yet his influence will be practically negligible. The accomplishment of such a purpose is not confined to proper grammatical, rhetorical or phonetical grouping of words into sentences and paragraphs. There must be the logical connection between the thought in a man's brain and the ability to present it in clear language.[44]

Relationship With Subordinates

As one World War II naval officer put it "Douglas MacArthur is a man many admire but few love." This is an appropriate appraisal for the vast majority of the people under his command. For the senior members of his staff, it was quite different.

"MacArthur treated you with great consideration," his Commandant of Cadets said when the former was Superintendent at West Point from 1919 to 1921, "you worked hard for him because you liked him." When Colonel W.A. Ganoe wrote *MacArthur Close-Up*, someone made the comment in General Danford's presence that Ganoe "was just a hero worshipper of MacArthur." Danford looked him in the eye and said very sternly, almost challengingly, "So am I."[45]

Once during the war in the Southwest Pacific, General MacArthur called a conference of his army commanders on board a navy cruiser during the invasion of Hollandia (Dutch New Guinea). General Robert L. Eichelberger, one of his corps commanders, reminisced, "There is one passion of the Ohio smalltown boy which I have never outgrown—an unquenchable appetite for ice cream. So, to celebrate our fortunate landings, General MacArthur produced not a magnum of vintage-year champagne but chocolate ice cream sodas! There at the Equator they certainly hit the spot. When I finished mine with celerity, the Allied commander grinned and gave me his own untouched, frosted glass. I polished off that soda too."[46]

When Lieutenant General Lewis H. Brereton reported to the Philippines in November 1941 as MacArthur's air chief, he remembered his reception quite well:

> After checking in at the hotel and talking to General Clagett, whom I was relieving, I 'phoned General MacArthur at his penthouse apartment on the roof of the Manila Hotel, announcing my arrival.
> "Where are you, Lewis?" General MacArthur asked.
> "Here in the hotel, sir," I replied.
> "Come up immediately," he said.
> I was very cordially received by General MacArthur, whom I apparently fished out of his bath inasmuch as he came out in his dressing gown. I had not seen him, except

under purely official circumstances, since the last war. He recalled the occasion on which we had served together. I was in command of the 12th Observation Squadron in the Vosges sector in the spring of 1919 and my first operations were in support of the 42nd Division, commanded at that time by General Menoher with General MacArthur as Chief of Staff.

Now General MacArthur, eager as a small boy to hear all the news, slapped me on the back and threw his arm over my shoulder.

"Well, Lewis," he said, "I have been waiting for you. I knew you were coming, and I am damned glad to see you. You have been the subject of considerable conversation between myself, George Marshall, and Hap Arnold. What have you brought for me?"[47]

General Kenney said of his many years with General MacArthur, "I found myself admiring him as a general, liking him as a man, and inspired by his innate gift for leadership. MacArthur leads—he does not drive. People who work for him drive themselves to carry out his wishes. They feel that they must not let 'the Old Man' down. You never feel that he has given you a direct order to do something, but at the same time his positive way of expressing himself never leaves you in doubt. I do not remember ever having been given a direct order by MacArthur during the whole time I worked for him, but I always knew exactly what he wanted done and knew he expected me to do it."[48]

In answer to "Why was MacArthur great?", Whitney replied it was because "he made his men feel that their contribution was an important one—that they were somebody." His consideration was not, however, limited to his staff. During World War II, he attempted to send a letter to the family of every soldier lost in battle, always saying something individual in the letter. Many families wrote back and told General MacArthur how much better they felt about losing their boy after receiving his personal note.[49]

Even though he had a burning hatred for the Japanese, they too learned of his consideration once victory was won. To those who clamored for a tough occupation policy towards Japan after the war MacArthur replied: "I am not concerned with how to keep Japan down but how to get her on her feet again."

Never has a commander done so much with so little. It was truly brilliant leadership that permitted MacArthur to make so much of his limited resources. Even the most severe critics of MacArthur have never questioned his professional competence. His defeat at Bataan was as brilliant as his greatest victory. He knew the people and terrain of the Philippines as no other American could. His battle plans during World War II in the Southwest Pacific were executed with such precision that there almost seemed to be a "MacArthur Style." He was the professional soldier's concept of what a professional soldier should be. He injected into every mission to which he was assigned, a sense of Destiny—a sense of history, indeed, the very name of greatness, MacArthur.

On June 1, 1898, his father was appointed a brigadier general of volunteers and sent to the Philippines. "I was anxious," Douglas MacArthur said, "to pass up my coming cadetship and enlist . . ." His father opposed his enlisting, saying to him, "My son, there will be plenty of fighting in the coming years, and of a magnitude far beyond this. *Prepare yourself.*"[50]

In his Memoirs, General MacArthur commented that the words of Elihu Root, spoken at his graduation in 1903, served as a constant reminder, particularly the phrase: "Before you leave the Army, according to all precedents in our history, you will be engaged in another war. It is bound to come, and will come. Prepare your country for that war."[51] He did just that, and the reason in his own words was, "preparedness is the key to success and victory."[52]

Although he was challenged in many capacities during his lifetime and did not always remain free from criticism, he certainly came through more than a half-century of service to his country with banners flying. "Despite the greatness of his intellectual gifts," Cardinal Spellman said of MacArthur after his death, "he was characterized by simplicity and directness. He will always stand as a towering symbol of what it means to be a loyal American." And one can well believe that MacArthur would be happy to be so remembered.

SOLDIER-STATESMAN-DIPLOMAT

The Leadership of
General of the Army
Dwight D. Eisenhower

Dwight D. Eisenhower graduated 61 out of 164 from his class at the Military Academy. This group who finished in 1915 was to later be called "The Class the Stars Fell On," by virtue of 58 members earning one or more stars by the end of World War II. The cadet from this class who achieved the highest rank was Eisenhower. In 1939 he was a lieutenant colonel; by 1943 he was a four-star general; in 1944 he became Supreme Commander of the Allied invasion of Europe and one of four American army generals to achieve the newly created five-star rank of General of the Army. There were many officers who enjoyed a phenomenal rise in rank during World War II, but none had the success of Dwight D. Eisenhower. Why was Eisenhower the graduate to achieve such great success? Why was he the one selected as Supreme Commander?

Pre-World War II Career

The answer to these questions are not simple; but undoubtedly, the most singularly important factor was his selection for the War Plans Division in December, 1941. The story of why he was picked for that position covers his entire pre-World War II career.

153

Dwight D. Eisenhower's first assignment after graduation
from West Point was to Ft. Sam Houston in San Antonio,
Texas. It was there that he met a slender, attractive young lady
with dark brown hair and violet eyes. Her name was Mamie
Geneva Doud, whom he later married. His introduction to this
young lady was through three young lieutenants, Leonard T.
Gerow, Wade H. Haislip, and Walton H. Walker. They were to
become lifelong friends, and two of them were destined to play
a role in the remarkable career of Eisenhower.

The most important of these three personalities to General
Eisenhower was Leonard T. Gerow, a 1911 graduate of Virginia
Military Institute. They were to have other assignments
together; one of the most significant was Command and General
Staff School at Ft. Leavenworth, Kansas, where Eisenhower was
first in the graduating class of 1926, a factor which marked him
as a strong contender for future command.

In 1940 Gerow, as a brigadier general, was head of one of the
most important departments in the United States Army, the
War Plans Division. On November 18, 1940, Gerow sent a brief
radiogram to Eisenhower, who was then on IX Corps staff at Ft.
Lewis, Washington:

I NEED YOU IN WAR PLANS DIVISION DO YOU
SERIOUSLY OBJECT TO BEING DETAILED ON THE
WAR DEPT GENERAL STAFF AND ASSIGNED HERE
PLEASE REPLY IMMEDIATELY[1]

Eisenhower did have serious objections. He wanted a field
command more than anything else in the world. His answer
could have been the most fateful decision of his life, and would
certainly have great bearing on his future career. If he accepted
Gerow's offer, it would probably mean the end of any opportunity to get command, and spending another World War as a
stateside officer. He wrote to Gerow the next day:

Dear Gee:
    Your telegram, arriving this morning, sent me into a
tailspin. I am going to tell you the whole story and then if

you decide that I should come to the War Plans Division, all you have to do is have the orders issued without any further reference to me.

In the first place, I want to make it clear that I am, and have always been, very serious in my belief that the individual's preference and desires should have little, if any, weight in determining his assignment, when superior authority is making a decision in the matter. So all the rest of this is because, by implication, you asked for it!

With this somewhat pompous-sounding preamble, here goes.

There is not another individual that ranks with yourself so far as my personal choice of commanders is concerned. You have known this for so many years that it seems redundant to repeat it. I have never been so flattered in my life as by the inclusion, in your telegram, of the word "need" as you used it.

Next, I have, in the few short months I have been allowed to serve with troops, completely reassured myself that I am capable of handling command jobs. I feel confident that my superiors' reports have and will show this, and certainly I have had nothing but the most splendid cooperation and loyalty from those who have served under me. But in this Army, today, such self-confidence (or egotism if you choose to call it that) does not appear to be sufficient when some of the ritualistic-minded people begin to scrutinize the record. They simply say, "He has had only six months' actual duty with troops since 1922. He cannot possibly be given a regiment or what have you."

As I wrote you when you were at Benning, I have resisted every suggestion that I leave troops, not so particularly because I felt that after so many years of staff duty I was entitled to my own turn at the more fascinating work of handling soldiers, but also in conformity with the War Department policy that requires a certain proportion of troop duty in order for a man to be considered a capable and rounded officer. In correspondence with friends in Washington, I have consistently indicated my desire to stay with troops, either with the 15th, or, if possible, in command of one of the mechanized units to be organized in the spring.

At various times I have had informal reports from Washington, to the effect that I had been requested for positions on certain corps and division staffs. My informants have told me that in each such instance the War Department (Chief of Infantry) has declined to give favorable consideration, on the ground that I needed duty with troops. In one instance, where I am told a corps commander (I believed to be General Krueger) asked for me as his chief of staff, the answer was that I was too junior in rank for that post.

I suppose that you have informally investigated the attitude of the Chief of Infantry and the Adjutant General, or possibly even the Chief of Staff, toward assigning me to the W.D.G.S. and are, therefore, sure that if you put in the request it will be approved. Incidentally, another question interjects itself and that is the one concerning the provisions of law affecting eligibility for the General Staff! Naturally, if a fellow is going to serve in a General Staff position, he would like to get official credit for doing so, and unless the Department has waived normal eligibility rules for the period of the emergency, it might be impossible to have me assigned. Again, however, I presume that you have investigated this particular point.

All the above seems to be a lot of beating the devil around the bush. However, it is almost necessary to recite these things to you so that you can understand the reasons for the somewhat confused state of mind in which I now find myself. Oh yes! Another thing I should probably tell you is that General Thompson is merely awaiting favorable action on a recommendation of his, regarding a new assignment for his present division chief of staff, before putting my name before the War Department to fill that position. I believe, however, that that particular request has not yet gone forward, as I am sure he is awaiting the result of his first recommendation.

To summarize, then, my ideas on the matter:

For both Mamie and me the thought of renewing our old close companionship with you is a delightful prospect.

From the official angle, assuming that all the obvious objections to my present assignment to the General Staff have been eliminated, I would like, before the matter is officially consummated, for those in authority to know that I have earnestly tried for many years to get an assignment to troops and to serve at least a normal tour with them. Unfortunately, General MacArthur would never allow those requests to be made of record. I know that General Marshall, in person, is not concerned with the assignment of such small fry as myself; but I would like to see the matter so handled that not only is the attention of the Chief of Infantry and the Adjutant General, but if possible, even that of the Chief of Staff attracted to the above facts. Particularly, I would like to see it clearly noted in the official records. I think it's just a matter of pride, but I don't want to be considered, on the basis of records, as *unfit* for duty with troops.

But, if you're satisfied that the matter is understood by all, as I've roughly indicated, go ahead!

Finally, if I am ordered to Washington, I would like to have the orders framed, if possible, so as to order me and my household goods there by rail. This would allow me to make a short visit with both Mamie's and my family on the way to my new station. I would need, of course, about ten days' leave on the way.

I hope that all of this does not sound too demanding or unreasonable. I do not need to tell you that whatever I am told to do will be done as well as I know how to do it, but since your radio seemed to request my complete reactions to your suggestion, I have tried to put them before you fully and frankly. Please send me advance notice, by radio, of the final decision.

P.S. By the way, if you are living in an apartment house in Washington, would there be any chance for Mamie and me to get into the same building? And if war starts, I expect to see you raise the roof to get a command, and I go along!

Gerow replied:

AFTER CAREFUL CONSIDERATION OF CON-
TENTS OF YOUR LETTER AND THE WISHES OF
GENERAL THOMPSON AS INDICATED TO G1 I HAVE
WITHDRAWN MY REQUEST FOR YOUR DETAIL TO
WAR PLANS DIVN WILL WRITE DETAILS LATER
REGRET OUR SERVICE TOGETHER MUST BE
POSTPONED.[2]

Colonel Eisenhower remained at Fort Lewis until he received
orders on June 24, 1941, assigning him to headquarters, Third
Army, San Antonio, Texas. Third Army was commanded at
that time by General Walter Krueger. It was to be a short tour
for Eisenhower; he was to be called again for the plans job, the
second time by General Marshall. This time he was not given the
chance to refuse. A week after Pearl Harbor Eisenhower was in
Washington as assistant to General Gerow, a step that was the
major turning point in Eisenhower's climb to the top.

General Gerow played a role in Eisenhower's selection, but so
did other personalities. One crucial officer was Douglas
MacArthur, under whom Eisenhower served indirectly for three
years, and directly for five years. "I came into contact with
General MacArthur," said General Eisenhower, "just shortly
after he'd become Chief of Staff. We were preparing a paper on
industrial mobilization over in my section of the War Department, which was the Assistant Secretary of War's office. At that
time I was studying the capacity of America to support a war,
the economic ability, and what you could do with these
factories that were making automobiles and other products. We
really wanted to get informal agreements with them, what
they'd be ready to do to prepare. We finally prepared the paper,
calling it a sort of basic plan for mobilization. General
MacArthur had the job of presenting the plan to a Congressional
Committee. He knew I had prepared the paper, and after de-
livering it he, from then on, gave me special jobs to do. Then

the second the Republicans lost control and I was no longer obligated to the Assistant Secretary of War, he promptly took me over in his office,"[3]

When working for General MacArthur, "I wasn't really an aide," he said, "The job really didn't have a name. I called myself his good man Friday. My office was right next to his, and he could just call me at anytime. He gave me chores—for example, I'd prepare the annual report of the Chief of Staff. He gave me a few ideas and I'd work them up." In addition to the opportunity to do high level staff work, "I was around men who were making decisions and listening to how they did it."[4]

Ike was so highly regarded by MacArthur that the General asked him to come as his senior assistant when he accepted the position as Field Marshal in the Philippines in 1936. Eisenhower accepted. His duties there were varied, but one of his most important tasks was drawing up the plans for the defense of the Philippines, a circumstance that made him the most knowledgeable military man in the United States in 1941 about the Philippine defense. As the picture looked in December 1941, it was only a matter of time before the Japanese would be invading the Philippine Islands.

When Eisenhower received a call in December 1941 from Colonel Walter Bedell Smith, Secretary of the General Staff, that the "Chief" wanted him to catch the next plane to Washington, Ike said:

I had probably been ordered to Washington, I decided, because of my recently completed tour in the Philippines. Within a matter of hours after their assault on Pearl Harbor the Japanese had launched against the Philippines an air attack that quickly reduced our inadequate air forces to practical impotence. It was the spot upon which official and public interest was centered, and General Marshall undoubtedly wanted someone on his staff who was reasonably familiar with conditions then current in the islands, who was acquainted with both the Philippine Department of the United States Army and the defense organization of

the Philippine Commonwealth, which war had caught half-
way in its planned development.[5]

Another influential person in Ike's selection to the War Plans
Division was General Mark Clark, long a close friend of General
Eisenhower. Clark said of Ike:

> He was two years my senior at West Point, but we had
> been in the same company and had lived in the same divi-
> sion of barracks. We saw a lot of each other . . . I had long
> admired his sterling qualities . . .[6]

When General Marshall was at Vancouver Barracks, Washington, Clark had so impressed him that he was marked by
Marshall as an officer he would call upon for positions of
responsibility. Clark also had made a distinguished record in the
amphibious maneuvers held in the Pacific in 1938-1939. Because of Marshall, Clark was selected as deputy to General
Lesley J. McNair (who was Chief of the General Headquarters)
in August 1940.

Not long after the Louisiana war maneuvers of 1941, Clark
related that General Marshall said to him one evening when they
were sitting alone that he was going to make some changes in
the staff in Washington. Marshall then said to Clark: "I wish
you would give me a list of ten names of officers you know
pretty well and whom you would recommend to be Chief of
Operations Division of the War Department General Staff"
(which was then headed by Gerow). Clark answered: "I'll be
glad to do that, but there would be only one name on the list. If
you have to have ten names, I'll just put nine ditto marks below
it."

"Who is this officer of whom you think so highly?" asked
General Marshall.

"Ike Eisenhower," answered Clark.

"I've never met him," Marshall said; but he quickly added
that he knew of Ike's brilliant record. General Clark noted that
"not long thereafter Eisenhower was ordered to Washington. . ."[7]

There was still another officer who undoubtedly played a part in General Eisenhower's selection, Lieutenant General Walter Krueger. "I had assumed command of Third Army on 16 May 1941," wrote General Krueger, "upon the retirement of Lieutenant General Herbert J. Brees. When, shortly thereafter, Brigadier General Joseph A. Atkins [Chief of Staff, Third Army] also prepared to retire, I asked General Marshall to let me have Colonel Dwight D. Eisenhower to fill the vacancy.[7a] He approved, and after Eisenhower reported, I detailed him as Deputy Chief of Staff on 2 July 1941, and as Chief of Staff of Third Army and of Southern Defense Command on 9 August 1941 . . . He proved to be invaluable, effectively coordinating the activities of the staff and handling much of the administrative work, thus enabling me to devote myself primarily to inspections, training, and tactical exercises, especially the great Louisiana Maneuvers of 1941 and the critiques of it. Upon my recommendation Colonel Eisenhower was promoted to brigadier general on 3 October 1941.

"Toward the end of the Louisiana Maneuvers, when General Marshall asked me whom I regarded as best fitted to head the War Plans Division which I had headed several years before, I named Eisenhower, though I was loath to lose him."[8]

Certainly it was the combination of factors rather than any single one which resulted in Ike's selection to the War Plans Division. His professional knowledge of the situation in the Philippines, his closeness to Gerow, the high regard of others for his ability, and his brilliant record all operated in his favor. But once he arrived it was his performance which accounted for his rise up the ladder of responsibility, though it would be naive to deny that there was a certain element of luck involved in his success.

When General Eisenhower was asked why he was selected for the position in the War Plans Division in 1941 he replied, "I think Gerow and Mark Clark and possibly Wade Haislip suggested me, pointing out that I had come out number one in the Leavenworth Class which was very competitive. I think Marshall rather respected the Leavenworth training."[9] Graduating first in this class at Leavenworth made Eisenhower a marked man. The competition was so keen among the officers attending this school and the pace so demanding that there was an average of a suicide a year among its students, and the Army even considered closing the school. More than any individual other than himself, the person responsible for his achievement was a tough, dedicated, and brilliant soldier by the name of Fox Conner. Ike first met Conner through then Colonel George S. Patton, Jr. in the fall of 1919 at the Infantry Tank School at Camp Meade. Eisenhower and Fox Conner immediately had great mutual respect for each other. Two years later when Conner asked Eisenhower if he would like to join his staff in the Canal Zone where he was commander of the 20th Infantry Brigade, Eisenhower assented; and in January 1922, he left for Panama.

"General Conner," Eisenhower said, "made up his mind [at Panama] he was going to give me ground work in making tactical decisions. Every day instead of having the usual general orders, the special orders to handle our command, he made me write the field orders. I wrote the field orders every single day for three years for everything we did. Having done this the writing of field orders just became second nature to me."[10]

Writing field orders was one of the requirements at Leavenworth. Another area of emphasis was war problems. Eisenhower had his first exposure to this type of problem in 1919 at Fort Meade through Patton. "George Patton and I," remarked General Eisenhower, "were great friends. He was getting prepared for Leavenworth and had sent for the back problems. Then he said to me, 'Lets you and I solve these together.' He was eight years senior to me, and Leavenworth was still years ahead in my career; but I worked the problems with him. We began to solve them; and I found that as long as you didn't have any pressure on you, they seemed very easy. I liked them and got a lot of fun out of it. We'd go to his house or my house and the two of us would sit down, and while our wives talked for the evening, we would work the problems.

Then I would open up another pamphlet, find the answer, and grade ourselves. Later, I used to send for these when I was teaching classes."[11]

Had it not been for Fox Conner, General Eisenhower might never had had the opportunity to attend Command and Staff School. Because of a dispute with the Chief of Infantry over the use of tanks, the then Major Eisenhower was apparently going to miss the chance to attend Leavenworth. Fox Conner, who appreciated the value of the school, decided to intervene. He had Eisenhower transferred to the Adjutant General's Department and put on recruiting duty at Fort Logan, Colorado. The Adjutant General had a quota of two openings a year for Leavenworth, and as a favor to Fox Conner, the Adjutant General gave Eisenhower one of those openings in 1924. "I got letters from some of my classmates," said General Eisenhower in reflection, "telling me I'd ruined myself, that the infantry would never have anything to do with me anymore. I think it sort of burned them up at the Chief of Infantry Office, but it did turn out wonderful."[12]

Major Eisenhower expressed some doubt to General Conner about his preparation for Command and Staff School since he had not been to the prerequisite company grade school at Fort Benning. General Conner told Eisenhower, "You quit worrying. You are better prepared for Leavenworth than any other man that has graduated from Benning because you have had to do the work required at Leavenworth. I know; I've been through that school, I've been an instructor there. You just go on and keep still when an order comes putting you on recruiting duty. Accept it and don't kick."[13]

A final factor in his success at Leavenworth was the area where the problems occurred. "Most of our problems," General Eisenhower said, "were on the Gettysburg three inch map. I had commanded a camp here in 1918, and I became more familiar with the country around here than you can imagine; so it never took me more than five minutes to stake out my problems where the others had to look up where the location of Seven Stars, Tawneytown, New Oxford and all the rest were. It would take the average fellow 40 minutes and I'd take five."[14]

Assignment to the War Plans Division was perhaps Ike's most significant assignment towards becoming Supreme Commander. It is ironical, however, with the benefit of hindsight, to note his initial reaction to the call to come to Washington in December 1941:

> This message was a hard blow. During the first World War every one of my frantic efforts to get to the scene of action had been defeated—for reasons which had no validity to me except that they all boiled down to "War Department orders". I hoped in any new war to stay with troops. Being ordered to a city where I had already served a total of eight years would mean, I thought, a virtual repetition of my experience in World War I. Heavyhearted, I telephoned my wife to pack a bag, and within the hour I was headed for the War Department.[15]

Ike's reaction was similar to Marshall's when he was pulled away from troop duty in 1938 to go to the War Plans Division. Had Ike not gone to the plans job in Washington he might well have retired as just one of many World War II generals. This officer who had a driving ambition to become a division commander was within three years to command the largest aggregation of forces in the history of the world.

One can see by Eisenhower's own account of his first assignment from Marshall that the approach he took would bring him increased responsibility:

> I reported to General Marshall early on Sunday morning December 14 (1941), and for the first time in my life talked to him for more than two minutes at a time. It was the fourth time I had ever seen him. Without preamble or waste of time the Chief of Staff outlined the general situation, naval and military, in the Western Pacific . . . General Marshall took perhaps twenty minutes to describe all this and then abruptly asked, 'What should be our general line of action'?"

Instead of giving him an immediate answer, Eisenhower said to the Chief of Staff: "Give me a few hours."

> I took my problem to a desk . . . Obviously, if I were to be of any service to General Marshall in the War Department, I would have to earn his confidence: the logic of this, my first answer, would have to be unimpeachable, and the answer would have to be prompt.[16]

Though he spent several hours on his answer, it was really a matter of organizing his thoughts. Years had gone into the preparation of his answer—the countless hours of study in the service schools he had attended; the training furnished by his many and varied assignments, particularly in years of work in the Philippines; the informal studying he did on his own time; his professional growth through association with such men as Fox Conner and MacArthur—all of this went into his answer. He reached his conclusions and took them back to General Marshall. The answer must have been what Marshall was looking for; he said to Ike, "I agree with you," and Ike said to himself, "His tone implied that I had been given the problem as a check to an answer he had already reached."[17]

Not long after Eisenhower's arrival on the Army Staff as Deputy of the Operations Division, he replaced his boss and good friend, Leonard Gerow. General Marshall related his reason for the change to a key officer on General Eisenhower's staff (in January 1943) when he was commanding the North African campaign:

> When I brought him to head the Operations Division after Pearl Harbor, I put him in the place of a good officer (Gerow) who had been in that job two years. I felt he was growing stale from overwork, and I don't like to keep any man on a job so long that his ideas and forethoughts go no further than mine. When I find an officer isn't fresh, he doesn't add much to my fund of knowledge, and worst of all, doesn't contribute to the ideas and enterprising push

that are so essential to winning the war. General
Eisenhower had a refreshing approach to problems. He was
most helpful.[18]

In any profession, the men at the top want men around them
who have ideas and imagination, and who can supplement and
contribute to and mature their own thinking. Eisenhower performed this function.

Eisenhower replaced Gerow in February 1942. Gerow's new
assignment was as a field commander (later the division commander of the 29th Division). As he left his parting words to
Ike were:

> Well, I got Pearl Harbor on the book, lost the P.I.
> [Philippine Islands], Singapore, Sumatra and all the N.E.I.
> [Netherlands East Indies] north of the barrier. Let's see
> what you can do.[19]

The next significant step in Eisenhower's rise was the
responsibility for drawing up a plan for a joint allied operation
in Europe. He was given this task in April and by June had
completed the staff work on the project. He took the report,
entitled, "Directive for the Commanding General, European
Theater of Operations," to General Marshall and suggested to
the Chief of Staff that it be read in detail. Marshall replied:

> I certainly do want to read it. You may be the man who
> executes it. If that's the case, when can you leave?[20]

Less than a week later Ike had his orders and left for London to
assume command of the European theater of operations. Ike's
strong belief in the invasion plan, and his basic optimism, contributed to his selection. There were few who believed that we
could invade Europe in 1942 or 1943 (we didn't), and the
British were violently pessimistic about the operation. The
strongest believer was Marshall, and anyone sent over to
represent us must have the fortitude to combat the eloquently

persuasive and determined Churchill. Marshall was convinced that Eisenhower, as planner of and therefore believer in this invasion, could properly represent us and hold to our army staff's position.

It is past history that Ike moved from the E.T.O. position to command of the allied invasion of North Africa in 1943, to become the Supreme Commander for the D-Day invasion in France. The leadership qualities which moved him from one success to another will be discussed in detail later; one of his biographers summed up in a few words, however, the qualities which contributed to Eisenhower's ascent to more and more responsible commands:

> This . . . was an entirely new kind of war, and its suc-
> cessful direction demanded a new kind of supreme com-
> mand. It called for a unique combination of soldier-
> administrator-coordinator-diplomat with a generous dash
> of native political talent.[21]

This was Eisenhower. But in any success story such as this there is usually an element of luck. In Ike's case, an unfortunate death may have been a factor in his selection for the job in Europe, the death of General Frank Andrews. General Arnold remarked in his memoirs:

> . . . Andrews left to head the American missions in the
> European Theater, where early in 1943 he was to lose his
> life when his transport plane ran into the side of a
> mountain in Iceland. I have always felt that if General
> Andrews had not been killed, he might well have been the
> overall Commander of the American troops in Europe in
> World War II, for he had all the attributes for that job.[22]

General Eisenhower was an immediate success with Marshall; and again, one finds that General Conner played an important part. General Conner had been General Pershing's operations officer during World War I, a position enabling him to observe

Marshall closely. "I had tremendous respect for Marshall," General Eisenhower said, "because of Fox Conner. Fox Conner was the greatest soldier I ever knew, a soldier who never had a chance to actually prove that he was. He was a terrific fellow. I was predisposed towards General Marshall because Fox Conner constantly said to me that Marshall was the ideal soldier and that he was a military genius."[22]

During General Conner's tutelage of Eisenhower at Panama, he constantly preached Allied command. "Fox Conner," stated General Eisenhower, "said that within a quarter of a century there would be another war. 'It is already written in the Treaty of Versailles. Systems of command are going to have to be worked out.' He always put up George Marshall as the model for handling it. He said Marshall will know how to do it."[24] When Eisenhower was given a task to perform during his three years at Panama, it was the highest praise Conner could give to say to him, "Eisenhower, you handled that just the way Marshall would have."[25] One might say that to a degree General Eisenhower was groomed to Marshall's way of doing things.

It was apparent that this tutelage was remembered. At the time he was given his first problem to solve by Marshall, Eisenhower reflected:

A curious echo from the long ago came to my aid. For three years, soon after the first World War, I served under one of the most accomplished soldiers of our time, Major General Fox Conner. One of the subjects on which he talked to me most was allied command, its difficulties and its problems. Another was George C. Marshall. Again and again General Conner said to me, "We cannot escape another great war. When we go into that war it will be in company with allies. We must not accept the 'coordination' concept under which Foch was compelled to work. We must insist on individual and single responsibility— leaders will have to learn how to overcome nationalistic considerations in the conduct of campaigns. One man who can do it is Marshall—he is close to being a genius."

With that memory I determined that my answer should be short, emphatic, and based on reasoning in which I honestly believed. No oratory, plausible argument, or glittering generality would impress anyone entitled to be labeled genius by Fox Conner.[26]

The Eisenhower career illustrates again that having the ability to lead is not enough; there must be an opportunity to demonstrate that ability and an influential superior to observe it. A combination of sponsorship, luck, and years of preparation and hard work gave Eisenhower the chance for significant leadership, a chance of which he proved himself worthy.

In the summer of 1942, Eisenhower's credentials for the job before him included knowledge of the European situation, strengthened by the circumstance of his primary responsibility for drawing up the plans, by a favorable British view of his military and diplomatic qualities (for surely he would not have been selected without British approval), and by his performance as an administrator.

Newspapers, to play upon the reader's imagination, often described Eisenhower as an obscure lieutenant colonel who in 1939 just seemed to come out of nowhere. They painted him as a Horatio Alger of the military profession. This concept was just as fictional as the personality of Horatio Alger. He was one of eight of his Class of 164 to be promoted to the rank of lieutenant colonel during World War I. He was one of only two to achieve this distinction in stateside duty. He received wide recognition for his performance at Leavenworth, was a key man on the Army General Staff for over five years, and was singled out by MacArthur. Eisenhower might have been obscure to the American people; but within Army circles, he was a brilliant officer destined for great responsibility in a time of crisis for his country.

Ike as an Allied Leader

All of Eisenhower's illustrious colleagues of World War II, in discussions with the author on Eisenhower's leadership, have given greatest emphasis to his success in accomplishing Allied unity: "Ike got more work out of the Allies than most anybody else would have," according to General of the Army Omar N. Bradley. "He could work with British and Americans and keep them both fairly happy. If Ike had not had that faculty we might have been fighting each other more than we were. When you get two Allies working as closely as we were with the British, where you were brought up under different systems, there were potential cliques, but Ike kept that to a minimum. That is one of his greatest contributions."[27]

General Mark Clark remarked, "There had to be a commander with an understanding of the nationalistic ambitions of the various nations, and Ike was well qualified for the job. I was a little more impetuous as Ike's Chief of Staff in North Africa, and when the British or French did this or that, I would get upset. Ike would say to me 'Keep your shirt on,' and it would always work out as he said it would."[28] His air chief, General Carl Spaatz noted that Eisenhower had successfully handled the campaign in North Africa, a combined British-American operation.[29] One of the war's most successful field commanders, General Anthony "Nuts" McAuliffe answered: "He had a very difficult problem of molding many nationalities in a single headquarters. I think this is where he excelled. you won't find any alliance in history as effective as his, and this was certainly his great contribution."[30] In the views of Generals Jacob Devers, Courtney Hodges, William Simpson, J. Lawton Collins, and many other officers who were under General Eisenhower's command during World War II, there is complete agreement on why he achieved such overwhelming success: his ability to accomplish Allied unity in World War II.

Field Marshal Montgomery in his *Memoirs* said of General Eisenhower, "I would not class Ike as a great soldier in the true sense of the word. He might have become one if he had ever had the experience of exercising direct command of a division, corps, and army—which unfortunately for him did not come his way. *But he was a great Supreme Commander—a military states-man. I know of no other person who could have welded the Allied forces into such a fine fighting machine in the way he did, and kept a balance among the many conflicting and dis-turbing elements which threatened at times to wreck the ship."*[31]

The man who was originally selected to be the Supreme Com-mander for the invasion of Europe, British Field Marshal Lord Alanbrooke, wrote in his diary on May 15, 1944, "The main impression I gathered was that Eisenhower was no real director of thought, plans, energy or direction. Just a coordinator, a good mixer, a champion of inter-Allied cooperation, and in those respects, few can hold the candle to him."[32] In a reflec-tion upon his comment on General Eisenhower, Lord Alanbrooke later said, "If I was asked to review the opinion I expressed that evening of Eisenhower, I should, in the light of later experience, repeat every word of it. A past master in the handling of allies, entirely impartial and consequently trusted by all. A charming personality and good coordinator. But no real commander."[33]

Lord Alanbrooke's comment, "But no real commander," could be interpreted as "sour grapes," or it might even be classed as ridiculous. It is really a problem of semantics. The Supreme Commander's role was unique, and required a rare combination of leadership qualities. Even his British counter-parts conceded that he succeeded brilliantly in achieving Allied unity, the job he was called upon to do in order to bring about victory. Each responsibility requires a particular type of leader-ship; General Eisenhower practiced that needed for the job of Supreme Commander. His success is history, the point to be discussed now is simple: How did he lead as Supreme Commander?

In the history of warfare there has been no certain factor for achieving victory. There has been a common denominator for failure: the attempt of relatively equal partners to achieve victory against a common enemy through coalition or allied effort. "Even Napoleon's reputation as a brilliant military leader suffered," General Eisenhower reflected, "when students in staff colleges came to realize that he always fought against coalitions—and therefore against divided counsels and diverse political, economic, and military interests."[34] World War II offered the same threat of allied disunity between the United States and Great Britain.

The differences in British and American political and military organization, in their approach to decision making, in tactical methods, command and staff procedures, national psychology, and language were potential causes of misunderstanding among the senior military officers of the two nations. There were also many problems among the lower ranking military personnel and the civilian population. American soldiers received much more money than their British counterparts; bad feeling was caused by the interest of British girls in the well-paid new arrivals. The fog and rain of England were appealing to few Americans. Traditions were not always compatible. There was sometimes a lack of appreciation by Americans of the British situation, particularly by those who had the attitude of, "Here we are again to fight your battles." In addition to everything else soldiers away from home were not always themselves, and neither the people of Great Britain nor the United States in time of war were seeing each other at their best.

One source of friction was the "ill-concealed amusement" with which the British officers viewed the fighting ability of American soldiers at the beginning of America's first clash with German forces in North Africa in 1943. Great Britain had been the predominant world power for centuries. The British had been fighting the Germans since 1939, and harbored doubts about what the untried armies of the United States could do. In addition to considering Americans inexperienced, they thought them loud and boastful; indeed, our cocky soldiers, who had never known defeat in war, were not always humble. The American soldiers, on the other hand, considered the British officers conceited, arrogant, and supercilious.

Both nations had strong men in the top military positions, men who staunchly held their beliefs and did not quickly accept the views of others. When there were differences of opinion the clashes were sometimes awkward, particularly for the Supreme Commander, who had to settle these differences. To resolve such conflicts, often based upon nationalistic differences, without showing undue favoritism for either his own country or the British, called for a balance difficult to maintain.

The leaders of the British Empire were looking beyond the end of World War II and were bidding to save face in the European invasion. Initially, the Supreme Commander was going to be British Field Marshal Lord Alanbrooke. This decision was changed when it became obvious that the United States would have an overwhelming superiority of men and material. In 1943, therefore, Roosevelt and Churchill decided the commander should be an American; and in December 1943, General Eisenhower was selected. Veterans of the services of Great Britain, who had been fighting for several years, now found they were to serve under an American officer who had never been in battle. Of this situation one senior British officer wrote: "Individual higher commanders as often as not have their idiosyncrasies as to methods of command as well as in other matters. It is often difficult for those who have held independent high commands to take kindly once again to a subordinate role. Higher commanders are just as prone as are other men to experience jealousies, likes and dislikes. . ."

General Eisenhower confronted a great challenge and responsibility. "There was no precedent to follow," he wrote, "no chart by which to steer. Where nations had been successful in concert against a common foe, one member of the coalition had usually been so strong as to be the dominating partner. Now it was necessary to produce effective unity out of concessions voluntarily made."[3 5]

Fortunately the primary prerequisites for Allied unity were accomplished early—the willingness of the leaders of both countries to adjust nationalistic differences in the making of strategic decisions on the conduct of the war and the allocation of resources, and their agreement that there should be a Supreme Commander for the military forces of both nations. With these matters settled, the war's success rested, in General Eisenhower's opinion, "in the vision, the leadership, the skill, and the judgment of the professionals making up command and staff groups."[36]

General Eisenhower decided the foundation of his command scheme should be the concept of Allied unity. He was warned by many old Army friends that with such a plan he was doomed to failure—commencing with the Greeks, five hundred years before the birth of Christ, allied coalitions had failed in war.

During his first assignment as commander of Allied troops in combat in North Africa in 1943, he committed what some of his fellow American officers considered an unpardonable sin—in piecemeal fashion, he placed American troops under British command. He was reminded by associates that General Pershing made his reputation during World War I by refusing to integrate American forces in Europe. "What such advisors did not recall," General Eisenhower wrote, "was Pershing's famous statement when stark crisis faced the Allies in March 1918. At that time, realizing the size of the stakes, he postponed integration of an American Army and said to Foch, 'Every man, every gun, everything we have is yours to use as you see fit.' I felt that here in Tunisia, on a small scale, we had a glowing opportunity comparable to the crisis of 1918, and I was quite willing to take all later criticism if only the Allied forces could turn over Tunisia to our people as a New Year's present!"[37]

The primary goal was to eliminate purely nationalistic considerations that conflicted with military requirements. This was particularly necessary in the decision over the time and place of the Allied second front. The British, for political reasons, wanted to defeat Germany by concentrating the main effort in the Mediterranean theater. This was a predominantly British show since they had more men and materiel in that area. The United States was adamant that victory would best be won in the shortest period of time and with a minimum loss in men and materiel by invading Europe.

After that argument was closed with the invasion of Europe
on June 6, 1944, Winston Churchill tried to divert the Allied
forces planned for the followup invasion of Southern France,
scheduled for August 15, 1944, to the Mediterranean theater.
Churchill felt so strongly about it that he told General
Eisenhower he might have to go to the King and "lay down the
mantle of my high office"[38] if his plan were not followed.
General Eisenhower was respectfully adamant that the invasion
of Southern France go off as scheduled. On August 15, 1944,
General Eisenhower had dinner with General Smith, Admiral
Ramsay, Lietenant General Ismay, and General DeWitt. General
Eisenhower's aide wrote in his diary that evening, "Before dinner, Ike told of his discussion with the Prime Minister, Ismay
sharing the good humor. Ike said that at his last meeting on
Friday the PM had practically wept and, in fact, actually had
rolled tears down his cheeks in arguing that the Americans were
adopting a 'bullying' attitude against the British in failing to
accept their, meaning primarily his, ideas as to grand strategy.
Both love the Prime, as they frequently speak of him, and their
comment about him is like that of two admiring sons discussing
a cantankerous yet adorable father."[39] The affection was
mutual. After Churchill lost the election in the summer of
1945, he decided to take a vacation. "I was pleased and
honored," General Eisenhower said, "that he asked me to put
him up; his suggestion implied that he felt for me some little
fraction of the great respect, affection, and admiration I had
developed for him."[40]

There were no formal rules outlining the authority of the
Supreme Commander. It would not have made any difference if
there had been, in Eisenhower's opinion:

> No written agreement for the establishment of an allied
> command can hold up against nationalistic considerations
> should any of the contracting powers face disaster through
> support of the supreme commander's decisions.
> Every commander in the field possesses direct disciplin-
> ary power over all subordinates of his own nationality and

of his own service; any disobedience or other offense is punishable by such measures as the commander believes appropriate, including the courtmartial of the offender. But such authority and power cannot be given by any country to an individual of another nation. *Only trust and confidence can establish the authority of an allied commander in chief so firmly that he need never fear the absence of this legal power.*[41]

One of the most quoted stories about General Eisenhower during World War II pertained to a rift between an American and British officer. The disagreement was so vehement that it came to the attention of General Eisenhower. In the interest of Allied unity he called both of them in for a few words. After he talked with them together, he dismissed the British officer and asked the American to remain behind. "I don't mind your airing your differences with this British officer," he told him; "I don't particularly mind that you engaged in fisticuffs with him. I must say that I think you were right in your position. Ordinarily I don't condone cursing and name-calling, and I forgive you for calling him a son-of-a-bitch. But I cannot forgive you for calling him a *British* son-of-a-bitch. Consequently, I am sending you home on a slow boat, unescorted."[42]

There were occasions when it was necessary to act quickly and ruthlessly for the cause of Allied unity. Early in the campaign in North Africa, General Alexander attempted to cut off the Germans retreating from an assault by British forces under Montgomery. The American II Corps were involved in the attack under a British Army commander. One American division in this attack was poorly trained, and had not worked together as a unit. It failed to perform as expected. The British corps commander who led the attack severely criticized to newspaper correspondents the poor showing of the American division. "With the help of Alexander," General Eisenhower related, "we quickly took steps to stop it. Nothing creates trouble between allies so often and so easily as unnecessary talk, particularly when it belittles one of them."[43]

The disputes Eisenhower was forced to settle were not all among diverse nationalities. One of the American members of the OVERLORD planning team said:

I observed General Eisenhower resolve a bitter dispute on mutual support among three top British commanders by patience. He made them talk and explain their positions for at least an hour without indicating any position himself. After letting them talk themselves out, he asked the most reasonable if he could not make a slight concession to the most irate participant. Then, he asked for a concession by another participant and so forth. After an hour and a half, they left in agreement, feeling they had solved the problems themselves. If he had announced a flat decision during the first hour, he would probably have lost two valuable British commanders.[44]

There were times when General Eisenhower received complaints from American Army commanders about being too pro-British, particularly when he held back an American Army to permit the British to move forward; but allied unity had to be accomplished. As Supreme Commander of Allied forces he could not expect to please everybody. His first real problem with American officers occurred during the planning of the North African invasion. They believed the United States had been persuaded by the British into that operation rather than invading Europe in 1943. "I stated and restated," General Eisenhower said, "at conferences during this planning phase, that Torch was an order from the Commander in Chief, the President of the United States."[45]

Releases to the press and radio had to be carefully watched to avoid an unfair story favoring one nation or the other. The problem was described by General Eisenhower as "delicate, tricky, and important." Matters pertaining to Allied unity were brought to his attention immediately.

While promoting Allied unity he never forgot, nor did he permit his subordinates to forget, that they were Americans. He continued to use American slang such as, "he knows the score", "GI", and "go peddle your papers", when talking with the British. If Americans started to use British terms such as, "bloody", "Cheerio", or "I say old boy", they were fined an English penny. But for military terms they purposely designed a common vocabulary, using some English and some American expressions, to ensure complete understanding.

There were two levels at which General Eisenhower needed to accomplish Allied unity: among senior officers, and the junior officers and enlisted personnel. For the latter group he arranged a series of lectures designed to educate the Americans to British traditions, political and military organization, psychology, language, and the magnificent sacrifice of the English people. To emphasize the latter point he arranged tours through the areas most severely devastated by German bombing, where Americans could see a people able to get along without refrigeration or central heating, or automobiles, willing to make do with very little food, and seldom complaining. Editorials were published in *Stars and Stripes* on British hospitality and courage. A "people to people" program was established through which Americans were invited into British homes so there would be a better understanding among the people of the two nations.

Allied unity and the ways and means of attaining it, in General Eisenhower's opinion, constituted the principal challenge and lesson of World War II. Although his job was made easier by the natural desire of the Allies to defeat Germany, he faced a demanding task; but he was determined to make Allied command work. He was quick to get rid of anyone who could not cooperate, and his reputation for toughness spread widely.

General Eisenhower's success with the British was phenomenal. After his assignment as the Allied commander for the invasion of North Africa, he received a note from Churchill on May 1, 1943, praising him for his "genius" in promoting harmony among the Allies.

General Eisenhower's success in accomplishing Allied unity was the result of his personality as well as his ability. As with most outstanding achievements, the man running it well makes it look easy. His charm, the warmth of his smile, his unpretentiousness, his complete honesty and frankness, backed up by his strength and conviction, thawed the coldest British skeptic. He was called by Winston Churchill, "probably the most optimistic person in the world," a refreshing change to a people who had four years of defeat and retreat.

It would be unjust to many individuals to give all the credit to General Eisenhower for accomplishing Allied unity; but it was his responsibility, and it required his leadership. He certainly would have borne the blame had Allied unity cracked.

General Eisenhower and His Commanders

Montgomery

Few senior leaders in the history of war have ever had the variety of commanders serving under them that General Eisenhower did in World War II. A constant challenge to his leadership was British Field Marshal Sir Bernard L. Montgomery. In Montgomery's own words—probably *the* understatement of World War II—to General Eisenhower at the end of the war: "I do not suppose I am an easy subordinate; I like to go my own way." Making the individualistic Montgomery into a team man was a real study in a leader's patience and understanding.

Great Britain wanted a British hero. The need was particularly urgent at the time of El Alamein in 1942. The best prospect was General Alexander; but he was a modest, retiring personality, who did not seek or fit the role of swashbuckler. Not so Montgomery. He was cocky, successful, and as a leader could raise the morale of soldiers to a high fighting pitch. The English newspapers were looking for a colorful personality, and Montgomery was ideal for their needs. Since he had nothing against favorable publicity, Montgomery accepted the adulation given him by the British press. Thus, from the days of the

Desert and Tunisian campaigns, Monty had been the general upon whom the British radio and press concentrated; and before the beginning of the invasion of Europe, he was being groomed by the media as the hero of the Second Front, perhaps he might even become the Napoleon of World War II! Unfortunately the newspapers exaggerated and built him up out of all proportion. He was described as one of the four greatest captains in history. He was a great crusader who read the Bible, didn't permit smoking in his presence, who wore a distinctive beret, and who had other habits which made him good copy.

This attempt to establish a British hero and the ensuing inflation in publicity brought about the first serious controversy between Eisenhower and Montgomery. For the initial landing in Europe in June 1944, it was decided by the Combined Staff that there should be a single operational ground commander. Montgomery was selected. After the Allies had established a base of operations the overall command was to go back to General Eisenhower as the Supreme Commander. Although it was planned to announce the return of command right after the invasion, General Eisenhower did not do so; he was concerned that the British people would interpret a change at that time as an affront to Montgomery. Although General Eisenhower did in fact take over, it was not made public.

The publicity given to Montgomery was not easy for the Americans to take. The British press portrayed the invasion as "Monty's show", and referred to the American armies as, "Monty's Right Wing". The situation came to a head on August 17, 1944, when Wes Gallagher of Associated Press in an article exposed the true command situation. General Eisenhower was furious. The thing he most feared happened. The British press viewed the announcement as a slap in the face to Montgomery and the British armies. Editorials claimed General Eisenhower could not be both administrator and strategist, that Monty should be brought back in to plan the strategy, that only Monty was the man to do battle with Von Rundstedt.

On September 1, 1944, General Eisenhower solved the dilemma in his usual manner. He called a press conference in

London and leveled with the press. Praising the work Montgomery had done, he stated that the extent of the total operation was too great for any field commander to handle. He was not taking overall command from Montgomery since it had belonged to the Supreme Commander all along. Presumably, therefore, it was clear to everyone that General Eisenhower was the tactical commander of all ground forces.

During this embarrassing episode, Montgomery was of very little assistance to Allied unity. In August of 1944, General Montgomery had proposed that he continue to exercise control of all ground forces as well as the 21st Army Group. This would have been impossible. He could not have run his own army and allocated supplies and divisions for the many operations without creating confusion. Had Montgomery gotten his wish it would have meant, in essence, that General Eisenhower had given up the position of Supreme Commander.

General Bradley said of this command controversy, "I was puzzled as to why Monty did not squelch it. He could have easily enlightened the British newsmen in an off-the-record explanation of our OVERLORD plans for ground command. At the risk of being unjust to Monty, I could only conclude that he did not wish to."[46]

This controversy was never really settled. During the winter of 1944-45, talk in British circles continued to advocate restoration of Montgomery. Following the Battle of the Bulge, the issue burst out again, with Montgomery supporters claiming the Bulge would never have occurred if Montgomery had been the single ground commander. Again General Bradley was disturbed that although "Montgomery could have curbed these backers he carefully ignored them. Indeed he even intimated during that phase of the campaign from the Seine to the Reich that if ground command were vested in him, he would shorten the span of the war."[47]

Another aspect of the controversy bothered General Bradley:

Monty lent substance to the canard that Eisenhower functioned in Europe primarily as a political commander,

unfamiliar with the everyday problems of our tactical war.
The inference was grossly unfair, for Eisenhower showed
himself to be a superb tactician with a sensitive and intimate feel of the front. With Bedell Smith to shoulder a
generous share of his administrative duties, Eisenhower
directed his major efforts to operations in the field. . .
Because Ike's labors were largely confined to private conversations with the Army Group commanders, only Montgomery, Devers, and I could attest to his rare astuteness in
this role as field commander.[48]

In addition, on August 31, 1944, the 12th Army Group,
under the field command of General Omar N. Bradley, was
removed from Montgomery's command; and coequal status was
assigned to the British and American Army Groups. With the
announcement of the change came other news that was irritating to American commanders—Montgomery was promoted
to the rank of field marshal, thus holding a higher rank than the
Supreme Commander.

In December 1944, there was another flareup in Allied relations. Monty requested that two American armies on the north
be assigned to him during the Battle of the Bulge to permit him
to run that side of the Bulge from 21st Group. General Bradley
fought this change because he believed it would discredit the
American command, but the best concession he could get from
Eisenhower was a promise that it was "temporary," lasting only
as long as the Bulge.

The change took effect at noon on December 20, 1944.
General Bradley said:

Had the senior British field commander been anyone
else but Monty, the switch in command could probably
have been made without incident, strain or tension. Certainly it would never have touched off the Allied ruckus it
subsequently did. But Montgomery unfortunately could
not resist this chance to tweak our Yankee noses. Even
Freddy de Guingand, his chief of staff, was later to chide
Montgomery for the manner in which he behaved. And

while Eisenhower held his tongue only by clenching his teeth, he was to admit several years after the war that had he anticipated the trouble that was to be caused by it, he would never have suggested the change.[49]

The trouble came when Montgomery, without prior approval from General Eisenhower, spoke to the press on January 7, 1945, after the German counter-attack of December 1944 had been thwarted. This was what he said in describing the Battle of the Bulge:

> Von Rundstedt attacked on December 16. He obtained tactical surprise. He drove a deep wedge into the centre of First US Army and split the American forces in two. The situation looked as if it might become awkward; the Germans had broken right through a weak spot and were heading for the Meuse.
>
> As soon as I saw what was happening I took certain steps myself to ensure that *if* the Germans got to the Meuse they would certainly not get over that river. And I carried out certain movements so as to provide balanced dispositions to meet the threatened danger; these were, at the time, merely precautions, i.e. I was thinking ahead.
>
> Then the situation began to deteriorate. But the whole allied team rallied to meet the danger; national considerations were thrown overboard; General Eisenhower placed me in command of the whole Northern front.
>
> I employed the whole available power of the British Group of Armies; This power was brought into play very gradually and in such a way that it would not interfere with the American lines of communication. Finally it was put into battle with a bang and today British divisions are fighting hard on the right flank of First US Army.
>
> You thus have the picture of British troops fighting on both sides of American forces who have suffered a hard blow. This is a fine allied picture.
>
> The battle has been most interesting; I think possibly one of the most interesting and tricky battles I have ever handled. . .

One would conclude from this that Montgomery had single-handedly done everything. The Americans were furious.

Again there was talk in British circles that Montgomery be made ground commander for both the British and American forces. General Bradley was so embittered by this experience that he told General Eisenhower that if Montgomery were given the top ground command, "You must know after what has happened, I cannot serve under Montgomery. If he is to be put in command of all ground forces, you must send me home, for if Montgomery goes in over me, I will have lost the confidence of my command." With this statement, "Ike flushed. He stiffened in his chair and eyed me hotly," said General Bradley. "Well," replied General Eisenhower, "I thought you were the one person I could count on for doing anything I asked you to." General Bradley answered, "You can Ike. I've enjoyed every bit of my service with you. But this is one thing I cannot take."[50] General Patton, who was present, clapped General Bradley on the arm and said, "If you quit, Brad, then I'll be quitting with you."

"I do not believe," General Eisenhower said of Montgomery's press conference, "that Montgomery meant his words as they sounded, but the mischief was not lessened thereby." "This incident," he continued, "caused me more distress and worry than did any similar one of the war. I doubt that Montgomery ever came to realize how deeply resentful some American commanders were. They believed that he had deliberately belittled them; and they were not slow to voice reciprocal scorn and contempt."[51]

A fair account of what actually occurred during the Battle of the Bulge, to undo the damage caused by Montgomery, was finally given by Churchill in a speech to the House of Commons on January 18:

I have seen it suggested that the terrific battle which has been proceeding since December 16 on the American front is an Anglo-American battle. In fact, however, the United States troops have done almost all the fighting and have suffered almost all the losses. They have suffered losses almost equal to those of both sides at the Battle of Gettysburg. . . The Americans have engaged thirty or forty men for every one we have engaged, and have lost sixty to eighty men to every one of ours. That is a point I wish to make.

Care must be taken in telling our proud tale not to claim for the British armies undue share of what is undoubtedly the greatest American battle of the war, and will, I believe, be regarded as an everfamous American victory. I have never hesitated to stand up for our own soldiers when their achievements have been cold-shouldered or neglected or overshadowed, as they sometimes are; but we must not forget that it is to American homes that telegrams of personal loss and anxiety have been coming during the past month, and that there has been a hard and severe ordeal during these weeks for our brave and cherished ally. . .

Our armies are under the supreme command of General Eisenhower, and we march with discipline wherever we are told to go. According to professional advice which I have at my disposal, what was done to meet von Rundstedt's counterstroke was resolute, wise, and militarily correct. The gap was torn open, as a gap can always be torn open in a line hundreds of miles long. General Eisenhower at once gave command to the north of the gap to Field Marshal Montgomery and to the south of it to General Omar Bradley. Many other consequential movements were made and rightly made.

Judging by the result, both these highly skilled commanders handled very large forces at their disposal in a manner which I think I can say without exaggeration may become a model for military students in the future.

Field Marshal Montgomery, at the earliest moment, acting with extraordinary promptitude, concentrated powerful British reserves at decisive strategic points; and, having been placed in command as he was by General Eisenhower of American forces larger than those he holds from the British Government or from the Canadian, larger than those he holds in the 21st Army Group, he fell unceasingly upon the enemy in the north and fought the

battle at the time from that part of the assailed front. The
United States First Army, which was one of a group of
Armies under General Bradley, was severed by inroads.

It was reinforced with extraordinary military efficiency
from the Metz area by General Patton's Army, who hurled
themselves on those intruders from outside of Bastogne.
All movement of commanders would have been futile but
for the bravery of the troops. General Omar Bradley was
commanding the American forces and so was Field Marshal
Montgomery. All these troops fought in magnificent
fashion, and General Eisenhower, balancing the situation
between his two commanders, gave them both the fairest
opportunity to realize their full strength and qualities.

Let no one lend themselves to the shouting of mischief
makers when issues of this momentous consequence are
being successfully decided by sword.

The fact that the calm and steady Omar Bradley expressed
himself so strongly about Montgomery was a significant indi-
cator of the degree of bad feeling among American generals for
some of Montgomery's antics during the war. That the aggressive and impetuous Patton felt antagonistic toward Montgomery, however, was a suprise to no one who knew him.

In Sicily General Patton's Army moved so rapidly, in comparison to the forces under Montgomery, that there was some
misinterpretation at home of the true military situation, and
resulting resentment on Patton's part. On one occasion John
Marquand, visiting Patton in Sicily in 1943, was asked by the
general: "You've just come out from Washington. What is the
reaction in the States to what American troops have done in
Sicily?" Marquand hesitated because he knew Patton would not
like what he had to say. Patton, however, said "No, no, don't
dress it up. Go ahead and tell me."

Marquand replied that as a reader he had gathered the impression that American troops faced only token resistance,
while the British faced the heaviest opposition. General Patton
reacted violently: "By God, don't they know we took on the

Herman Goering division? Don't they know about Troina? By God, we got moving instead of sitting down, and we had to keep moving every minute to keep them off balance, or we'd be fighting yet; and what were they doing in front of Catania? They don't even know how to run around end. All they can do is to make a frontal attack under the same barrage they used at Ypres."[5][2] Patton, who believed American success was a result of speed and aggressiveness, resented the fact that his troops did not get proper credit. The resentment was projected towards Montgomery and his tactics of caution and thorough preparation.

As the Allies were pushing through Germany, Montgomery suggested the northern route toward the Ruhr as the best route to Berlin. The British field marshal also suggested to General Eisenhower that he should "bed Third Army down on the Meuse and let Patton hold," while he raced on to Berlin. "The proposal," Bradley said, "was reminiscent of Monty's tactics during the Sicilian campaign, when he recommended that U.S. forces sit out the war on a defensive front while he went on alone to take Messina."[5][3]

While the Allies were rich in resources, there was not always enough materiel to supply the armies as quickly as they would like. It was necessary, therefore, for General Eisenhower to allocate available supplies of men and materiel. When he gave gasoline to the British, there was less for the Americans. When the gasoline for an army was exhausted, the army was stopped. And when Third Army was forced to stop because supplies went to Montgomery, Patton's anger was almost uncontrollable.

As the war developed General Patton grew bitter towards Montgomery. The American general was little interested in inter-Allied politics or in balancing the forward movement of Allied armies. He wanted to meet and defeat the enemy with *his* army as quickly as possible. It was only by an extraordinary exercise of leadership that General Eisenhower was able to keep the outspoken Patton toned down, but he did usually manage to restrain his utterances. Patton recorded in his diary on December 16, 1943: "General Sir Henry Maitland-Wilson had returned and was at dinner. He is a very large man and quite jovial. I was more impressed with him than with almost any other British officer I have met. All of them [present at dinner], including the General, were very much interested in my reaction to General Montgomery, but I was very careful in what I said and refused to be drawn out."[54] General Eisenhower had obviously ordered Patton to keep quiet about Montgomery, and he did so remarkably well.

Patton and General Eisenhower had been friends for some time. When Montgomery offered himself as the single ground commander, General Patton was not pleased that "Montgomery had the nerve to get someone in America to suggest that General Eisenhower was overworked and needed a Deputy Ground Force Commander for all troops in Europe, and that he, Montgomery, was God's gift to the war in this respect."[55]

American commanders frequently resented Montgomery's attitude toward the Supreme Commander. On one occasion, for example, a conference of Army Group commanders was called at SHAEF for September 22, 1944. As the time for the meeting approached, bets were placed among the SHAEF staff that Montgomery would not come. He did not come, but instead sent someone to represent him. "Although Eisenhower appeared unperturbed," remarked General Bradley, "Monty's absence was viewed by the other commanders as an affront to the Allied chief. The situation at Arnhem was nearing its crisis, but I do believe the war could have spared Monty for a few hours that one afternoon. . . If Monty's absence exasperated Ike, the latter restrained his irritation with uncommon self-control."[56]

The root of the problem was easy enough to understand. It was best summed up by General Bradley who said, "With Montgomery obviously partisan toward those maneuvers that would benefit or bring prestige to his British troops, I was unabashedly Yankee in my outlook and feelings. To Eisenhower there fell the difficult task of fusing these national differences into an Allied effort."[57]

All the fault certainly was not Montgomery's. Part of the problem rested with the American attitude. General Bradley had a set idea about what the relationship should be between American and British troops.

> Remembering General Pershing's troubles in World War I, I was determined to fight any proposal for the assignment of American troops to British field command. Not only were we competent to direct our own battles, but I could not forget the calamitous results of extranational assignments in the Tunisian campaign. Much as I opposed the assignment of American corps and armies to British army or group command, I objected even more strenuously to the far more perilous practice of assigning individual divisions. For while the larger units could probably retain their integrity, a division might too easily become lost.[58]

Another factor was the difference between the military structure of the American and British armies. Just after the campaign in Sicily, General Patton visited Monty at the latter's headquarters. During conversation Patton complained about the injustice of one of the orders that had been issued during the battle. With an amused look, Monty replied to Patton, "George, let me give you some advice. If you get an order from Army Group that you don't like, why just ignore it. That's what I do." General Bradley commented in his memoirs on this statement:

> Montgomery, of course, had oversimplified his explanation. He was first a good, if sometimes perverse, soldier. He didn't ignore his orders though sometimes he seemed to skirt them, while being careful to avoid a showdown. Basically Montgomery's comment to Patton reflected a common attitude in the British command, a view sometimes difficult for an American soldier to understand. Unlike the U.S. Army where an order calls for instant compliance, the British viewed an order as a basis for dis-

cussion between commanders. If a difference of opinion developed, it would be ironed out and the order might be amended. In contrast, we in the American army sought to work out our differences before issuing an order. Once an order was published it could not be changed except by the issuing authority.[59]

Through all of this General Eisenhower had great patience. Only his closest staff officers knew whether he was irritated and upset with Montgomery. A measure of his success as a leader was the infrequency with which the Allies were embroiled in such disputes. The best testimonial to General Eisenhower's success was a letter written by Montgomery himself on June 7, 1945:

Dear Ike:
Now that we have all signed in Berlin I suppose we shall soon begin to run our own affairs. I would like, before this happens, to say what a privilege and honor it has been to serve under you. I owe much to your wise guidance and kindly forbearance. I know my own faults very well and I do not suppose I am an easy subordinate; I like to go my own way.
But you have kept me on the rails in difficult and stormy times, and have taught me much.
For all this I am very grateful. And I thank you for all you have done for me.

Your very devoted friend,
Monty[60]

Perhaps the best way to close the discussion of Montgomery is with the words of Winston Churchill, who said of Field Marshal Montgomery that he "was magnificent in defeat, and insufferable in victory."
Too much should not be made of the friction between Montgomery and the U.S. generals. While this dispute went on in Europe there was a far more bitter feud between the two

American generals, Joseph Stilwell and Clare Chennault, in China. And as far as difficult subordinates were concerned, none was more obstreperous than General George S. Patton, Jr.

Patton

A great deal has been written about a particular episode that caused General Eisenhower much grief, a slapping incident involving General Patton and two enlisted men in Sicily in 1943. Every biography on Patton covers it in length, and none of the significant memoirs of World War II generals in Europe failed to mention it. At the time it occurred, there was, of course, extensive coverage of the incident in the press and on the radio. No two people tell the story the same way. Since the episode has been subjected to such extensive coverage, and because of distortions brought about in retelling, only the brief account given by Patton himself will be used to introduce the incident:

> During the attack on Troina, I drove to the Headquarters of General Bradley, who was conducting the attack, accompanied by General Lucas. Just before we got there, I saw a field hospital in a valley and stopped to inspect it. There were some three hundred and fifty badly wounded men in the hospital, all of whom were very heroic under their sufferings, and all of whom were interested in the success of the operation.
>
> Just as I was leaving the hospital, I saw a soldier sitting on a box near the dressing station. I stopped and said to him, "What is the matter with you, boy?" He said, "Nothing; I just can't take it." I asked what he meant. He said, "I just can't take being shot at." I said, "You mean that you are malingering here?" He burst into tears and I immediately saw that he was an hysterical case. I, therefore, slapped him across the face with my glove and told him to get up, join his unit, and make a man of himself,

which he did. Actually, at the time he was absent without leave.[61]

The news of Patton's outburst first reached General Eisenhower's office in Algiers on August 17, 1943. Brigadier General Thomas J. Davis, the Adjutant General, called Butcher and told him in confidence that the Surgeon General, Brigadier General Fred Blesse, had received a report from a medical officer in Sicily involving General Patton. General Davis suggested that Blesse see Eisenhower about the matter right away. "Blesse came in around noon," said Butcher, "and showed Ike the report, the gist of which was that Patton had visited evacuation hospitals and had routed out certain patients by the 'scruff of the neck,' presumably suspicious they were laggards."[62]

For the offense of slapping an enlisted man, Patton was liable to a courtmartial. It was an absolutely unforgivable display of temper for an American general officer. Within two days, the story had leaked to the newspaper reporters. Quentin Reynolds informed General Eisenhower that in Sicily there were 50,000 American soldiers who were so mad they would shoot Patton if they had the chance. Charles Daly of the Columbia Broadcasting System thought Patton had gone temporarily crazy. But in this difficult time, confidence in General Eisenhower's leadership was displayed by the American correspondents, who, although General Eisenhower refused to censor the story, voluntarily withheld it to save one of his ablest and most aggressive generals for the war.

What to do with Patton was a great dilemma, and General Eisenhower scarcely slept for several days worrying about the situation. He finally decided upon a burning letter of reprimand, requiring Patton to apologize to the two soldiers he slapped, and ordered Patton to publicly apologize to his command in Sicily. General Eisenhower sent a major general to tell Patton what he must do. Patton's immediate, impetuous reply was, "Go to hell." The emissary talked some more and finally gave Patton ten minutes in which to change his mind before he returned to General Eisenhower with his answer. General Patton returned in less than ten minutes and said he would apologize. Having heard of Quentin Reynolds' comment that his soldiers would shoot him on sight, Patton said to the gathering of men in his command to whom he was to apologize, "I just thought I'd stand up here and let you soldiers see if I'm as much a son-of-a-bitch as you think I am." The cheers of the men for him were described as "spontaneous, thundering, and sincere."

"To assault and abuse an enlisted man in a hospital was nothing less than brutal," General Eisenhower said, "except as it was explained by the highly emotional state in which Patton himself existed. His emotional tenseness and his impulsiveness were the very qualities that made him, in open situations, such a remarkable leader of an army. In pursuit and exploitation there is a need for a commander who sees nothing but the necessity of getting ahead; the more he drives his men the more he will save their lives."[63]

Just before the slapping incident occurred Eisenhower had sent a visiting officer from the States, Lieutenant General Alvan C. Gillem, Jr., to Patton's headquarters. General Gillem reports:

He directed me to stay with Patton and observe him for the next few weeks. He instructed me that upon my return to Tunis he desired my first hand report as to Patton's physical condition, state of mind and general attitude. At this particular moment in Sicily Patton's Seventh Army was on the left with General Montgomery's Army on his right. Patton and Montgomery seldom agreed and coopera-tion was difficult. The British were at that time being held up in the area of the volcano which dominated the terrain in central Sicily. Patton on the contrary had been emi-nently successful in his swing to the North and West. Eisenhower had directed Patton to halt and wait in place for the British to resume their advance. Patton had pro-tested this order and, in fact, when I flew over he flew back to Tunis to protest in person. It is this situation which General Eisenhower very likely contemplated for he said when I departed, "you know Patton is unbeatable on the beaches and unsurpassed as an offensive leader, but

when he is required to stop and regroup he is another man
and quite difficult. It is for this reason I would like to get
your personal report when you return."

Patton knew his old friend. The evening before General
Gillem's return to Eisenhower's headquarters at the end of his
two weeks or so of visiting, General Patton looked him in the
eye and said, "Gillem, what are you going to report to Ike? I
know you have been instructed to look me over and give him
your opinion."

"My reply," commented General Gillem, "was that in my
judgment it was evident to all concerned that he represented the
best in a field leader."[6][4]

Military friends and correspondents cautioned the Supreme
Commander that to put Patton in command of an invasion
Army might ruin Eisenhower—that the feeling of resentment
toward General Patton in America and Britain because of the
slapping incident in Sicily was still too strong. But Eisenhower
decided to take the chance.

On November 22, 1943, three months after the slapping incident occurred, Drew Pearson broke the story; and again
General Eisenhower was faced with severe criticism. Accusations were made that Army censorship had prevented release of
the story, but war correspondents emphatically denied this.
Many in Congress and other official positions demanded the
recall and courtmartial of Patton. But General Eisenhower,
strongly supported by Secretary Stimson and General Marshall,
waited out the protests and kept Patton in Europe.

When it was all over Patton wrote a letter to General
Eisenhower, saying in part, "I am at a loss to find words with
which to express my chagrin and grief at having given you, a
man to whom I owe everything and for whom I would gladly
lay down my life, cause to be displeased with me."[6][5]

No single decision during World War II received such trium-
phant vindication as General Eisenhower's decision to keep
Patton. When Patton's name was released along with the story
of Third Army's success in Europe, Eisenhower's good judgment was acclaimed by everyone. The press was fulsome in its

praise; and the Senate, which had held up Patton's promotion to the permanent rank of major general, quickly confirmed the appointment.

General Patton was deeply concerned that the slapping incident might keep him out of the war in Europe. After Patton learned of the attempted assassination of Hitler, he rushed to General Bradley's headquarters at Colombieres and pleaded, "For God's sake, Brad, you've got to get me into this fight before the war is over. I'm in the doghouse now and I'm apt to die there unless I pull something spectacular to get me out."[66]

General Bradley, in reflecting upon the slapping incident, said, "I've often wondered how much this nothing-to-lose attitude prodded Patton in his spectacular race across the face of France. For certainly no other commander could have matched his in reckless haste and boldness. Some day a definitive biography of Patton will go into the issue more exhaustively than I. Until then I shall go on believing that the private whose face he slapped in a Sicilian hospital ward did more to win the war in Europe than any other private in the Army."[67]

Although General Patton apologized to the troops for the incident, he did not regret it. "I am convinced that my action in this case was entirely correct," he wrote, "and that, had other officers had the courage to do likewise, the shameful use of 'battle fatigue' as an excuse for cowardice would have been infinitely reduced."[68]

General Patton, in the opinion of the Germans, was America's most dangerous commander. General Eisenhower realized this; so in order to deceive the Germans into thinking that the invasion of June 6, 1944 was a feinting action, he did not announce that Patton was commanding Third Army. The Germans, therefore, held back sixteen divisions in reserve to meet the main attack to be led by Patton. General Eisenhower maintained the censorship on General Patton's role as commanding general of the Third Army that was making such exceptional progress in August 1944. On August 12, General Bradley went in to see the Supreme Commander about lifting the ban on publishing Patton's name. His reasoning was that

"George was stimulated by headlines, the blacker the headlines the more recklessly he fought."

General Eisenhower replied, "Not yet, after all the troubles I've had with George, I have only a few gray hairs left on this poor old head of mine. Let George work a while longer for his headlines."[69]

To keep the impetuous Patton in line, General Eisenhower was forced very often to be quite tough with him. Recorded in Captain Butcher's diary were such comments as, "Ike spoke vigorously to Patton about the inadequacy of his reports of progress reaching headquarters at Malta . . . when we left General Patton I thought he was angry. Ike stepped on him hard. There was an air of tenseness." (July 13, 1943)[70] On January 27, 1944, Butcher wrote, "General Patton, cloaked in censorship for a few days, came to dinner last night. Ike had seen him during the afternoon at the office and told me before Patton arrived at the house last evening that he had given him a severe bawling out for failing to follow Ike's instructions of counting ten before issuing an order or by taking an abrupt action."[71]

On April 18, 1945, he recorded, "I told Ike of the flurry at PRD amongst the censors because General Patton had arbitrarily fired one of them for passing stories that we had captured some of the German loot and of an expedition Patton ordered to liberate some American prisoners. General Ike said he had heard this chapter and verse while he was visiting Patton, and had made clear to 'George' that he had no right to relieve a SHAEF censor, over whom he has no authority, anyway . . . Ike had taken Patton's hide off. But I think Patton must have as many hides as a cat has lives, for this is at least the fourth time that General Ike has skinned his champion end runner."[72]

There were numerous times when Patton presented problems for General Eisenhower, but some of the occasions were more aggravating than others. In May 1944, while still in difficulty over the Sicilian slapping incident, Patton made an "off the record" speech at a British gathering in which he suggested that

after World War II and Allied victory it would be necessary for
the United States and Great Britain to rule the world. The next
day his speech was in the newspapers of the United States and
Great Britain, and again Patton was in trouble. General
Eisenhower had ordered Patton to avoid press conferences and
public statements because "I well knew," he said, "that it
would be far easier to keep him for a significant role in the war
if he could shut off his public utterances. He promised faith-
fully to do so."[73]

Because of the slapping incident the statement attracted a
great deal of attention. "For the first time," General
Eisenhower wrote, "I began seriously to doubt my ability to
hang onto my old friend, in whose fighting capacity I had
implicit faith and confidence. However, my concern was not so
much for his particular statements, which were the object of
criticism at home, as it was for his broken promise with the
resultant implication that he would never improve in this
regard."[74]

General Patton went to the Supreme Commander and offered
to resign his commission to relieve him of embarrassment. When
the Third Army commander learned that Eisenhower was going
to drop the matter, he was moved to the point of tears. Patton
then apologized, not only for the speech, but also for his
criticism of General Eisenhower when he thought he was going
to be relieved. Eisenhower's reply was, "You owe us some
victories; pay off, and the world will deem me a wise man."[75]
There were many inquiries from Washington over the affair; but
Stimson and Marshall left the decision over Patton's fate
completely up to General Eisenhower. The Supreme Commander learned that before the start of the meeting at which he
made his ill-considered talk, Patton had refused to make a
speech. When the group insisted, and promised there were no
reporters present and nothing would go outside the room, he
relented. Unfortunately, his belief in the good faith of others
was misplaced.

There was a limit to the Supreme Commander's patience,
however, and Eisenhower told Bradley after this incident, "I'm

just about fed up. If I have to apologize for George once more, I'm going to have to let him go, valuable as he is. I'm getting sick and tired of having to protect him. Life's much too short to put up with any more of it."[7][6]

Fifteen months later General Patton tried Eisenhower's patience for the last time. During the early occupation of Germany, Patton failed to abide by his instructions, and he hired former Nazis to restore the railroads and public works and to serve as civil government officers. He was criticized for this in the press. He explained his actions to newsmen by saying: "This Nazi thing, it's just like a Democratic-Republican election fight," and, "The outs are always coming around saying the ins are Nazis. . .more than half the German people were Nazis, and you'd be in a hell of a fix if you tried to remember all the Party members." This was too much. Patton was relieved as Commanding General, Third Army, and the Eastern Military District. He was then assigned as Commanding General, Fifteenth Army, which was involved in studying and writing about World War II to make recommendations for the future.

The reason for General Eisenhower's great patience was simple: Patton was a superb leader of men in combat. He could be counted upon for relentless pursuit of the enemy, driving his men to heights and victories of which they never believed themselves capable; but keeping him under control was a task very nearly as demanding as that of maintaining harmonious Allied relations.

The Political Leadership of the Supreme Commander

As Supreme Commander of the Allied forces General Eisenhower had two wars to fight at the same time, one military and one political. The political battle required at least as much leadership ability as the military. Throughout the war it was necessary, in addition to maintaining American-British unity, to deal with political problems concerning the Soviet Union, France, and Spain. Problems were bound to arise in any military force encompassing units, and soldiers from Brazil, Scotland, India, Newfoundland, South Africa, Ireland, Canada, Poland, New Zealand, and even Italy.

In November 1942, Generals Eisenhower and Clark during a bull session, "lamented the necessity of dealing in such high matters politic as they have been compelled [to] since this operation [invasion of North Africa] was started. Both said that they would be happier running divisions."[7] Eisenhower didn't really mean it. Actually he was proud to have a responsible role in the conduct of the war and to have the opportunity to make a mark in history; but for any man burdened with great responsibility there are times of exasperation.

North Africa

General Eisenhower's first political problem, and almost his last, occurred in North Africa. He was faced with the necessity, after the Allies had routed the Germans, to fill the governmental vacuum left by the removal of the Vichy machine; and the responsibility for filling the vacuum fell to General Eisenhower. It would have been a challenge for the most sophisticated and experienced diplomat; for a politically inexperienced military officer, it was a nightmare.

There were several alternatives for establishing a civil government in North Africa. The first was to permit Charles De Gaulle and his followers to set up the government; a second choice was to place General Henri H. Giraud in charge; and the third was to continue with members of the Vichy government. General De Gaulle had proclaimed his leadership of the Free French. General Giraud, who had been smuggled out of France by submarine in the hope that the citizens of North Africa would rally behind him and rise against the Vichy government, was described by an enemy as being politically a child and as a "good divisional commander, nothing more." This proved to be true. Just as the invasion was to be launched Giraud refused to cooperate with the Allies and told them he would be a spectator in the affair. Giraud later changed his mind and decided to help out; but unfortunately, the French Army and people in North Africa had no desire to follow his lead.

General Eisenhower therefore decided to deal with Admiral Jean Francois Darlan, the number two man in the Vichy government, because he was the only Frenchman who could achieve the cooperation of French forces in North Africa with the Allies. "I realized," General Eisenhower said, "that the matter was one that had to be handled expeditiously and locally. To have referred it back to Washington and London would have meant inevitable delays in prolonged discussions. So much time would have been consumed as to have cost much blood and bitterness and left no chance of an amicable arrangement for absorbing the French forces into our own expedition."[7][8]

There was a violent reaction to his decision when it was made public. General Eisenhower was called a Fascist and a betrayer of the common people, among other things. On November 14, 1942, Eisenhower cabled President Roosevelt fully explaining his decision regarding Darlan.

Existing French sentiment in North Africa does not even remotely resemble prior calculations and it is of utmost importance that no precipitate action be taken which will upset such equilibrium as we have been able to establish.

The name of Marshal Petain is something to conjure with in North Africa. From highest to lowest, everyone attempts to create the impression that the shadow of the Marshal's figure dominates all his actions and, in fact, his very life. The military and naval leaders, as well as the civil governors, agree that only one man has the obvious right to assume the mantle of Petain and that man is Admiral Darlan. Even General Giraud clearly recognizes this overpowering consideration and he has modified his own ambitions and intentions accordingly. . .

It must be understood that if we repudiate Darlan and attempt from the outside to dictate the personnel of the coalition to run North Africa, the following will be the consequences:

a. French armed forces here will resist us passively and, in certain instances, actively.

b. The hope of securing cooperation in this area will be lost at great cost to us in stagnation of operations and in requirements for additional troops.

c. The opportunity for gaining some assistance from remaining French naval and military units in North Africa will disappear.

d. The last glimmer of hope with respect to the Toulon Fleet will be gone.

e. Admiral Esteva, in Tunis, will not cooperate and our hope of getting Tunisia quickly will not be attainable. Admittedly, Esteva may already be helpless, but there is still a chance of his being able to assist.

Admiral Cunningham and General Clark, together with my full staff, have assisted me in making what we consider to be the only possible workable arrangement designed to secure advantages and avoid disadvantages. No one who is not on the ground can have a clear appreciation of the complex currents of prejudice and feeling that influence the local situation. Also, it should be clear that General Giraud's earnest participation in this arrangement indicates the necessity for the agreements we have made.

In the event the British and U.S. Government, after analysis of this radio, are still dissatisfied with the nature of the agreement made, I suggest that a mission of selected U.S. and British representatives (including the Free French if deemed advisable) be dispatched immediately to Algiers where they can be convinced in short order of the soundness of the moves which have been made.

He received advice from many sources—the press, the people, and high ranking government officials. Advice from this latter group took such form that President Roosevelt had to scold the Cabinet "for trying to butt in and interfere with the civilian government of the occupied territories in North Africa."[79]

But the problem was Eisenhower's, and he solved it remarkably well. President Roosevelt was satisfied with the outcome of the Darlan affair. If he had not been, he would have selected a new Allied Commander for the invasion of Europe.

Churchill was also pleased with General Eisenhower's political leadership as Supreme Commander, a real mark of success in view of the magnitude of some of the Prime Minister's nationalistic machinations during the war. Churchill guarded him carefully, saying often that the only other man who could do the job General Eisenhower was doing was General Marshall. While in England, Eisenhower met twice a week with the Prime Minister, who had a special underground shelter built in London for the General, consisting of an entire apartment with kitchen, living room, bedroom, and secret telephones to insure proper protection. Churchill was a great challenge to all who dealt with him, including Eisenhower. General Eisenhower said:

> He was a man of extraordinarily strong convictions, and a master in argument and debate. Completely devoted to winning the war and discharging his responsibility as Prime Minister of Great Britain, he was difficult indeed to combat when conviction compelled disagreement with his views. In most cases problems were solved on a basis of almost instant agreement, but intermittently important issues arose where this was far from true. He could become intensely oratorical, even in discussion with a single person. . .
>
> I admired and liked him. He knew this perfectly well and never hesitated to use that knowledge in his effort to swing me to his own line of thought in any argument . . . If he accepted a decision unwillingly he would return again and again to the attack in an effort to have his own way, up to the very moment of execution.[80]

But as borne out by the invasion operations, OVERLORD and ANVIL, General Eisenhower was steadfast in his military approach to the war. Although it was true that give and take were necessary in negotiating with the British, there are no grounds

to accuse Eisenhower of compromising too much or too frequently in the name of Allied unity.

The Invasion Decision

Only a few weeks after France surrendered to Germany on
June 22, 1940, the time and place of the Second Front in
Europe were discussed in London, in July 1940, at the first
conference on wartime cooperation between the United States
and Great Britain. The American military mission was sent by
General George C. Marshall, United States Army Chief of Staff
and Admiral Harold R. Stark, Chief of Naval Operations, with
the approval of President Roosevelt. The talks of a highly secret
nature, were to be of a purely "exploratory" character with the
British Chiefs of Staff.[81] Out of these conversations came the
basic Anglo-American policy of going on a strategic offensive in
Europe and on a strategic defensive in the Pacific, should the
United States become involved in the war against the Axis.
Neither the United States nor Great Britain was at war with
Japan at that time; but the Axis Tripartite Pact stated that
"Japan recognized German and Italian leadership in creating the
'New Order' in Europe, and Germany and Italy recognized
Japan's leadership in organizing the 'Greater East Asia Co-
Prosperity Sphere'." This made such planning necessary.

When it was decided that Europe had priority, then future
planning of operations would determine the area of strategic
concentration in Europe. These early talks, however, were not
to be considered a final decision on continental operations by
the Allies.

The next staff conversations furthering the strategic preparedness of the United States occurred in Washington, from
January to March 1941. These talks were kept secret. The agreements reached were embodied in a plan known as ABC1
(American-British-Canadian Staff conversations). These discussions concluded that in the event the United States and Great
Britain become involved in war with both Germany and Japan,

"the concentration of force should be on Germany first, while a containing war of attrition was to be waged against Japan pending Germany's defeat."[8 2] The plans called for operations in the Mediterranean to drive Italy out of the war, and "for the concentration of Allied ground forces in Great Britain to prepare for an invasion in Western Europe."[8 3]

General Eisenhower, as head of the War Plans Divisions in 1941, played a key role in the plans for the invasion of Western Europe. He believed very strongly that this was the best way to defeat Germany. His belief in this plan, and his strength, were the two most important reasons for his selection by Marshall for the position of Supreme Commander. Holding the reluctant British to their agreement to invade Western Europe was undoubtedly General Eisenhower's greatest leadership accomplishment in World War II.

The United States first considered a cross-Channel attack for 1942, an operation highly thought of by the American Chiefs of Staff.[8 4] However, with the entry of the United States in the war, Churchill was quick in acquainting the Americans with a new military objective. This plan he outlined in a paper sent to President Roosevelt, dated December 16, 1941, proposing "that the main effort of the Allies in 1942 be devoted to the occupation of the entire seaboard of North Africa, stretching from Dakar to the Middle East."[8 5]

In June 1942 Churchill talked with then Major General Eisenhower about the cross-Channel attack at length. Churchill agreed to such an invasion for 1943, showing the American general a paper outlining his thoughts. Eisenhower, to commit Churchill to it in writing, asked the British Prime Minister to send a copy of the paper to General Marshall.[8 6]

Churchill revealed his thinking on the issue in his book *Hinge of Fate*:

> ... I had made a careful study of the President's mind and its reactions from some time past, and I was sure that he was powerfully attracted to the North African plan. This had always been my aim, as was set forth in my

papers of December, 1941. Everyone in our British circle
was by now convinced that a Channel crossing in 1942
would fail. . .[87]

A sample of Churchill's machinations occurred in July, 1942
in a story told by General Mark W. Clark:

> Ike and I . . . accepted an invitation for an overnight
> visit with Prime Minister Winston Churchill at
> Chequers . . . At that time a controversy was just starting
> that was to last for several months and involve periods of
> rather bitter recrimination. It had to do with the question
> of whether the Allies should try to open a second front by
> crossing the English Channel to invade western Europe . . .
> It was typical of the Prime Minister that he lost no time
> in stating his views. He stressed to us that he was in favor
> of postponing the cross-Channel operation and under-
> taking an invasion of northwest Africa at the earliest
> possible date. A European operation, even of a limited
> nature would be too hazardous he said, until a later time.
> Both Ike and I felt that direct action was the best idea and
> that it was necessary to carry the war to the European
> continent as directly and quickly as possible. We were,
> therefore, noncommittal about Churchill's suggestions be-
> cause we felt that his African plan would detract from
> whatever hope there was of striking directly at Europe
> with a limited invasion program in 1942, or of mounting a
> large-scale invasion operation in 1943.[88]

Eisenhower and the other American military leaders lost that
round to Churchill, consoling themselves that the British Prime
Minister promised a cross-Channel attack in 1943. Eisenhower
was so depressed that he thought the date of the decision would
become known as " the blackest day in history."[89]
Within less than two months after it was decided that there
would be no cross-Channel invasion in 1942, the British started
to delay it for 1943. The British, in starting discussions of the
post-North African invasion, started to suggest further invasions

in the Mediterranean, with Sardinia, Sicily and Italy as the goals. Churchill won the second round by getting the Allies to invade Sicily and then Italy. Churchill also started talking about some Allied activity in the Balkans.

From May 12-25, 1943, the United States and Great Britain held the TRIDENT Conference in Washington, D.C. A firm commitment came out of this meeting for the invasion of Europe on May 1, 1944. Then on July 25,1943, when Mussolini was ousted from power, Churchill again argued that the Allies should exploit the opportunities in the Mediterranean at the expense of the cross-Channel attack. Secretary of War Henry L. Stimson, Generals Marshall and Eisenhower had a constant battle to fight off Churchill's attempt to divert Allied activities. The American who carried the burden in the discussions with Churchill was, of course, the Supreme Commander, Eisenhower. If Churchill could win "Ike" over to his way of thinking, he would win the day. Matching wits with the eloquent, driving, tenacious, likeable, and persuasive British Prime Minister was probably General Eisenhower's greatest challenge.

Before the Cairo Conference scheduled for November 22, 1943, Churchill went to Cairo early to work on General Eisenhower again. The conversation which the General reports to have been carried on was the usual:

> He dwelt at length on one of his favorite subjects—the importance of assailing Germany through the "soft underbelly" . . . He seemed always to see great and decisive possibilities in the Mediterranean, while the project of invasion across the English Channel left him cold. How often I heard him say, in speaking of Overlord's prospects: "We must take care that the tides do not run red with the blood of American and British youth, or the beaches choke with their bodies."
>
> I could not escape a feeling that Mr. Churchill's views were unconsciously colored by two considerations that lay outside the scope of the immediate military problem . . . The first of them was his concern as a political leader for the future of the Balkans. For this concern I had great

sympathy, but as a soldier I was particularly careful to exclude such considerations from my own recommendations...[90]

At the Big Three meeting at Teheran in November 1943, Great Britain and the United States "irrevocably" committed themselves to OVERLORD. But Churchill never really gave up. He next fought the transfer of landing craft from the Mediterranean to Europe for the forthcoming cross-Channel attack. He wanted continued use of them for the Anzio invasion. When General Eisenhower refused, emphasizing they must start transferring them to Europe now, Churchill went over Eisenhower's head to Roosevelt. But it was made clear to the Prime Minister this was the last delay.[91]

Only with the Allied D-Day invasion on 6 June 1944 was the issue finally closed. It was General Eisenhower's leadership accomplishment.

Berlin

The most important military-political objective of the war was Berlin. The question has been raised often why American troops did not capture Berlin before the Russians. There was even a statement alleging that the United States did not do so because of a political agreement with Russia. This is not entirely true. Eisenhower's reason for not seizing Berlin was military. He considered himself a military commander; and he took his orders from the President of the United States and the Combined Chiefs of Staff. SHAEF had received intelligence reports that the Nazis intended to move into the Bavarian Alps for their final fight, a move General Eisenhower wanted to prevent. His Chief of Staff has said of the Berlin situation in 1945:

> Battles are fought to defeat armies, to destroy the enemy's ability to go on fighting. Only when a port, such as Cherbourg, or an area, such as the Ruhr, is so vital to the enemy that it is protected with large numbers of

troops, or when a particular locality, such as Foggia in Italy, provides great advantages for the further development of a campaign, are "terrain objectives" of justified military importance. With the German Government evacuated, Berlin was a terrain objective empty of meaning. To send our armies crashing into its western suburbs could have no tactical significence. General Eisenhower felt that such a campaign would have its only importance in headlines, and no battle was ever fought by the Allied Expeditionary Force for headlines.[92]

Nevertheless, it is also true that it had been decided by the heads of government of the United States, Great Britain, and the Soviet Union that Berlin would be in the Soviet zone of occupation. Based upon the "Allied" concept of 1945, it would have been a violation by the Americans of their part of the political agreement if they had attempted to capture Berlin to keep the Russians out, or to have kept our troops there without Russian agreement. During four years of favorable propaganda, the Soviet Union had been a valued ally; to have said overnight that she was a potential enemy would have created a violent public reaction among the people of all the Allied nations. The possibility of a new war would have been too much to expect nations to face when they were weary from four to six years of war.

General Eisenhower was authorized to communicate directly with Moscow on exclusively military matters. This authorization was challenged by Churchill when late in 1945 the Supreme Commander presented a plan to Stalin for the Allied and Russian armies to meet somewhere along the Elbe. Churchill believed that, since the war was almost over, the maneuvering of the armies had acquired political significance and that the political leaders should be brought in on the decisions. The Prime Minister wanted the Americans and British to go beyond the Elbe and to capture Berlin; and since he could not persuade General Eisenhower, he took the matter to President Roosevelt, who supported General Eisenhower.

Political Philosophy

All of Eisenhower's political difficulties were not with the British. He was surprised to find in July 1942, that the Ambassador from the United States to Great Britain had wired Washington to request that he, the Ambassador, be allowed to establish a committee to select targets for strategic bombing. This was interference in the military sphere, and General Eisenhower was most displeased. He immediately stepped into the situation and, without causing any friction between himself and the Ambassador, saw that the latter was removed from the target selection business.[93] Eisenhower would not tolerate any jumping of the chain of command when military matters were at issue.

Just before French Morocco was captured, for example, he requested of Washington that a civilian governor be appointed. He made it very clear, however, that this administrator was to be on his staff and was not to have a direct line to Washington. General Eisenhower was in charge, and all communications would go through him. He followed this policy with all his civilian advisors.

Eisenhower's philosophy about the political aspects of his job was a factor in his military success. He told President Roosevelt in Casablanca during their discussions of his handling of the Darlan affair in December 1943, "I believe in a theatre commander doing these things without referring them back to his home Government and then waiting for approval. If a mere General makes a mistake, he can be repudiated and kicked out and disgraced. But a Government cannot repudiate and kick out and disgrace itself—not, at any rate, in wartime."[94] In other words, the general was the "fall guy" if a mistake were made; it was a part of the job.

The role of Supreme Commander called for a unique set of qualities. A soldier, trained to command and obey without question, often sees issues only in black and white, and performs according to established rules. The diplomat or statesman must have an open, flexible mind, accomplishing his mission through persuasion and the compromise of conflicting national interests. General Eisenhower was able, on occasion, to call upon the attributes of both soldier and statesman.

Command Responsibility

General Eisenhower was fortunate in that Marshall believed in assigning a theater commander a job, giving him the necessary men and materiel to get the job done, and then leaving him alone as much as possible to accomplish the mission. As Chief of Staff, Marshall had personally selected General Eisenhower; and he believed that the man in the field knew more about the tactical situation than did he in Washington, thousands of miles from the front. The Supreme Commander was in complete agreement with this philosophy. "If results obtained by the field commander become unsatisfactory, the proper procedure is not to advise, admonish, and harass him, but to replace him by another commander."[95] General Eisenhower followed the same practice with his Army commanders. He gave them their job and left them alone; with responsibility for millions of men and billions of tons of materiel he had to. By contrast, the British chiefs maintained daily contact with their field commanders and interfered consistently in tactical plans.

Coordination of Forces

As Supreme Commander, Eisenhower had to coordinate the sea and air forces with the Army; fortunately, he was blessed with superb rapport with the other services. When he left Washington in June, 1942, there was little doubt in his mind about how he would get along with the senior naval officers. He went by to see Admiral King, who had replaced Admiral Stark as Chief of Naval Operations. The Navy chief informed General Eisenhower that he would do everything in his power to help him out. "He said," General Eisenhower remarked, "that he wanted no foolish talk about my authority depending upon 'cooperation and paramount interest' (meaning which service, Army or Navy, had primary responsibility in a theater of war). He insisted that there should be a single responsibility and authority, and he cordially invited me to communicate with him at any time that I thought there might be intentional or unintentional violation of this concept by the Navy."[9][6]

The senior naval officer in Europe was Admiral Harold R. Stark, formerly Chief of Naval Operations in Washington. Although the Navy command was independent of General Eisenhower's headquarters, this presented no problem for the Supreme Commander. When Admiral Stark arrived he told General Eisenhower, "The only real reason for the existence of my office is to assist the United States fighting forces in Europe. You may call on me at any hour, day or night, for anything you wish, and when you do, call me 'Betty,' a nickname I've always had in the service."[9][7] An Army commander could hardly ask for better cooperation than that from another service.

The American air commander from 1942 until the war ended in Europe was General Carl "Tooey" Spaatz. "From the time of his arrival at London in July—[1942]." General Eisenhower said of his air chief, "he was never long absent from my side until the last victorious shot had been fired in Europe. On every succeeding day of almost three years of active war I had new reasons for thanking the gods of war and the War Department for giving me 'Tooey' Spaatz. He shunned the limelight and was so modest and retiring that the public probably never became fully cognizant of his value."[9][8]

General Eisenhower as a leader was tremendously considerate of the welfare of his commanders. In December, 1942, General Mark W. Clark, deputy to General Eisenhower for the North African invasion, attended a conference with his superior in Algeria. General Eisenhower had to leave the conference hurriedly to fly back to Gibraltar. At the airfield, there were many newspaper reporters and photographers hoping for a press conference; but time was so short that Eisenhower did not have time to answer any of the reporters' questions. "He did, however," said General Clark, "make one of the friendly and thoughtful gestures that are so typical of him. When the reporters and cameramen were crowding around, he said he had time for just one thing. Then he fished a star out of his pocket and pinned it on my shoulder. 'I've been waiting for a long time to pin on this third star, Wayne,' he said. 'I hope I pin on the fourth.' "[9]

He seldom asked his commanders in the field to come see him; he preferred to go to them and save them the inconvenience of leaving the battlefield. When he traveled to the front, he always insisted that his temporary headquarters be set up away from the battle commander's headquarters, to ensure that he would not be a burden upon the officers busy with the actual fighting.

Relations with Staff

When General Eisenhower organized a headquarters, he was very careful in the selection of his staff. He told them after they were set up, "You are handpicked experts in your fields. I expect you to get your jobs done without supervision. Otherwise, I made a mistake in selection." After he had done this, he relied upon the staff to relieve him of administrative details. His Chief of Staff for most of World War II, General Walter B. Smith, described General Eisenhower's ability to delegate authority to his staff as, "beautiful". Duties were delegated; but there was never any doubt that General Eisenhower was boss. In interviews and correspondence, all of his staff officers stated in one way or another that, "He was a commander who would listen to all points of view with the ability to analyze a problem, extract its core, and work out a solution. He was so gifted that he could literally put his finger quickly and accurately on the crux of a situation."

General Eisenhower had two U.S. personal aides. His senior aide was Commander (later Captain) Harry C. Butcher, United

States Naval Reserve. Before the war Harry Butcher had been a vice-president of Columbia Broadcasting System. General Eisenhower had met Butcher in Washington prior to World War II through his brother Milton. It was unusual for an Army general to have a naval officer as an aide; but Admiral King, Chief of Naval Operations, was glad to consent to General Eisenhower's request. Captain Butcher was wonderful for General Eisenhower. He was a public relations counselor extraordinary, with a sense of humor. One friend of General Eisenhower's quoted him as saying, "I keep Butcher around just for laughs."

But Butcher was good for much more than laughs. He was a friend in whom General Eisenhower could confide. He was trustworthy, was not subservient, and was not at all reluctant to talk back to the Supreme Commander who had a strong dislike for "yes" men. He helped Eisenhower relax; he talked when the general needed someone to talk to and kept still when all he wanted was silence. He relieved his boss of numerous administrative details. "Sometimes," General Eisenhower said during the war, "I get back from the office to my quarters and I just want to curl up in a corner like a sick dog, but Butcher won't let me. Butcher's job is simple. It is to keep me sane."[100]

His other personal aid was Captain Ernest R. Lee of the United States Army. Prior to the war Lee, nicknamed "Tex", was sales manager of a Chevrolet agency in San Antonio. A reserve officer since 1932, he went on active duty in 1940. He first served with then Colonel Eisenhower in June 1941 in the office of the Chief of Staff of the Third Army. Some described Lee as insincere, but actually he was just shy. He was a hard worker and intensely loyal to General Eisenhower. His job consisted of arranging for the Supreme Commander's travel and overseeing the details of running the office.

General Eisenhower's "superorderly" was Sergeant Michael "Micky" McKeogh, who had gone to work for Colonel Eisenhower in 1941. He had been a bellhop at the Hotel Plaza in New York City before entering the Army and was wise in the ways of the world. General Eisenhower said in his memoirs:

Sergeant Michael McKeogh accompanied me always and was close to my side, day and night. One day in Africa I had to make a hurried trip to the front and I telephoned Sergeant McKeogh to bring a bag to the airfield. Flying conditions were deplorable and, in the total absence of flying aids in the mountainous country of Tunisia, the prospect of the flight was not enjoyable. When I got to the plane I found Sergeant McKeogh also prepared to make the journey. I said, "Mickey, I intend to return tomorrow, and I doubt that I will need you before then. Flying conditions are not comfortable and there is no use in both of us being miserable. You may go back to quarters."

The sergeant seemed to pale a bit but he looked me squarely in the eye and said, "Sir, me mother wrote me that my job in this war was to take care of you. And she said also, 'If General Eisenhower doesn't come back from this war, don't you dare to come back.' "

The impact of such loyalty and devotion, not only on the part of the sergeant but on the part of the mother who could say such a thing to her son, left me almost speechless. All I did say was, "Well, hop into the plane. We're late."[101]

Sergeant McKeogh fell in love with a WAC corporal named Pearlie Hargrave, who served as a driver for General Eisenhower. On December 16, 1944, Sergeant McKeogh and Corporal Hargrave were married in the Chapel of the Great Palace at Versailles. The bride was given away by Tex Lee. The guests included General Eisenhower, Lieutenant General Walter B. Smith, and many other high ranking officers from SHAEF.

Consideration for his staff was a natural part of General Eisenhower's leadership. On October 23, 1943, he went to Paddington Station in London to meet Mrs. Eleanor Roosevelt who was arriving for a visit. Also at the station to meet her were the King and Queen of England. When the King recognized General Eisenhower, he took him aside for a talk. General Eisenhower noticed his Chief of Staff, General Walter Bedell Smith, a few feet away "standing stiffly at attention, so called him over," his aide said, "and introduced him to the King as informally as a traveling salesman."[102]

The consistent display of consideration and thoughtfulness by General Eisenhower inspired superior performance by his staff. When operations were particularly demanding and crucial they rose to meet the situation. "During the week that ended May 6, 1945," General Walter Bedell Smith wrote, "developments occurred so rapidly that they can hardly be catalogued in chronological order. This period was a single unit of time for the Supreme Commander and the Staff. Scarcely anyone left headquarters. We ate when we felt hungry, slept when we could no longer keep awake. Twelve o'clock on the dial of a watch might mean noon or midnight. A man looked toward the window to find out."[103]

When they worked at this pace they were often preparing staff studies. These reports were handled by General Eisenhower in an interesting manner. One of his officers commented:

> With the tempo stepped up, the pace accelerated, there was no time for leisurely processes because time was of the essence. When a staff study on a critical matter was prepared and presented by an officer having primary interest, it was referred to other officers who were specialists in certain phases of the problem. On occasion the latter might not agree with the recommended action. But this was not acceptable to General Eisenhower who held that to disagree in itself was insufficient unless the officer so disposed could come up with something better. Therefore a more adequate plan had to be submitted when disapproval was recommended. This made for more careful scrutiny and analysis.[104]

During the normal conduct of the war General Eisenhower rarely left his office before seven, and expected his staff to stay until he was gone for the day. General Eisenhower had spent many years as a staff officer, and he had never left the office until his superior did; he expected his staff to do the same. He was exacting and detested inefficiency.

The staff knew that General Eisenhower was under great pressure. During the early phases of the first Allied invasion Butcher wrote in his diary. "Ike still hard at it, and so are we satellites, but we don't have to make the decisions. He's iron. I've seen a lot of top-flight executives doing supposedly important things under considerable stress. Despite the pressure on Ike and the irritation caused by the current confusion on political problems, he operates just as coolly as during the planning."[105]

But General Eisenhower was not always cool and patient. There were other comments in Butcher's diary that show the Supreme Commander to be human: "D Day for assault to take Tunis and pen up Bizerte was postponed 'for a week or ten days' by General Anderson. Disappointing to Ike, who is irritated at any delays. If he ever gets Tunisia, he'll be a changed man; now he's like a caged tiger, snarling and clawing to get things done" (December 9, 1942). "In any event, the succession of political difficulties, the setback in Tunis, the bombing of Bône, where the cruiser *Ajax* took a dive bomb down her funnel and got her guts strewn around sufficiently to require four to five months for repair, the loss of four supply ships in one day, the apparent ability of German air to hit us effectively and our air's apparent inability to hit commensurately hard with its proportionately larger forces—all these, plus the repetition of monotony of office to house and vice versa, contributed to Ike's foul frame of mind last evening." (January 4, 1943). "Today, Ike, John, and Lee returned from the Advance Command Post before lunch, weather again having prevented Ike's trip across the Channel. The weather was not too rough for the U.S. destroyer, but the waves were too high on the other side to permit disembarkation. Ike will make his third try tomorrow. The fruitless delays do not improve his disposition."[106]

It was rare that anyone other than General Eisenhower's closest intimates knew when he was upset. His staff recognized that though he was cool, patient, and understanding, when aroused he had a dangerous temper. There was an explosive force in abeyance behind his kindness and consideration, and with its eruption his temper was a force to behold. Apparently it never erupted at crucial moments.

A member of his staff of long standing remarked:

It was notable that in his dealings with the British, French, and Russians, General Eisenhower never allowed himself to make any show of temper, no matter how angry he may really have been. For such cases, if the matter seemed important enough to require correction, he would send a subordinate commander or a member of his staff in whom he had confidence to the headquarters of the erring commander to try and adjust the matter through his staff. This usually succeeded, and it was not allowed to appear that the emissary was intrenching under the direction of General Eisenhower, thus good relations were preserved.[107]

When he set up his headquarters in England in July 1942, he moved it out of London into the country "where all hands," said an aide, "could live together like a football team and think, plan, and execute war all our waking hours."[108] To further develop the concept of teamwork he often had his staff officers eat their meals with him, at which time they discussed business.

It was General Eisenhower's thesis that in all commands the high commander's success *will be measured more by his ability to lead and persuade than by his adherence to fixed notions of arbitrary command practices.* This truth applies with particular force during the time necessary to build up confidence—a confidence that reaches back to governments at home as well as throughout the length and breadth of the command."[109]

An officer who was with General Eisenhower through most of World War II states:

I know of no instance during the entire war where General Eisenhower made an independent or arbitrary decision. Invariably, as far as I could see, he only considered and decided a matter that came up to him through and after study by his staff, or from one of his senior subordinate commanders. During the latter stage of the war, he came more and more to want council and advice from General Omar Bradley who had impressed him with his high intelligence, good judgment, and strength of character. I never felt, nor knew of others who felt, that this procedure implied any weakness or lack of confidence on the part of General Eisenhower, but stemmed from his great anxiety to get the best information and advice available before making a decision.[110]

Relations with the Press

In a democracy, no military officer in a position of high responsibility, in war or peace, can be successful in accomplishing his mission without a knowledge of how to work with the press, radio, and television media. Captain Butcher, who, as noted earlier, had been a vice-president of the Columbia Broadcasting System prior to the war, wrote in his diary on September 20, 1942, "I have a feeling that I will gain a reputation as an expert in this field. I'll be getting the credit for Ike's good sense, for he is the keenest in dealing with the press I've ever seen, and I have met a lot of them."[111]

Because of General Eisenhower's modesty, he had some difficulty in his early dealings in public relations. He believed the less his name and picture appeared in the press the better, though he was very gracious in throwing bouquets to his subordinates for their work. The unfortunate consequence of this policy was that it left the impression in the United States, that perhaps General Eisenhower was not doing anything.

Though shunning publicity himself, Eisenhower noted that "an Army fights just as hard as the pressure of public opinion behind it." He also believed that, "In the last analysis public opinion wins wars." The primary agency for informing public opinion was the press. After World War II was over, General Eisenhower wrote in his memoirs that it was essential "in modern war, for a commander to concern himself always with the appearance of things in the public eye as well as with actual accomplishment. It is idle to say that the public may be ignored in the certainty that temporary misunderstandings will be forgotten in later victory."[112]

General Eisenhower realized that complete rapport was impossible between the press and the military authorities. The military saw the need for secrecy to maintain the element of surprise so important for victory and to minimize the loss of men and materiel. The means for controlling the flow of military information was censorship, a measure most antagonistic to the freedom of speech and press known in America, even though the need of censorship in time of war was recognized by everyone. General Eisenhower solved this area of potential friction by seeking to understand the viewpoints of both the press and the military. The military viewpoint he was naturally aware of. To hear from the other side he permitted the press to register complaints and asked the association of correspondents to draw up their own proposals for a plan to control censorship, proposals which General Eisenhower took into consideration in formulating censorship rules for SHAEF. But, even though he solicited their opinions, there was never any doubt about the relationship between the press and any command run by General Eisenhower. One of the war correspondents assigned to his headquarters remarked of him, "He's a swell guy, democratic and all that, but you know all the time that he could get hard as hell if he wanted to."

Eisenhower held his first press conference after the announcement of his selection as Supreme Commander in England in January 1944. He opened by telling them, "You correspondents have a role in this war just as much as I do." He then made very clear the relationship that would exist between himself and the press. "I will not," he said, "tolerate in my theater an atmosphere of antagonism between myself and the newspaper people." He established the rules that would be used between his headquarters and the press: a censor would delete only what would violate military security; there would be no censorship of stories that criticized himself; newsman were to have unhampered—except where military security prevented it—access to his headquarters. He wanted the public to be honestly informed of the conduct of the Supreme Commander and his Headquarters; and if the people wanted a new man for the Supreme Command job, they should have him.

He did a number of other things to establish smooth relations. He met with the press in large briefing rooms, although he preferred to meet correspondents informally in his office. But he thought transporting the more than one hundred reporters to his headquarters was too dificult; so he went to them rather than have the reporters come to him.

Captain Butcher was of great value to General Eisenhower in his relations with the press. Butcher knew and understood the problems of the correspondents; they considered him their friend, and he was at every press conference. Often complaints of the press were taken to General Eisenhower through Butcher; and if the gripes were legitimate, the problem was removed immediately.

One of the most common grievances on the part of newsmen was impatience with what seemed to them to be useless red tape. Eisenhower was even able to do something about that. The *Chicago Daily News* wrote in an editorial about General Eisenhower's Headquarters, "Correspondents with experience in Paris, London and Washington from the outset of the war claim they have never seen such an absence of red tape."

The atmosphere at his press conference was a factor in his success. On November 21, 1944, Ike was scheduled to give a press conference in the briefing room at the "Scribe" building in Paris. Ike arrived and his new public relations chief, Brigadier General Frank A. Allen, Jr., announced very simply, "Gentlemen, I present the Supreme Commander." General Eisenhower's aide, Captain Butcher, was present. "I winced," Butcher said, "because I recalled Ike telling me that he would much prefer not to be introduced, as he thought the formality entirely unnecessary."

Sometimes General Eisenhower would reverse the questioning at a press conference. After the liberation of Paris, the French were allowed to resume governing themselves immediately. Ike was bothered by this; he didn't know whether he had done the right thing. At a press conference, after he had initiated the policy of Frenchmen governing Frenchmen, he interviewed the reporters. He asked them such questions as: What has been the reaction of the French people? What about the man on the street? What do the French think of DeGaulle? Is there any threat of revolt by the French people? What do you (the reporters) think of the situation?

On June 12, 1943, General Eisenhower held one of the most unique press conferences in the history of war. The war correspondents for the Mediterranean theater were called for a conference at 3:30 in the afternoon and were informed that the next Allied invasion would be Sicily, "sometime next month." As General Eisenhower took the reporters into his confidence, trusting them implicitly, there was a stunned silence. "Mouths fell open as I began the conference," said General Eisenhower, "by telling the reporters that we would assault Sicily early in July, with the Seventh Army under General Patton attacking the southern beaches and the British Eighth Army under General Montgomery attacking the eastern beaches south of Syracuse."[113] Brigadier General Robert A. McClure, the Director of Information for the United States Army, was shocked. Even though General Eisenhower had emphasized the necessity for absolute secrecy, General McClure got up after he finished and informed the correspondents that even most of the officers at Allied Headquarters did not know the time and place of the next allied invasion.

"I felt," said General Eisenhower, "I had to stop speculation by war reporters as to the future intentions of the Allied Force ... During periods of combat inactivity reporters have a habit of filling up their stories with speculation, and since after some months of experience in a war theater any newsman acquires considerable skill in interpreting coming events ... I do not believe that speculation by self-styled military analysts in the homelands, far removed from a theater of operations, is of any great benefit to the enemy ... But in an active theater it is an entirely different matter, and because of an inborn hatred of unexplained censorship and, more than this, because of the confidence I had acquired in the integrity of newsmen in my theater, I decided to take them into my confidence."[114]

General Eisenhower's approach of trusting the correspondents was a complete success. The reporters felt a part of the commander's responsibility, and ceased writing speculative stories in the Mediterranean theater over what would be the next Allied move after North Africa. It was a risky thing to have done, and General Eisenhower knew it. He said of the event, "I would not particularly like to repeat" the experiment. Even newsmen asked General Eisenhower, "Please don't ever do that again." Reporters became reluctant to talk to each other about it; and as a precautionary measure, some gave up drinking. This test of the correspondents' patriotism and loyalty placed a great deal of pressure upon them. The experiment had a long range impact—before other major Allied offensives there were very few speculative stories by correspondents. They had learned a valuable lesson.

Ike was thoroughly honest with the press and the American people. He would not even permit dishonesty in press reporting for propaganda purposes. In June 1943, during the fighting in North Africa, the Allies had thought 11,000 prisoners were captured on Pantelleria. A quick count, however, revealed that there were at least 15,000 prisoners. At a press conference on June 12, 1943, General Eisenhower asked the press to say that "more than 10,000" had been "hastily" accounted for, although he did not doubt the 15,000 estimate. "He doesn't want," Butcher wrote in his diary, "to be in the position of permitting the Axis to say we were guilty of exaggerations."[115]

At his initial press conference as Allied Commander for the North African invasion, which he held in England in 1943, he immediately was presented with his first challenge. American Negro soldiers were dating white British girls. "When I learned," Ike said, "at the press conference that stories of this kind were on the censored list, I at once revoked the order and told the press men to write as they pleased—urging them only not to lose their perspective. To my astonishment several reporters spoke up to ask me to retain the ban. . . They said that troublemakers would exaggerate the importance of the incidents, and that the reports, taken at home, would cause domestic dissension. I thanked them but stuck to my point, with the result that little excitement was ever caused by ensuing stories. It was a lesson I tried always to remember."[116] This set the pattern of frankness in dealing with the press which General Eisenhower followed throughout the war.

As has already been discussed, Montgomery was ground commander for both the American and British forces for the invasion of Europe. In August 1944, the story appeared in American newspapers stating that Montgomery was no longer the ground commander and that General Bradley and he were on equal status. This delighted the Americans who did not relish our forces in a subordinate role to a British commander, even if Ike was the Supreme Commander of all the Allied forces, ground, sea and air, in the European theater.

British irritation was as great as American elation; they believed that Montgomery had been demoted. The whole story was immediately denied by SHAEF, and confusion was rampant. General Marshall sent a wire from Washington asking for an explanation. General Eisenhower was displeased with the commotion. "It wasn't enough," he said in his wire to General Marshall, "for the public to obtain a great victory, the manner in which it was gained seemed to be more important." General Eisenhower was human, and there were times when the press was an irritant; but he understood the reasons. He said about the above situation, "The reaction in both countries was completely normal." He even saw good in the situation. "Were it not," he said, "for the intense patriotism and spirit that create this kind of nationalistic pride, the task of organizing and maintaining armies in the face of losses would be an impossible one. The incident became just one more profitable lesson in handling matters in which the public was certain to have great concern."[117]

General Eisenhower was successful in dealing with the press because he was honest with them. He knew they wanted to end the war just as quickly as everyone else did. The correspondents, in turn, appreciated the confidence and trust that General Eisenhower had in their integrity, patriotism, and good judgment. He was direct and forceful. He was considerate of the reporters. Newspaper men are known for their toughness, but this shell was broken by General Eisenhower. He spoke to them on a personal basis in an informal manner. He made them feel they were soldiers in the American Army, doing their part to win the war. He refused fanfare, and did not like any attention given to his high rank. He was a humble man and the press knew that his modesty was genuine. Honest and natural publicity was to him the best and the normal and natural thing to do.

In his handling of the press, Eisenhower compared favorably with men who had many years of experience in the business. In February 1945, Steve Early, who had handled press conferences for President Roosevelt and other top officials for years, attended a press conference given by General Eisenhower at Rheims. "It was," said Early, "the most magnificent performance of any man at a press conference that I have ever seen. He knows his facts, he speaks freely and frankly, and he has a sense of humor, he has poise, and he has command."[118]

The General and the Troops

General Eisenhower did not spend all of his time with his senior commanders and his staff; it was part of his function to frequently visit the soldiers in his command. In the fall of 1944, General Eisenhower went to the front to talk with several hundred men of the 29th Infantry Division. He spoke to them on a very muddy and slippery hillside. After he had finished talking, he turned to go back to his jeep and suddenly slipped and fell with a plop on his back. He was thoroughly covered with mud. The soldiers he had been talking with could not refrain from laughing; but this did not upset General Eisenhower. "From the shout of laughter that went up," he reflected," I am quite sure that no other meeting I had with soldiers during the war was a greater success than that one."[119]

It was his policy, once his headquarters for SHAEF was set up, to devote about one third of his time to visiting the troops. When he did so, he ordered that no parades or formal inspections would be held, since he wanted training to continue as usual. His visits were normally made without press coverage. He spent very little time with the brass, concentrating his attention on the soldiers in the ranks, their food and quarters.

If he was scheduled to inspect a unit of men, the standard procedure was to have them open ranks. Then he walked along, neither fast nor slow, up one line and down the other. About every dozen or so men, he would stop and talk with one of the soldiers. The conversation with the soldier would usually go like this:

General Eisenhower: "What did you do in civilian life?

Soldier: "I'm a farmer, sir."

General Eisenhower: "Fine, so am I. What did you raise?"

Soldier: "Wheat."

General Eisenhower: "Good. How many bushels did you get to the acre?"

Soldier: "Oh, about 35 bushels when we have a good year."

General Eisenhower: "You do? Well, when the war is over I'm coming to you for a job."

Then he would usually close by saying to the soldier, "Do me a favor, will you? Go and finish this war, fast, so I can go fishing."

His jeep had a loudspeaker which he would use to groups of soldiers. He generally emphasized their importance in the war by saying, "You are the men who will win this war." He told them it was a privilege to be their commander. "A commander," he would say, "meets to talk with his men to inspire them. With me it is the other way around. I get inspired by you."

Once, visiting the front when the Allies were getting ready to cross the Rhine, he encountered a soldier walking along the bank of the river. The man was very depressed. General Eisenhower asked, "How are you feeling, son?" "General," the soldier replied, "I'm awful nervous. I was wounded two months ago and just got back from the hospital yesterday. I don't feel so good!"

"Well," General Eisenhower said, "you and I are a good pair then, because I'm nervous too. But we've planned this attack for a long time, and we've got all the planes, the guns, and airborne troops we can use to smash the Germans. Maybe if we just walk along together to the river we'll be good for each other."[120]

There was a pattern as well as a purpose to General Eisenhower's visiting. Lieutenant General Alvan C. Gillem, Jr., who was Commanding General of the XIII Corps during the Battle of the Bulge, decided after the Bulge crisis was over to get away for a day or so to relax, since he had been under considerable strain and needed a brief change. General Gillem went to Paris, checked into the Ritz Hotel and after dinner went to the Follies and several other night clubs, returning to the hotel about 1:00 A.M. As he entered his room, the telephone was ringing urgently; it was a call for him to return to his Headquarters immediately. No reason was given except to return at great speed. After a hazardous flight in a light plane in miserable weather, bumping along at treetop level for several hours, he landed on an unimproved field. He was met by a noncom in a jeep; and with a surface ride that was as hazardous as his flight, he arrived at his Command Post. There he was informed that General Eisenhower was present and at the time was at the officers' mess having lunch. "I hastened to the mess hall," General Gillem said, "and as I arrived General Eisenhower and several staff officers emerged. I reported and stated my regrets at not being present to meet him when he arrived. He informed me, with a broad smile, that his visit was unexpected and that, as a matter of fact, it was better to inspect a Headquarters when the Commander was away, for if it could not function under such circumstances it was not efficient. He further stated he was eminently satisfied and that he would not return, that he had obtained the viewpoint he wanted and that he regretted he must leave. He congratulated me on my

command and expressed his pleasure at what he had seen of the
conduct of the Corps during the recent battle. We shook hands
and he departed. That was the last time I heard from him or his
Headquarters until the final days on the Elbe River."[121]

Eisenhower often made a point of arriving unannounced to
insure informality and minimize disruption. Once he stopped by
to see his First Army Chief, General Omar N. Bradley, at Cherbourg. "With Ike," General Bradley remembered, "I drove up
into the sector of the 79th Division in the center of Collins'
line. There we picked up the division commander and drove on
to a regimental bivouac. A captain knelt in his OD undershirt
over a helmet of water, lathering his face for a shave. He looked
up in annoyance as we walked to the clearing. His eyes bugged,
then rolled in despair, as they traveled from the broad smile of
Ike to the agonized face of his division commander. The captain
stumbled to his feet and, with a towel still tied around his neck,
saluted, and reported to the Supreme Commander. As Eisenhower moved briskly among the troops, the captain fell in behind him. Hands on his hips, head cocked, Ike frowned as he bit
off his words in conversation with the men."[122]

"The importance of such visits by the high command",
General Eisenhower stated, "including at times, the highest
officials of government, can scarcely be overestimated in terms
of their value to a soldier's morale. The soldier has a sense of
gratification whenever he sees very high rank in his particular
vicinity..."[123]

He had a style of visiting with the men that developed an
informal and friendly rapport. It was impossible for him to visit
all the men in his command; but when he talked with individual
soldiers or to small groups of them, it established a closeness
with those men, who in turn told their story to others. In this
way, the word spread throughout thousands of men. The stories
were exaggerated as they spread, but the account always
described General Eisenhower as personal and human. It disturbed him when he read a story about his visit in the newspaper. If the men concluded he was doing it for publicity, he

would lose his effectiveness. He therefore would not permit the
press to accompany him during his visits.

But he could not always keep his actions out of the newspapers. Once during the drive through Paris in January 1945, he
performed an unintentional act of showmanship that reached
millions of American soldiers through the military journal, *Stars
and Stripes*:

> At SHAEF last week, an appeal was made to head-
> quarters men for contribution of type O blood, needed
> immediately at the front.
>
> A couple of days later, volunteers were lined up in the
> dispensary. No one paid much attention at first as an
> officer walked into the room. He lay down on a litter and
> a nurse bustled over to wrap a tourniquet around his arm.
>
> A soldier on the next litter looked over idly, looked
> back, then did an astonished double take. The guy next to
> him was General Eisenhower.
>
> "It was just like any other GI", said T/4 Conrad J.
> Segrin, one of the dispensary's medics. "He wasn't a
> special case at all. Ike came in, they took his blood, he got
> a cup of coffee and he left. Just like that."
>
> There was a private in the waiting line who saw the
> Supreme Commander on his way out. He turned to the
> man beside him and said, "Hey, that'd be the blood to get.
> Maybe I could make General with it."
>
> Ike overheard him, turned around and grinned. "If you
> do, he said, "I hope you don't inherit my bad disposition."

Contact with the troops played a role in Eisenhower's decision making. Just before he was to transfer from the Mediterranean area to London to assume his duties as Supreme Commander of the Allied invasion of Europe, he became uneasy
over the Anzio project. He was disturbed to hear that his plan
for concentrating Air Force headquarters in Caserta was to be
dropped. "To me this decision," General Eisenhower commented, "seemed to imply a lack of understanding of the situation and of the duties of the highest commander in the field:

regardless of preoccupation with multitudinous problems of great import, *he must never lose touch with the 'feel' of his troops. He can and should delegate tactical responsibility and avoid interference in the authority of his selected subordinates, but he must maintain the closest kind of factual and spiritual contact with them or, in a vast and critical campaign, he will fail. This contact requires frequent visits to the troops themselves.*"[124]

As the momentum of preparation built up before a big battle, so did the visiting by General Eisenhower and his senior commanders. In the four months before the invasion of Europe, for example, from February 1, to June 1, 1944, General Eisenhower visited twenty-six divisions, twenty-four airfields, five ships of war, and numerous depots, shops, hospitals, and other important installations. The visiting schedules of Generals Bradley, Montgomery, Spaatz, and Tedder followed his example. Their visits were squeezed in among countless conferences and staff meetings during a period when the top generals were overwhelmed with work; but they always made time to see the men.

Friends of General Eisenhower urged him to give up or to at least curtail his visits with soldiers. They told him he could at best only hit a small percentage of the total. They said he was wearing himself out without accomplishing anything. He did not agree with or follow this well meaning advice. "In the first place," he said in reply to these suggestions, "I felt I gained accurate impressions of their state of mind. I talked to them about anything and everything. . . so long as I could get the soldier to talk to me in return. This, I felt, would encourage men to talk with their superiors, and this habit, promotes efficiency." He believed that if men were aware they could talk to the "brass", they would not be afraid to talk with their lieutenant. He hoped his example would encourage the officer to seek information from his men. "There is," General Eisenhower said, "among the mass of individuals who carry the rifles in war, a great amount of ingenuity and initiative. If men can naturally and without restraint talk to their officers, the products of their resourcefulness become available to all." For this reason, one of his favorite questions was to ask a soldier if his squad or platoon had found any new trick or gadget which improved their fighting in combat. The overall effect of this was to promote "Mutual confidence, a feeling of partnership that is the essence of *esprit de corps*."[125]

In December 1944, General Eisenhower found, because certain decisions relative to Allied unity had been made in favor of the British, that some American soldiers were saying, "Eisenhower is the best general the British have." This bothered him. Shortly after this comment started he paid a visit to the front. After his visit Wes Gallagher, correspondent for Associated Press, sent a note to Captain Butcher which stated in part: "Thought you might like to know that Ike's recent trips to the front, coupled with the recent U.S. activity, appear to have completely silenced that 'best general in the British Army' business."[126]

From the time General Eisenhower became Commanding General, European Theater of Operations, in the spring of 1942, until he returned to the United States after the war in Europe was over in the spring of 1945, he was never late for an appointment to review the troops. He just did not believe in keeping those men waiting.

In May 1945, Senator Homer Capehart was traveling with General Eisenhower as he was inspecting the troops. They were walking through an American Army camp in Paris to their aircraft; and as they walked, the word spread among the soldiers that Ike was there. Huge crowds gathered, making passage very difficult. The Supreme Commander spoke briefly to every fourth or fifth man. After he spoke the man would turn around and tell the others excitedly what was said. One said, "GI sure stands for General Ike." As Senator Capehart observed this he commented, "I hope that fellow never decides to run against me in my state. He's got what it takes. I can see now why the GIs worship him. He speaks their language; he isn't high hat like you expect from brass, and he knows their problems and they know it."[127]

He also made a point to visit the wounded in hospitals, where he would ask each soldier his name, shake his hand, ask him how and where he was wounded and when he hoped to get out of the hospital. It was necessary in World War II to set aside some hospitals and camp facilities for soldiers who were suffering from self-inflicted wounds, real or put-on hysteria, psychoneuroses, and deliberately contracted venereal disease. General Eisenhower believed:

It is profitable for a commander to visit these places. to talk with individuals, to understand something of the bewilderment, the fear, the defeatism that affect men who are essentially afraid of life, though believing they are afraid of death. An astonishing number of these individuals react instantly and favorably to a single word of encouragement. more than one has said to me, immediately upon discovering another's interest in him, "General, get me out of here; I want to go back to my outfit." Harshness normally intensifies the disease, but understanding can do much to cure it and in my opinion, if applied in time, can largely prevent it.[128]

Eisenhower recorded in his memoirs a major reason for his attention to the troops:

Soldiers like to see the men who are directing operations, they properly resent any indication of neglect or indifference to them on the part of their commanders and invariably interpret a visit, even a brief one, as evidence of the commander's concern for them. Diffidence or modesty must never blind the commander to his duty of showing himself to his men, of speaking to them, of mingling with them to the extent of physical limitation. It pays big dividends in terms of morale, and morale, given rough equality in other things, is supreme on the battlefield.[129]

He viewed such contacts as part of the basic equipment of a commander. "Attention to the individual is the key to success. Our service schools have a definite duty to instruct officers in this field. Regardless of any progress made in the country's educational institutions, the Army's business is success in war, and the Army cannot safely neglect any subject that experience has shown to be important to that success."[130]

On one of his visiting trips he traveled from Paris to Cherbourg, north up the coast to Antwerp, and then back to his command post. While motoring to an old French port near Antwerp, he noticed a group of men boarding a ship, stopped to talk to a few of them, and learned that they were going home on rotation. Within five minutes he was surrounded by some 400 men. He told them that he hoped they would find their friends well and happy; that they should have a good time; to get a good rest, and to come back to him ready to do another big job. Then General Eisenhower noticed a captain who had been decorated with five wound stripes. He asked the captain where he wanted to go when he returned. The captain replied, "To my old outfit, sir." General Eisenhower liked his attitude and spirit. The Supreme Commander's car hadn't moved 50 yards from the place where he had talked with the men when he turned to General Ben Lear who was with him, and said in a deeply concerned voice: "Lear, that captain has had five chances. You please see that he doesn't take any more of them."[131]

Eisenhower's professional competence—accomplished by his years of hard work, study, and preparation, particularly the tutelage under Major General Fox Conner, his smile, his warmth, his genuine interest in other people, his consideration, his patience properly balanced with toughness, his vision, his sense of perception that saw quickly the root-of-the-matter, his flexibility to perform as an able statesman as well as a military man, his rapport with the press—were all factors that made an almost impossible job of leadership look easy.

BLOOD AND GUTS

The Leadership of
George S. Patton, Jr.

"Patton's greatest quality as a leader was his ability to infuse his troops with his own martial ardor." The literature on General George S. Patton, Jr. is filled with such comments. "He could stamp his personality on a whole army and, though they sometimes hated him, they acted and thought and fought as he did." "The Third Army was molded in the image of its general—tough, cocky, daring, proud." "Patton's genius lay in his ability to accomplish the impossible with his men."

Patton himself claimed that "In a week's time I can spur any outfit into a high state of morale;" and as he said to one officer during World War II, "I am stupid in many particulars, but there is one quality I know I have—the ability to exercise mass hypnotism."

The men of the Third Army were ordinary human beings. They were inexperienced and unschooled in war. They were not volunteers. Yet they fought with a morale and spirit that made them one of the most successful armies in World War II. "Patton," said an officer, "had the ability to deliver that indefinable something which makes men want to go out and give their all for him; to do just a little bit more than it is humanly possible to do."

How did Patton impress his own dynamic personality on his troops? Why were his men able to accomplish the impossible? What was the secret of his mass hypnotism of his soldiers? Were his accomplishments as a military commander based on something "indefinable"? The answers to these questions sketch a picture of leadership, depicting the most successful and unforgettable combat general of World War II, George S. Patton, Jr.

Early Career

George Patton started on the road to success as quickly as possible for any young officer. Soon after his graduation in 1909 and while still a second lieutenant, he became aide to General Leonard Wood, Army Chief of Staff from 1910 to 1914. This assignment was of great importance in the light of the personality of Wood, under whom young and impressionable Patton was to serve. Leonard Wood was an unusual officer. He was a physician by training but a soldier at heart. After graduation from Harvard Medical School and a brief Boston practice he decided he wanted to be a soldier. He was commissioned as an officer and embarked upon a military career. Although an assistant surgeon, he won the rare distinction in 1886 of receiving the Congressional Medal of Honor for heroic action during the Indian Wars of the latter part of the 19th century, in what was certainly a non-medical capacity. The official citation of Wood read:

Voluntarily carried dispatches through a region infested with hostile Indians, making a journey of 70 miles in one night and walking 30 miles the next day. Also for several weeks, while in close pursuit of Geronimo's band and constantly expecting an encounter, commanded a detachment of Infantry, which was then without an officer, and to the command of which he was assigned upon his own request.[1]

As President William McKinley's physician, Wood continued to be "the frustrated military commander." While on active duty in Washington, D. C., and with the advent of the conflict with Spain he sought to command a regiment of cavalry. He was turned down on numerous occasions. President McKinley would not help because he wanted his wife's physician to stay in Washington. But finally he got a regiment with the aid of Teddy Roosevelt. Roosevelt had been seeking the opportunity to get into the war, and when the Governor of Arizona, who had been pleading to send a regiment of volunteers from his state, finally met with success he offered Roosevelt the command. Roosevelt turned down command of the regiment, and used his influence to put Wood in charge, with himself as the assistant commander. This regiment was ultimately to become known as the "Rough Riders". Thus Wood got his line command, even though it was referred to in the press as Roosevelt's regiment. The two were a wonderful balance and worked in great harmony.[2] On July 9, 1898, Wood was commissioned a Brigadier General of Volunteers, and less than two weeks later he became the Commanding General of the city of Santiago which the Spanish Army had surrendered to the U.S. on the 16th.

Serving as aide to Leonard Wood had a definite impact upon Patton. General Wood's greatest influence, however, was indirect since it was through his aide's position that Patton made what was perhaps the most important friendship and contact of his life. The President at this time was Taft and his Secretary of War was Henry L. Stimson. The young officer selected to be Stimson's aide or escort for many official functions at Fort Myer and in Washington, was Patton. It was no coincidence that Patton became one of Stimson's aides. Patton made a point, since he knew Stimson was an avid horseman, to find where the Secretary of War rode. As a result of their riding together, Stimson quickly became attached to Patton, for the latter exemplified the code of the officer and gentleman, a code which Stimson himself followed. He had all the social graces, was knowledgeable in his profession, dedicated to serving his country; and both were fond of the outdoors and were avid horsemen. A friendship was started here that grew stronger through the years and later had great bearing on Patton's career.

Patton was unique in his army career in having been in on every significant peacetime event in which an Army officer could participate. The first of these was the border skirmish between the United States and Mexico, precipitated by the bandit Pancho Villa. When Villa moved across the border and raided Columbus, New Mexico, President Wilson decided to take decisive action—he ordered General Pershing to take a contingent of troops to follow Villa into Mexico, to capture him and to put a stop to his activities.

At the time, Patton was stationed with the 8th Cavalry at Fort Bliss, Texas, near El Paso and right on the border, living next door to General Pershing. The troops at Fort Bliss were all anxious to get into action to avenge the deeds of Villa, but only a small group was chosen. When Patton learned that the 8th Cavalry was not selected for the expedition he was terribly dejected. Rather than accept the inevitable, he decided to do something about it. He parked himself on a chair outside Pershing's office for almost forty continuous hours. Finally the aloof Pershing noticed him and asked him what he was doing there. Patton answered, "I have been waiting for a chance to speak with you, sir."

"Well, you've got it. What do you want?"

"I want to go to Mexico with you, as your aide, sir."

"I have already chosen my two aides."

"You can use a third one, sir, and if you take me I promise you will never regret it."

"There's no use staying around here any longer. Go back to your quarters. You may hear from me."³

In a few days Patton did hear from him. His "modest insistence of his own excellence," as his fellow officers described it, and his determination to fight impressed the General sufficiently that he decided to take Patton along. Pershing did not regret his decision. Patton distinguished himself in service to the General and managed to work in a couple of daring episodes as well.

Here is the newspaper story of one of his exploits in Mexico:

On the afternoon of Sunday, May 14, a fight that will go down as unique in the records of this [the Mexico] expedition. For it was there that Lieutenant George S. Patton of Los Angeles with a scout and nine enlisted men, in three automobiles encountered and killed three Villistas, including Captain Julio Cardenas, in what army men would call one of the prettiest fights of the campaign.

Patton with three Dodge cars rode up to a "suspicious" dobe house, and came to an abrupt stop in the road, immediately behind the ranch house. Patton sprang from the car, and drawing a six-shooter, ran east in the lee of the north wall of the ranch house until he reached the front of the group of buildings. There four Mexicans were skinning a beef, and Patton was on the point of speaking to them when three horsemen, with rifles drawn from saddle boots, rode out through an arched sallyport of dobe from the corral formed by the ranch building.

The horsemen opened fire immediately, cutting chunks of dobe from the wall over the Lieutenant's head . . . Patton raised his six-shooter, which by the way is a beautiful weapon, cased and ornamented, and fired. He shot five times.

The leading horseman lurched in his saddle, then, wheeling his mount, rode back through the archway. He was wounded. Patton, his revolver empty, dodged back behind the wall to reload, and as he did so the second horseman, putting spurs to his mount, made a dash for it, riding diagonally across the ranch yard to the left of the Lieutenant and his party, firing over his shoulder as he fled.

"I remembered then," Patton relates, "what an old Texas ranger had told me. That was to kill a fugitive's horse, which was the surest way of stopping him."

With this axiom in mind Patton sent a bullet from his pistol crashing through the hip of the fleeing horse.

The horse, hip broken, stumbled, fell, and rolled over his rider. The Mexican struggled to his feet, game, facing the Americans. Lieutenant Patton fired . . . The Mexican sank down in the sand without a word, dead. [There was also a presage of the future here.]

Three Villistas is not a big bag, even in this campaign where the guerrilla warfare does not make for large casualty totals, but the fact that Patton and his men fought from the automobiles, that is to say, sprang directly from their cars into the fight, put the encounter in a class by itself.[4]

In 1917, the United States entered World War I and prepared to send troops to fight in Europe, the Army Chief of Staff, Major General Hugh L. Scott, selected General John J. Pershing to command the American Expeditionary Force. Remembering his outstanding work in Mexico, Pershing asked Patton if he would like to command his Headquarters troops. With obvious excitement and enthusiasm Patton jumped at the chance that would guarantee him the opportunity to get into the fighting of World War I. With the position went a promotion to the rank of captain. With great fervor Patton exploited his opportunity, and within a year had risen to the rank of full colonel.

As Headquarters Commander Patton became a tank expert. He went to the French Tank School at Champs Lieu; and with what he had learned there, he set up a tank school to train American soldiers at Langres. While carrying out this assignment, he also managed to attend the French General Staff College at Langres where he was pleased to be able to renew his friendship with Henry L. Stimson, who was attending the same school as a lieutenant colonel.

When Patton got into action he proved again to be a most courageous soldier. He was awarded the Purple Heart for wounds of shrapnel and machine gun bullets during one tank battle, won the Distinguished Service Cross for extraordinary heroism in action, and the Distinguished Service Medal "for exceptional, meritorious, and distinguished services" in organizing and directing the Tank Center at the Army Schools at Langres.

Patton never forgot the chance Pershing gave him in the Mexican conflict and in World War I. Before he sailed from the

United States for action in North Africa he went to see General
Pershing, saying, "I can't tell you where I'm going, but I
couldn't go without coming to ask you for your blessing." The
old General replied, "You shall have it. Kneel down." After the
blessing, Patton stood at attention and snapped a salute to his
mentor. It is reported that Pershing rose from his chair and
"twenty years dropped from his shoulders as, standing erect, he
returned the salute."[5]

While George Patton was winning medals and gaining combat
experience, there was a young lieutenant colonel from the West
Point Class of 1915 who was much less fortunate. This officer,
Dwight D. Eisenhower, had tried desperately to get overseas,
but was destined to finish out the war as Commander of Camp
Colt, at Gettysburg. This was the Tank Training Center in the
United States. When Patton returned to the United States, it
was almost inevitable that this veteran of tank combat should
meet Eisenhower who had the responsibility for stateside tank
training. They met at the Tank Center at Camp Meade, Maryland, in March 1919 and quickly formed a close friendship
which lasted until Patton's unfortunate death in 1945. The two
took correspondence courses and often met at each other's
homes to work out their lessons together and to discuss military
affairs in general.

When the U.S. prepared in World War II to send our forces
overseas, Patton, as one of our few experienced tank battlefield
commanders, was one of the first officers considered for action
in the desert of North Africa. The importance of the long and
close friendship of Patton and Eisenhower played a role in his
selection. Eisenhower related in his memoirs:

> For commander of such a unit (i.e., a tank division for
> the Egyptian desert) my mind turned instantly to one of
> my oldest friends, Major General George S. Patton, Jr.,
> who was not only a tank expert but an outstanding leader
> of troops. I was astonished to find my choice flatly op-
> posed by a considerable portion of the staff, but I was
> convinced that this was due entirely to Patton's rather

bizarre mannerisms and his sometimes unpredictable actions. He conformed to no pattern—a circumstance that made many fearful of his ability to fit into a team. Such doubts had no influence on me because of my confidence in his fighting heart and my conviction that he would provide effective leadership for combat troops. I felt that I knew him well because at the end of the first World War, he and I had formed a fast friendship that could even include heated, sometimes almost screaming, arguments over matters that more often than not were doctrinal and academic rather than personal or material.[7]

As events developed, an American division was not sent at that time to Egypt because of a lack of available shipping. But it must be emphasized that Patton was being selected not simply because he was a friend, but because their friendship permitted Eisenhower to know the real Patton and to have confidence that he was the man for the job. Indeed Patton was to find that when Eisenhower was his boss in World War II in Europe, that friendship could be a disadvantage. Patton wanted a certain officer for Corps Commander and General Eisenhower initially refused the selection because the officer was a graduate of the Class of 1915 and he did not want to be accused of showing favoritism towards a classmate. It was only after strong arguing that Patton won his point.

Patton was terribly disappointed to have missed the opportunity to get into action at such an early date, but some sound advice was given to him by his old friend, Henry L. Stimson, who had once again been called upon to contribute his outstanding ability to the nation, this time as Secretary of War for President Franklin D. Roosevelt. Stimson wrote in his diary:

General George Patton who was to command the Armoured Division if we had sent it to Libya was out there watching the demonstration and I took him home to dinner. He may have been a little disappointed at not getting his chance to go to Libya but I pointed out to him how important it was for him and our tank forces to get a real good chance the first time they go into action and he agreed with me. Mabel [Stimson's wife] and I had a pleasant evening with him.[8]

Again it should be noted that knowing the right people was only one key factor in Patton's success since all the "right" people were not in his camp. It has been already mentioned that when Eisenhower wanted Patton to command the first armored division to be sent into action against the Germans he found opposition to the assignment. Stimson too was surprised to learn in 1941, when Patton was up for promotion to major general, that there were elements of opposition not only within the Army but in the White House as well. He decided to assist Patton's cause by sending to Roosevelt, along with the list of generals to be promoted if the President approved, a personal letter specifically recommending Patton's promotion.[9]

Patton later learned of the personal intervention by Stimson and wrote him a letter of thanks. Stimson's reply, in a personal and at that time confidential letter revealed the overriding consideration in his intervention: [10]

My Dear General:

I have received your very kind letter of April 11th.

When I especially endorsed your candidacy for your recent promotion, I did not do it because of my regard for you—although you must know that I have a very warm feeling for you. But I did it because I was very confident that under your command the Second Armored Division will be instilled with a vigorous fighting spirit and I expressly wanted to have that done.

My best wishes go with you.

Very sincerely yours,

/s/

Henry L. Stimson
Secretary of War

When Patton received command of his first corps he again wrote Stimson to thank him and received the reply, "You have won your promotion to the Command of the I Armored Corps solely upon your own merits and the fine way in which you performed in your duties in your previous assignments."[1] When Patton got into his most serious trouble in World War II over slapping an enlisted man, Stimson came to his aid, less out of friendship than because the United States could not afford to lose the officer whom General Eisenhower called his "best fighting general."

One can see in his own writings the comfort which Stimson derived from having a leader like Patton in command. Though few people knew it then, there was strong doubt about the North African invasion. Our Army Staff strongly opposed this "political" decision by Churchill and Roosevelt. Even Stimson, who confessed his doubts only to General Marshall, remarked in his diary, "We are embarked on a risky undertaking but it is not at all hopeless and, the Commander in Chief having made the decision, we must do our best to make it a success."[2]

During this period of doubt another Stimson comment revealed his faith in Patton's ability.

> I had a conference with General George Patton who had just got back from Europe. He is to command Torch [the North African landing] and I had a very intimate and thrilling talk with him. He has no illusions but he thinks with luck he can do it and I gave him my best wishes and blessings. He has been extremely loyal and grateful to me throughout his career in the Armored Corps and this now is the culmination of it. I feel rather somber but was very much bucked up by the actual advent of the crisis and my talk with him over the whole situation. He has just the right spirit and I believe will do everything that humanly can be done to make the matter a success.[3]

Patton's World War II Leadership

How did General Patton lead? How did he stamp his dynamic personality on his troops, accomplish the impossible, and hypnotize his men? By word, example, training and discipline, personal leadership, and concern for the soldier's welfare.

Word

Aboard a transport which was moving slowly through a choppy Mediterranean Sea in July 1943, an Army Colonel climbed atop a gun mount. Gathered around him were hundreds of grim faced American soldiers. The men wore helmets, boots and fatigues. M-1 rifles were slung over their shoulders. Around the waist of each was a belt heavily loaded down with ammunition, K-rations and a canteen. They were dressed for war. In a few minutes they would be given the signal to climb over the side of the ship into their launches and the invasion of Sicily would be on.

In nervous anticipation they stood waiting to hear the Colonel read the Order of the Day from Lieutenant General George S. Patton, Jr., Commander of the United States Seventh Army. This was what they heard:

> We are teamed with the justly famous Eighth Army, which attacks on our right, and we have for the Army Group commander that veteran and distinguished soldier, General Sir Harold Alexander.
>
> When we land we will meet German and Italian soldiers whom it is our honor and privilege to attack and destroy.
>
> Many of you have in your veins German and Italian blood, but remember that these ancestors of yours so loved freedom that they gave up home and country to cross the ocean in search of liberty . . .

Remember that we as attackers have the initiative. We must retain this tremendous advantage by always attacking rapidly, ruthlessly, viciously, without rest. However tired and hungry you may be, the enemy will be more tired, more hungry. Keep punching. God is with us. We shall win . . .

A similar scene was going on on hundreds of other troop transports in the thousand-ship convoy, implementing a typical Patton leadership tactic. He talked personally, or through his commanders and Orders of the Day, to his men in training, before a campaign, during battle, and after a campaign was over. He talked to infantry soldiers, armored soldiers, air corps personnel, officers, sergeants, truck drivers, supply men behind the lines, communications men, cooks, and all the other personnel who were part of his army.

When the first contingent of Third Army landed at Normandy Beach on July 28, 1944, there was a steady stream of hundreds of launches coming ashore to unload men and material. As the men jumped off the boat immediate commands were shouted out by officers and NCO's giving the men their instructions for the move forward to the front lines. Supplies were being stacked on the beaches or loaded into trucks. There was a constant roar of tanks, trucks, and jeeps as they were driven off barges. In the background was the sound of artillery fire, machine guns, mortars, and M-1 rifles. Overhead, tactical airplanes were coming in low to strafe the battle lines with machine guns and to drop their bombs.

Amid all this activity the Third Army Commander, General George S. Patton, Jr. landed. In spite of the noise and confusion he was immediately recognized by his men. The landing operation came to a standstill as the soldiers of Third Army crowded around General Patton's jeep, anticipating a speech. He did not disappoint them. He stood up, looked around, and said to them: "Men, I'm proud to be here to fight beside you. Now let's cut out the guts of these Krauts and get the hell on to Berlin." There was a cheer from the men. General Patton's driver threw the jeep into gear. The vehicle jumped forward and their general was on his way to the front. As he traveled throughout the battle area, he always took the time to speak to individual soldiers, squads, platoons, companies, divisions, or whatever size group could be collected.

Speech-making was a tested Patton leadership technique, employed from the early days of World War II. In 1942, he had the responsibility for preparing one of the first American units to go into offensive action against the Germans in World War II. As the unit progressed to a high level of proficiency, the men became restless. Finally, Patton received word from Washington that his outfit was to go into action in Europe. He immediately called his men together to speak to them:

> Well, they've given us a job to do. A tough job, a mansize job. We can go down on our bended knees, every one of us, and thank God the chance has been given to us to serve our country, I can't tell you where we're going, but it will be where we can do the most good. And where we can do the most good is where we can fight those damn Germans or those yellow-bellied Eyetalians, And when we do, by God, we're going to go right in and kill the dirty bastards. We won't just shoot the sonabitches. We're going to cut out their living guts—and use them to grease the treads of our tanks. We're going to murder those lousy Hun bastards by the bushel.

Soon after landing in England these men, who were now in the II Corps, were aboard a convoy for the invasion of North Africa. As they went into battle for the first time against the Germans, they could remember General Patton's departing words: "If we are not victorious, let no one come back alive."

There were two occasions when Patton gave special emphasis to speaking. He always tried to talk with a unit just before the start of a difficult attack, as on March 5, 1945, when he paid a visit to the 65th Infantry Division, about to go into action against the Germans at the Siegfried Line. Major General Stanley E. Reinhart, Commander of the 65th Division recalled:

We assembled such officers and top three grade NCO's
as we could to hear him. He addressed them from a
packing box in the village of Ennery with the usual manure
piles for background. It was cold, I wore a lined parka
myself, but he shed his short overcoat and made his
splendid figure in perfectly groomed uniform, which with
his usual profane delivery was calculated to make a vivid
impression upon these new soldiers of his, and comments
which I heard showed that he had thoroughly succeeded.[14]

Another occasion when General Patton made a special effort
to talk to the soldiers of his army was after a significant victory.
Marking the feat of the U.S. Seventh Army which had routed
the German and Italian soldiers in Sicily in an unexpectedly
brief period of 38 days, he delivered this message to his men:

Born at sea, baptized in blood, and crowned with
victory, in the course of thirty-eight days of incessant
battle and unceasing labor, you have added a glorious
chapter to the history of the war.
Pitted against the best the Germans and Italians could
offer, you have been unfailingly successful. The rapidity of
your dash, which culminated in the capture of Palermo, was
equaled by the dogged tenacity with which you stormed
Troina and captured Messina.
Your fame shall never die.

After the Third Army successfully emerged from the
Germans' most challenging counter-offensive of the war at
Ardennes, the Battle of the Bulge, in the winter of 1945, he
told his men "Neither heat, nor dust, nor floods, nor snow have
stayed your progress . . .Under the protection of Almighty God
and the inspired leadership of our President and the High
Command, you will continue your victorious course to the end
that tyranny and vice shall be eliminated, our dead comrades
avenged, and peace restored to a war-weary world . . . "

General Patton did not direct all his talks to the fighting man. Many men were required to keep the man on the front line fighting, and Patton never forgot that support troops played an important role in any victory. His attitude towards the non-combatant was expressed in a speech to his men in England in July 1944, just before they were to go into action:

All the real heroes are not storybook combat fighters, either. Every man in the Army plays a vital part. Every little job is essential to the whole scheme. What if every driver suddenly decided that he didn't like the whine of shells and turned yellow and jumped headlong into a ditch? What if every man said: "They won't miss just one man in the thousands." What if every man said that?
Where the hell would we be now? No, thank God; Americans don't say that.
Every man, every department, every unit is important in the vast scheme of things. The ordnance men are needed to supply the guns, the QM to bring up the food and clothes for us. Every man in the mess hall, even the one who heats the water to keep us from getting diarrhea, has a job to do.

After the victory in North Africa Patton called a meeting of his staff officers. They snapped to attention as Patton entered. Telling them to take seats, he then sat on a table and looked into the eyes of the men gathered in the room. In a quiet voice he said:

Gentlemen, you have done well. Mistakes were made. We should not have fallen into ambushes. Some of the troops are too slow. Too many of them want to sit on their arses and stick their heads in holes. But the operation was on the whole successful. I want to say my job and your job is not over. We have thousands of miles of territory to take care of, including the Spanish border. I'm going to do something about that. So you must work hard, every one of you. I won't have my staff sitting around their damn offices, chewing the fat. I have no use for a staff officer who doesn't know which end of an M-1 to put

against his shoulder. Get out in the field and see what is
the real problem. I don't want a lot of officers who get
varicose veins and waffle-tails from sitting in chairs all day.
That is all, gentlemen.

When he spoke to his officers and men his high-pitched,
almost feminine-sounding voice was harsh. As he continued it
grew harsher and more penetrating. He spoke of reality in
violent words: "War is a killing business. You've got to spill
their blood, or they'll spill yours. Rip 'em up the belly, or shoot
'em in the guts." "Hit hard soon." "When you stick your hand
into a bunch of goo that a moment before was your friend's
face . . . " "Carry out your objective even if you have to crawl
there on your goddam hands and knees." "A pint of sweat will
save a gallon of blood." "Americans do not surrender." "If we
go forward with desperation, if we go forward with utmost
speed and fight, these people cannot stand against us."
"Americans love to fight . . . the sting and clash of battle."
"Death must not be feared." "We'll win this war, but we'll only
win it by fighting and showing our guts . . . " "Retreat is as
cowardly as it is fatal." "We don't want yellow cowards in this
army."

There was a reason behind this kind of talk. "The only
quality," General Patton wrote during the war, "which he [the
American soldier] does not have is that of being a fanatic. This
is a big disadvantage to us as we are fighting fanatics."[15] Patton
attempted to create a fanaticism through salty, raw, profane,
and vulgar exhortations. He was trying to build hatred towards
the enemy. He acted on the principle that it was his mission to
kill Germans—quickly, violently, ruthlessly. War was not a nice
thing. It was hell. You didn't approach it in a nice way because a
nice guy doesn't fight as well as the man fired up with hate and
the desire to kill.

The profanity in General Patton's speeches was constant and
startling. "He sounded," said Major General Frank L. Culin,
Commander of the 87th Division, "like a Missouri mule-skinner
trying to coax his charges out of their well-known stubborn-

ness." The eight chaplains of the 6th Armored Division, under the command of Major General R. W. Grow, were so disturbed when they first heard General Patton's profanity that they drew up a petition requesting his relief as Commander of the Third Army. General Grow, who had been with General Patton since the fall of 1940, assured them that General Patton's foul language was forced and that he was a very strong Christian. The chaplains were persuaded to forget the petition.

There was almost unanimous consent among General Patton's World War II Division Commanders that his profane language was a part of his leadership, though not all of them considered it laudable. Major General Orlando Ward, a Commander in the II Corps in the North African campaign, said he was "ashamed" when he heard the "vulgar" language Patton used. And General Patton was aware that his profanity was offensive to some. When asked why he used it he replied, "Goddamit, you can't run an army without profanity." To him it was language the soldiers understood. It might offend a few of them, but it was the group that counted. A soldier's personality in combat is different from the way he acts, talks, and thinks at home. The language appealed to the roughness a man must cultivate if he is to fight a war. Most of them ate it up; it reassured them of their toughness—real or assumed. It was Patton's objective to make his troops as tough as possible. Profanity was a means.

Example

General Patton wrote to his cadet son at West Point, "Be particularly spooney [flashy], so spooney that you not only get by *but attract attention.* Why do you suppose I pay so much attention to being well dressed? Have your clothes well pressed; when I was boning [working to achieve cadet rank] I alway had one uniform that I never sat down in."[16]

Patton was the beau ideal in his military dress. As a general officer he wore a magnificently tailored, form fitting battle jacket with brass buttons. Above the left pocket were four rows of campaign ribbons and decorations and on each shoulder and shirt collar were pinned oversized general's stars. His trousers were pink whipcord riding breeches. He wore high-topped cavalry boots, shined to a mirror-like finish, and spurs. Around his waist was a hand carved leather belt with a gleaming brass buckle. On each side rested a pearl-handled pistol ornamented with the stars of a four-star general. In his hand he carried a riding crop. His helmet was shellacked to a lustrous finish, and it too had stars. One officer in describing General Patton's dress said, "The first time you see him, 'boom!' " There is no doubt that his appearance in uniform attracted attention. His dress seemed to say "I'm Patton—the best damn general in this or any other army."

As Patton traveled over the army forward areas he rode in an open jeep so all his men could see him. Mounted on a platform in the rear of the highly-polished jeep was a 50-calibre machine gun, manned by his aide. The upholstery was bright red, and on the front and back were oversized stars signifying his military rank. As he sped along the road visiting and inspecting, the driver announced Patton's presence by running a loud siren or sounding a multiple tone French horn. The distinctive sound of the horn was recognized as Patton's by all within hearing distance. His jeep, like his military dress, seemed to announce "Here comes General Patton, commander of the best damn army in the world."

When a town was captured, he was among the first to enter even though there was danger of sniper bullets and delayed bombs. After an amphibious invasion, he would leap into the surf before his landing barge was grounded, wading ashore amidst zinging bullets, artillery shells and mortar fire, yelling encouraging remarks to the men. He waded across many a river as his army moved over France and Germany. He even practiced to perfection his facial expressions. Once his sister Nita asked him, "Why do you look so mean and ornery in your pictures?" Patton laughed and replied, "That's my war face."

One cold, rainy afternoon during the war Patton came upon a group of men at work repairing a tank which had been hit by enemy fire. The tank, bacause of the heavy movement of traffic forward towards the line of battle, had pulled about ten yards off the road. Seeing this, Patton ordered his driver to stop. He jumped out of his jeep, went over to the disabled tank and crawled underneath it. The two mechanics, busy working on the necessary repairs, were awe-struck to see the shiny silver stars of a general in the mud. Patton, according to the assistant division commander whose area he was touring at the time, remained under the tank for twenty-five minutes. When he returned to his jeep, he was covered with mud and grease. His aide asked, "Sir, what was wrong?" Patton replied, "I don't know, but I am sure that the word will spread throughout the division that I was on my belly in the mud repairing the tank."[17]

Sometimes the effectiveness of Patton's showmanship was based on simplicity. In Berlin, just after the war was over, Patton and Marshal Zhukov were representing their respective countries at the dedication of a Russian war memorial. Zhukov's uniform blouse was completely covered with medals on both sides. By contrast, General Patton wore only a few campaign ribbons. An observer of the ceremony commented that "Patton looking so neat and trim was more lethal than even the big Russian tanks."[18]

Patton's showmanship as a general was not new to him or to colleagues in the military leadership rank. As a cavalryman in the twenties, General Patton was known as "Horse George" because of his antics in polo and riding. One friend said of his junior officer relationships with Patton, "We always seemed to be charging." When Patton took command of the 2nd Armored Division he designed a special green uniform for tank personnel, which earned him the nickname of "Green Hornet" and "Flash Gordon". Others found such names as Buck Rogers, Man from Mars, and Iron Pants fitting for his personality. In one of his speeches he told the men in his command that it took only two things to win a war—blood and guts. This earned him another name as Army Commander in World War II, "Old Blood and Guts." To him such names were indicative of successful show-manship, of the notoriety that he considered vital to the leadership of an army. With a command of almost 500,000 men Patton necessarily had to exert his leadership from a distance, and flamboyance helped to spread the image he wanted his men to see.

Major General Reinhart, commander of the 65th Infantry Division, wrote of his action under Patton in Germany that the advance "was extremely rapid and was in the nature of a pursuit. Our flanks were seldom secure and we were threatened by envelopments ... So much so that my three infantry regimental commanders once in a group protested informally to me that they did not like our situation. 'We have been riding all the way up here with our shirt tails out' [meaning their exposed flanks], was the way they expressed it." General Reinhart asked them if they did not believe that, if worse came to worst and they were surrounded, "Georgie" would be on the way to pull them out. "This idea," said General Reinhart, "seemed to satisfy them completely and I never heard another word about it from any of them."[19] These officers had never met Patton, but they knew his reputation. Loud and colorful, even from a distance, he was able to create a personal leadership.

General Eisenhower noted that Patton's showmanship "was a shell that was worn constantly and carefully." Everything Patton did had a purpose. He believed that a leader, in order to make himself known in the lower echelons, should exhibit an individualism calculated to cause men to talk about him. His soldiers knew him as a personality and thought of him as one of themselves, not a "rank" at a remote desk. Having created the image, he assiduously preserved it. He told Major General Robert C. Macon in North Africa in 1943, "During training I wore two pearl handled revolvers. They called me 'Two Gun Patton'. Well, when I came ashore here, I was not going to let them down. I wore the damn two guns."[20]

Those who were close to Patton saw that he was an actor. He could turn his showmanship on or off as the situation required. For the dedication of a cemetery, for a speech of praise to his officers and men, or for biting criticism of a unit which performed poorly, he had different but appropriate acts. He was not, however, insincere. Nor did his showmanship seem awkward; though admittedly a costume, it was a tailored and well-fitted one.

Training and Discipline

The most challenging job that faced Patton and other American military leaders in 1941 was the changing of ordinary, peaceful civilians into disciplined, bellicose fighting men. This transition Patton accomplished by training—training with the objectives of instilling discipline and creating a killer instinct. This had to be done at the expense of their bodies, minds, and souls, to the point where they could, if necessary, fight like automatic machines in spite of physical and mental exhaustion. "All through your Army career," Patton said in a speech, "you men have bitched about this chicken drilling. That drilling is all for one reason, instant obedience to orders. It creates instant alertness. I don't give a damn for a man who is not always on his toes. A man to continue breathing must be alert at all times."

Patton insisted that the training conditions of the men simulate the conditions the troops would face in actual combat. To prepare his men for fighting in the African desert he took them to a tract of scorched and lifeless American desert which ran from the Colorado River westward to Indio, California. The temperature during the day averaged 120°. Inside the tanks it averaged 145°. The men were limited to a single canteen of water per day. In this inferno the troops marched, maneuvered the tanks, fired their guns, dug trenches, laid mines, and built fortifications. Patton drove them hard and the men grumbled. It would take combat to prove to them the value of this type of training. At the end of the day, when everyone was hot, tired, and hungry, Patton made the officers run a mile while he himself would run a mile and a quarter. No matter how hard the men were driven, Patton drove himself harder—and he made sure the men knew it.

An experience in World War I taught Patton the value of training. While leading a group of men against a German position a burst of machine gun bullets hit him in the thigh. Still in the open he fell to the ground. A sergeant who was close behind dragged him into a shell hole. Patton was bleeding profusely and in great pain; but, in spite of this, he continued to lead his men by writing instructions which he sent out to his officers. Patton said of this experience, "I had no memory of issuing those orders. I was only partly conscious at the time, but I reacted automatically to years of training."[21] This was the automatic reaction he wanted his officers and men to display during World War II. It could only be developed through training.

An intrinsic element of military training is discipline—discipline, according to Patton, "so ingrained that it is stronger than the excitement of battle or the fear of death." Discipline, as he understood it, was based on pride in the profession of arms, on meticulous attention to detail, and on mutual respect and confidence.

"There is only one kind of discipline," said General Patton in the instructions he issued to his commanders, ". . . PERFECT DISCIPLINE. If you do not enforce and maintain discipline, you are potential murderers." Why was he so insistant upon discipline? It was essential to the high morale of the men, and hence to their maximum fighting potential. When Patton took over in North Africa, after the defeat of the Americans at the Kasserine Pass, the men were unshaven and dirty, they needed haircuts, their shoes and boots were crusted with mud, they wore all types of non-regulation uniform combinations, they failed to salute and say "sir" to officers. Why?—because they just didn't care. They didn't care about themselves, about fighting, or about their country. They would just as soon forget the whole war. This was the attitude Patton was determined to eradicate by instilling unquestioning discipline.

As already indicated, Patton's personal dress was part of his showmanship. His requirements for the dress of his men were no less stringent. One of the favorite stories told about General Patton during World War II pertained to his high standards for a soldier's apperance. A young lieutenant and several enlisted men, so the tale went, had climbed up a high rock ledge to act as observers in directing our artillery onto German positions. Gaining the position with daring and skill, the men were doing a superb job in assisting accurate fire. The lieutenant was aware that General Patton had observed his outstanding performance. He saw General Patton dispatch an aide in his direction, obviously to deliver a message. Expecting a compliment for his brave deed, when the runner arrived the lieutenant asked him "What is the General's message?" To his surprise the reply was, "The General says for you to put your leggings on."

This story was meant to be funny, but Patton did not consider it so. One of his favorite mottos was, "Sloppy soldiers don't win battles." Both in and out of combat he issued the order that helmets and neckties would be worn at all times. Leggings and side arms were to be worn according to regulation. All men who were old enough to shave would do so once a day.

When Patton went into North Africa he was commander of the I Armored Corps. After the initial invasion this Corps, composed of two divisions, was given the mission of staying put in order to discourage Franco from entering into the conflict by closing the Straits of Gibraltar. But when Spain refused to get involved Patton became bored and restless. The II Corps, which was battling the Germans deep inside North Africa, was doing very badly in combat and to give them a shot in the arm General Eisenhower gave command of the Corps to Patton. It was Patton's assignment to get the troops of II Corps up to a "fighting pitch".

"By the third day after his arrival, the II Corps staff was fighting mad—but at Patton, not at the Germans," wrote General Omar Bradley.

For George had set out deliberately to shock II Corps into a realization that the easy-going days were ended. Rather than wait for the effect of this change in command to filter down to the divisions, Patton sought a device that would instantly bring it home to every GI in the corps. He found what he was looking for in uniform regulations.

After several months in combat, American front-line troops had affected the British soldier's casual disregard for conventional field dress. While not under fire, an increasing number removed their heavy helmets and wore only the OD beanie that had been issued for wear under the helmet. To Patton this beanie had become the symbol of slovenly discipline within II Corps. He set out to banish the beanie and make it the first of his corps reforms.

The blow fell with an order that prescribed the wearing of helmets, leggings, and neckties at all times in the corps sector. Rear-echelon units were not exempted from the wearing of helmets and front-line companies were not to be spared the wearing of neckties while in combat. To enforce the regulation Patton established a uniform system of fines that ran as high as $50 for officers, $25 for enlisted men. "When you hit their pocketbooks," George used to say, "you get a quick response."[2 2]

Patton, to emphasize that he meant business, would personally go out on occasion and "round up a handful of offenders." How did Patton imprint his personality and leadership upon this command? "Each time a soldier knotted his necktie," said General Bradley, "threaded his leggings, and buckled on his heavy steel helmet, he was forcibly reminded that Patton had come to command the II Corps, that the pre-Kasserine days had ended, and that a tough new era had begun."[2 3] He made no exceptions to the rule on helmets and neckties. Ordnance asked General Patton if it applied to mechanics when they were working on their trucks. He answered "You're goddam right— they're soldiers, aren't they." It even applied to nurses as they worked in the hospital tents. Everyone knew Patton was there. No one doubted who was boss.

His next command after North Africa was Sicily, where he used the same technique of discipline of dress. While the soldiers in Montgomery's Eighth Army wore light desert uniforms, the American soldiers wore thick regulation shirts and pants even though the days were extremely hot. In these hot clothes the men sweated and as they did they thought of Patton. There was no love for him then; but as their fighting ability improved, they started to understand that there was a purpose in his discipline, that men lived when they followed his stringent rules. They began to appreciate that he had their interests at heart and that uniform regulations were not just arbitrary cussedness. Patton wasn't looking for popularity. He wanted American victories with minimum loss of American lives; and, as his men realized this, they grew to respect him and later to love him.

One of the most controversial points in uniform regulations was whether or not an officer should wear his insignia in combat. Some officers did not do so, believing it made them prime targets for snipers and any other form of fire and reasoning that a dead military leader could have little impact on the effectiveness of his troops. But, whenever Patton took command of an outfit, he immediately ordered all officers to paint their rank insignia on the front of their helmets; this usually generated a wave of protests. The lieutenants called their bars "aiming stakes" for enemy snipers; senior officers claimed that if they were killed or wounded they would be of no use to the allied cause.

One senior colonel, after Patton took over the II Corps in North Africa, protested the order. He maintained that to paint the eagle on his helmet would be tantamount to suicide. He told Patton, "I am up on the battle line frequently; and if I am killed, I am of no further use to you or to my unit."[24] Patton at that time wore the rank of a three-star general on his helmet, on each shoulder, on both collars, and on his pistols. Dressed in this attire, he led the colonel to his jeep and drove to the front lines. As his jeep traveled along and the men recognized Patton, they snapped to attention and saluted. Men stopped their work and cheered him as he drove by. At the front, bullets and shells were hitting all around Patton's jeep. As he pointed to some soldiers he explained to the colonel his reasoning: "Those men are looking to you for leadership. But without the insignia of your rank, you are nothing to them. Or to me. A leader should be up ahead leading, even if he gets killed. And his men have to know he is their leader. Put your insignia on."[25]

In his uniform requirements, as in most all other things, Patton knew when to forget the rule book. During the winter of 1944-1945 the cold weather in Europe was particularly severe and American soldiers used their ingenuity in order to keep warm, but in the process their uniform appearance became sloppy. As Patton toured and inspected his Army he commented, "I noticed that the Army was going to hell on uniform. During the extremely cold weather it had been permissible, and even necessary, to permit certain variations . . ." It was the only practical thing to do, but he added later that ". . . with the approach of summer I got out another uniform order."[26]

Patton wrote in his diary: "There has been, and is now, a great deal of talk about discipline, but few people, in or out of the Army know what it is, or why it is necessary." Patton knew what discipline was and why it was necessary.

When a man enters the Army, he leaves home, usually for the first time, and also he leaves behind him the inhibitions resulting from his respect for the opinion of his parents and his friends; which inhibitions, unknown to himself, have largely guided his existence. When he joins a unit and lacks this corrective influence, he is apt to slip in morals, in neatness, and in energy. Administrative discipline must replace the absent inhibitions.

All human beings have an innate resistance to obedience. Discipline removes this resistance and by constant repetition, makes obedience habitual and subconscious . . . No sane man is unafraid in battle, but discipline produces in him a form of vicarious courage which, with his manhood, makes for victory. Self-respect grows directly from discipline. The Army saying, "Who ever saw a dirty soldier with a medal?" is largely true.[27]

He would often tell this story to illustrate his philosophy on discipline:

Æons and æons ago a small band of natural fighters
arose in their might and beat all the timid, primitive men
into submission. At last, however, because there were more
of them, the timid men organized into armies and beat the
fighters. The fighters in turn had to figure out a way to
regain prestige. Unfortunately there were not enough of
them to make up a great army, so they resorted to hiring
soldiers. This, however, did not work either. The mercenaries ran away. At length they hit on the solution. They
simply beat the heads of the deserters together until their
brains fell on the ground. Then the other mercenaries
obeyed them and defeated the timid men. The fighters had
learned the art of discipline.

In a radio broadcast from Rabat, North Africa in 1943,
Patton even more explicitly stated his belief:

Of all the things West Point gives us, nothing is so
important as the training we get in discipline, because
discipline demands and produces alertness, instant obedience, and self-confidence. At the terrific tempo of mechanized war lackadaisical men, lacking in self-confidence and
slow to obey, are lost. And we, who lead in battle and fail
to demand and secure the type of discipline we learned at
West Point, are both murderers and suicides.

Personal Leadership

On the morning of November 9, 1942, General Patton was
making an inspection trip of the beach at Fedhola, North
Africa, to observe the unloading of supplies for his Army. The
beach was under a constant strafing attack from French aviators. Boats were landing with men and supplies but were not
being pushed off. Every time an aircraft came in to strafe the
men would run for cover, delaying the unloading. Only fifteen

hundred yards inland a major battle was going on, and the
ammunition and other supplies these boats were carrying were
badly needed. After observing the situation for several minutes,
General Patton jumped out of his jeep and began working with
the men. "By remaining on the beach," he said, "and personally
helping to push off boats and by not taking shelter when the
enemy planes flew over, I believe I had considerable influence in
quieting the nerves of the troops and on making the initial
landing a success. I stayed on that beach for nearly eighteen
hours and was wet all over all of that time. People say that army
commanders should not indulge in such practices. *My theory is
that an army commander does what is necessary to accomplish
his mission*, and that nearly eighty per cent of his mission is to
arouse morale in his men."[28] It was this type of leadership that
drove men beyond the limit of whatever capabilities they
thought they had. It was this type of leadership that resulted in
Patton's stamping his drive and personality upon his men.

The number one instruction General Patton issued to his
commanders and officers was: "Each, in his appropriate sphere,
will lead in person." Patton himself led in person. He was
always all over the battle area. Some army commanders
operated on the theory that juniors should come to visit them.
Patton did not concur. "The more senior the officer," he would
say, "the more time he has. Therefore, the senior should go
forward to visit the junior rather than call the junior back to see
him. The exception to this is when it is necessary to collect
several commanders for the formulation of a coordinated plan.
In that case, the juniors should report to the superior headquarters."[29] It was Patton's thesis that "the days of running
your unit by telephone or a comfortable dugout are over. From
now on, you have to run it from a tank, motorcycle or jeep—
you have to stay up with your men, and never ask them to do
anything you wouldn't do yourself."[30] He utilized a unique
visual aid to illustrate his concept of leadership. Placing a piece
of wet spaghetti on a table, he poked his finger into the middle
of it and pulled it forward, saying "That is leadership. You can't
move that line forward by pushing on its ends. It will just

buckle in the middle. So will a line of troops, unless they are led."

General Patton was particularly emphatic that his commanders practice personal leadership. Every division commander in Patton's Army agreed with one who remarked, "I have always been glad that when Patton visited my outfit he never caught me hanging around the Command Post." One commanding officer, when asked if he was afraid to be caught at his Command Post when Patton visited, replied, "No, but I was sure as hell scared to be found anywhere but with the troops when we were involved in active fighting."

In making visits to the front lines to see what was going on, Patton was constantly exposing himself to the danger of being wounded or killed; but he considered this a necessary risk. It was his belief that danger only enhanced the value of the visit. He emphasized this in one of his World War II letters when he wrote: "In any of these fights, a general officer who does his duty has got to expose himself. Otherwise, he cannot look himself in the face and order men to do things that he is afraid to do himself. I am sure that whatever success I have had has resulted from my adherence to this belief, and if you will study history, you will find that with the exception of the war of 1870 and the one of 1914-1918, the successful generals have always obeyed this rule and have in a large measure survived."[31] He commented on one of the occasions when he purposely exposed himself to fire that "It was purely a motion on my part to show the soldiers that generals could get shot at."[32]

Patton's constant visits to the front lines were a source of encouragement and inspiration to the men. One observer of Patton during World War II wrote of his visits to the troops:

When they recognized the stern and lonely figure sitting in the back of the three-starred jeep, the first echelons raised a shout that echoed across the muddy field and rolled on down the line. The sight of their general sent a wave of confidence surging through the whole division, and as his jeep passed the tanks and half-tracks, the mobile guns and truckloads of soldiers, their wild cheering was for victory already won because they trusted him.[33]

The same reporter wrote that several years after the war one of the soldiers in Patton's Third Army said to Mrs. Patton, "I knowed your husband well. We was on a truck that had gone into the ditch, when his jeep came up with him standing in the back screaming, 'Get out of that, you blank-blank sons of bitches, and heave her out!'

"We tumbled out fast and began to push. The next thing, I saw that the man pushing alongside of me was the General himself.

"Yes, ma'am, I knowed him well!"[34]

Several division commanders in Third Army commented that Patton's visits were sometimes too inspiring. When Patton visited the 76th Infantry Division according to the commander, Major General W. R. Schmidt, "My division came to a standstill. The men stopped fighting the Germans, and some of them were jumping out of their foxholes yelling 'Patton,' 'Patton,' 'Patton is here.' I tried to calm them down and cautioned them that they were exposing themselves to danger. They didn't care. It was not until Patton had gone that order was restored."

There were times when Third Army moved so fast that Patton's visiting was the only means of central communication. When his Army was flowing through the Brittany peninsula he was out of contact with three of his divisions for several days because their advance was too rapid for the telephone wiremen to keep pace. Nevertheless, Patton ordered his men to keep driving, no matter what resistance they encountered or where they ended up. He was confident that he had the situation under control.

In a military unit in time of war there is often great resentment between the fighting men and the staff of a headquarters, based upon the supposedly soft, safe job of the staff members compared to the men in battle. There was no such resentment in General Patton's Army. It was avoided by his requirement that each staff section send at least one officer to visit a front line division or small unit every day to learn their problems and furnish assistance.

General Patton recognized that personal leadership could be overdone. "I find," he wrote, "that people get used to you if they see too much of you."[35] He had an extensive front to cover and was careful to avoid being seen too often by any single unit. He maintained a careful balance to prevent over-exposure and an accompanying decreased interest and impact.

Patton's objective in visiting so often was twofold. First, it was one of the means by which he knew what was going on—it gave him a "feel" for the situation. Secondly, as noted, it served as an inspiration to his men and provided an example to other officers. When III Corps Headquarters was formed he said to its officers at a briefing, just before they became active in combat: "Don't become desk-bound. Get up in the lines and see what's going on. Those are your men fighting up there and you can't know what the hell they're up against unless you go up and see it with your own eyes. That's what we do in this Headquarters [i.e. Army] and that's what I require every other Headquarters in my command to do." Though Patton was a frequent visitor at the Corps and Division Headquarters of the Third Army he did not interfere with their operation. He believed you should "never tell people *how* to do things. Tell them *what* to do and they will surprise you with their ingenuity."[36]

Nor did he surround himself with "yes" men. His commanders were not afraid to speak up to him. Major General Leroy H. Watson described how he worked up training problems which "Patton checked with me and in each case I had to explain why I did this or that. He never ordered me to change anything, but often he gave me his views—sometimes I used them and sometimes I didn't."[37]

The Soldier's Welfare

Within the military service in World War II there were measures for the punishment of the undisciplined soldier who refused to carry out orders. He was jailed, fined, courtmartialed, or in a flagrant case, shot. There were appropriate measures for the men who failed to perform in the manner expected —stagnation or reduction in rank, or return to innocuous stateside duty. These methods of punishment served to create a fear within soldiers that provided an incentive to perform their duty. It was seldom, however, necessary for General Patton to use fear; he found that a more effective way to get results was to look out for the welfare of the men in his army. Patton said:

> Officers are responsible not only for the conduct of their men in battle, but also for their health and content- ment when not fighting. An officer must be the last man to take shelter from fire, and the first to move forward. He must be the last man to look after his own comfort at the close of a march. The officer must constantly interest himself in the welfare of his men and their rations. He should know his men so well that any sign of sickness or nervous strain will be apparent to him. He must look after his men's feet and see that they have properly fitting shoes in good condition; that their socks fit, for loose or tight socks make sore feet. He must anticipate change of weather and see that proper clothing and footgear are asked for and obtained.

It was a basic hypothesis of Patton's leadership that a well cared-for soldier made the best fighting man, and he spent considerable time inculcating this principle in his juniors. He would often say that knowing how to take care of their men was "more important for young officers to know than military tactics." He told his commanders to never spare ammunition because "it is much better to waste ammunition than lives. It takes at least eighteen years to produce a soldier, and only a few months to produce ammunition."[38]

To the officers of III Corps Headquarters he emphasized: "You must make your men take care of themselves. Men in the lines, men who are tired and hungry are apt to get careless about that ..." He then told a story to indicate the ingenuity required: "I was up in the lines the other day and a regimental commander told me he had no way to dry his men's clothes. When he told me that, we were in a room that was so god-damned hot it would have dried all the clothes in his regiment in a couple of hours. I pointed that out to him and also the fact that *there always is a way to do things if you've got the brains and guts to want to do them.*"[3][9]

One of the greatest causes of non-battle casualties was trench-foot. Medical instructions were issued on how to avoid it, the key element being to change into dry socks frequently and to massage the feet to keep up circulation. Patton watched the medical reports closely; and if a unit had too many cases of trench-foot, the commander was relieved.

It was important to conserve a soldier's strength. Patton followed a technique of not letting a man walk in combat if he had a chance to ride. To do this he utilized every available vehicle—tanks, armored cars, gun carriages, AA guns, and trucks. He was motivated in part by consideration for his men but more importantly by the obvious fact that a soldier tired from marching has less strength for fighting. To generals who thought an army looked unsightly "traveling in such a manner," Patton answered, "While the sight of a division moving under this system is abhorrent to the best instincts of a Frederickian soldier, it results in rapid advance with minimum fatigue."[40] His primary concern was with results.

In drawing up his war plans Patton considered the human element upon which success depended. He believed the courage of his forces was a factor to be considered in deciding where to place them in battle. Soldiers experienced in combat have more courage than green troops. If the experienced soldiers were emotionally keyed to a high pitch of hatred, to the point of fanaticism, they were unbeatable. The second human factor he considered was the endurance level of the soldier. If a fighting man was tired, hungry, and cold, he was generally a poor soldier.

When Patton's Third Army captured German stores of food, military clothing and liquor, the combat troops shared in the booty. In many armies the front line soldiers were so busy fighting they didn't have the opportunity to share the wealth; instead the rear echelons grabbed it up. This did not happen in Patton's Army. When enemy stores were captured he had the items distributed to the troops. At Reims in August 1944, a store of liquor was captured. He held it under guard for three months; and on Thanksgiving Day, every soldier in his Army received either seven bottles of wine or cognac, depending upon his preference. Between Verdun and Metz, Third Army captured 3,000,000 pounds of beef at a German meat-refrigerating depot. Again the soldiers benefited from this good fortune and enjoyed steaks, roasts, and stew in place of K-rations.[41]

There are many other instances of the consideration that was an intrinsic part of Patton's leadership and his success. Some commanders were indifferent to keeping soldiers waiting for inspections, or on occasion might even not bother to inspect after the troops had spent many hours in preparation. Patton followed a policy of always thoroughly inspecting a unit which had been alerted to expect it, and he was always on time. "When soldiers have gone to the trouble of getting ready to be inspected, they deserve the compliment of a visit."[42] If they deserved credit, it was given publicly. If they were bad, he told the commander in private. When performing the inspection, he always made a point to speak to all enlisted men who had won decorations or who had been wounded; and in doing so, he asked them how they earned the decoration or received the wound.

He at times reached the point of "pampering" the troops, although they never knew it. He instructed his staff officers that "the chief purpose of the General and Special Staffs is to insure that the troops get what they want in time. In battle, troops get temperamental, and ask for things which they really do not need. However, where humanly possible, their requests, no matter how unreasonable, should be answered."[43] Sometimes staffs get the idea that the soldiers exist for them rather than the other way around. There was never any doubt that in Patton's hierarchy the troops came first.

And he realized that it was important to let them know they had done well. He often told his commanders and staff officers that "All a soldier desires to drive him forward is recognition and appreciation of his work." In one of his war letters to a friend Patton described a tank fight in which a single U.S. medium tank attacked and destroyed five German Panther tanks. It was, Patton said, a phenomenal accomplishment by the American tank crew. "The tank," he wrote, "was hit several times and every man in it was killed except the Lieutenant, who was wounded. He was immediately decorated by me. It was one of the finest feats of arms I have ever seen."[44]

Decorating the Lieutenant on the spot was not an unusual thing for Patton to do. He was always quick to recognize outstanding action, either the bravery of a soldier in combat or the competence of a staff officer. He would award a medal and have an aide take notes on the event he observed at the front that justified the award of a decoration. At the end of the day when he returned to his headquarters these notes were used to provide the facts for the citation for the decoration he had already awarded. He considered awards and decorations very important in building and maintaining morale; and in the Third Army, he required that they be handled directly and as rapidly as possible by G-1 without using the usual time-consuming administrative channels. In the case of seriously wounded men, he frequently decorated them on the spot in the battlefield or in a hospital bed, with decorations carried by an aide who brought in the necessary facts to back up the citation. In fact, Patton instructed all of his commanders during World War II to "have a definite officer on your staff educated in writing citations and see that they get through."[45] Patton was a believer in the Napoleonic adage, "If given enough medals, I could conquer the world."

He was even this way with his division commanders. General Oliver remembered an incident that occurred when his division was leading the advance toward Argentan. He was returning in his jeep from the front, passing tanks and other vehicles along the dusty road on a hot August day. Sweaty and dirty from his travels, he entered the orchard where his CP was set up and found General Patton there. Patton was greatly pleased at the progress the 5th Armored Division was making. He went up to General Oliver and slapped him on the back and said, "Bug, you are the dirtiest damn general I ever saw, but one of the best. I'm awarding you a Bronze Star. I haven't one with me, but you get one pinned on as soon as you can. I want your men to see it. The order awarding it will be issued before the day is over."[46]

He was careful, however, to insure that a brave man did not push his luck too far. One of Patton's most considerate acts was an order that men who received the Medal of Honor or Distinguished Service Cross were not to go to the front anymore—"It has been my unfortunate observation that whenever [he receives one of these awards] . . . he usually attempts to outdo himself and gets killed . . ."[47]

Another way in which he insured recognition for his men was through press releases. He directed that war correspondents attached to his Army be given the details of all operations for immediate publication, including the name of every division, unit, and commander taking part in the action. This was a very radical policy at the time. Most of the allied armies held up such details for two months, fearing the information would be of assistance to the enemy. Patton's answer to this thinking was, "The enemy knows what units are opposing him within twelve hours after most battles, so what good does a policy of secrecy do?"[48] He thought immediate publication of the news would boost the morale of his men and, as a result, improve their fighting ability.

It also helped to develop the prestige which Patton and Third Army had back home in the States. The impact of this policy was far reaching. "I could tell you many stories about General Patton," wrote Major General Norman D. Cota, Commander of the 28th Infantry Division of the Third Army, "however, there is one story that left a tremendous impression on me. At the close of the war in Europe the Division I commanded was ordered to Camp Shelby, Mississippi, to prepare for a combat mission in the Pacific Theater. Mrs. Cota and I took a weekend and went to New Orleans. We had a room at one of the hotels. Our chambermaid was an elderly lady. She asked me where I had been during the last year. I told her. She stood erect, looked me straight in the eye and said, 'My grandson helped General Patton win the war in Europe!' "

When it came to recognition for excellent performance, Patton believed that a general officer should "assume the responsibility for failure, whether he deserves it or not;" and if things went well, he should "invariably give the credit for success to others, whether they deserve it or not."[49] His reasoning was that a general who took all the blame and gave everyone else all the credit would get more out of his subordinates. This was the policy Patton practiced.

Relations with Subordinates

Admiral Ernest J. King, Chief of Naval Operations during World War II, remarked to Patton at a dinner party in 1943, "I trust that when you appear, the lions continue to tremble in their dens." This was an accurate depiction of Patton the flaming warrior; but Patton the man and Patton the image were two different persons. "I was his Chief of Staff," said General John M. Devine, "when he first made Corps Commander . . . I had not known him before except by reputation, and I was sure we would never get along. I soon discovered that the man and his reputation were miles apart. I developed a great admiration, respect, and affection for him."[50]

This change in attitude toward General Patton was not unusual. Contrary to popular belief, he was not at all harsh with commanders unless they made an uncalled-for error. In Normandy, in late July of 1944, the 5th Armored Division under Major General Lunsford E. Oliver, after crossing the channel, was assembled and ready for action. They soon received orders from Third Army Headquarters to proceed by a certain road through the St. Lo breakthrough to an area between the Sees and Selune Rivers. The move was to be made at

night and they were told that the road over which they would
travel would be available for their exclusive use. But it didn't
work out that way. The road was crowded with troops from
other divisions, vehicles of all sorts, and supply convoys. The
5th Armored Division had a very difficult time making progress,
and General Oliver soon lost radio contact with one of his
combat commanders. The situation was serious. General Oliver
said, "I soon received orders to pull my division off the road
and report to General Patton at his command post. I proceeded
to it with difficulty in the darkness and confusion and with
considerable foreboding. I knew our deplorable situation was
not my fault, but I was afraid George would think it was. I
knew that if he thought I had failed, our friendship would not
save me. George finally assembled his staff, corps commanders
and division commanders, and opened the conference. He began
by saying, 'We are in a hell of a mess, and it is my fault. I
wanted to get going and therefore I had my staff issue orders
without taking time to work out necessary schedules, and the
result is this mess. Now we shall just sit tight until the staff can
work out schedules and restore order.' "⁵¹

Patton was not perfect; he was continually learning. His
impetuousness sometimes brought about mistakes. But when *he*
made them, he didn't cut someone else's head off. For an Army
Commander who had just become operational to admit he had
made a bad mistake and to free his commanders of all blame
took moral courage. Patton did not lose his officers' respect for
his mistake. He did win their loyalty by showing his own.

Patton had very little patience with division commanders
who did not follow his orders. On one occasion, he relieved a
division C.O. for going around a town instead of through it; it
was vital that that particular town be captured. For violating his
orders the division commander was ousted, setting an example
that was not lost on other commanders who might consider
violating a Patton order.

As noted previously, General Patton believed in telling his
commanders what to do, but not how to do it. Sometimes he
would forget, however, and start telling a man what to do *and*

how to do it. General Macon remembered, "Before one attack General Patton said to me, 'I have not been able to give you any medium tanks, but you go ahead and use your light tanks as you would the medium. If you lose some it will be all right.' Then he started to give some additional advice but stopped and departed after the remark, 'Oh Hell! You know more about how to do it than I do. I made you a general, prove I am right.' "⁵² The commanders in Patton's outfit had great freedom in developing ideas and exercising their ingenuity in training units for combat. They could try (and did) about anything in the line of training, as long as they worked hard at it and got good results. As one division commander put it, "He was always reasonable in his attitude as long as you delivered the goods, but God help you if you didn't." Almost every division commander in Third Army commented in one way or another that "Patton knew what he wanted and recognized it when he got it." He would sometimes assign tasks to his commanders that seemed impossible, realizing that they had enough intelligence to try for the objective to the best of their ability.

Certainly Patton knew how to express gratitude. On the morning of May 8, 1945, his staff assembled, at the usual time of 0800, in a German barracks for its regularly scheduled briefing. General Patton, followed by his two aides and his pugnacious looking English bull terrier dog, Willie, walked briskly to his chair and sat down. The war in Europe was all but over. The briefers for the various sections—intelligence, logistics, supply and public relations, covered their material quickly. When they were finished the staff waited for Chief of Staff General Hobart Gay to rise and make the announcements for the day before the final adjournment of the meeting. To the surprise of the staff, General Patton arose, walked over to the situation map and looked at it for several minutes. He turned towards his men and looked at them. Then he said quietly:

This is the last of our operational briefings in Europe. I trust we shall have the privilege of renewing them in another and more distant theatre of war. One thing I can promise you: if I go, you go.

He went on to discuss the record of Third Army, emphasizing to the men of his staff,

> You made history in a manner that is glory to you and to our country. Probably no Army Commander in history ever did less work. You did it all, and the imperishable record of Third Army is due largely to your unstinting and outstanding efforts. I thank you from the depths of my heart for all you have done.

Then he stood silently for several minutes looking at his staff. He suddenly broke the silence by snapping his fingers, waking Willie who was curled up asleep under a chair during this historic moment. The staff officers jumped to attention. Patton marched off the platform and down the steps, while his dog scampered along after him.

He later went on to personally thank each member of his staff for what he had done. "No one man," he wrote after the war, "can conduct an army . . . success of any army depends on the harmonious working of its staff and the magnificent fighting ability of the combat officers and enlisted men. Without this teamwork, war cannot be successfully fought."[5][3] Be it ever so small a role he gave credit to everyone: his staff, his officers, to the soldiers, to the air corps protecting his unguarded flanks, to the navy putting his men and material ashore, to wire stringers, cooks, dish washers, truckdrivers, and everyone else who was part of the team. No one was unimportant.

In his first briefing to Third Army Staff he had informed them, "I've won in battle and I'm going to win again. I won because I had good commanders and staff officers." The officers on his staff never had any doubt about what was required of them. "I don't fight for fun," he said, "and I won't tolerate anyone on my staff who does. You are here to fight . . . you can't afford to be a goddamned fool, because in battle fools

mean dead men. It is inevitable for men to be killed and
wounded in battle. But," he went on to say, "there is no reason
why such losses should be increased because of the incompetence and carelessness of some stupid son-of-a-bitch. I don't
tolerate such men on my staff."[54]

There was no show or sham on Patton's staff. He was interested in one thing—results. One of his staff officers said of his
Third Army Headquarters, "You had a feeling that Third Army
was going in only one direction—forward." The men worked
night and day when necessary to get a job done. They were on
call 24 hours a day. But when the work was done they relaxed;
they felt no compulsion to look occupied or to take part in
"busy work". They were a quiet, smooth, and efficient staff.

"A number of persons," said staff member Brigadier General
Wallace, "have asked if General Patton was difficult to work
for, always driving you on. He was just the opposite and . . . his
spirit carried through the whole staff." He went on to say that
to be on Patton's staff and remain there "you either knew your
job, or you didn't. If you didn't or if you were the cause of any
friction in the Headquarters, you were quickly and quietly
gotten rid of, 'rolled' as we called it—sent to some other
organization. But if you knew your job you were allowed to
perform it in your own way and were never told how to do a
thing, only requested in a quiet gentlemanly way to do it. The
rest was up to you. Results were all that counted."[55] In
running his staff Patton's axiom was "staff officers of unharmo-
nious disposition, irrespective of their ability, must be removed.
A staff cannot function properly unless it is a united family."[56]

Patton was organized, systematic, and purposeful. He was
briefed every day at 0800 and 1700 with the most up-to-date
information available. These briefings had a twofold objective:
to keep him and the staff informed of plans and operations, and
to knit all of the staff sections together. They were short
briefings, never lasting over 20 minutes. After he was informed
of the latest intelligence, personnel, logistics and air data, he
asked questions or advice of his staff members, outlined that

day's action, and left for the front line area. Upon his return he was briefed on the day's events.

When Eisenhower visited Third Army Headquarters in March 1945, he told them, "I warmly congratulate you, General Patton, and all your officers. Since last summer, when you became operational in Normandy, the Third Army has not made one mistake!"[57] This was a great compliment to both Patton and the staff which had prepared the information used as the basis for Third Army decisions.

Were they a brilliant staff? How should we evaluate Patton's words at the May 8, 1945 briefing—"no Army Commander in history ever did less work. You did it all . . ." Did they really? General Patton's superior during the European campaign had an answer to this question. "Until the Battle of the Bulge," said General Omar Bradley, "I did not share George's enthusiasm for his Third Army staff which, unlike those of both the First and Ninth Armies, lacked outstanding individual performers. Indeed, I had once agreed with the observation of another senior commander who said, 'Patton can get more good work out of a mediocre bunch of staff officers than anyone I ever saw.' "[58] Full recognition, consideration, delegation of responsibility—all of these qualities were part of Patton's success with his staff as well as with his commanders, officers, and men. But even with a large, efficient, and loyal staff to assist him in carrying out his duties of command, all basic decisions, policies and the responsibility for their execution were his. By outside observers he was credited for the success of his army and would have received full blame for its failure. He knew it and so did his staff.

Forward, action at any cost

General Patton believed in movement forward. He did everything possible to get his Army to drive, drive, drive. A town that could not be captured swiftly was bypassed to be strangled to death while his troops pressed after the quarry like hounds baying for a kill. The shorter the action, the fewer the casualties. There would be time for rest after the war was won.

Drive was always in his speeches. On the eve of the Battle of Morocco in 1943, Patton issued the battle orders: "We shall attack and attack until we are exhausted, and then we shall attack again." Aboard almost a thousand ships carrying the U.S. Seventh Army into Sicily under Patton's command, the order of the day was read just before the invasion: "Remember that we as attackers have the initiative. We must retain this tremendous advantage by always attacking rapidly, ruthlessly, viciously, without rest. However tired and hungry you may be, the enemy will be more tired, more hungry. Keep punching." Other orders on other occasions were in the same vein: "In war nothing is impossible, provided you use audacity"; and the most frequently repeated statement of all was Patton's motto (which was also the motto of Napoleon): "Audacious, audacious, audacious, always audacious. Remember that. From here on out, until we win or die in the attempt, we will always be audacious."

You can almost feel the forward surge in Patton's statements urging his men on. He was the epitome of the Clausewitz statement, "Theory leaves it to the military leader, however, to act according to his own courage, according to his spirit of enterprise and his self-confidence. Make your choice, therefore, according to the inner force; but *never forget that no military leader has ever become great without audacity*."[5][9]

Constantly he said to his officers and men, "Attack rapidly, ruthlessly, viciously, and without rest." He told them that their:

fire reduces the effectiveness and volume of the enemy's fire, rapidity of attack shortens the time of exposure. A pint of sweat will save a gallon of blood. Our mortars and artillery are superb weapons when firing. When silent, they are junk.

Infantry must move in order to close with the enemy. It must shoot in order to move. When principle targets were not visible, the fire of all infantry weapons must search the

area probably occupied by the enemy. Use marching fire.
It reduces the accuracy of the enemy's fire, and increases
our confidence. Shoot short. Ricochets make nastier
sounds and wounds. To halt under fire is folly. To halt
under fire and not shoot back is suicide.

Drive was a component of his personal conduct. As Patton
progressed, alleged complaints filtered into Ike's headquarters
indicating, if the reports were true, that he was driving forward
unmercifully. One story related that Patton drew his pistol on a
slovenly American soldier lying in a field without his socks,
leggings or boots. Another told of a cart pulled by a mule which
was blocking a convoy of truck supplies, so he shot the mule
and helped push the cart and dead mule off the road. These
complaints were ignored by Supreme Headquarters.

He even fought with Americans to keep up the momentum of
his Army. In order to drive forward Patton needed more and
more men and materiel. Whenever higher headquarters attempted to take divisions away from him, he raised hell. He
recorded in his diary one day: "I made an unsuccessful attempt
to delay the withdrawal of the 17th Airborne Division. I believe
that a good deal of my success and a great deal of my un-
popularity is due to the fact that I fought every order to take
troops away from me, and frequently succeeded in holding on
to them or in getting others to replace them."[60]

Patton would do almost anything to get additional men if the
attack was going slowly. During one operation, he said he wrote
to General Bradley asking for from one to three additional
divisions because, "I felt very keenly at that time that history
would criticize us for not having been more energetic." He got
approval for one extra division (10th Armored), but for that
operation only. Patton said to himself, "It always makes me
mad to have to beg for opportunities to win battles."[61]

Replacements of men during the push through France and
Germany by Third Army did not keep pace with the casualties,
but Patton refused to let this stop his advance. To overcome the
shortage, he issued a request to the Headquarters units and

Army and Corps troops for combat volunteers. This raised only 5,000 of the 11,000 troops needed; so to obtain the remainder Patton ordered the drafting of men from each non-combat section. Thus men who had been quartermaster troops, clerks, and headquarter troops became front-line combat soldiers. When Patton announced this decision at a staff meeting he explained why he was doing it: "This Army is faced with the unhappy task of making its own grease. There are no replacements and it is clear now there won't be any for some time. We have licked shortages of gas and ammunition and other handicaps in the past. We are not going to be stopped now by lack of replacements."

To solve the gasoline shortage Patton initiated one of the most ingenious operations of the war—the Red Ball Express. This was a fleet of trucks which formed a convoy hundreds of miles long. Carrying only gasoline, they drove around the clock the 1000-mile round trip from the front lines to the gas dumps. One war correspondent who observed this operation wrote: "I well remember passing these supply trains on the Verdun-Paris highway in September 1944, and being struck with the almost nightmarish quality of the task they were trying to perform. In the cab of each truck sat the driver, usually a negro, with a mate beside him. They drove like maniacs, hitting the bumps at full speed, rounding curves on the wrong side of the road, roaring through towns; and always the air was filled with the screeching of their brakes and gears . . . these truck drivers usually ate on the road and slept in their cabs. They were an epic fraternity . . ."[62] It was a typical Patton operation—fast, reckless, but efficient.

When on occasions his ingenuity failed he ordered his division commanders to fight "until lack of supplies forces you to stop," and when this happened he told his men to dig in. In a directive to General Eddy when he was running out of ammunition, one again sees his overwhelming desire to move forward: "Eddy called me to state that his allowance of shells for the eighteenth was nine thousand, but I told him to go ahead and shoot twenty thousand, because I could see no reason for hoarding

ammunition. You either use it or you don't. I would lose more
men by shooting nine thousand rounds a day for three days
than I would by shooting twenty thousand in one day—*and
probably not get as far*."[63] Again, his usual concern for the
number of casualties and his fervent desire to advance against
the enemy.

The supply item which finally slowed Patton to a standstill in
Europe was gasoline for his armored vehicles. For a period, it
stopped entirely. He noted that "at first I thought it was a
backhanded way of slowing up the Third Army. I later found
this was not the case, but the delay was due to a change of plan
by the High Command, implemented, in my opinion, by
General Montgomery."[64] Patton said of this turn of events:

> It was my opinion then that this was the momentous
> error of the war. So far as the Third Army was concerned,
> we not only failed to get back gas due us, but got prac-
> tically no more, because, in consonance with the decision
> to move north, in which two corps of the First Army also
> participated, all supplies—both gasoline and ammunition—
> had to be thrown in that direction.[65]

Patton's drive continued, however; he told his commanders "to
continue until the tanks stopped, and then get out and
walk . . ."[66]

Patton then called upon another aspect of American ingenuity for help. He promised three-day passes to the men who
could steal the most gasoline drums—full or empty, American or
enemy. The U.S. divisions of First and Ninth Armies not assigned to Third Army were on occasions stolen blind. Any
shortages which existed in Patton's Army were supplemented in
every possible way; and it was not unethical to get supplies
from other American outfits, even though they were "bor-
rowed" without permission. No questions were asked by the
recipients.

He overlooked nothing to keep his Army going fast. The
selection of his combat headquarters served as a prod to his

staff. When Undersecretary of War Robert Patterson was on an inspection trip in France he was very much surprised to see that Patton's trailer served as his headquarters. He said to Patton, "Well, I can't say much for your housing. Why don't you find yourself a chateau?" Patton replied, "To hell with 'em! Too comfortable. Get in a chateau, and those birds [his staff] never would want to get a move on. When it's like this they're glad to hop along, hoping the next halt will be better. But it *won't*."

In the latter part of the invasion of France, Patton came up with the idea of convoying infantry battalions on tanks to hasten the speed of the advance. He mentioned this to the visiting Undersecretary Patterson. A little puzzled, Patterson asked, "But how in the name of heaven are they going to hang on?"

"That" replied Patton, "is their problem."

In his almost fanatical driving, Patton has been accused of careless planning. This accusation reflects a lack of knowledge of Patton's staff and of the value of his intensive study and preparation for war. Patton did make quick decisions and plans; but speed did not mean, in his case, that quality was sacrificed. His mode of operation was pragmatic:

> If the doings of the Third Army and its General are subject to inquiry by future historians, the two points just mentioned [concerning a quick change in tactical plans] should be a warning. In the space of two days I had evolved two plans, wholly distinct, both of which were equally feasible. The point I am trying to bring out is that one does not plan and then try to make circumstances fit those plans. One tries to make plans fit the circumstances. *I think the difference between success and failure in high command depends upon the ability, or lack of it, to do just that.*[67]

Patton also believed that "a good plan violently executed *now* is better than a perfect plan next week."[68]

Several of Patton's division commanders and a corps commander called him a "careless" planner. Neither Patton nor his staff would agree with this accusation. "There is a great difference," commented Patton, "between the two words haste [implying carelessness] and speed. Haste exists when troops are committed without proper reconnaissance, without the arrangement for proper supporting fire, and before every available man has been brought up. The result of such an attack will be to get the troops into action early, but to complete the action very slowly. Speed is acquired by making the necessary reconnaissance . . . artillery and other tactical support . . . and then launching the attack with a predetermined plan. . . "[69]

The Third Army drove forward so rapidly in Europe that its flanks were often exposed to the enemy. During the advance through France one of Patton's corps commanders, Lieutenant General Wade H. Haislip, became concerned that his corps had thirty miles of open flank threatened by sixty thousand Germans. He brought the matter up with Patton, who thought for a moment and then replied, "I'll tell you what you do, Ham, just ignore them!"[70]

Patton was not recklessly indifferent, however, to the security of his flanks. He was counting upon air support for protection. This was the first war in history in which ground forces relied upon airpower to protect their flanks. Another reason for Patton's suggesting to Haislip that the flanks be ignored was brought out in a conversation between Patton and division commander Major General Manton S. Eddy. Eddy, a veteran of the North African Campaign, was jittery over the XII Corps' long, exposed, south flank. He brought the matter up with Patton, who said to him: "Manton, if I had worried about flanks, we'd all still be sitting in the hedgerows in Normandy. You have an open flank, but it's nothing to worry about. First of all, the enemy is on the run. Second, he has nothing south of you mobile enough to make an attack in strength before our Air can spot it."[71]

Obviously this refusal to permit any let-up of the forward movement was a factor in the remarkable victories of his Army. Patton even questioned whether or not the whole concept of the need for protecting extended flank was valid in modern warfare. He said in a speech to his staff, before Third Army was operational in France:

> There's another thing I want you to remember. Forget this goddamned business of worrying about our flanks. We must guard our flanks, but not to the extent that we don't do anything else. Some goddamned fool once said that flanks must be secured, and since then sons-of-bitches all over the world have been going crazy guarding their flanks. We don't want any of that goddamned crap in the Army. Flanks are something for the enemy to worry about. Not us.[7 2]

Regardless of how thoroughly an action was planned, Patton knew it was inevitable for men to be killed and wounded in battle. In his relentless drive forward he was willing to risk his life and the life of anyone else, because in the long run immeasurably more lives would be saved.

It was common belief among the American battle commanders is Europe in World War II that the British generals, because of consistent defeats early in the war, were "defensive" minded. This made them reluctant to move forward with the optimism of American military leaders who had never known defeat. Some Americans also were of the opinion that British reluctance to aggressively enter into battle until they were so strong that victory was certain was based more on the desire to save their reputation than the lives of their troops.

Patton had an attitude of contempt toward defense. He was forever making comments such as, "Nobody ever successfully defended anything." and "An Army is defeated when it digs in." To prove his point he would refer to the historical examples of the Great Wall of China, Troy, Syracuse, and the Maginot Line. In a letter he wrote during World War II he said, after a discussion of German pillboxes, "The whole thing proves that people who build walls or ditches or pillboxes, or think that the ocean can defend them are gullible fools. No form of defense is worth a damn."[7 3]

Patton so hated the concept of defense that he seldom permitted his commanders to allow their soldiers to dig trenches. To him, it was psychologically bad because a soldier who thought he had to dig in to be safe must have thought the enemy dangerous. Such thoughts were not conducive to maximum performance in the offensive drive forward. There were practical considerations as well: chances of getting killed sleeping on top of the ground were quite remote, and in addition, he wanted the soldiers to conserve their strength and energy for fighting. The efficacy of slit trenches was not worth the energy expended.

One reason for the unbelievable speed with which Third Army moved through enemy-held territory was Patton's refusal to permit his corps and division commanders to retreat. Indeed, he would not even let them stand still. He told his officers before the invasion started for Third Army in Europe, "I don't want to get any messages saying, 'I am holding my position!' We're not holding anything. Let the Hun do that. We are advancing constantly and are not interested in holding anything, except onto the enemy. We're going to hold onto him and kick the hell out of him all the time."[74]

Retreat was out of the question in Patton's code. He wrote to a friend on October 4, 1944, "On the 30th we almost had a bad accident. One of the divisions got hysteria and decided they were beaten and got permission from one of the Corps Commanders to retreat. Fortunately, I found out about it, went up, and had a counterattack, with the result that in about two hours we killed 700 Germans in one place and an undetermined number in the woods." His aggressive leadership paid off, for the next day he said, "I went to see this division and it had completely reversed itself and was full of ferocity and had forgotten all about the day before when it was on the point of retreating."[75]

On July 31, 1944, General Patton was visiting VIII Corps Headquarters. Corps Commander General Troy Middleton reported to Patton that he had obtained his objective, which was the Selune River. Upon finding that he had not crossed the river, Patton pointed out that "throughout history, many campaigns had been lost by stopping on the wrong side of a river," and directed him to go across at once.[76] Middleton said the bridge was out; but while they discussed ways and means of getting across, a message came in that the bridge was usable. Patton directed Middleton to cross it, which he did successfully. Patton's reaction was, "it shows that a little extra push at a critical moment is sometimes useful."[77]

Even when Patton was ordered by higher headquarters to go on the defensive he would define the command to mean "active defense" or "creeping defense" and continue his forward advance at a somewhat slower pace. He was taking a risk and he knew it. He wrote to a friend in February 1945: "We are having a very funny battle right now. I am taking one of the longest chances of my chancey career; in fact, almost disobeying orders in order to attack, my theory being that if I win nobody will say anything, and I am sure I will win . . ."[78]

Patton felt so strongly about being ordered to go on the defensive that he threatened to resign on one occasion. As he described it, "On the tenth, Bradley called up to ask me how soon I could go on the defensive. I told him I was the oldest leader in age and in combat experience in the United States Army in Europe, and that if I had to go on the defensive I would ask to be relieved."[79] Bradley calmed him down by telling him he owed too much to the troops and he would have to stay on. Bradley also looked the other way when Patton practiced his "active defense". Certainly Bradley's leadership and understanding were contributing factors to Patton's success.

There was a philosophy behind Patton's offensive driving methods; "Soldiers fight primarily for two reasons: hero worship for a commanding officer and desire for glory. All good soldiers have it. *Patriotism is not enough.* The desire to do something heroic, which will be remembered by their friends, will drive soldiers forward even to death. *You can defend a position with patriots but you can't take a position with them.* I am not interested in defense. My motto in battle is "GO FORWARD."[80] In other words it required something extra to

stay on the offensive. Patton's leadership supplied that something extra. This driving attitude was also clear in a story that
Patton told about General Eddy.

> "The nineteenth, instead of being the day I hoped it
> would be, was bad. The 35th Division had been pushed off
> a hill northeast of Nancy, so the enemy had observation
> and could fire into the town. The 4th Armored was being
> heavily attacked and the XV Corps had not yet reached
> Luneville. To cheer Eddy up, I told him two stories: first,
> that Grant once said, "In every battle there comes a time
> when both sides consider themselves beaten; then he who
> continues the attack wins," second, what Lee is supposed
> to have said at Chancellorsville, "I was too weak to defend,
> so I attacked." As a result, Eddy retook the hill at once.[81]

Patton would not let his generals think tired; he would not let
them quit; he drove them to the limit and beyond.

Though he drove his men at an inhuman pace, Patton did not
fail to understand human nature. He had an excellent knowledge of the human mind and body, and his insight in this area
was a large factor in his success. He knew that "fatigue produces
pessimism." He realized that when men were extremely tired
they had less confidence in their combat ability. They might
want to quit, but Patton would not let them quit. Often a
division commander would tell Patton that his division was too
tired to launch an attack that night, or the next morning.
Patton would say to him, "All right, who did you recommend
be your replacement." The division commander always re-
considered, did as Patton originally ordered, and found that he
was right—the division was not too tired to perform the assigned
task. Since "of course . . . corps and division commanders suffer
from greater physical fatigue and danger than does an Army
Commander, . . . it is the duty of the Army Commander to
supply the necessary punch when fatigue starts sapping the
energy of the other officers."[82] Patton personally never seemed
to feel any loss of energy. He did appreciate that there was a
limit to how much the troops could be pushed. "Troops can

attack continuously for sixty hours. Frequently much time and
suffering are saved if they will do so. Beyond sixty hours, rather
a waste of time, as the men become too fatigued from lack of
sleep."[8][3]

Fatigue could affect the best of soldiers. When his Army was
advancing on Messina, General Patton ordered an amphibious
operation. General Bradley, commanding the II Corps, and
Major General Lucian Truscott, commanding the 3rd Division,
considered the operation too dangerous to attempt and therefore requested to postpone it. Patton said no and immediately
went to their headquarters. They discussed the matter at length,
but Patton was adamant. He observed as they talked that
General Truscott, a most capable officer, was suffering from
physical fatigue which caused his pessimism about the operation. The conversation closed with Patton saying to Truscott
that he would carry out the operation; if it succeeded Truscott
would get full credit and if it failed, "I will take the blame." He
called General Bradley at Corps and told him the same thing
and that he was returning to his Headquarters since, "If I stayed
around, I would fail to show confidence." Next morning, after a
restless night, Patton was informed by telephone that the attack
was a complete success.[8][4]

George S. Patton, Jr. got his men to give their all for him—to
do just a little bit more than they thought humanly possible. He
did it through his speeches in which he waved the flag, emphasizing that it was a privilege and an honor to fight and die for
one's country. He talked to everyone—cooks and dishwashers as
well as men on the front. No one had an unimportant role in
fighting the war. He inspired in his men an almost fanatical
hatred of the enemy, encouraging them to attack ruthlessly,
viciously, and without rest. He told his men what a wonderful
job they were doing, but that they needed to do better; and in
his speeches, he convinced them that their fame would never
die.

Through his showmanship—his guns, his flashy dress, his jeep,
and other ways of gaining attention—he reached down; and he

became known to the lower echelons, creating an individual impact on hundreds of thousands of soldiers.

Generals have been successful without using showmanship, but they will not be remembered as is General Patton. Generals Alexander Patch, Courtney Hodges, and William Simpson were not showmen. Many have commented that these generals accomplished just as much as Patton. Others contend they did not; that the other American general's armies did not conquer as much territory, they did not kill as many of the enemy, they had more casualties. When you asked a man in First, Sixth, Seventh, or Ninth Army what outfit he was in, he would give you the battalion, regiment, or perhaps the division. It was seldom he could tell you who the Army Commander was. When you asked a soldier in Third Army what outfit he was in he would answer—usually with pride, sometimes with hatred, but never with indifference—"Patton's Third Army."

He changed ordinary, peaceful civilians into bellicose, fighting men through training and discipline. As a result more soldiers came home alive, a fact they soon realized when they entered combat.

Patton was a personal leader; his men saw him everywhere, but never too often. He was on the beaches helping to unload supplies; he was at the front being shot at, visiting his commanders at *their* command posts, helping soldiers push trucks out of the mud. He was vitally concerned about the welfare of his men. He was always certain they were well-fed, that they were not exposed to unnecessary danger, that they were warmly clothed and got sufficient rest. When feats of bravery were performed, he gave recognition on the spot; but he prevented the courageous fighter from pushing his luck too far. Patton loved his country passionately, and he loved the men he was leading. As one of his Division Commanders said, "Patton fought as hard for his men as he fought against the enemy."

Some have an image of Patton as a tough, harsh, and unmerciful man. Those who served under him knew better; they were aware that his hardness was a shell, and that Patton the man was the soul of consideration. Actually successful leadership is based more upon consideration and respect of men than anything else. Just as an artisan must understand how to use his tools, so must the military leader, whose tools are his men. He can accomplish some things with one man but not with another, and for others he must turn to still a third method. The leader discovers by a deep feeling for his men what method to use for each man and what service each man can best render for the unit. This takes time and a deep interest on the part of the commander. Patton told his commanders, "General officers must be vitally interested in everything that interests the soldier. Usually you will gain a great deal of knowledge by being interested." He was always genuine and sincere about the welfare of his men; but he advised the officer who was not, that "even if you do not [have an interest] the fact that you *appear* interested has a very high morale influence on the soldier." At best, combat is filled with hardships, but soldiers in any war will endure hardships with very little complaint if they sense that their commander cares what happens to them. Soldiers quickly feel a commander's loyalty and devotion to them and respond with loyalty and respect for him. No soldier in Third Army doubted he had a "home" in Patton's outfit.

Many persons have referred to Patton as a driver rather than a leader. It would be more accurate to say that he was a leader, and drive was one of the means by which he led. To anyone who served under General Patton in World War II, it was no surprise that his closest aide and confidant in World War II, Lieutenant Colonel Charles R. Codman, entitled his book on Patton, *Drive*. Drive was personified in Patton. It was a technique which was fundamental and vital to his leadership success, and it answers in part the question of how Patton impressed his personality and dynamism upon his men. It was a technique that brought him success, but it also caused problems for himself and for his senior commanders. It brought about the slapping incident, the abortive speeches, and quarrels with American as well as Allied commanders. Seldom would Patton be found going down the middle of a stream. He lived, he talked, he acted at the extremes. At his best he was superb; at

his worst he was impossible. In the Allied Army that fought in
Europe in World War II, there was room for only one leader like
George S. Patton, Jr.

THE MILITARY CHARACTER

There is absolutely nothing which can take the place of the qualities in a man which are referred to as character. Generals such as George Washington, Robert E. Lee, John J. Pershing, Stonewall Jackson, to mention but a few, are remembered not only as great field leaders, but as generals whose character transcended the wars in which they fought.

To some, success is the only common denominator applicable to eminent commanders because success signified leadership and created conscience. But General Washington lost many battles before the final victory, and the majority of his men did not lose confidence in him. General Robert E. Lee was the commander of the losing side, but his name is synonymous with leadership. Why? Because both were men of character.

Of all the components of leadership discussed thus far the most important is the quality of character. Leadership is really the unconscious expression of the character and personality of the leader. But what is character, and what is its role in leadership? General Eisenhower, in a discussion of military leadership, stated that "character in many ways is everything in leadership. It is made up of many things, but I would say character is really integrity. When you delegate something to a subordinate, for example, it is absolutely your responsibility, and he must understand this. You as a leader must take complete responsibility for what that subordinate does. I once said, as a sort of wisecrack, that leadership consists of nothing but taking responsibility for everything that goes wrong and giving your subordinates credit for everything that goes well."[1]

To General Omar N. Bradley character means "dependability, integrity, the characteristic of never knowingly doing anything wrong, that you would never cheat anyone, that you would give everybody a fair deal. Character is sort of an all inclusive thing. If a man has character everyone has confidence in him. Soldiers must have confidence in their leader."[2]

General Mark Clark remarked about the qualities necessary for successful leadership, "I would put character way up on the list. If you want to select an officer for your command you want one who is confident of his abilities, who is loyal and who has got good character. It is the man of good character that I am going to seek out. There are a lot of people who know the 'smart' way of getting things done, but they also ride roughshod over people that they are supposed to be working with. I don't want that."[3]

"Character," said Lucian K. Truscott, "as we used to say when I was in elementary school, is what you are. Reputation is what others think you are. The reason that some fail to climb the ladder of success, or of leadership if you want to call it that, is that there is a difference between reputation and character. The two do not always coincide. A man may be considered to have sterling character. Opportunity might come to that man; but if he has the reputation for something he is not, he may fail that opportunity. I think character is the foundation of successful leadership."[4]

To General Carl Spaatz, first Chief of Staff of the Air Force and air commander in Europe during World War II, character is a strong will. "You can't be wishy-washy as a military leader," he commented. "You must be able to size up the situation and make a decision. Indecisiveness is weakness of character. You must be able to have confidence in what a leader tells you."[5]

General J. Lawton Collins stated, "I would place character as the absolutely number one requirement in leadership. By character, I mean primarily integrity. A man whose superiors and, even more important, whose subordinates can depend upon that leader taking action based on honesty and judgement.

If he does not base his actions on honor, he is worthless as a leader."[6]

General William H. Simpson believes that "there are many qualities that go into a man of sterling character. I don't know how to break it down. A man of high character has integrity, he is honest, he is reliable, he is straightforward in dealing with people. He is loyal to his family, his friends, his superiors."[7]

"I get accused all the time," General Jacob Devers answered when asked what character meant to him, "of using the word integrity when I mean character and character when I mean integrity. I think character is everything in leadership. It is what we try to build in all our young officers. It means the truth to me. That's the only way I can put it. To stand up and tell the truth and not be in the gray area."[8]

The personal meaning of character to General Albert Wedemeyer is, "an officer who stands up under fire, who has the courage to defend his convictions, not arrogantly, not stubbornly, but intelligently. Someone who does not believe he knows all the answers, who will listen to others with different experiences and different knowledge. It means a deep sense of loyalty. Unless an officer has character nothing he can do can cause his men to love and respect him."[9]

"Character plays a tremendous role in military leadership," said General Anthony "Nuts" McAuliffe; "It's a combination of many things—personality, clean living, presence. I just don't know; it's a very difficult word to describe because, as everyone knows, leaders come in all shapes and sizes and all sorts of personalities. I don't suppose I ever knew two men whom I knew well who differed as much as General MacArthur and General Patton, yet both were tremendous leaders of mass armies, both were men of great character."[10]

Seldom, in any group larger than two, can one find unanimous agreement on a point. As reflected in the above comments from military officers who achieved the highest pinnacle of leadership distinction—as Army commanders in time of war and as Chiefs of Staff—there is unanimous concurrence that character is the foundation of military leadership. The belief in the importance of character in leadership was also unanimous among over five hundred other general officers with whom the author has talked and corresponded. But agreement on what the word means is not unanimous. Actually, character defies definition; it must be described.

Perhaps the need for character was greater during the years of peace than in time of war. The four generals in this comparative study were dedicated men, but they were also human. There were times when they were tempted—because of slow promotions, poor pay, frequent moves, inadequate equipment for training their men, and other hardships—to leave the service.

General Marshall, after he had served as Chief of Staff of the Army, Secretary of State, and Secretary of Defense, was once asked what the most exciting moment of his life had been. "Being promoted to first lieutenant," he replied. He had spent five years as a second lieutenant. In spite of his outstanding success in various assignments and schools, Marshall at 35 years of age was still a first lieutenant in 1915, fourteen years after his graduation from VMI. In a mood of despondency, that year, he wrote to the Superintendent at VMI, General Edward W. Nichols:

> The absolute stagnation in promotion in the infantry has caused me to make tentative plans for resigning as soon as business conditions improve. Even in the event of an increase as a result of legislation next winter, the prospects for advancement in the Army are so restricted by law and by the accumulation of large numbers of men nearly the same age all in a single grade, that I do not feel it right to waste all my best years in the vain struggle against insurmountable difficulties.[11]

Marshall did not leave the service in 1915 and, upon his return from the Philippines in 1916, he was pleased to be assigned, a second time, as aide-de-camp to a man for whom he had tremendous respect and admiration, General J. Franklin

Bell. This challenge and World War I undoubtedly were factors in his decision to remain in the Army.

Because of his brilliant performance as a staff planner and operations officer in World War I, Marshall came to the attention of several prominent and wealthy businessmen who were patriotically serving in responsible positions on Pershing's staff. One of these men offered Marshall, in 1919, a starting salary of $20,000 to leave the service and go with the J.P. Morgan financial firm. He turned it down, even though he knew he would soon lose his wartime rank of colonel. In 1920, he was reduced to the rank of major, and a salary of $3,000 a year. Still, he remained in the service.

In 1947, after General Eisenhower had retired as Chief of Staff of the Army to become President of Columbia University, the Eisenhowers bought their first new car. It was delivered to their home; and, after he inspected it, the former Chief of Staff wrote a check for the full cost of the automobile, almost wiping out their savings. Getting up from the table where he wrote the check, he took Mamie by the hand and walked with her to the door, saying "Darling, there's the entire result of thirty-seven years' work since I caught the train out of Abilene."[1][2]

A man certainly did not stay in the Army for money.

"There were three times," General Eisenhower said, "when I was offered what you might say were attractive opportunities to leave the service. The first was right after World War I. I was right here in this town (Gettysburg). There was a man whose name, strangely enough, was Patton, who was a manufacturer in Ohio or Indiana—someplace in the Midwest—who wanted me to go with him at double the salary I was getting then as a lieutenant colonel. For a while our Army pay looked pretty low. Mamie had quite an influence upon me. I was very disheartened that I hadn't gotten over into the battle; and I thought my army career was ruined. I was fed up. After all the studying and hard work, I wouldn't get into the war. Mamie kidded me a little bit, and we decided to go on in the Army."[1][3]

The next offer for then Major Eisenhower came in 1927; a group of people were forming a new oil company. The man who was putting up a large part of the money was someone Eisenhower had met only a few times; but the investor said he wouldn't contribute unless Eisenhower agreed to enter the new firm, not as the top man, but as one of the executives. The backer wanted Eisenhower because he considered him honest and believed he would watch his money for him. Again, Eisenhower turned down the temptation of more money.

In the Philippines, several men who wanted Eisenhower to enter business with them offered to put $300,000 in escrow in the bank if he would join them, the money to be used by Eisenhower if things didn't work out.

As the offers came forth he always discussed them with Mrs. Eisenhower; "We always said we got this far in the Army and we're going to stay with it. The only offer I really considered was the first one because of my disappointment over not getting into the war."[14]

There was probably only one occasion when General MacArthur ever gave thought to leaving the service. He did not get married until he was a brigadier general, at the age of forty-two. His wife was a rich divorcee with two children, and right after their marriage he was assigned to the Philippines. Mrs. MacArthur, who was used to the gay, exciting social life of New York and Washington, became bored. She believed her husband to be too brilliant, so the story goes, to waste himself by making a career of the Army; she wanted him to leave the Army to enter the business world. It finally reached the point where MacArthur had to decide between the Army and his wife. He decided to remain in the Army, and the marriage ended in divorce.

George Patton was never really tempted to leave the service. He had independent means which provided all the money he could want, and his wife also had considerable wealth. It was truly remarkable for a man of such opulence to make the service—a life so filled with hardship and frustration—his career. But a soldier's life was what Patton wanted, and that was the life he led.

Service life before World War II involved constant sacrifice; nevertheless, fortunately for the United States, we had a group of outstanding military leaders who were ready when Pearl Harbor was bombed on December 7, 1941. Why did these men remain in the service?

When General of the Army Omar N. Bradley was asked that question he replied, "Well, just the fact that I liked military work. I like working with men. I like to teach; and, you know, most of your service involves teaching your own men or instructing at some service school. I liked the outdoors—and you spent a great deal of time outdoors in the Army. There is another angle to it, which was more true then than now. In the old days, you had a rather small Army; and you knew practically every officer in the Army, either personally or by reputation. You usually lived on the post, you were one big family, the atmosphere was pleasant, and you had a nice group to work with. Your contemporaries spoke the same language. There was the feeling that in serving your country you were accomplishing something. There was always something to be done, something to learn."[15]

General Mark W. Clark, who spent sixteen years as a captain, felt much the same way. "I like," he said, "working with men, training young people. That is why I took it up [he was then President of the Citadel, a state military school in South Carolina] after I retired from the Army. I like the outdoors. I was fond of hiking, riding and all kinds of outdoor activity. I had been raised on an Army post and I liked the life an Army officer led—the fine families you met, the children you associated with, because they were invariably raised in Christian families and they were always well disciplined."[16]

General J. Lawton Collins was a lieutenant for seventeen years! He almost left the Army in 1919 to study law. He wrote to a friend who advised him that he would be "crazy" to leave the service for law, since good lawyers could be hired for $250 a month. "Your natural bent," that friend said, "is military service. You would be crazy to give it up." General Collins decided, since he was stationed in Europe, to postpone resigning for a year. "I evaluated the situation very carefully," he said of his position at the end of that year; "I finally decided that there were three things that appealed to me about military service which I could never get anywhere else. The first was that I was not competing with my fellow officers for money. I was actually holding down jobs that normally went to more senior people. Even though I was drawing just a captain's pay, I was given the opportunity to do things irrespective of my age and rank; and that appealed to me. The second thing that I liked was the people I was associated with. They were men of high caliber, men of integrity; and at no time in my then two or three years of service did anybody ask me to do anything that didn't meet my own standard of conduct."

"At the same time," he continued, "I met the girl I later married, and that had considerable influence. I decided then I would stick it out in the service for better or worse, and I gave up any thought of resigning from the Army."[17]

During the thirties General Spaatz almost left the Army Air Corps along with General of the Army H. H. Arnold, to join the embryonic Pan American Airways. But they both stayed. General Spaatz remained because he liked the life, his friends, and the flying. "There really wasn't any incentive to stay in the service between World War I and World War II as there is now. There was no apparent threat of war in those days. There was, however, a feeling among most of us who came into the old aviation section, the Signal Corps, that there was going to be a growth in military aviation. We had confidence that it was going to get its due position, and we decided to stay with it."[18]

The answers given by the other outstanding World War II generals were the same: they liked the life, working with men in the outdoors, teaching, the association with people of integrity, the reward of giving service in a dedicated manner to something that counted. There were surely men who remained in the service during time of peace because it was a soft life, but Army life was not a leisurely, lazy life for those men who reached the top. While others played, they were working, studying, and preparing. The real explanation of why they stayed is that these men had character; they possessed the feeling of belonging to something greater than themselves; they believed in the code, "Duty, Honor, Country."

One aspect of character is the answer to the question, "Was he there?" Had it not been for the duty to country concept of Marshall, MacArthur, Eisenhower, and Patton, they would not have been around to accept the top positions of responsibility in World War II. How fortunate our country has been that these men were sufficiently patient with the slow promotions, poor pay, inadequate housing, inadequate money for training, the hardship of many moves, the unhappiness of children uprooted from friends, and the many other difficulties. Only a dedicated and selfless man would make such a sacrifice.

Humility

Robert Payne, in the introduction to his biography of General George C. Marshall, *The Marshall Story*, wrote regard ing U.S. generals, "Too often the military autobiographers suffer from the first of the seven deadly sins, which is pride; they ascribe their successes to their superb intelligence and their occasional failures to unkindly fates. They speak of the soldiers under their command as one might speak of robots, and they very rarely speak of the soldiers . . . Humility," he said, "is not characteristic of generals . . . "[19]

Such a statement generalizes from an apparent lack of knowledge about the real character of American World War II general officers. Many examples can be cited to refute Payne's allegation.

Marshall

As World War II progressed, country after country decorated Army Chief of Staff George C. Marshall. This embarrassed him. He first tried to handle the situation by not wearing any

ribbons; but then military missions from the awarding countries
began to question whether this American General valued their
awards, and General Marshall finally felt forced to wear every
medal he received. But he had them reproduced in miniature
size. They were so compressed that forty of the miniature
ribbons fitted into the space that sixteen decorations would
normally occupy.

Marshall was never one to court the honors and privileges due
his rank and position. During a European inspection trip in
February 1945, he wired ahead to General Clark that he was
coming to Italy, and requested, "Do not meet me at airport. I
will come to your headquarters. No honors." General Clark
replied that he planned to have a minimum of honors. Quickly
General Clark heard again from the Army Chief of Staff:
"Don't meet me. No honors, repeat, no honors."

General Clark had honors anyway. Upon arrival at Fifth
Army Headquarters near Florence, Marshall found a large honor
guard waiting. "His lips," General Clark said, "pressed together
in a thin line." General Marshall barked at General Clark,

"Didn't you get my message?"

"Yes, Sir."

"Didn't I say no honors?"

"Yes, sir."

"Well?"

"It will only take a few minutes and you'll not regret it."

General Clark, whose Army Command was composed of
many nationalities and races, had assembled an honor guard
including: Negroes from the 92nd Infantry Division; representatives from the Brazilian Expeditionary Force; the lst Argyll
and Sutherland Highlanders; the 318 Punjabs of the 8th Indian
Division; the 166th Newfoundland Field Regiment; the 6th
South African Armored Division; the 24th Guards Brigade,
Welsh Guards; the 2nd Battalion, Inniskillings, Irish; lst Armored Brigade, lst Canadian Corps; the 2nd Polish Corps; the
2nd New Zealand Division; and members of the Women's Army
Corps and women of the American Red Cross. General Marshall

was opposed to any fanfare, but he concurred with General Clark that this was a most appropriate honor guard.[20]

As the war progressed General Marshall proposed a single Chief of Staff to cover both the Army and the Navy. Secretary Stimson and Harry Hopkins believed that Marshall was the only man on the horizon suitable for that position; but, Stimson said, "Marshall rules himself out because he thinks the Navy would not accept the situation unless there was a Navy man appointed."[21] General Marshall considered it vital that the "Joint Chief" position be created. The mission was the important thing, not personal rank or glory. Stimson noted that "The President recognized Marshall's generosity on this point and spoke warmly of it." Stimson's own reaction was that it was "an act of great magnanimity on Marshall's part."[22] At Marshall's suggestion, Admiral William D. Leahy was appointed.

Marshall's air of confidence was accompanied by an attitude of humility, not arrogance. He never considered himself a great leader. When men asked his opinion, listened, and accepted his advice, he considered that they listened because they believed he was better informed on the subject than they were.

During his first important meeting as Chief of Staff, in 1939, with President Roosevelt, a number of other top political and military leaders were present. The President discussed with them his plan to build 10,000 airplanes, to which Marshall was opposed—because of his desire for a balanced air-ground build-up. The majority of the political and military leaders, Marshall said, "agreed with him [Roosevelt] entirely [and] had very little to say and were very soothing...He finally came around to me...I remember he called me 'George'. I don't think he ever did it again...I wasn't very enthusiastic over such a misrepresentation of our intimacy. So he turned to me at the end of this general outlining...and said, 'Don't you think so, George?' I replied, 'I am sorry, Mr. President, but I don't agree with them at all.' I remember that ended the conference. The President gave me a startled look, and when I went out, they all [the politicians and other military leaders] bade me good-bye and

said that my tour in Washington was over. But . . . that didn't
antagonize [Roosevelt] at all. Maybe he thought I would tell
him the truth . . ."[23]

Marshall had an innate dignity. He was considerate, thoughtful, even kind in his association with others, but no one would
venture upon a familiarity with him. Some interpreted his
reserve as egotism, others thought him a "stuffed shirt".
Reserve could work to an officer's disadvantage if he were
considered cold. A leader who is cold and indifferent does not
inspire men; but an officer who, though reserved, is clearly
interested in his men and their welfare does. It was obvious to
all who counted that Marshall was interested in American
soldiers and their welfare.

George C. Marshall was complete within himself. Doing his
job well was its own reward; he did not need the compliments
of others to evaluate his performance. He was eminently fit for
the responsibilities and loneliness of command, intellectually
and psychologically.

MacArthur

John Gunther, in his book, *The MacArthur Riddle,* called
General MacArthur an egotist. Others have said the same thing
about him, but never has any colleague who really knew and
worked with him made such a comment. "I have heard,"
General Wedemeyer said, "General MacArthur criticized as
being a vain man, very vain. I don't think he is a vain man. I
think, however, that he has a great deal of confidence in his
knowledge and in his experience that gives one the impression
he knows that he knows, and I think that that has given the
impression to his detractors that vanity is one of his characteristics. I personally don't think so. I say many people who
criticized him were either jealous, envious of his knowledge, or
were those who wanted to detract from his greatness as a
leader."[24]

General Eisenhower, who worked intimately with General MacArthur for six years, said of him: "I don't think he ever had a conscious egotism. He has a tremendous amount of self-confidence and he's damned able; there's no mistake about that. I would never be party to criticism of General MacArthur."[25]

During his entire military career, MacArthur avoided social functions. As Superintendent of West Point, he rarely joined his staff in their homes for dinner; but he often had military officers in his home for discussions of tactics, strategy, the future of the Army, and other aspects of professionalism. As Chief of Staff, he avoided the "prestige" activities of Washington society. Some interpreted this as meaning that he thought he was too good for others. This was not so; he just wanted to be left alone to enjoy a private life, a life dedicated to one thing—his profession. It is probably the fate of any non-convivial and dedicated professional to be branded proud and egotistical, less from malice than from inability to comprehend such a man.

The army strategy in the Pacific in World War II was called by newsmen, "hit-'em-where-they-ain't." When General MacArthur, who master-minded this strategy, was asked by the Army's historical section to comment on it he took no credit for it. "The system," he said, "is as old as war itself. It is merely a new name, dictated by new conditions, given to the ancient principle of envelopment."[26]

He was called aristocratic, both by people who did not know him and by those who did. He was indeed something special, in a sense a king, and he was in fact sometimes called this unofficially by those who had the greatest love, respect, and admiration for him. But he was a king who never lost the common touch. General McNarney has related an incident showing that MacArthur's interest in people was real:

I never served with General MacArthur. He was Chief of Staff when in Washington. My wife and I called on him when we came to Washington, as everyone did since he was Chief of Staff. I didn't see him more than fifteen minutes,

but a year later I got into an elevator in the munitions
building. There was someone else in the elevator as I
stepped in. It was General MacArthur and he said, 'How
are you, McNarney?' I had not seen him for a year! It
made quite an impression upon me.[27]

When the press of the United States and England began to
imply in 1943 that General MacArthur's command was going to
be reduced to a secondary role, he remarked: "It makes little
difference whether I or others wield the weapon just so the
cause for which our beloved country fights is victorious.
However subordinate may be my role, I hope to play it
manfully . . ."

When he was awarded the highest decoration the United
States can bestow to a soldier, the Congressional Medal of
Honor, he said that he regarded it "not so much for me
personally as it is a recognition of the indomitable courage of
the gallant army which it was my high honor to command."

He was brilliant; but because he was human like others, he
too made mistakes. Early in the war in the Far East, MacArthur
and several of his key officers were talking one evening at
Government House. General Kenney, MacArthur's air chief, and
General Sutherland were involved in an argument over a
separate Air Force. Sutherland opposed a separate air arm.
"Much to my surprise," said General Kenney, "General
MacArthur broke into the conversation and said that he agreed
with me. I replied that he had certainly changed his mind since
1932 when such a bill had been proposed. He said, 'Yes, I have.
At that time I opposed it with every resource at my command.
It was the greatest mistake of my career!"[28] It takes a big man
to admit his own mistakes; and certainly, such admission is not
a quality one would expect in an egotist.

Actually MacArthur was a terribly shy man, and this was one
of his reasons for keeping to himself. He told Courtney Whitney
that he always signed his correspondence, Douglas MacArthur,
rather than, MacArthur, because the latter sounded "too egotistical." Whitney, MacArthur's longest close aide, stated to the

author, "I have never seen the slightest egotism in Douglas MacArthur." He never "paraded" his brilliance; he never made you think he knew more that you; indeed, "he made an excessive effort to make others count."[29] He never wore his ribbons during World War II and was never seen any more dressed up than his open collar khaki uniform.

That he possessed a certain amount of pride cannot be denied. There was an account given of a disagreement on the Army budget between MacArthur when he was Chief of Staff in the early 1930's and President Roosevelt's budget director, Lewis Douglas. The latter asked MacArthur, "General, do you expect a serious epidemic of dysentery in the U.S. Army?" MacArthur replied "No," and the budget director asked then why his budget for toilet paper was so high, accusing the Army of padding their appropriation request. MacArthur was so furious he got up and walked out of the room without saying a word in reply. He would not even lower himself to discuss such an insult to his character. Mr. Douglas later apologized to MacArthur.

Seeing him at the zoo with his young son, or quietly pushing his boy in a swing in a public park, as was often the case years ago, would not be something one would expect of an egoist.

Patton

When General Patton wrote the diary that was later to be the basis of his book, *War As I Knew It,* he began "Part II, Operation Overlord" by saying it was "... a hastily written personal narrative for the benefit of my family and a few old and intimate friends. I apologize for the frequent appearance of the first pronoun . . ."[30]

At a dinner given for several officers at a private gathering, General Omar Bradley commented on the brilliant maneuvering by Patton's Third Army during the Battle of the Bulge and gave high praise to Patton. The latter replied very quickly, "All the credit, *all* of it, one hundred percent, goes to Third Army Staff, and in particular to Hap Gay, Maud Miller, Nixon and Busch."[31]

This type of laudatory credit from Patton was not confined to small, private groups of military officers who knew the important role Patton's leadership had played in his Army's success; at a press conference after the Bulge Operation, Patton said the same thing:

"The purpose of our initial attack can be stated briefly. We hit the sons-of-bitches on the flank and stopped them cold. Now that may sound like George Patton is a great genius. Actually, he [meaning himself] had damned little to do with it. All he did was to give the orders. It was the Staff of this Headquarters and the troops in the line that performed this matchless feat."[32]

It was this humility and recognition of teamwork that enabled military officers to get along with each other as well as they did. General Patton, who graduated from West Point in 1909, was senior to General Mark Clark. a 1917 graduate, by eight years. When Clark was still a lieutenant in 1918, Patton had received the wartime rank of full colonel; but World War II brought about a strange reversal. "When I took command of the Fifth Army," General Clark wrote of his World War II experiences, "it occurred to me that the dashing Patton, who had known me when I was in knee pants and he was a young officer just out of West Point, would be under my command. I had a high regard for him, but I entertained some fears that he might resent being in a subordinate position to me. My fears were completely groundless. He not only accepted the situation pleasantly but went out of his way to be helpful on every possible occasion, and my feeling of admiration and friendship for him increased instead of suffering any strain."[33]

Eisenhower

There is an old military saying that "Rank has its privileges." Seldom do top leaders ever claim that privilege. During his stay in London prior to the D-Day invasion, General Eisenhower, instead of living in a plush hotel in London made available for his comfort, lived in Telegraph Cottage, a small, old, and poorly heated house outside London. On one occasion, Eisenhower was on board a naval ship observing an allied beach landing on enemy territory; because of enemy fire from the shore, the ship's Captain and many of the crew were very protectively guarding the Supreme Commander. Seeing this Eisenhower said to his staff, "I don't want anybody to get hurt on my account. Let's go under."[34] In Algiers, in February 1943, he was returning to Algiers from an inspection in Constantine. It was a short trip by air; but whenever he flew in his B-17, the Air Force always sent a heavy fighter escort along. Because fighters were badly needed for combat, he decided to drive back—a hard, eight-hour drive over a rough, twisting Algerian road.

During the North African fighting in January 1943, General Sommervell strongly advocated that General Eisenhower spend more time at the front so he would get credit for Allied successes. It was suggested the Allied Commander move his Headquarters from Algiers to Constantine. He would not do this. He believed his commanders at the front were doing a superb job, and he knew that moving his headquarters up to the front would overcrowd an already congested area. Communications would be easier with Europe and the United States if he remained in Algiers. At the core of his decision, though, was a belief that there were too many people already looking for credit. Personal acclaim was not his goal. He stayed in Algiers.

As a matter of fact, avoiding personal publicity was almost an obsession with General Eisenhower. When it was announced on November 7, 1942, that he was Commander-in-Chief of the Allied forces, he insisted that communiqués from that theater not be datelined with his name. As Supreme Commander for the invasion of Europe he directed that news dispatches from his headquarters be datelined "Allied Headquarters" or "SHAEF," never "General Eisenhower's Headquarters." Throughout the war there was a pool of war correspondents at his Headquarters. General Eisenhower had the pool reduced to one representative of each major outlet (AP, UP, CBS, ABC, NBC). One reporter said it was unusual to find a general insisting that coverage be reduced. General Eisenhower felt the same way about pictures; in his opinion, the less he was before the public in newspapers and magazines the better. On only two occasions throughout the war could he be coerced into sitting for a portrait painting, and then it took the personal insistence of some high-level people.

When he was in a position to give help to others he did not want personal credit for it. One of the Americans who had joined the British Royal Air Force as a fighter pilot in 1939 returned badly wounded from a mission. While in the hospital, with his chances of living still uncertain, he asked for transfer to the American Air Force. It was a warm and touching story. When the flier's desire came to his attention, General Eisenhower immediately granted permission, but he insisted that the transfer be attributed to the Theater Headquarters and not to him. He wanted no personal credit, "especially", he said, "at the expense of this unfortunate flier."[3][5]

On one occasion a newspaper syndicate secured and published some of his personal correspondence, including letters to his family. General Eisenhower was positively bitter about it. He considered it an unjust invasion into his personal and private life. It was difficult for him to understand that he had become a person in whom the public had great interest, that everything he did was news. He was a sincerely modest man, and personal publicity went against the grain.

On September 29, 1940, Eisenhower, then a colonel, received a wire telling him he had been promoted to the rank of temporary brigadier general. He wrote to his friend, Leonard Gerow, "Things are moving so rapidly these days that I get almost dizzy trying to keep up with the parade. One thing is certain—when they get clear down to my place on the list, they are passing out stars with considerable abandon."

After his first meeting, in August 1942, with General Sir Harold R.L.G. Alexander, the famous British field commander in North Africa, General Eisenhower said of him, "That guy's good! He ought to be Commander-in-Chief instead of me."[36] When he was selected in December, 1943, as Supreme Commander, he wrote to Secretary of War Stimson, "I have always agreed with you that General Marshall was the logical choice to do the OVERLORD job, but as long as it has been assigned to me you need have no fear but I will do my best. It is heartening indeed to have your expression of confidence."

Eisenhower was certainly not indifferent to his success. He was pleased to make the rank of brigadier; and when he was promoted to the rank of full general on the field of battle, he was overjoyed to be in the company of Grant, Sherman, and Pershing. But he was too busy trying to win a war to think about it very long; and his fifth star was too anticlimactical to cause any excitement.

In May 1945, the war in Europe ended. After the surrender documents were appropriately signed, General Eisenhower's staff prepared numerous drafts of possible victory messages to be given by the Supreme Commander to the world. General Eisenhower turned down all the various proposals and closed out the most devastating war in history by saying: "The mission of this Allied force was fulfilled at 0241 local time, May 7, 1945." The simplicity of the message was characteristic; he did not seize the opportunity for personal acclaim. He did not seek to impress the world with words that would live on forever. He had been assigned a job to do. It was over with and so was the necessity for talk. Modesty, he believed, was a virtue for the individual. A nation in victory should be equally humble.

Upon his return to the United States after the victory in Europe he asked that official functions be held to a minimum. He wanted to go fishing. In his post-war speeches, he constantly emphasized that "My position was merely that of a symbol. I am not a hero."

"Professional military ability and strength of character," General Eisenhower later wrote in his memoirs, "always required in high military position, are often marred by unfortunate characteristics, the most frequently encountered and hurtful ones being a too obvious avidity for public acclaim and the delusion that strength of purpose demands arrogant and insufferable deportment. A soldier once remarked that a man sure of his footing does not need to mount a horse!"[37] This was a philosophy that he practiced as well as preached, as did all the great American military leaders of World War II. Their attitude is best described by a statement of General Eisenhower's in 1945: "Humility must always be the portion of any man who receives acclaim earned in the blood of his followers and the sacrifice of his friends."

Religion

An essential part of the character of successful American military leaders was their religious belief. Religion has varied meanings to different people. To some, it means going to church; to others, it means reading the Bible; and to many, it means a belief in God without doing either. Religion can be defined as: "the service and adoration of God or a god as expressed in forms of worship"; "devotion or fidelity"; and "conscientiousness". A fourth definition of religion, and the one most appropriate for this study, is "an awareness or conviction of the existence of a supreme being, arousing reverence, love, gratitude, the will to obey and serve and the like."

Generals Marshall, MacArthur, Eisenhower, and Patton were religious men in the sense of believing in the existence of a supreme being who aroused reverence, love. gratitude, and a commitment to obedience and service. To understand the leadership of these four generals, one must look into the role that religion played in their conduct.

MacArthur

In combat some men die, others are wounded, a few become mentally ill. Some go through combat without a scratch, either mental or physical. The question arises concerning the fate of men in combat: "Why do some escape without noticeable harm while others do not?" Many have answered this question for themselves satisfactorily, others are still searching for an answer. MacArthur had an answer—he believed God was the reason for his survival in combat. During his tour as Superintendent at West Point, MacArthur, in a reminiscing mood, reflected back upon his experiences during World War I in a conversation with his Chief of Staff, William A. Ganoe. Major Ganoe had asked General MacArthur a question about his battle experiences; the reply illustrated the role that he thought faith played in his surviving in battle:

Chief, God led me by the hand—led me by the hand. There were so many times I shouldn't have escaped. The Forty-second was stopped. We'd tried to take a hill in our front but the Boches had it so heavily fortified and armed, we were held up each time. The losses would be too costly. I felt we must get more information on the details of their position. I organized a night reconnaissance patrol. I accompanied it because I felt my presence would help morale and I could personally direct the movements so as to obtain specifically what we needed.

We had not gone far in the darkness over no-man's land when the enemy opened up with everything he had. Automatically, we hit the dirt and dropped into shell holes. I lay there till things got quiet and the darkness was blackest. Then I called in muffled voice, "Each one of you get up when I give the signal, take the hand of the man on his right. I will lead off to get back to our lines!" I waited till the time was ripe and gave the command. No one stirred, and there wasn't a sound. I called again. No action

or reply. I crawled along from shell hole to shell hole. I
took hold of each man and shook him, thinking it not
unlikely his extreme fatigue had caused him to sleep.

Chief, they were all stone dead. I was the only one left
there alone. I made my way back with God's help.[38]

Napoleon believed that God was on the side with the most
troops. General MacArthur did not agree with this maxim, but
he did believe that God played a role in his military success.
During World War I, when he was leading a battalion of men in
combat, his description of one of his battles revealed this belief:

> Before I dared contemplate my action, I crawled up
> over the top and called, "Follow me!" I walked forward
> not looking back, with utter silence behind me . . . I never
> felt so alone and naked in my life. The enemy was opening
> up, and I was a solitary human being against nests of
> machine guns. But way down I felt my men, who had
> previously shown devotion to me, would not see me
> sacrifice myself. I must have taken only a few steps, which
> seemed to me like a hundred, when I heard them scramble
> up with a little cheer.
>
> We won that day, but if ever God led me by the hand, it
> was then.[39]

In addition to believing that God was responsible for his
survival and for his success as a leader, he found that God was a
source of guidance and strength. MacArthur once told an
interviewer during World War II that "only God or the Government of the United States can keep me from the fulfillment
of my mission." MacArthur's conviction that God had a guiding
role was shown on mnay other occasions. One was the eve of
the American invasion of the Philippines in 1944:

> It was eleven p.m., and black as only the Pacific can get
> on a dark, starless night, when we reached our position off
> Leyte Gulf. We would be off Leyte until dawn. The ships

of the convoy were dark silhouettes gliding past us. On each of them, nervous soldiers, sailors, and marines fidgeted as the night wore on toward the dawn that might be their last. For the hundredth time rifles were checked, landing nets were tested, maps were carefully folded and refolded. Each man was alone with himself ... Fully 150,000 men and 1,500,000 tons of general equipment plus 235,000 tons of combat vehicles and 200,000 tons of ammunition were poised to strike. And in his bunk in his cabin aboard the Nashville, MacArthur had fallen asleep, an open Bible in his lap.[40]

MacArthur believed in God, but he did not attend church services. According to General Kenney, MacArthur's wife Jean "did the churchgoing in the family." MacArthur did, however, hold religious services in his own home. Eight in the morning was the time for family prayers. The service was conducted from the Anglican Book of Common Prayer with General MacArthur reading the Bible passage.[41]

When reading through General MacArthur's speeches and dispatches of World War II, one finds constant references to God and an association between God, democracy, and patriotism. He wrote to the editor of a religious journal, "I am absolutely convinced that true democracy can exist only on a spiritual foundation." He made such frequent reference to God a fellow officer once suggested that it might provoke ridicule. MacArthur in his reply summed up the role religion played in his leadership: "In war when a commander becomes so bereft of reason and perspective that he fails to understand the dependence of arms on Divine guidance, he no longer deserves victory."[42]

Patton

It might strike as strange those who have followed General Patton's fiery career in only a cursory manner to find that he was a religious man, indeed a devoutly religious man. Since

General Patton was such a showman one might justifiably
suspect that his overt devotion to religion displayed during
World War II was only a front. However, a close study of his
early life reveals that he had long been deeply religious. Two
cousins had entered the ministry, and one biographer maintains
that Patton himself gave serious thought to that calling. Since
he had already decided he wanted to be a soldier more than
anything else, he prayed that "he would not get the call" for
the ministry.

As a cadet at West Point, his roommate, Philip S. Gage, said
Patton "was very religious, though he did not 'wear it [his
religion] on his sleeve.' I believe he felt his religion was a very
personal matter, and I can't recall that he ever discussed his
convictions with anyone, not even with me. He used to say his
prayers nightly, and I'm positive he called on Divine guidance
quietly in his inner person whenever he felt he needed it."[43]

Patton was an avid polo player during his early military
career. Before a game, he habitually knelt beside his bed to
pray. "His helmet hung on the bedpost, his mallet leaning
against the wall, and his polished boots stuck out behind him
with the naked spurs upturned." Once his wife asked him when
he prayed like this before a match if he was praying to win the
game and he answered, "Hell, no! I'm praying to do my
best."[44]

General Patton's first combat was under General John J.
Pershing in the Mexican Campaign of 1916. Before leaving for
this assignment he gave his wife, Bea, a keepsake which had the
word MIZPAH engraved upon it. The translation testifies both
Patton's religious belief and his close attachment to his wife:
MIZPAH means, "The Lord watch between me and thee while
we are parted from one another."[45]

Nevertheless, some of Patton's religious practices were char-
acteristically unorthodox. During World War II, Patton was still
saying his prayers at night, and their content was on occasion of
questionable virtue by usual standards of Christianity. After he
had been relieved of command in Sicily, he became bored and
restless and asked General Mark Clark, who was commanding

the American Army in Italy, for permission to visit his theatre. Clark, who had idealized Patton since his junior officer days, assented and he put up Patton in his quarters. The first evening they were together, Patton kneeled down to say his prayers before going to bed. After he was through, Clark, who had watched the reverent scene, asked him what he said in his prayers. Patton answered with a smile, "I prayed, Mark, that you would fall flat on your face and that I would be assigned to take your place."[46]

When the then Colonel Patton was stationed at Fort Clark in Brackettville, Texas, before World War II, he insisted that no sermon given at the post chapel should be longer than ten minutes and so indicated to the chaplain. Then, on Sunday, he would sit in the front pew and look conspicuously at his watch when the sermon had been in progress for eight minutes. The sermons, it was reported, always finished within the allotted ten minutes.[47]

General Patton also maintained this policy in combat during World War II. In a letter dated September 26, 1943, to his father-in-law, who was also a close friend, he said, "I had all the non-Catholic chaplains in the other day and gave them hell for having uninteresting services. I am convinced that man does not want to be preached to on the Divinity of Christ or the efficacy of prayer—certainly not preached to for half an hour. I told them that I was going to relieve any preacher who talked more than ten minutes on any subject. I will probably get slapped down by the Church Union, but I am absolutely right."[48]

While Patton's limitation on the length of sermons might shock some devout church members, it does not repudiate his deep and emotional faith in God. Many a theological school and seminary counsels its students that "no soul is saved after the first twenty minutes of a sermon."

The episode of the "dry weather" prayer offers an interesting insight of General Patton's independent religious outlook. In December 1944, during the critical Battle of the Bulge, Patton called on his Chief of Staff and the Third Army Chaplain, Colonel James H. O'Neill. Colonel Harkins, his Chief of Staff, reports the conversation:

> General Patton: "Chaplain, I want you to publish a prayer for good weather. I'm tired of these soldiers having to fight mud and floods as well as Germans. See if we can't get God to work on our side."
>
> Chaplain O'Neill: "Sir, it's going to take a pretty thick rug for that kind of praying."
>
> General Patton: "I don't care if it takes the flying carpet. I want the praying done."
>
> Chaplain O'Neill: "Yes, sir. May I say, General, that it usually isn't a customary thing among men of my profession to pray for clear weather to kill fellow men."
>
> General Patton: "Chaplain, are you teaching me theology or are you the Chaplain of the Third Army? I want a prayer."
>
> Chaplain O'Neill: "Yes, sir."

Outside, the Chaplain said, "Whew, that's a tough one! What do you think he wants?"

It was perfectly clear to me. The General wanted a prayer—he wanted one right now—and he wanted it published to the Command.

The Army Engineer was called in, and we finally decided that our field topographical company could print the prayer on a small-sized card, making enough copies for distribution to the army.

It being near Christmas, we also decided to ask General Patton to include a Christmas greeting to the troops on the same card with the prayer. The General agreed, wrote a short greeting, and the card was made up, published, and distributed to the troops on the twenty-second of December.

Actually, the prayer was offered in order to bring clear weather for the planned Third Army break-through to the Rhine in the Saarguemines area, then scheduled for December 21.

The Bulge put a crimp in these plans. As it happened, the Third Army had moved north to attack the south flank of the Bulge when the prayer was actually issued.

PRAYER

Almighty and most merciful Father, we humbly beseech Thee, of Thy great goodness, to restrain these immoderate rains with which we have had to contend. Grant us fair weather for Battle. Graciously hearken to us as soldiers who call upon Thee that, armed with Thy power, we may advance from victory to victory, and crush the oppression and wickedness of our enemies, and establish Thy justice among men and nations. Amen.

Whether it was the help of the Divine guidance asked for in the prayer or just the normal course of human events, we never knew; at any rate, on the twenty-third, the day after the prayer was issued, the weather cleared and remained perfect for about six days. Enough to allow the Allies to break the backbone of the Von Rundstedt offensive and turn a temporary setback into a crushing defeat for the enemy.

We had moved our advanced Headquarters to Luxembourg at this time to be closer to the battle area. The bulk of the Army Staff, including the Chaplain, was still in Nancy. General Patton again called me to his office. He wore a smile from ear to ear. He said, "God damn! look at the weather. That O'Neill sure did some potent praying. Get him up here. I want to pin a medal on him."

The Chaplain came up next day. The weather was still clear when we walked into General Patton's office. The General rose, came from behind his desk with hand out-stretched and said, "Chaplain, you're the most popular man in this Headquarters. You sure stand in good with the Lord and soldiers." The General then pinned a Bronze Star Medal on Chaplain O'Neill.

Everyone offered congratulations and thanks and we got back to the business of killing Germans—with clear weather for battle. P.D.H.

The day before the prayer was passed out to the troops another member of General Patton's staff pointed out to him

that the prayer had been printed three weeks earlier. To this
Patton replied, "Oh, the Lord won't mind. I know He will
understand. He knows we're too busy right now killing Germans
to print another prayer. It's the spirit that counts with the
Lord. And He knows I mean well."[49]

In countless interviews and in correspondence with members
of the General's staff, his corps commanders, division commanders, and GI's it was brought out that he attended the field
worship services regularly. While showmanship was part of his
leadership technique, there was no sham or show in his worship
of God. People who had heard of his frequent use of profanity
were surprised to find a Bible on the desk of his living quarters
in the field. During a lull in the North African Campaign,
General Patton took time to visit Jerusalem and he wrote that,
"While I was in the chapel, I secured a rosary for Mary Scally
and had it blessed on the altar."[50] Mary Scally had been his
childhood nurse and was then ninety-six years old. This action
was also indicative of Patton's thoughtfulness.

Patton's belief in God's help was an important source of
strength to him in battle. The evening before the North African
invasion he wrote in his diary, "Sea dead calm—no swell. God is
with us." His reliance on divine guidance is further illustrated
by an earlier entry in his diary: "In forty hours I shall be in
battle, with little information, and on the spur of the moment
will have to make the most momentous decisions, but I believe
that one's spirit enlarges with responsibility and that, with
God's help, I shall make them and make them right."[51] When
things went well in the North African invasion he commented,
"I guess I must be God's most favorite person."

In one of his war letters to a friend, General Patton put his
finger upon a vital aspect of the meaning of religion to the
fighting man:

> Ever since I got to Sicily I have been going to Catholic
> churches largely for political reasons but also as a means of
> worshipping God, because I think He is quite impartial as
> to the form in which He is approached.

This morning I went to the Episcopal Church and for the first time in my life found it crowded with American soldiers and sailors. I had very strange feelings in watching the faces and types of men who went to Communion.

There were men with the shoulder patch of the 9th Division beside aviator ground crews who had never fired a shot or been in danger. There was an Irish Guardsman and a Navy cook; a 6'2" Coldstream Guard kneeling beside a little runt from the 1st Division who, to my certain knowledge, had killed a dozen men. It was a very strange mixture. Whether it is faith or superstition I do not know, but certainly it comes out in war and is coming out faster all the time.[52]

After Patton's victorious return to the United States in 1945, his final act before returning to Europe was to go to the church in Los Angeles where he had been baptized and confirmed, stating, "God has been very good to me, and I'd like to go there and give thanks to Him." While there he spoke to a Sunday school class and told them how religion had given him great comfort during battle. He strongly encouraged them to develop their religious faith, "for if the day of war does come again, you will find strong support in religion."

Eisenhower

General Eisenhower had had a strict religious upbringing. His grandfather and father held prominent positions of responsibility in the Church of Brethren of Christ; and during Eisenhower's youth, his family devoted one night a week to reading and studying the Bible. A study of Cadet Eisenhower's extracurricular activities at West Point reveals that he was in charge of the Sunday School class for the dependents.

During the Mediterranean Campaign of World War II General Eisenhower took a two-day trip through the lower Nile Valley and a one-day trip by plane to Jerusalem. He thoroughly impressed the members of his staff with his knowledge of Biblical history. When Ike was asked about this he replied, "I practically had to memorize the Bible when I was a kid."[53]

Like Patton, General Eisenhower was also known to use profanity, a fact which disturbed some religious men. Indeed when Clark Lee, a wartime aide of Ike's, wrote an article on General Eisenhower which said that he was "capable of using all of the normal and some of the super-American cusswords," Ike received a letter from an irate American citizen who said Ike was not a fit general to lead men into battle, that he was not sufficiently religious. Captain Butcher, General Eisenhower's military aide, brought this criticism to his attention and Ike answered, "Why dammit, I *am* a religious man."[5][4]

Like the other generals in this study Ike found strength for battle in his belief in God. During the gloomy days of the Ardennes attack by the Germans, General Eisenhower said in one of his very few written orders of the day, on December 22, 1944:

> By rushing out from his fixed defenses the enemy may give us the chance to turn his great gamble into his worst defeat. So I call upon every man, of all the Allies, to rise now to new heights of courage, of resolution and of effort. Let everyone hold before him a single thought—to destroy the enemy on the ground, in the air, everywhere destroy him. United in this determination and with unshakable faith in the cause for which we fight, we will, with God's help, go forward to our greatest victory.

In looking back at World War II there is a tendency for Americans to forget that we could have lost the war and that it took hard fighting to win it. When the Allies were launching their first attack in North Africa in World War II, they lacked the confidence of success in battle and, therefore, were apprehensive. The operation went off extremely well; and when the initial landing was successful, Eisenhower said a prayer of thanks: "At no time during the war did I experience a greater sense of relief than when I received a meager report to the effect that beach conditions were not too bad and the Casablanca landing was proceeding as planned. I said a prayer of thanksgiving, my greatest fear had been dissipated."[5][5]

Marshall

Religion meant a great deal to General Marshall. His Chief of Chaplains during his entire tour as Chief of Staff of the Army from 1939 to 1945 was Major General William Arnold. "General Marshall," Arnold said, "was very much interested in the religious welfare of people in the services. When I was made Chief of Chaplains he told me, 'Now I want you to come here to my office whenever it is necessary, but at least once a month and tell me what the situation is and what you need.' He considered the spiritual welfare of the men important; it made them better soldiers. When I'd get there he'd motion me to come into his room where the desk was and sit down. We discussed the situation and what I needed. Every time, without a single exception, when we were through he'd get up and walk to the door with me and he'd say, 'Please pray for me.' He was a very religious man."

"Sometimes," Arnold remarked, "I had to deal with people who weren't very much interested in the religious worship of our men, but when those individuals found out that Marshall was, they quickly became interested. I used to tell my Chaplains they should appreciate what Marshall was doing for them and their men and to say prayers for him."[5 6]

Religion in combat, where one faces life and death every minute, does not rely on the established institutions or denominations, but rather implies a sincere belief and dependence on a supreme being without whose existence life would have no meaning. All four of these generals had a belief in God which was as fundamental and as necessary to them as the foundation to a building. It seemed to give them a sense of completion. There appeared to be a need not only for the physical and mental attributes of successful leadership, but for spiritual attributes as well, which served as a guide to shape their actions. Man is by nature selfish. and the man who does things for self-interest only is liable to go astray. These men reached for spiritual guidance to provide them with a good compass and rudder to reach their destination.

War *is* hell, as only those who have fought in war can know. There are moments of profound discouragement for the battle-field commander. The man who has the strength of conviction supplied by religion can always find it easier to pull himself out of the depths with the help of God. The man who relies on his resources alone is more apt to give up.

The battle leader is perhaps the loneliest man in the world. His subordinates may refrain from too intimate an association for fear of being accused of bootlicking. The leader, for his part, stays aloof to avoid criticism for showing favoritism. To make decisions that will result in the death of others is not easy. The man occupying the lonely peak of leadership often finds refuge in the knowledge that he can appeal to a higher power.

Politics

Traditionally the military officer is completely disassociated from politics. He takes no sides in political disputes, he does not run for office, often he does not vote. In his acceptance address after receiving the Sylvanus Thayer Award at West Point on May 12, 1962, General MacArthur expressed a political philosophy that had been an element of the American military heritage for over a century:

Yours is the profession of arms—the will to win, the sure knowledge that in war there is no substitute for victory; that if you lose, the nation will be destroyed; that the obsession of your public service must be Duty-Honor-Country. Others will debate the controversial issues, national and international, which divide men's minds; but serene, calm, aloof, you stand as the nation's war-guardian, as its lifeguard from the raging tides of international conflict, as its gladiator in the arena of battle. For a century and a half you have defended, guarded, and protected its hallowed traditions of liberty and freedom, of right and justice. Let civilian voices argue the merits or demerits of our processes of government; whether our strength is being sapped by deficit financing, indulged in

too long, by federal paternalism grown too mighty, by
power groups grown too arrogant, by morals grown too
low, by taxes grown too high, by extremists grown too
violent; whether our personal liberties are as thorough and
complete as they should be. These great national problems
are not for your professional participation or military
solution. Your guidepost stands out like a ten-fold beacon
in the night, Duty-Honor-Country.

These eloquent words summarized the "non-political" code
of the majority of American military leaders. It was subscribed
to by all the top World War II military commanders. General
Marshall stirred up a great deal of criticism in 1952 when he
stated he had never voted during active duty as an officer, and
that he would not vote in the coming election. When he was
asked, on occasion, during his military career about his political
allegiance he replied humorously, "My father was a Democrat,
my mother was a Republican, and I am an Episcopalian." It was
Marshall's conviction that a career officer should not be identified with any political party.

"Eisenhower once told me (it was in London in March,
1944)," wrote Robert Sherwood in his book *Roosevelt and
Hopkins*, "that his family had always been Kansas Republicans
but that he himself had never voted in his life. He felt that since
an Army officer must serve his government with full loyalty and
devotion regardless of its political coloration, he should avoid
all considerations of political partisanship."[5][7]

General Patton also refused to vote. To him it was contrary
to his code of honor. "I am in the pay of the United States
government," he said. "If I vote against the administration I am
voting against my commander-in-chief. If I vote for the administration in office I am being bought."

General Spaatz commented, "I have always felt that career
officers of any of the services should not be concerned with
politics. If they vote that means they are siding with one party
or the other. I think there should be the same separation of the
military from the political part of the government as they say
there should be of separation of church and state."[5][8]

In addition to conviction, many pre-World War II officers did not vote because of constitutional limitations. General William H. Simpson, who said it was his belief that as a soldier ". . . it didn't make any difference to me who the constituted government was. I was dedicated to the service of my Country," added, "I could not have voted if I wanted to. As a native of Texas I was prohibited from voting. The Constitution of Texas in my day had a provision stating convicts, imbeciles, and officers could not vote." Then he showed his native Texas pride by saying, "Since I was blocked from voting by my home state, I just dismissed it from my mind."[59] Absentee balloting, something the service officer takes for granted today, was virtually nonexistent in state statutes prior to World War II.

There was also the problem of property ownership, a stipulation required for residency in many states. Few military officers were stationed anywhere long enough to buy property, nor were they that well paid. It was also difficult, because of frequent moves, to become knowledgable about state and local politics. "I couldn't cast an intelligent ballot," was Lucian Truscott's conclusion, "because I was out of contact with the situation in my home state, Oklahoma." In national elections General Truscott adhered to the same philosophy held by the vast majority of the Army officers of his day. "In presidential elections I never bothered to vote," he said, "because regardless of my own personal opinion, as a regular Army officer I carried out the orders of whatever adminstration was in."[60]

History, particularly with the benefit of hindsight, will continue to criticize the American World War II generals for their political naivete. The position of the Americans, however, was a traditional one. Politics was not their concern. This was up to statesmen; and when statesmen failed, they called upon the military to handle their failures. During World War II, the assignment of the top military officers was to defeat the enemy expeditiously and professionally; decisions were not made on nationalistic and political grounds. When the constitutional authorities—the executive, the legislature, and even the courts— see fit to change the military role, then the military will acquiesce; but such a change would be the precursor of trouble.

General Marshall refused to write his memoirs. Why? He did not want to embarrass or contradict anyone. He particularly wanted to avoid tarnishing the image of any high civilian leaders. This was another indication of his absolute loyalty to the American system of government and to the complete subordination of the military to civil authority.

In a personal interview in 1954 which included a discussion of Yalta and its blunders, General Marshall very frankly stated, "People think that I was in on everything, but that is not true. I had the Army to think about. My thinking was military thinking. *I would make a decision without considering the political consequences*. That was for the politicians."[6] [1]

Germany, Japan, and France have historically placed their generals in an exalted position. In the past, this has often resulted in the officers of these nations developing an attitude of aloofness and arrogance in their dealings with their military subordinates and, even more unfortunately, with civilian authorities and the general public. They were given or they usurped sufficient power to make decisions for their country, decisions which frequently led to war against other nations in order to extend their power and influence. American generals have not done this. It is part of our national code that the military is subordinate to the President, his key cabinet officers and, most of all, to the people.

The American military officer is always prepared to "take the rap" for risky political decisions. For example, the politically astute Roosevelt wanted to avoid holding the bag for the unpopular Darlan decision made by General Eisenhower. But the general realizes this is part of the military officer's role, and if he is unwilling to accept this aspect of the job he has no business being in a top leadership position.

An officer finds it hardest to bow to civilian authority when his expert military judgment is being ignored or overruled. This happened on one significant occasion during World War II. In 1942, at the conference between President Roosevelt and Prime Minister Churchill, it was decided that the United States must

enter into offensive action that year. An invasion of Europe was
ruled out, largely because of Churchill's insistence that such
action would be unsuccessful and therefore fatal to the whole
subsequent war effort. He just did not believe in the readiness
of American troops. The two leaders at this Conference decided
upon the invasion of North Africa for 1942 and gave it the code
name of GYMNAST. American military leaders were strongly
opposed, believing that such a diversionary action would delay
the invasion of Europe which they hoped to undertake in 1943.
General Marshall and his staff presented their position as
strongly as possible; but the decision was made by the Commander-in-Chief, President Roosevelt, that there would be an
invasion of North Africa in 1942. The political reasons were
obvious, and the Allied pressures compelling. It was one of the
very few decisions of World War II that President Roosevelt
made entirely on his own and over the opposition of his
military advisers. General Marshall and his staff, without further
discussion, started planning for the invasion as ordered.

The North African operation was scheduled for November
1942. "Today," Secretary Stimson wrote on August 9, 1942, "I
asked Marshall if he was President or Dictator whether he would
go on with Gymnast, and he told me frankly no."[6 2] A month
later, on September 28, 1942, Secretary Stimson received a
briefing from General Mark W. Clark, General Eisenhower's
second in command of the North Africa invasion. "When we got
down to the bottom of the matter," Secretary Stimson said of
the interview, "Clark agreed with me about the hazards and
unwisdom of the whole movement." But orders were orders.
Stimson said at that time of the character of American generals,
"It is a superb tribute to our leaders to see the vigor and
enthusiasm they are putting into a job of which they really
disapprove."[6 3]

Probably it is fair to say that a major strength of the
American theory and practice of government is that not often
must the general be asked to support an operation of which he
really disapproves. Though he has no direct political voice, both

he and the politician spring from the same traditions and answer, in one way or another, to the same constituency.

Attitude Toward War

The American professional soldier is sometimes called a "warmonger" by pacifists and by certain left-wing groups. Isolationists are suspicious of our soldiers and fear they will in some way maneuver the United States into a war. They assume that when so much time is spent preparing for combat, it will not be possible to resist the temptation to use the training and equipment. One of the considerations, supposedly, is the desire of the officer for promotion, which comes faster in war. This attitude is very unfair—it is based upon inadequate information or, occasionally, unreasoning prejudice; but it is part of the soldier's code to refrain from answering criticisms such as these.

What is the American general's attitude toward war? This work will be concerned only with World War II personalities. It is necessary, however, in order to understand them, to look briefly at the attitude held by the European generals of World War I. Such a comparison shows a definite change in outlook. The World War I approach was a more callous one. Soldiers were referred to as "bodies", as if they were merely freight—or even more shocking, as if they were corpses. This obviously signified a very cold and callous feeling toward the men doing the fighting. The French generals' "realistic" analysis of war was that it would be won "by the side that can last fifteen minutes longer than the other." This leaves one with the impression that military leadership consisted of the indifferent trading of human lives. There was an attitude of detachment and dedication to harsh discipline for the men who had to fight and die, while the general himself was usually free from the threat of death.

Some World War I commanders ordered frontal assaults of infantry troops into the fire of massed machine guns and artillery. The tactic achieved little success and was therefore a stupid maneuver causing unnecessary slaughter. Intelligent leadership would have devised different tactics. Winston Churchill once said that "Battles are won by slaughter and maneuver." He then put the emphasis upon where leadership fits into the Western general's attitude toward war: "The greater the general, the more he contributes in maneuver, the less he demands in slaughter." Men are the decisive element in war, and they must be dealt with as human beings and not as items of material. This is the consideration which in time of war puts the emphasis upon leadership.

Patton

What was the attitude towards war of the generals in this comparative study? General George S. Patton, Jr., had the reputation of being a "go for broke" type of general. This did not mean, however, that he was reckless about the lives of his men. When Patton was given command of the first tank unit in World War I he said to General Pershing, "Sir, I accept my new command with particular enthusiasm because with the eight tanks, I believe I can inflict the greatest number of casualties on the enemy with *the smallest expenditure of American life.*"

The smallest expenditure of American life while inflicting great casualties upon the enemy was the basic purpose of Patton's tactics. He drove himself more tirelessly than his men because it was his belief that the shorter the action, the faster the enemy retreated and the fewer the Allied casualties.

At one point during World War II, Patton became irritated because he said "three divisions of Marines in the Pacific were getting great credit by reporting their tremendous losses, while twelve or thirteen divisions in our Army were getting no credit because we did not have tremendous losses." Patton was not proud of the loss of American lives, and he considered tremendous losses to be indicative of poor generalship. He had a policy of issuing a "score sheet" for the newspapers to publish which showed the American casualty list and compared it to the

estimated German casualty list. The overwhelming losses of the
Germans compared to the Americans spoke for themselves.

During the Battle of the Bulge, in Bastogne, which was
occupied by the American Rangers and completely surrounded
by the Germans, there was an urgent need for ammunition,
medicine, and other supplies. Convoys of trucks were prepared
to truck them in, but driving to Bastogne meant running
through deadly German fire power. Patton decided, because of
the suicidal nature of the mission, to cancel the convoy of
trucks. "We have a corridor," he said, "but it's under fire. I'm
taking no chances on losing men and supplies that way. There's
a big difference between wading in and slugging the enemy and
letting him sit off and pot shot you. The Germans expect us to
try to send in convoys tonight, and they'll be laying for them
with everything they've got. We're not going to play into their
hands that way. Tomorrow, when the corridor has been
widened and reinforced, we'll start trucking. Until then we'll
continue to supply by air. It's a lot better to be sure than
sorry."[64]

During the battle of St. Lô, there occurred the unfortunate
bombing of American troops by our own aircraft. Because of
this, Patton, a great believer in the potency of tactical air power,
personally took part in all air planning connected with the
movement of his Third Army. At one conference on targets he
was informed, after he laid down the rule for the safety zone
for his troops, that the rule of thumb for the bomb lines was
2,000 yards for medium bombers and 3,000 for heavies. He was
adamant in insisting that this be changed. "That's not enough,"
he said, "raise them to 3,000 for the mediums and 4,000 for the
heavies. We're out to kill Germans, not our own men. We want
all the air support we can get. But it would be a lot worse on
the morale of our men to bomb them than not to bomb at all. I
don't want any St. Lô fiascoes in this Army. I'd rather attack
without bombing than with it, if there is any danger of bombing
our own men."[65]

As Patton's Third Army approached the Rhine he pushed his
troops unmercifully.

Every day we save means saving hundreds of American
lives. The enemy is in chaos on our front. But if we delay
72 hours, he will reorganize, and we'll have to fight to
push him out of the way. We must not give him that
chance, regardless of what political machinations are going
on up above. I don't give a good goddamn what they're
planning. I don't propose to give the Hun the opportunity
to recover from the killing we've just given him. We
destroyed two armies in one week with a handful of losses
to ourselves, and I don't propose to give the bastards the
chance to reorganize on the east bank. I owe that to my
men.

We're going to make a crossing at once. I don't care how
or where we get the necessary equipment, but it must be
got. Steal it, beg it, or make it. But I want it, and it had
better be where we need it, when we need it. We're going
to cross the Rhine, and we're going to do it before I'm a
day older.

Patton would often break into tears when he saw his men
dying in battle and when he visited the wounded in hospitals.
After the war in Europe ended in 1945 he returned briefly to
the United States to see his family and to make a series of
inspirational speeches. In Boston, he said to one crowd, "It is
foolish and wrong to mourn the men who died. Rather we
should thank God that such men lived." He was so moved by
his memories as he said this that he began to cry, and he could
not go on. Within five minutes after he had gotten up to speak
he had to sit down, wiping the tears from his eyes and face.

In July 1945, after the war in Europe was over, Patton spoke
to all of his divisions some thoughts which summed up his
attitude toward war:

It is certain that the two World Wars in which I have
participated would not have occurred had we been prepared. It is my belief that adequate preparation on our
part would have prevented or materially shortened all our
other wars beginning with that of 1812. Yet, after each of
our wars, there has always been a great hue and cry to the

effect that there will be no more wars, that disarmament is the sure road to health, happiness, and peace; and that by removing the fire department, we will remove fires. These ideas spring from wishful thinking and from the erroneous belief that wars result from logical processes. There is no logic in wars. They are produced by madmen. No man can say when future madmen will reappear. I do not say that there will be more wars; I devoutly hope that there will not, but I do say that the chances of avoiding future wars will be greatly enhanced if we are ready.

He closed his speech saying "it is my profound hope that we shall never again be engaged in war, but also let me remind you of the words attributed to George Washington; 'In time of peace, prepare for war!' That advice is still good."

MacArthur

The assault force for recapturing the Philippines in 1944 was huge. There were one hundred and fifty thousand soldiers and a total of 200,000,000 tons of equipment, vehicles, and ammunition. The fleet was composed of 650 battleships, aircraft carriers, cruisers, destroyers, transports, and landing-craft. As this force set poised for the strike, General MacArthur stood at the rail watching the ships which stretched as far as the eye could see; his aide, Brigadier General Courtney Whitney, said, "General, it must give you a sense of great power having such a mighty armada at your command." General MacArthur's answer was: "No, Court, it doesn't. I cannot escape the thought of the fine American boys who are going to die on those beaches tomorrow morning."[66]

MacArthur's strategy in the Far East during World War II was to hit the enemy where they were weakest and to bypass and encircle enemy strongholds, to strangle them until they withered on the vine. The basis of this strategy was his concern for the welfare of American troops. The first thing General MacArthur did in his daily routine during World War II was to examine the casualty reports. "Therein, to his mind, largely rested the balance between success or failure."[6] [7]

MacArthur's troops were so widely spread out that Washington expressed concern about the thousands of enemy troops which were *behind* his line of advance. His reply again illustrates his desire to minimize casualties:

The enemy garrisons which have been by-passed in the Solomons and New Guinea represent no menace to present or future operations. Their capacity for organized offensive effort has passed. The various processes of attrition will eventually account for their final disposition. The actual time of their destruction is of little or no importance, and their influence as a contributing factor of war is already negligible. The actual process of their immediate destruction by assault methods *would unquestionably involve heavy loss of life, without adequate compensating strategic advantages.*

His strategy paid off. American losses were very small. A commander conducting offensive operations expects to lose twice as many casualties as the enemy. Thanks to the leadership of General MacArthur the reverse was true in the Far East— Japanese losses were twice as great as ours.

MacArthur was also concerned about the welfare of the Philippines. When his troops entered Manila in February 1945 the Japanese pulled out of the eastern part of the city and retreated into the walled city of Intramuros. Here they made their last stand. One could admire their brave and stubborn stand were it not for the fact that they enclosed five thousand Filipino men, women, and children with them. These innocent civilians were exposed to the siege of Allied forces and to killing and torture at the hands of the Japanese. General Kenney, MacArthur's Air Chief, who did not know that the Philippine citizens had been forced to remain behind the wall, asked MacArthur to let him bomb Intramuros into oblivion. The General replied "No, I can't let you do that. You would probably kill off the Japs, all right, but there are several thousand Filipino civilians in there who would be killed, too. The world would hold up its hands in horror if we did anything like that. It will take a lot longer, of course, for I'm not going to let our troops rush the place and take heavy casualties. We will use plenty of artillery to breach the walls, and take our time so that we keep our losses to a minimum."[68] General Kenney replied that he agreed, but that the Japs would probably fight to the last man and would kill all the civilians anyhow. MacArthur said to this, "Yes, they will fight to the last and then probably commit suicide rather than surrender. I expect, too, that they will kill a lot of the civilians, but not all. We will rescue well over half of them."[69]

A month before the invasion of the Philippines was launched General MacArthur, because of his love and concern for the Filipino people, warned the air, naval and ground personnel that: "One of the purposes of the Philippine Campaign is to liberate the Filipinos. They will not understand liberation if accompanied by indiscriminate destruction of their homes, their possessions, their civilization and their own lives. Humanity and our moral standing throughout the Far East dictate that the destruction of lives and property in the Philippines be held to a minimum, compatible with the assurance of a successful military campaign."

MacArthur was deeply moved and angered by the uncalled for atrocities of the Japanese towards American POW's and Filipino citizens. He said it was "violative of the most sacred code of martial honor and stains indelibly the creed of the Japanese soldier. No other belligerent of modern times has so debased an honorable service . . ." The profession of soldier has been a proud one; the epitome of its honor was a man like Douglas MacArthur, and he resented the shame brought upon the profession by the brutal savagery of the Japanese soldiers in World War II.

As the invasion of the Philippines progressed, the Japanese prison guards increased their brutality. As General Whitney commented, "The thought of their [POW's] destruction after so many years and with deliverance so near, struck him to the soul." MacArthur drove himself unmercifully because every day brought new reports of savagery by the Japanese towards our POW's. On one occasion General Kenney dropped in to talk with MacArthur about the progress of the campaign. They had dinner together, but MacArthur ate almost nothing. When Kenney asked him about it MacArthur replied, "George, I'm so darn tired I can't eat."[70] They talked quite some time, and the next morning General Kenney, who was leaving before dawn, asked the duty officer to apologize for him to MacArthur for leaving without saying goodby. The O.D. replied, "Oh, General MacArthur left for the front two hours ago."

In later life he summed up his philosophy when he said, "Could I have but a line a century hence crediting a contribution to the advance of peace, I would gladly yield every honor which has been accorded me in war."

Eisenhower

General Eisenhower, since he had the responsibility for the strategic planning for Allied operations, was in a very favorable position to look out for the lives of American soldiers. He was conscious of the fact that men had to fight and would die by his orders. He realized that if he made a mistake men would die unnecessarily. He did not consider himself an impersonal, aloof commander; and he could not divorce himself from personal responsibility for lives of his men.

It was because of his personal love for his men that he was able to hate the enemy so strongly. When inspecting in Sicily in 1943, he told a group that if he should catch Mussolini he would have him shot, and stated vigorously, "I am not one who finds it difficult to hate my enemies."

Many of Ike's decisions were controlled by his concern for American lives. The battle for the Ruhr near the end of the war furnishes an excellent case in point. Hitler had decided that the Ruhr would be treated as a fortress; Goering stated after his capture that "the troops in the Ruhr were given instructions not to surrender under any circumstances."[7] [1] This meant that in taking the Ruhr there would be heavy casualties because of expensive building-to-building fighting in one of the world's most heavily developed and populated industrial sections. Hitler anticipated that twenty Allied divisions would be tied down attempting to take the Ruhr; but General Eisenhower, to avoid the costly and vicious in-fighting, ordered the Ruhr encircled, to die on the vine while the Allied spearhead moved on to the east.

Ike's concern for the lives of Americans was well known to his staff and to many back home in the United States. At a dinner given in honor of Eisenhower in New York City on June 19, 1945, Irving Lehman said: "We who have greeted you so tumultuously today also silently love you deep in our hearts because never for a moment have you forgotten that American soldiers are not mere pawns in a game of war but are loved youths, and because you have loved them as we do; and we honor you, sir, because you—the man trained in the arts of war, commander of embattled nations, who in righteous wrath took up their arms to defend their right to live in peace [have] brought the day nearer when all men shall live in security in their own homes, fearing none and hating none."

One of the meetings between General Eisenhower and Marshal Zhukov just after the close of the war in Europe, is worthy of mention because it provides a comparison of the attitude of Americans and Russians toward the lives of their soldiers. Marshal Zhukov had described, among other things, Russian tactics. General Eisenhower said:

> Highly illuminating to me was his description of the Russian method of attacking through mine fields. The German mine fields, covered by defensive fire, were tactical obstacles that caused us many casualties and delays. It was always a laborious business to break through them, even though our technicians invented every conceivable kind of mechanical appliance to destroy mines safely. Marshal Zhukov gave me a matter-of-fact statement of his practice, which was, roughly, 'There are two kinds of mines; one is the personnel mine and the other is the

vehicular mine. When we come to a mine field our infantry
attacks exactly as if it were not there. The losses we get
from personnel mines we consider only equal to those we
would have gotten if the Germans had chosen to defend
that particular area with strong bodies of troops instead of
with mine fields.[72]

General Eisenhower summed up the difference by saying,
"Americans assess the cost of war in terms of human lives."

This difference was illustrated during another conversation.
Eisenhower commented to Zhukov that German prisoners were
fed the same rations as were our own soldiers. In great
astonishment, Zhukov asked, "Why did you do that?" Ike
answered, "Well, in the first place my country was required to
do so by the terms of the Geneva Convention. In the second
place the Germans had some thousands of American and British
prisioners, and I did not want to give Hitler the excuse or
justification for treating our prisioners more harshly than he
was already doing." Ike reported that "again the Russian
seemed astounded at my attitude." Zhukov replied to Ike, "But
what did you care about the men the Germans had captured?
They had surrendered and could not fight any more."[73]

"As the months of conflict wore on," Ike reflected of World
War II, "I grew constantly more bitter against the Germans,
particularly the Hitler gang. On all sides there was always
evidence of the destruction that Hitler's ruthless ambition had
brought about. Every battle, every skirmish demanded its price
in broken bodies and in the extinction of the lives of young
Allied soldiers."[74]

Eisenhower hated war. "During the war," he said, "hundreds
of broken hearted fathers, mothers, and sweethearts wrote me
personal letters, begging for some hope that a loved one might
still be alive, or, at the very least, for some additional detail as
to the manner of his death. Every one of these I answered, and *I
know of no more effective means of developing an undying
hatred for those responsible for aggressive war than to assume
the obligation of attempting to express sympathy to families
bereaved by it.*"[75]

A study of General Eisenhower's World War II speeches leaves no doubt about his attitude toward war: "There is no glory in battle worth the blood it costs"; "Total war would be the suicide of our generation"; "Your business [in speaking to a civilian audience] is to put me out of business"; "We must train the youth of America to avert World War III."

When American professional soldiers argue for preparedness they do not do it because they seek anything for themselves— they aren't looking for promotion or for money to throw away. Our military leaders are seeking the protection of our people and our way of life. And as General Eisenhower said at the end of World War II, "Weakness cannot cooperate with anything. We have got to be strong."

General MacArthur, as a professional soldier, had long been a proponent of strength and preparedness. When discussing the unreadiness of the United States for World War I, he said to his executive officer that "it was our inexcusable neglect before-hand which caused so much needless mortality—so many lives— so many lives!" His face, contorted with emotion, he continued, "men shot down who didn't have a chance—young, strapping youths who didn't know their weapons or how to protect themselves."[76]

General Patton, also a strong supporter of preparation, reached a paradoxical conclusion when he heard of the atomic bomb. In a letter to a friend dated August 21, 1945 he said, "So far as the atomic bomb is concerned, I think that its advent was most unfortunate because now it will give the pacifists a chance to state that there can be no more wars, which has been their favorite thesis and chief means of producing wars for the last 6,000 years."[77] In other words, since war had become so horrible that it would be impossible, there was no need to prepare for something that will never come about. Patton's answer to this was that "the advent of the atomic bomb was no more startling than was the act of the first man who picked up a rock and bashed out the brains of another man, thereby spoiling the age-old method of fighting with teeth and toenails"; and that "the atomic bomb was not as startling as the first cannon

or the first gasoline motor or the first submarine."[78] Patton
died before the development of more powerful nuclear
weapons, but there is little reason to believe that even these
more terrible weapons would change his agreement with Plato's
comment: "Only the dead have seen the end of war."

Why are American officers concerned over American casualties and POW's? For one thing, of course, those who live fight
another day, and they fight harder. They have the security of
knowing someone cares about them, that as POW's they will not
be ignored. Although they believe there is something worth
dying for, they have confidence that their commanders would
rather that they live.

There is no contradiction in an American officer's wanting
both success in battle and minimum loss of life. Those who
think there is are misled by the facade into believing that the
military are *in* our democracy but not *of* it. Whatever the
trappings, institutional or personal, the man behind them
knows, perhaps better than the civilian who mistrusts him, that
the votes will be with him only as long as he realizes that his
constituency is composed of individuals who have been brought
up to believe that each of them deserves to live.

Selflessness

On June 12, 1944, a week after the D-Day invasion, General
Marshall, along with General H. H. Arnold and Admiral King,
made an inspection trip to Europe. With General Eisenhower as
their escort, the officers went over and up and down the
beachheads in jeeps. They stopped at noon at a field lunch
mess; and as they sat on ammunition boxes, General Marshall
turned very suddenly to the Supreme Commander and said,
"Eisenhower, you've chosen all these commanders or accepted
the ones I suggested. What's the principal quality you look
for?" General Eisenhower reports that "without thinking, I said
selflessness."

Selflessness was certainly part of Marshall's character, and the
epitome of this was never illustrated more sharply than by his

actions during the discussions of who would lead the Allied invasion force—the most overwhelming aggregate of arms and men in the history of warfare.

It was agreed upon by President Roosevelt and Prime Minister Churchill early in 1942 that the Supreme Commander of the Allied invasion would be a British officer. As the war developed, however, it became obvious that there would be a preponderance of American troops and material in the invasion force. This presented an awkward political position for both Roosevelt and Churchill. The former would have to inform the American people, should the commander be British, that a foreigner would command an invasion force composed largely of American soldiers. On the other hand, Winston Churchill would find it politically difficult to explain to the British people that an American would be commanding a European invasion to end a British war. Churchill relieved Roosevelt from this embarrassing situation by voluntarily saying to him that the commander should be an American.

The selection of the Supreme Commander, a matter of vital interest to everyone, required a long and indecisive two years. After it was agreed that it would be an American, Roosevelt deferred naming him for eighteen months, during which time Churchill pressed frequently for a decision. At Teheran in 1943, Stalin asked peremptorily, "Who will command OVERLORD?" (the code name replacing ROUNDUP for the Allied invasion of Europe). The President replied he had not yet decided. Stalin declared his preference for General Marshall as supreme commander and tried to pressure Roosevelt into a decision by saying it was clear to him that until a supreme commander was named he could not consider the Allies were sincere about invading Europe. Stalin was desperate, but Roosevelt would not be pressured.

General Marshall was indeed the primary American contender for the role. On July 31, 1942, Winston Churchill sent a wire to President Roosevelt stating, "It would be agreeable to us if General Marshall were designated for Supreme Command of ROUNDUP." On August 10, 1943, in a letter to President

Roosevelt, Secretary of War Stimson gave his position on the selection of the D-Day Commander:

> Finally, I believe that the time has come when we must put our most commanding soldier in charge of this critical operation at this critical time. You are far more fortunate than was Mr. Lincoln or Mr. Wilson in the ease with which that selection can be made. Mr. Lincoln had to fumble through a process of trial and error with dreadful losses until he was able to discover the right choice. Mr. Wilson had to choose a man who was virtually unknown to the American people and to the foreign armies which he was to serve. General Marshall already has a towering eminence of reputation as a tried soldier and as a broad-minded and skillful administrator. This was shown by the suggestion of him on the part of the British for this very post a year and one-half ago. I believe that he is the man who most surely can now by his character and skill, furnish the military leadership which is necessary to bring our two nations together in confident joint action in this great operation. No one knows better than I the loss and the problems of organization and world-wide strategy centered in Washington which such a solution would cause. I see no other alternative to which we can turn in the great effort which confronts us.
>
>   Faithfully yours,
>   HENRY L. STIMSON
>   Secretary of War

Almost two weeks later, on Sunday, August 22, 1943, Stimson and Roosevelt discussed the matter at lunch. Stimson said of the lunch, "He told me that Churchill had voluntarily come to him and offered to accept Marshall for the Overlord operation. This, the President said, relieved him of the embarrassment of being obliged to ask for it. He also discussed with me Marshall's successor [as Chief of Staff], mentioning Eisenhower."[79]

General Marshall was clearly Roosevelt's number one choice
for the Supreme Command position. In November 1943,
Roosevelt visited North Africa. While there he had a long talk
with General Eisenhower. "Ike," the President said, "you and I
know who was the Chief of Staff during the last years of the
Civil War but practically no one else knows, although the names
of the field generals—Grant, of course, and Lee, and Jackson,
Sherman, Sheridan, and the others—every schoolboy knows
them. I hate to think that 50 years from now practically
nobody will know who George Marshall was. That is one of the
reasons why I want George to have the big Command—he is
entitled to establish his place in history as a great General."[80]

As it became clear that the Allies would soon have to name
the D-Day commander, rumors began to spread in Washington,
most of them naming General Marshall. Since his appointment
had been more or less decided at Quebec in August 1943, it was
true at the time. But when the news leaked out that General
Marshall was going to leave to take command of the invasion, it
created a furor of discussion in Washington. Three senior
members of the Military Affairs Committee, Senators Warren R.
Austin, Styles Bridges, and John Gurney protested that General Marshall was too important to Congress to leave Washington. "They told me," Stimson said, "how much they relied on
him not only individually, but how they were able to carry
controversial matters through with their colleagues if they could
say that the measure in question had the approval of
Marshall."[81] The Senators were concerned that there was an
ouster movement, aided and abetted by enemies who wanted to
remove Marshall from the position of Chief of Staff because his
influence was great with the President and the Joint and
Combined Chiefs of Staff.

The Washington *Times Herald* even carried an article on the
"rumor", maintaining that General Marshall was going to be
taken away from Washington and sent abroad because he had
attacked the President. On September 28, 1943, another story
accused the President of a plot to get Marshall out by "kicking
him upstairs" and putting General Somervell in as Chief of

Staff. Roosevelt was doing this, so the story went, to enable
General Summerville to use the patronage of his position for
Roosevelt's 1944 Presidential campaign.

General Pershing too was opposed to General Marshall's
leaving the position of Chief of Staff. In a letter to President
Roosevelt, Pershing expressed his conviction that it "would be a
fundamental and very grave error in our military policy" for
Marshall to be transferred. President Roosevelt replied to the
AEF commander of World War I that he wanted General
Marshall to be the Pershing of World War II.

Admiral Leahy, General Arnold, and Admiral King had all
gone to President Roosevelt, individually and privately, to urge
the President to keep General Marshall in Washington. All three
believed Marshall to be too important to the harmony of the
Joint and Combined Chiefs organizations to be spared. He was
recognized by all the service chiefs as the dominant figure,
particularly in deciding upon and implementing joint strategic
decisions. He was vital to service unity in these decisions. He
was, according to General Arnold and Admiral King, the
acknowledged leader in the Joint Chiefs of Staff.

Admiral King informed President Roosevelt, "We have the
winning combination here in Washington, why break it up?"
General Arnold stated that no one else could have General
Marshall's "extraordinary sense of the requirements of global
war, his knowledge of land, sea and air logistics, his balanced
judgment as to the importance of one theater or one ally or one
arm of the service as opposed to another."[8][2]

An editorial in the unofficial organ of the services, the *Army
and Navy Journal*, said that to remove General Marshall as Chief
of Staff "would shock the Army, the Congress, and the nation
at large."

Finally Secretary Stimson took a strong position on the
stories about General Marshall. "I can make a statement," he
said at his press conference on September 30, 1943, "about
some of the reports that have come out . . . I am in a position to
say with absolute confidence that whatever duties General
Marshall may hereafter be called upon to perform will be

decided by the President in a spirit of entire confidence in
General Marshall and with the sole purpose of placing this
superbly able officer in the United States Army in the position
where he can render the best service towards a successful
conclusion of this war."

Often a man performs a responsible job in such a brilliant
manner that he makes it look easy. This was the way General
Marshall performed as Army Chief of Staff. The result was
sometimes that his outstanding job was taken for granted.
Certainly the rumors about his transfer gave emphasis and
public recognition to the brilliant work General Marshall was
accomplishing.

At the Cairo Conference in December 1943, President
Roosevelt announced his decision. General Dwight D.
Eisenhower was going to be Supreme Commander. He made the
decision in favor of General Eisenhower over General Marshall
in spite of the "impassioned" advice of two of his closest
advisors, Harry Hopkins and Secretary Stimson, both of whom
wanted General Marshall in the job. Stalin and Churchill also
had made known their preference for Marshall.

Why then was Eisenhower selected and not Marshall? Part of
the answer lies in the character of General George C. Marshall.
Had General Marshall indicated at any time his preference for
the job as Supreme Commander he would have had the
position. At Cairo in December 1943, before the decision had
been finally made, President Roosevelt called him to his villa.
General Marshall wrote of this meeting at which the President
asked him about the Supreme Commander position: "I recalled
saying that I would not attempt to estimate my capabilities; the
President would have to do that; I merely wished to make clear
that whatever the decision, I would go along with it wholeheartedly; that the issue was too great for any personal feeling to be
considered. I did not discuss the pros and cons of the matter. If
I recall, the President stated in completing our conversation, 'I
feel I could not sleep at night with you out of the country'."[8 3]

Secretary Stimson recorded Roosevelt's account of this conversation. "The President," during lunch with General Marshall

at Cairo, "brought the subject [of Supreme Commander] up in
a rather noncommittal way and asked Marshall what he wanted,
or what he thought ought to be done. Marshall, as usual, dug his
feet in and said it was not for him to say what should be done.
But then, he added, on one subject he would give his opinion
and that was that if he, Marshall, went to Overlord, the
President should not leave the position of Chief of Staff open
but should put Eisenhower there as full Chief of Staff [they
were considering putting Eisenhower in as "acting" Chief of
Staff], that any other course would not be fair to Eisenhower
or to the Staff."[84]

Then the President announced his decision. He told General
Marshall, "I've been thinking this matter over and have decided
that I will keep you as Chief of Staff and put Eisenhower in as
head of Overlord."[85] Marshall accepted the President's decision
without displaying any emotion. He discussed the meeting with
McCloy, right after it had taken place, and McCloy observed
that Marshall did not "seem as if he were a very greatly
disappointed man." But Stimson averred that "I think I know
better. I know his deepest ambition in his heart is and it was to
command the invasion into France. It was simply his matchless
power of self-sacrifice and self-control that gave the other
impression."[86]

On December 18, 1943, President Roosevelt told Stimson in
detail about his conversation with Marshall in Cairo. Secretary
Stimson reported his lunch with President Roosevelt in detail:

> The President described how he reopened this matter
> [of the Supreme Commander] with Marshall at their
> solitary luncheon together and tried to get Marshall to tell
> him whether he preferred to hold the command of Over-
> lord or whether he preferred to remain as Chief of Staff.
> He [the President] was very explicit in telling me that he
> urged Marshall to tell him which one of the two he
> personally preferred, intimating that he would be very glad
> to give him the one he preferred. He said that Marshall
> stubbornly refused, saying that it was for the President to
> decide and he, Marshall, would do with equal cheerfulness

whichever one he was selected for. The President said that he got the impression that Marshall was not only impartial between the two but perhaps really preferred to remain as Chief of Staff. Finally, after having been unable to tell him his preference, the President said that he decided on a mathematical basis that if Marshall took Overlord it would mean that Eisenhower would become Chief of Staff but, while Eisenhower was a very good soldier and familiar with the European theater, he was unfamiliar with what had been going on in the Pacific and he also would be far less able than Marshall to handle Congress; that, therefore, he, the President, decided that he would be more comfortable if he had Marshall at his elbow in Washington and turned over Overlord to Eisenhower.

Stimson himself was disappointed. "I was staggered," he told President Roosevelt, "when I heard of the change . . ." Stimson had thought Marshall to be the best man for the job. He would be able to overcome the obstacles and delays of launching the invasion which "I felt certain he would meet in Great Britain on account of the attitude of the Prime Minister and the British Staff." A second reason for Stimson's desire to see Marshall as D-Day Commander was based upon his understanding of Marshall's true feeling. "I knew," he said to the President, "That at the bottom of his heart it was Marshall's secret desire above all things to command this invasion force into Europe; and I had had very hard work to wring it out of Marshall . . ." He then laughingly said to Roosevelt, "I wish I had been along with you in Cairo. I could have made the point clear."

Stimson then went on to say of his conversation with President Roosevelt, "I had had great difficulty in getting Marshall to speak on such a subject as his personal preference, but that I had finally accomplished it [he got General Marshall to say, 'Any soldier would prefer a field command'] "; and that "when he was on the point of leaving for the Teheran Conference I had begged him not to sacrifice what I considered the interest of the country to the undue sensitiveness of his own conscience in seeming to seek a post."[87]

Stimson recorded his continuing efforts over several months to get General Marshall to express his preference: "I called in Marshall who has been very reluctant to talk about the matter at all and has not helped me a bit in my decisions and efforts, and told him that he had to help me . . ." The next day there were further discussions between the two. Stimson said of that day's talk, "Marshall himself is very reticent on the matter because he is personally and directly involved, and I have therefore to make a good deal of effort to be in a position to help him . . ."[88]

As the rumors grew about General Marshall as D-Day Commander, he became even more reluctant to discuss it. He was "so upset and shy about it that the President," Stimson remarked, "complained to me rather wistfully at our last talks that he couldn't get any advice out of him on the subject."[89]

The rumors of late 1943, prior to Roosevelt's announcement of the Supreme Commander, were very harmful to British-American relations. They had, among other things, alleged that the Supreme Commander role was going to be more than a European position; it was to be a global command of all Allied forces in the world. It was difficult enough for Churchill to explain an American general in the key role in the European theater. The global command was too much.

General Marshall had a solution calculated to soothe British wounded pride. He suggested to Stimson that he would be willing to serve under Field Marshal Sir John Dill as Supreme Commander. This, Marshall thought, would ease the opposition facing Churchill at home. Stimson said no to this proposal because he thought it would have the opposite effect in the United States; as he remarked, "Our peoples' faith in Marshall is one of the things that will carry us through the tragedies that may go with Overlord."[90]

After the decision was made that General Eisenhower would be Supreme Commander, by mutual consent, further discussion of Marshall's commandership of Overlord was dropped in conversations between Stimson and Marshall. Stimson's comment on Marshall's reaction to the decision was that he showed "his usual bigness about the whole darn thing."[91] In all probability, Marshall had decided that, regardless of his personal desire, his duty was in Washington.

Marshall had made his reputation as a staff officer. Would he have been successful as D-Day Commander? There seems no doubt that he would have. As Supreme Commander his primary responsibilities would have been dealing with statesmen, generals, and other high-ranking officers. He was not a flamboyant character; the job did not call for flamboyancy. He had proved as Army Chief of Staff that he had the respect of American generals, of political figures, and of Allied officers. He had proved his competency to deal with the press. And, as attested by the fact that both the British and Russians had advocated his selection for the supreme command post, he had proved his ability to get along with the Allies.

Apparently the most important factor in the decision was President's Roosevelt's conviction that General Marshall could not be spared, as evidenced by his comment, "I could not sleep soundly at night with General Marshall out of Washington." Marshall was needed in Washington by the President, by Congress, by the Joint Service Staffs, and by the American people who had so much confidence in him. To them the job of the Chief of Staff was more important than that of the invasion commander. For them, at that time, Marshall was the indispensable man.

This example, of Marshall refusing to express his strongest desire, was the epitome and the high point of a life of selflessness. The same life of selflessness was led by MacArthur, Eisenhower, and Patton.

The Role of Character

There is a high purpose for the American military man. He does not want war. He only desires the opportunity to live in a democracy, free from tyranny and secure from those nations who seek to destroy our way of life. Their high purpose was based not only on patriotism; as observed, it was also founded on deep religious faith and selfessness.

In writing this manuscript the author discussed the quality of character with over five hundred officers who achieved the rank of brigadier general through five-star general. Each was asked, "How do you define character?" There were many, many definitions given for this word. There are men of "no" or "bad" character; but when there is no qualifying adjective used with the word character, it was agreed that it implies a favorable connotation. Character is a personal attribute that encompasses all of the admirable qualities of human nature. Character is the ennobling attribute of man. But really, as it has already been stated, character is a word that should not be defined; it should be described.

These generals were also asked, "What role does character play in American military leadership?" In reply there were statements such as, "Without character there is no true leadership;" "Character and leadership are like the popular 'Horse and Carriage.' Both go to make marriage. You can't have one without the other." "Character is the base on which leadership is built;" "Character is the number one attribute of leadership;" "I cannot separate leadership from character except that you can have character without leadership, but not leadership without character;" and that "Character is leadership."

More briefly others said that the role of character in leadership is "all important," "vital," "the keystone," "the basis," "the most important factor," "the basic element," "the major role," "the whole work," "decisive," "dominant," "indispensable," "a must," and, as General Eisenhower summed it up, "everything."

Although these answers give emphasis to the importance of character, they do not specifically come to grips with just what role character plays.

Lincoln once said that you can fool some of the people some of the time, but never can you fool all of the people all of the time. In the military, you can't fool a soldier *any time*. You might fool the people above you as to what you are, but never the men under you. Character is a state of mind that reflects the inner qualities of an individual. With the close association most men have in a military unit it doesn't take long for a soldier to size up his leader. Men do not want to trust their lives or reputations to leaders whom they consider to be unqualified. A person with a low, weak, immoral or vacillating type of character may have a brilliant mind; but this intellect won't make them leaders. Men instinctively rally to the leadership of strong, bold, and inspiring leaders who demonstrate their qualification for leadership by adopting sensible courses of action and who have the will to follow through and overcome all difficulties until victory is obtained.

A man of strong character will honorably follow his conscience under all conditions, regardless of public opinion, if he is convinced he is right. The weak man will be swayed by public or private opinion because he fears what effect his actions may have on his reputation. It is not necessary to be right all the time, as long as the followers know that the leader did *what he thought was right* for the situation. Men must believe that their leader knows what he wants, means what he says, that he'll do what he says to the best of his ability, that he can be depended upon to be consistent.

But there must be a proper balance. As one general put it, "The individual who, in the face of adversity, makes the least compromise with what he believes to be right has the finest character. The individual who makes no compromise doesn't exist." There must be give and take in life as long as no one is perfect. If a leader is too positive he can lose his effectiveness—unless he is always right, a quality that only one man has been known to have in the history of the world.

Good character is necessary to gain respect, and respect is a requirement for leadership, particularly for the long run. When a commander has the respect of his subordinates they will emulate his actions, habits, mannerisms, and dress. It can almost be said that personnel will react in direct ratio to the character of its commander, whether good or bad.

Men have confidence in leaders they respect and trust, knowing that the leader will always have their well being in mind under all conditions.

The leader will succeed or fail by the example he sets. If he is disciplined, his followers will be. If he disciplines in such a fashion that the recipient believes he has been treated fairly and without bias, there will still be respect even though there will not be any popularity. Unless there is a sense of fair play, men will not follow long.

Any organization reflects the character of its leader. Character is reflected directly in the morale of an organization, and without high morale an organization will be unable to accomplish its mission in an above average manner. Morale is a state of mind that causes men to give their all to the leader and to the mission, regardless of the cost. With the leader who has character the men do it because "the old man wants it." It could be done by driving fear into the men, but then a subordinate will do no more than is necessary to get by. You can buy a man's time; you can, within the military, "order" a man's time, but not his loyalty and enthusiasm. These latter two qualities are part of the difference between mediocrity and above average results.

When the statement is made that character is the foundation of leadership, it might come to the reader's mind, "Well, how about Napoleon or Hitler or Stalin or the gangland dictator, Al Capone? Were they not leaders?" In the first place, it must be emphasized that the statement is made that character is everything in *American military leadership*. This study is concerned with why Marshall, MacArthur, Eisenhower and Patton were successful; it is not about dictators. It should be emphasized, however, that Napoleon, Hitler, Stalin, and Capone *failed*; they did not accomplish their ultimate objective in their lifetime. The character of the leader must be compatible with the desired goals and in harmony with the dominant motivating forces of those whom he seeks to lead. France and Germany under Napoleon and Hitler collapsed. Capone went to jail and died there, a broken man. The Soviet Union under Communist rule has fallen terribly short of its evil goals and is presently losing the gains it has made, rather than gaining. These dictators failed to understand men, and their purpose was not a really noble one that people would willingly give their all for or die for. "When Napoleon started to fight for Napoleon, and not France," General Eisenhower remarked, "France fell."[9][2]

Character produces enduring leadership. Someone might attain limited success despite obvious character deficiencies; but generally, only the men with sound character attain the top positions. If a man of low moral character reaches high rank, there is always the possibility that his subordinates will be influenced by his bad characteristics to the detriment of the mission. If the leader kills, lies, steals, or cheats, why should the followers do otherwise?

The leader is someone who is set apart from his followers. Character implies traits that set a man apart from the crowd. No strong man is without weaknesses (and no weak man is without strengths!); but a man of high character can be depended upon at all times. If a follower can say of his leader, "I can depend on him, not necessarily always to be right, but to do his best and what he considers to be right. I know his word is good. I can depend upon him to be honorable in his dealings with me. I can depend upon his moderation, his temperance, his fairness, his judgment. I trust him. I admire him," that is the type of leader men have confidence in and whom men will die for. Decisions are not easy in time of war, and the follower must believe in a decision that means life and death.

In summary, character shapes the actions of the individual leader, it offers an example to follow for those he leads, it commands respect, it promotes confidence in those whom he commands, it sustains him in moments of great crisis, it causes him to do instinctively the honorable and right thing when he is confronted with great decisions, and it instills in those he commands the desire to obey because they know that the orders they receive are just, sound, and necessary.

While the word character is difficult to define, if one were forced to decide on a definition, or a description, there is no better way to express either than to cite the historic motto of West Point—Duty, Honor, Country.

DECISION AND COURAGE

The Role of Decision

The wartime leader is a lonely man. At no time does he feel his loneliness more deeply than when he has to make a critical high-level decision dealing with life and death, success or failure, victory or defeat. It is an overwhelming responsibility which few people desire and one for which considerably fewer people are qualified. But making decisions is part of leadership; and, hopefully, in time of war the general who does not have the strength to make decisions and the judgment to be right a large percentage of the time does not remain long in a position of high leadership. Generals are human and are subject to the strains and stresses of the mind just as lesser men are, particularly since the general's responsibility is greater than that of the lesser man. His mistakes can be counted in death and destruction, and this is a responsibility that no sane man takes lightly.

The generals of World War II were faced daily with innumerable difficult and grave decisions. It would not serve any useful purpose, even if it were possible, to discuss all of these decisions; but several should be discussed to illustrate the importance of decision in military leadership. Before embarking upon this discussion, however, there are two points of caution that need special emphasis. The first is that although in time of war a high commander has to make critical decisions which change the course of history, very seldom were the generals' decisions based upon all the information that one has available in later years to evaluate those decisions retrospectively, with the benefit of historical hindsight; the commander must act upon the facts which are available at the time of decision. The second caution is that to one who has never experienced making high decisions it looks easy. Those below are often ignorant of the full complexity of the problems and are impatient when they receive late, or do not receive at all, a clear-cut decision. It is easy to criticize and to come up with an answer when *the responsibility* is not yours. But the same individual, should he be given this responsibility, would soon realize how magnanimous and overwhelming the task is when the power of decision *and* responsibility for the decision is his.

There is a third factor in high command decision that should be mentioned—normally, the commander in time of war can select his key staff members who advise him. If wise he will select the most competent people possible. This means that they will be dedicated professionals who are all strong men. They will have strong opinions backed up by proven professional ability and years of experience. One cannot take the advice of such people lightly, and when they are all opposed to a top general's conclusion, the decision making process is far more difficult.

Eisenhower

The greatest decision faced by Eisenhower during World War II, as has already been discussed, was the place, day, and hour of the Allied invasion of the European continent. There were also many other complex decisions during the war, for example, the question of sending two airborne divisions into the Cherbourg peninsula as a preliminary operation to the invasion of France. These divisions would be used to secure our landings at Utah Beach on the Contentin Peninsula. The reasons for the action, according to Ike's Chief of Staff, General Smith, were "... compelling. Behind the landing area stretched the low ground the Germans had flooded. A few roads crossed the marshy, mile-wide strip, but unless airborne troops were put down on the firm ground behind to seize the roadheads and engage the defenders, the narrow causeways across the marshes could be raked by enemy fire. Our troops would take heavy casualties forcing their way inland from the beaches."[1]

The senior air adviser on Eisenhower's staff, British Air Chief Marshal Leigh-Mallory, was very much opposed to the airborne operation because in his opinion it would result in the useless slaughter of two fine divisions. It was the Britisher's contention that the strong antiaircraft defenses of Cherbourg and the small area in which the airborne divisions had to be dropped would result in the loss of seventy-five percent or higher of the gliders going in and fifty percent of the paratroopers. It would result in the death of thousands of men; and the mission in his opinion, would fail because of these excessive losses.

On May 30, 1944, Leigh-Mallory came to General Eisenhower to make one final protest against carrying out the operation. After the Air Marshal presented his case these were the thoughts that went on in Eisenhower's mind:

> To protect him [Leigh-Mallory] in case his advice was disregarded, I instructed the air commander to put his recommendations in a letter and informed him he would have my answer within a few hours. I took the problem to no one else. Professional advice and council could do no more.
>
> I went to my tent alone and sat down to think. Over and over I reviewed each step . . . I realized, of course, that if I deliberately disregarded the advice of my technical expert on the subject, and his predictions should prove accurate, then I would carry to my grave the unbearable burden of a conscience justly accusing me of the stupid, blind sacrifice of thousands of the flower of our youth. Outweighing any personal burden, however, was the possibility that if he were right the effect of the disaster would be far more than local: it would be likely to spread to the entire force.[2]

In considering what should be done, Ike weighed the factors:

1) he was convinced that the operation was vital to the success of the assault on Utah Beach;

2) without the Utah Beach landing to immediately get the base of the Cotentin Peninsula, the entire operation was too risky to attempt; and

3) he just didn't believe, in his own judgment, that the Germans could inflict such heavy losses.

He called Leigh-Mallory and told him the attack would go on as planned. History proved Ike was correct. The losses to the airborne elements in the first drop were less than two percent, and less than ten percent for the whole operation. Captain Butcher cited in his book that "in typical British sport fashion," Air Chief Marshal Leigh-Mallory admitted he was wrong and that "the Marshal frankly said that it is sometimes difficult in this life to admit that one is wrong, but he has never had a greater pleasure in doing so than on this occasion. He congratulated General Ike on the wisdom of his command decisions."[3]

There was another incident quite similar to this experienced by General Eisenhower. The Allies were collecting our forces after the abortive Ardennes counter-offensive; and he wanted to follow through with the effective campaigns west of the Rhine because he believed we would destroy a large portion of Hitler's effectiveness before storming the river barrier. Field Marshal Sir Alan Brooke, who was originally selected as Supreme Commander, was opposed to this strategy because such an operation would result in a dispersal of Allied forces and divert divisions from the northern crossing of the Rhine by Montgomery's forces aimed at the Ruhr. Brooke had very strong feelings about the matter, but Ike stuck to his decision. Several weeks later Brooke was to say to General Eisenhower, "You were completely right, and I am sorry if my fear of dispersed effort added to your burdens. Thank God you stuck by your guns!"[4]

The D-Day Decision

The discussions which decided the time and place of the Second Front in World War II were conducted for over two years. After much controversy, particularly British reluctance to embark upon the project, the date was changed from 1942 to 1943, and then to 1944. The place also required considerable Allied argument because of Churchill's inclination towards the so-called, "soft-underbelly". When Ike was named Supreme Commander, the place, France, had been decided upon; and the staff planners had selected the month of May (1944) for the invasion. This date was indirectly to be Eisenhower's first change. He concluded that there would be a need to increase the number of assault divisions from three to five for the initial invasion. This meant, in order to accomplish the personnel and logistic changes (particularly the need for additional landing craft), a postponement from May until June 1944. The month's delay was significant because the good spring weather was advantageous to offensive fighting. Time would be looked upon as golden in the months of winter fighting ahead.

The critical aspect of the date was the weather. When General Eisenhower had to decide on "go" or "no go" in North Africa, weather was a problem. Sicily was worse. The decision had been made that the Allies would invade; but the evening before the Sicilian invasion the wind, instead of dying as it was predicted, rose to forty miles an hour. This wind would make many of the soldiers sea-sick riding into what would be a hazardous landing because of the high waves. Nor was it encouraging for the 82nd Airborne Division, which was going to drop into the midst of the enemy. General Marshall wired wanting to know, "Is attack on or off?" Ike said to himself, "My reaction was that I wish I knew!"[5] But the decision was his to make. Again he was alone; and again, he calculated the risks. If he were to call off the invasion now, there would be many isolated catastrophes among the units which, because of their particular mission, departed early. These forces, should they not receive the message to return, would be slaughtered. The element of surprise, upon which they were counting heavily, would be lost. Outside, he gauged the wind once more, went into his office and ordered: "It's on. There's a high wind, but think we'll have good news tomorrow." As the evening wore on the wind velocity, however, increased. During the lonely and desperate hours of waiting, he fingered his lucky coins; and, in his own words, "There was nothing we could do but pray, desperately."[6]

Because the Normandy invasion required the right combination of moon, tide and time of sunrise, the target date for the attack, after the month of May had been abandoned, would be on 5, 6, or 7 June. The decision on which of these days would depend upon the weather—another overwhelming decision to make. General Eisenhower said of the situation:

> If none of the three days should prove satisfactory from the standpoint of weather, consequences would ensue that were almost terrifying to contemplate. Secrecy would be lost. Assault troops would be unloaded and crowded back into assembly areas inclosed in barbed wire, where their original places would already have been taken by those to follow in subsequent waves. Complicated movement tables would be scrapped. Morale would drop. A wait of at least fourteen days, possibly twenty-eight, would be necessary—a sort of suspended animation involving more than 2,000,000 men! The good-weather period available for major campaigning would become still shorter and the enemy's defenses would become still stronger.[7]

To prepare for this momentous decision, beginning in April, Ike had numerous dry weather runs. He would say to his weather experts, "I want to invade tomorrow. What will the weather be like?" Based upon the weather man's prediction he asked the air, ground and sea commanders how the predicted weather would affect their operations. Then Ike would decide "go" or "no go", and they were in a position to criticize the performance when they actually had the opportunity to see what weather developed.

Unfortunately for the Allies they were having some of the worst June weather in the Spring of 1944 that the area had experienced in decades. It is no wonder that Eisenhower refuted the old adage that "The weather is always neutral." In his opinion, nothing could be more untrue: "Bad weather is obviously the enemy of the side that seeks to launch projects requiring good weather, or of the side possessing great assets, such as strong air forces, which depend upon good weather for effective operations. If really bad weather should endure permanently the Nazi would need nothing else to defend the Normandy Coast."[8]

It was tentatively decided that the invasion would be launched on June 5. The final meeting to decide was held at 0400 on June 4, even though some of the forward elements had already embarked. The weather was bad; there were low clouds, high winds and waves, all of which indicated a hazardous landing—air support would be impossible and naval gunfire inaccurate. General Eisenhower consulted his key advisers: Admiral Ramsay was neutral from the naval side, Montgomery said "go" and Air Marshall Tedder said "no go". But they could only advise—the final decision was Eisenhower's. He decided to postpone the attack.[9]

The staff met again the next morning. The weather outlook for June 6 was good, but would probably last only about thirty-six hours. General Walter B. Smith vividly described the scene on the morning of June 5:

All the commanders were there when General Eisenhower arrived, trim in his tailored battle jacket, his face tense with the gravity of the decision which lay before him. Field Marshal Montgomery wore his inevitable baggy corduroy trousers and sweat shirt. Admiral Ramsey and his Chief of Staff were immaculate in navy blue and gold.

The meteorologists were brought in at once. There was the ghost of a smile on the tired face of Group Captain Stagg, the tall Scot.

"I think we have found a gleam of hope for you, sir," he said to General Eisenhower, and we all listened expectantly. "The mass of weather fronts coming in from the Atlantic is moving faster than we anticipated," the chief meteorologist said and he went on to promise reasonable weather for twenty-four hours. Ike's advisers then started firing rapid questions at the weather man. When they had finished asking questions there was silence which lasted for a full five minutes while General Eisenhower sat on a sofa before the bookcase which filled the end of the room. I never realized before the loneliness and isolation of a Commander at a time when such a momentous decision has to be taken, with full knowledge that failure or success rests on his judgment alone. He sat there quietly, not getting up to pace with quick strides as he often does. He was tense, weighing every consideration of weather as he had been briefed to do during the dry runs since April, and weighing with them those other imponderables.

Finally he looked up, and the tension was gone from his face.

He said briskly, "Well, we'll go!"[10]

What goes on in a commander's mind after such a monumental decision? Ike said of the occasion in his memoirs, "Again I had to endure the interminable wait that always intervenes between the final decision of the high command and the earliest possible determination of success or failure in such ventures."[11]

He then occupied himself with visiting troops, receiving joshing comments from the men that he had no cause to worry.[12]

In spite of all the people around him during, before, and after decisions, it is easy to see why Ike wrote to a friend during the war, "The worst part of high military command is the loneliness . . ."

MacArthur

Discussions with members of General MacArthur's World War II staff illustrate that MacArthur's brilliance in decision making could be equaled by very few. One of his staff officers remarked that during World War II MacArthur was given the castoffs nobody else wanted. The author asked him, if this were true why were MacArthur's decisions so sound? The reply was that

MacArthur was so brilliant he didn't need a staff. He could make the best decision without them. This does not mean he did not listen to his advisers. It does mean that he had a feel or sixth sense of knowing what to do, when to do it, and in being correct.

MacArthur had a habit of listening quietly while his staff briefed him on the facts pertaining to the big decisions which had to be made. When the briefing was over, he would sometimes ask a few pertinent questions and then announce his decision.

The author interviewed a collection of officers in order to cover General MacArthur over his entire military career; it revealed a consistent pattern in his decision making. An officer would present the problem requiring a decision; and without any hesitation, MacArthur would give a decisive answer with clock-like precision.

General Kenney summed him up as a decision maker when he said, "MacArthur is a positive individual. There is nothing vacillating about him. He believes in himself, his destiny, and in his place in history. While he will truly admit his mistakes after they have happened, he is sure that his decisions are correct at the time he makes them."[13]

MacArthur was faced with many critical decisions during World War II; one of them well illustrates his concept of the war in the Pacific and his ability to make difficult decisions. Against the advice of many of his senior commanders and staff, MacArthur ordered a landing at Hyane Harbor on eastern Los Negros. Here is General Courtney Whitney's description of the situation:

In order to move our naval forces forward, it was necessary to obtain and hold an advanced naval base. Truk and Rabaul with their excellent harbors were such bases, but were firmly held by the enemy. To attack either would involve staggering losses both in men and material. Manus, in the Admiralties, hundreds of miles behind them and hundreds of miles nearer the final objective, was not so strongly held because the enemy could not visualize a movement to his rear such as MacArthur contemplated. Manus had a magnificent harbor capable of holding the entire American fleet. MacArthur's plan was the epitome of his concept of deep envelopment to the rear of the enemy in order to achieve complete surprise and isolate the enemy's forces by severing his lines of supply. With no material resources, these forces would then, as he expressed it, "wither and die on the vine."[14]

Just before the invasion army was ready to depart General MacArthur held one of his "rare councils of war". One of his key commanders was again recommending that the operation be cancelled, stating that it was "a military gamble with the deck of cards in the enemy's hands as dealer." MacArthur replied, "Yes, but a gamble in which I have everything to win, little to lose. I bet ten to win a million, if I hit the jackpot."[15]

Patton

Obviously Patton was a man who could make decisions, and his judgment proved to be superb—a really outstanding individual makes the difficult look easy. But one should not be misled by this; Patton himself said of one of his decisions, "The making of such a decision sounds easy, but is, in my opinion, quite difficult."[16]

As with Eisenhower, one can also with Patton see loneliness. Just before an attack by his army during the critical Battle of the Bulge he commented: "As usual on the verge of action everyone felt full of doubt except myself. It has always been my unfortunate role to be the ray of sunshine and the backslapper before action, both for those under me and also those over me. I can say with perfect candor that, at that time, I had no doubt as to the success of the operation . . ."

Further insight into decision making is gained by Patton's account of the release of his division commanders:

A general who had been relieved came in at his own request and tried to explain why he was no good. I offered him a lesser command in another division but he told me he needed forty-eight hours to consider it. I did not tell him so, but I realized that any man who could not make up his mind in less than forty-eight hours was not fit to command troops in battle.[17]

On November 6, 1942, just before the Allied invasion of North Africa, General Patton noted in his diary, "In forty hours I shall be in battle, with little information, and on the spur of the moment will have to make most momentous decisions; but I believe that one's spirit enlarges with responsibility and that, with God's help, I shall make them and make them right. It seems that my whole life has been pointed to this moment. When this job is done I presume I will be pointed to the next step in the ladder of destiny. If I do my full duty the rest will take care of itself."[18]

This statement by Patton almost sums up his concept of decision making. In essence he has said that he has also prepared all of his life to become a military (battlefield) decision maker, that if his decisions are good ones he will be called upon to make bigger decisions, that the man grows with the challenge and rises to meet the situation, and that God is a big help along the way.

Feel or Sixth Sense as a Quality of Decision Making

"One day during the latter part of the Sicilian Campaign the boss," wrote General Patton's World War II aide, Colonel Charles R. Codman, "was suddenly called upon, or felt he was, to make a critical decision. It was one of those decisions where if you guess right others get the credit and if you guess wrong you and you alone get the blame. Well, he was right and it wasn't a guess, either, but that sixth sense made up of intuition and conviction which goes to make a *grand chief*."[19]

Even the strongest opponents of the thesis that there is a pattern to leadership concede that all truly great military leaders have a "feel" or "sixth sense."

"Patton," said Omar Bradley, "had that sense. I remember when Third Army was going up the Rhine to Cologne and turned right to flank the people who were holding up the American Seventh Army on our right. Patton went for about two days, meeting only token resistance, then he suddenly stopped. Some members of my staff said, 'Why doesn't he keep going?' 'He senses something,' I said, 'that we can't sense because we don't have all the information.' The next day he was hit by three German divisions. But he had stopped to prepare for them; he bounced them off, and then he moved forward again."

Is this feel or sixth sense a quality a man is born with? Patton, who called this sense, "military reaction," wrote to his son at West Point on June 6, 1944, "What success I have had results from the fact that I have always been certain that my military reactions were correct. Many people do not agree with me; they are wrong. The unerring jury of history, written long after both of us are dead, will prove me correct.

"Note that I speak of 'military reactions.' No one is born with them anymore than anyone is born with measles. You can be born with a soul capable of correct military reactions or a body capable of having big muscles, but both qualities must be developed by hard work . . ."

"My theory," General Bradley said regarding his feel in decision making, "is that you collect information, little bits of it, and it goes into your brain like feeding information into a 1401 IBM calculator. It's stored in there, but you are not conscious of it. You hear some of it over the phone, you see some of it on the map, in what you read, in briefings. It is all stored in your mind, then suddenly you are faced with a decision. You don't go back and pick up each one of the pieces of information, but you run over the main items that are involved and the answer comes out like when you push the button on an IBM machine. You have stored up this knowledge as it comes in and when you are suddenly faced in battle with a situation needing a decision you can give it. When people would call me on the phone and give me a situation I would push a button, and I would have an answer right then. You can't go back and pore over the maps for two or three days."

There is more to feel than solving a problem that comes up at the moment. "Maybe there is such a thing as intuition," J. Lawton Collins remarked in a discussion of the quality of feel, "but I don't believe it is really intuition. I think it is a quality based on sufficient intelligence to make a careful evaluation of the situation—to know where the trouble spots are likely to develop. All good commanders that I knew had that faculty. They could anticipate where there would likely be trouble and they went there. They went there to be sure that they could do something about that trouble as it developed. If there is such a thing as intuition it is based first of all on knowledge, knowing the tools you have available. You have got to know your business. You know your business by working hard and studying as a younger man."

General Simpson expressed a similar conclusion when he stated that this feel "comes from several things. One is your background of training. As I look back on my long career and the first eight or ten years of basic work that I did, seven long weary years of which was as a second lieutenant, I realize it gave me a background of knowledge and experience that helped me understand situations that came up. I think it prepared me for anticipating things that might occur."

General Truscott said that to him "Knowledge is the basis for feel. Your training; your study; your knowledge of men, your understanding of the capability of what they can do for themselves, their physical limitations, their reaction to discipline. It requires an interest in people."

General Wade Haislip said the same thing, "I think feel is the result of education, of thoroughly knowing your profession. When I was over in Ireland in 1944 with a Corps, we were waiting and training for the invasion of Europe. I was to be in the second echelon to cross; so I had from the 9th to the 1st of

August to observe the fighting. I got permission, while my men were training, to go to Italy on a sight seeing trip. This was of the utmost value to me, and I saw there was nothing mysterious about it. It was exactly what I had been studying all my life. So when my Corps got into action nothing changed; we did exactly what we had been doing in all of our maneuvers and command post exercises. The only difference I knew was that people were shooting at us."

General McAuliffe's comments were no different: "A combat leader has to be something of a psychologist, both in the mass training of men and in the handling of his subordinate commanders. Some do better with a pat on the back while others need a kick on the backside. I think this is something a man learns over the years as he serves in the military. It requires an understanding of men. Experience has a great deal to do with it. You meet many people in your military career and you learn to measure people."

This feel, sixth sense, military reaction, or whatever one chooses to call it, is not limited to battlefield situations. Omar Bradley said that "George Marshall was a great character. He had great foresight. He had imagination. It's hard to define imagination. It is the faculty of foreseeing what is going to happen as a result of certain things. In battle you call it the feel of the battle, a sixth sense."

Sir Winston Churchill wrote in his book on Marlborough:

> The success of a commander does not arise from following rules or models. It consists in an absolutely new comprehension of the dominant facts of the situation at the time, and all the forces at work. Every operation of war is unique. What is wanted is a profound appreciation of the actual event. There is no surer road to disaster than to imitate the plans of bygone heroes and fit them to novel situations.

If Churchill meant by the last sentence that a leader could not learn from the past then he would find the beliefs of the top American military leaders to be in opposition.

General MacArthur, when he was Chief of Staff of the Army, wrote in his report of 1935 to the Secretary of War:

More than most professions the military is forced to depend upon intelligent interpretation of the past for signposts charting the future. Devoid of opportunity in peace, for self-instruction through actual practice of his profession, the soldier makes maximum use of historical record in assuring the readiness of himself and his command to function efficiently in emergency. The facts derived from historical analysis he applies to conditions of the present and the proximate future, thus developing a synthesis of appropriate method, organization, and doctrine.

But the military student does not seek to learn from history the minutiae of method and technique. In every age these are decisively influenced by the characteristics of weapons currently available and by the means at hand for maneuvering, supplying, and controlling combat forces. But research does bring to light those fundamental principles, and their combinations and applications, which, in the past, have been productive of success. These principles know no limitation of time. Consequently, the army extends its analytical interest to the dust-buried accounts of wars long past as well as to those still reeking with the scent of battle. It is the object of the search that dictates the field for its pursuit. Those callow critics who hold that only in the most recent battles are there to be found truths applicable to our present problems have failed utterly to see this. They apparently cling to a fatuous hope that in historical study is to be found a complete digest of the science of war rather than simply the basic and inviolable laws of the art of war.

Were the accounts of all battles, save only those of Genghis Khan, effaced from the pages of history, and were the facts of his campaigns preserved in descriptive detail, the soldier would still possess a mine of untold wealth from which to extract nuggets of knowledge useful in molding an army for future use. The successes of that amazing leader, beside which the triumphs of most other commanders in history pale into insignificance, are proof sufficient of his unerring instinct for the fundamental qualifications of an army.

He devised an organization appropriate to conditions then existing; he raised the discipline and the morale of his troops to a level never known in any other army, unless possibly that of Cromwell; he spent every available period of peace to develop subordinate leaders and to produce perfection of training throughout the army, and, finally, he insisted upon speed in action, a speed which by comparison with other forces of his day was almost unbelievable. Though he armed his men with the best equipment of offense and of defense that the skill of Asia could produce, he refused to encumber them with loads that would immobilize his army. Over great distances his legions moved so rapidly and secretly as to astound his enemies and practically to paralyze their powers of resistance. He crossed great rivers and mountain ranges, he reduced walled cities in his path and swept onward to destroy nations and pulverize whole civilizations. On the battlefield his troops maneuvered so swiftly and skillfully and struck with such devastating speed that times without number they defeated armies overwhelmingly superior to themselves in number.

Regardless of his destructiveness, his cruelty, his savagery, he clearly understood the unvarying necessities of war. It is these conceptions that the modern soldier seeks to separate from the details of the Khan's technique, tactics, and organization, as well as from the ghastly practices of his butcheries, his barbarism, and his ruthlessness. So winnowed from the chaff of medieval custom and of all other inconsequentials, they stand revealed as kernels of eternal truth, as applicable today in our effort to produce an efficient army as they were when, seven centuries ago, the great Mongol applied them to the discomfiture and amazement of a terrified world. We cannot violate these laws and still produce and sustain the kind of army that alone can insure the integrity of our country and the permanency of our institutions if ever again we face the grim realities of war.

The aspect of leadership in the conduct of war that is unchanging is people. Patton told his son on the eve of D-Day, June 6, 1944, "To be a successful soldier you must know history. Read it objectively—dates and even minute details of tactics are useless. What you must know is how man reacts. Weapons change, but man, who uses them, changes not at all. To win battles you do not beat weapons—you beat the soul of every man . . ." Certainly the plans of yesterday have current application with a slight twist or a varied nuance.

Omar Bradley said in answer to the question how does a man get this feel or sixth sense: "You first study the theoretical handling of troops; you study the principles of war, principles of tactics, and how certain leaders applied them. You are never going to meet with that exact situation, but when you know all these principles and how they were applied in the past, then when a situation faces you, you apply those principles to your present situation and hope you come up with a good solution. I think the study of military history, and what the great leaders did, is very, very important for any young officer in developing this quality."

The Role of Courage

Another quality that Generals Marshall, MacArthur, Eisenhower, and Patton all had in common was courage. It is one of the few characteristics, along with character and decision, to which there is absolutely no disagreement that all top generals have possessed. The crux of this quality is covered in the ancient fable, "A flock of sheep led by a lion will prevail over a herd of lions led by a sheep."

MacArthur

MacArthur's reputation for courage goes back to World War I. His bravery in that war was so unusual that his division

Commander said of MacArthur, "Where acts of heroism and valor were commonplace, his were outstanding." The famous Rainbow division, which he was commanding by the end of the war, thought so highly of his courage they presented him with a solid gold cigarette case with the inscription:

From the Division
"To the Bravest of the Brave"

During World War II he was equally courageous, particularly in the last ditch defense in the Philippines in 1942. President Roosevelt ordered that the Philippine Islands should be defended to the last. MacArthur's reply to this command was, "I plan to fight to the complete destruction of our forces on Bataan and then to do the same on Corregidor"; and he added, "I will remain and share the fate of the garrison."[20]

Throughout the seige of Bataan he was contemptuous of danger. His courage was contagious and an inspiration to the men. He had his headquarters on the highest point of the island of Corregidor, with the American Flag flying conspicuously in front of his headquarters. His staff became concerned about such a blatant display of his headquarters, and they asked that the flag be lowered. His reply to them was, "Take every precaution, but keep the colors flying." When the Headquarters was bombed the staff was sent down to an air-raid shelter; but "the General would remain in his office, or take a leisurely walk out on the terrace of the old wall to chat with the anti-aircraft gunners and observe the enemy." During the heaviest bombing, he never moved from his office.[21]

One time, he was out inspecting fortifications when a flight of Japanese bombers flew over. The troops jumped for cover; but as the men looked back they saw MacArthur standing there "studying the planes through binoculars, and (the troops) climbed sheepishly out of their slit trenches."[22]

For his conduct at Bataan he received our country's highest award for bravery—the Medal of Honor. The citation read:

For conspicuous leadership in preparing the Philippine Islands to resist conquest, for gallantry and intrepidity above and beyond the call of duty in action against invading Japanese forces, and for the heroic conduct of defensive and offensive operations on the Bataan Peninsula. He mobilized, trained and led an army which has received world acclaim for its gallant defense against a tremendous superiority of enemy forces in men and arms. His utter disregard of personal danger while under heavy fire and aerial bombardment, his calm judgment in each crisis, inspired his troops, galvanized the spirit of resistance of the Filipino people and confirmed the faith of the American people in their armed forces.

This was the third time MacArthur was recommended for the Medal of Honor. The first time he won the recommendation was for bravery in Vera Cruz in 1914. He did not receive it then because technically the United States was not at war with Mexico. The second time was for his bravery in World War I. This time he failed to receive the award because the recommendation came after the war had ended, and it had been decided that the award would not be given to any general officer.

General MacArthur displayed an indifference to danger that was unbelievable. Shortly after the landing in the Philippines the General had an office—bedroom combination arrangement as his working place. One day, while MacArthur was sitting at his desk, a Japanese plane strafed the building he was in, sending bullets through the window into the wall just above his desk where he was working. An aide rushed into MacArthur's office and found him still at work and obviously not in the least disturbed. The General looked up from his desk at the aide and asked, "Well, what is it?" The shaken aide said, "Thank God, General. I thought you were killed." MacArthur replied, "Not yet. Thank you for coming in."[2 3]

A similar nonchalance was shown during the invasion of Borneo. General MacArthur had ordered a barge be sent to his ship to take him ashore just after the initial invasion. He had instructed that it be ready for him at 0930, but at the appointed time the barge was not there. His aide sent a message of inquiry to the senior naval officer who replied, "Have delayed barge as beach is under enemy mortar fire, and it is not safe for the commander-in-chief to proceed." MacArthur answered, "Send barge at once." It was there in five minutes.[24]

On shore, as MacArthur was studying a map of the terrain with an Australian officer, a Japanese machine gun opened fire; and "Bullets whined about us, spurts of dust were kicked into the air. MacArthur and the Australian officer coolly continued to study the map until finally MacArthur folded it carefully and handed it to the Australian. Pointing to another hill near by, he said: 'Let's go over there and see what's going on.' As we went down the hill, with bullets slicing the leaves above us, I overheard MacArthur say: 'By the way, I think it would be a good idea to have a patrol take out that machine gun before someone gets hurt'."[25]

On several of the invasions of islands during World War II, MacArthur insisted upon going along. General Kenney went in to see him on one occasion to get permission to accompany his airplanes which were going to drop paratroopers onto an enemy held island. MacArthur, who normally did not permit this, was persuaded and said to Kenney, "You're right, George, we'll both go. They're my kids, too." Kenney became alarmed at the danger MacArthur would be exposed to and said to him, "No, that doesn't make sense. Why, after living all these years and getting to be the head general of the show, is it necessary for you to risk having some five-dollar-a-month aviator shoot a hole through you?"[26] The answer was simply that this was the way MacArthur led—he would expose himself to situations which required the same courage that was required of his men. He set an example for them. MacArthur replied to Kenney in a very serious tone of voice, "I'm not worried about getting shot. Honestly, the only thing that disturbs me is the possibility that when we hit the rough air over the mountains my stomach might get upset. I'd hate to get sick and disgrace myself in front of the kids."[27]

He was in on many of the Allied landings in the Far East in World War II. His staff tried to prevent it, without any success. For one particularly dangerous landing his Army Commander, General Walter Krueger, argued with him that he (Krueger) had been forbidden to take part in the landings; and he said, "I argued that it was unnecessary and unwise to expose himself in this fashion and that it would be a calamity if anything happened to him. He listened to me attentively and thanked me, but added, 'I have to go'."[28]

One of MacArthur's most daring and courageous ventures was his entry into Japan by way of Atsugi in August 1945 to set up his headquarters. Winston Churchill told the American Ambassador, Winthrop Aldrich, that "of all the amazing deeds of bravery of the war, I regard MacArthur's personal landing at Atsugi as the greatest of the lot." MacArthur came in unarmed, and he would not permit any of the token staff which accompanied him to carry arms. He entered a nation which had almost 3,000,000 troops still armed, many of them fanatics who were not certain they would go along with Japanese surrender. Was it a gamble? Perhaps not—it was the result of forty years of preparation through serving in and the study of the Orient. He knew the character of these people and how he should conduct himself. Obviously, he was correct in his analysis.

In this story, however, one can see a confident belief by MacArthur that God was deciding his fate. On MacArthur's first night in now occupied Japan he ordered a steak dinner at the hotel where he was staying. MacArthur's aide, General Whitney, said of this experience, "I found it difficult to resist the impulse to snatch MacArthur's plate away from him that first night in Japan and make sure the food had not been poisoned." When Whitney expressed his concern over the possibility of the food being poisoned, General MacArthur laughed and said, "No one can live forever." Again, one can see his attitude of "when you are going to die," just as he believed that "The bullet that is designed for me has not been cast."[29] This philosophy was part of his courage.

The high respect General MacArthur had for the quality of courage was made clear in a speech he gave to a soldier upon whom he was pinning the Medal of Honor: "Of all military attributes, the one that arouses the greatest admiration is courage."[30]

The full story of MacArthur's courage can be summed up by his decorations. He received twelve separate recognitions for risking his life in two World Wars. He was awarded the Medal of Honor on the third recommendation (for three separate acts), three Distinguished Service Crosses, seven Silver Stars, and two Purple Hearts. There is no officer living or dead in the history of the American Army who can match this record.

Patton

Patton's combat courage was partially based upon his being a fatalist. He believed that when his number came up he would die, and not before then. He had fear, but he could control it. He wrote to a friend during World War II:

> It is rather interesting how you get used to death. I have had to go to inspect the troops every day, in which case you run a very good chance—or I should say a reasonable chance—of being bombed or shot at from the air, and shelled or shot at from the ground.
>
> I had the same experience every day, which is for the first half hour the palms of my hands sweat and I feel very depressed. Then, if one hits near you, it seems to break the spell and you don't notice them anymore. Going back in the evenings over the same ground and at a time when the shelling and bombing is usually heavier, you become so used to it you never think about it . . . ."[31]

It was Patton's theory that this was why "veteran troops have such an advantage over green ones. They think more clearly under fire. In fact, the green ones do not think at all . . ."[32] Patton did not believe the soldier should be fearless. To him, part of a soldier's strength, however, was fear of fear. Experience served as a great maturer.

Patton, when his Army was widely spread throughout Germany, often was forced to travel in a cub aircraft. One evening when he was returning from a Corps Command Post, a British Spitfire aircraft, flown by a Polish volunteer for the R.A.F., dove at his cub plane and attempted to shoot it down. The pilot had mistaken it for a Storch, which was a German cub plane. Fortunately the pilot was a poor one, and he missed all of three passes at the cub. Patton's aide described the incident very vividly:

> My cub is behind the General's and high. The fighter makes a pass. He misses. Now he has the General's Cub lined up. The General is pointing something at him. His pistol? No, his camera. What a man. Rat, tat, tat, tat. Over and past, another miss, another zoom. Both Cubs are down low now, contouring the fences, the hollows, and the treetops. A terrific whining scream, guns chattering. Another miss? Yes, thank God. Pull-up? No, too fast, too low. The fighter hits a knoll in the field ahead, ricochets like a flat stone on the surface of a still pond. Hits again, slows, disintegrates. "Finis."[3 3]

The interesting aspect of this event was Patton's reaction, which indicates his fatalistic attitude: "After the first pass I decided I might as well take some pictures of my impending demise. There wasn't anything to do, so I thought I might as well use the camera. But after it was all over, I found I had been so nervous I had forgotten to take the cover off the lens."[3 4] It is no wonder that one of Patton's aides, who experienced with him many events such as these, commented that on more than one occasion "It was an unpleasant experience."[3 5]

Patton was often cautioned by Ike's Headquarters against recklessness. Ike realized Patton wanted to see every portion of his troops and the positions they occupied, but he did not want Patton to become a casualty.

Patton was not always oblivious to the threat of death, even though he was a fatalist. When he was prepared to fly on an inspection trip of the troops at the front line one day (in August 1944) he reflected, "I never recall getting into a plane with more reluctance, because I had been assured by all the Staff that, if the Germans failed to shoot me from above, the Americans would get me from below, as they were trigger--happy, due to considerable bombing. It was one of the few days, in fact, that I have had a premonition of impending death." He did not stop to take counsel of his fear, and on this particular day said Patton concerning his premonition of death, "It failed to materialize."[36]

On October 24, 1944, when Patton was located in Nancy, the Germans were shelling the area; and Patton noted in his diary, "Three of the shells hit in the immediate vicinity of our headquarters; none, I should say, more than thirty-five yards from my house. One struck the house exactly across the street from us, and...I heard quite a lot of screaming in the ruins." Patton went over to help the civilians who were buried in the ruins, and while doing so he said a "near-miss arrived and threw quite a lot of rocks on us. I believe that I was more frightened that night than at anytime in my career."[37]

What went on in Patton's mind when he was making decisions in combat? Did he ever worry? Was he afraid that they might not work out and therefore cause unnecessary deaths or possibly defeat? He stated in his book that "The plans, when they came into my mind, seemed simple, but after I had issued the orders and everything was moving and I knew that I had no reserve, I had a feeling of worry and, as usual, had to say to myself, 'Do not take counsel of your fears'."[38]

Patton knew fear, but it was his concept of battlefield courage that "If we take the generally accepted definition of bravery as a quality which knows not fear, I have never seen a brave man. All men are frightened. The more intelligent they are, the more they are frightened. The courageous man is the man who forces himself, in spite of his fear, to carry on."[39]

Eisenhower

During the war, Eisenhower had the greatest need for courage when making decisions. Against the advice of his air chief, Leigh-Mallory, who feared overwhelming losses, General Eisenhower had the courage of his convictions to send two airborne divisions into the Cherbourg peninsula. In opposition to Field Marshal Sir Alan Brooke he took Allied forces west of the Rhine, opposition for which the British leader later apologized; "I am sorry if my fear of dispersed effort added to your burdens." And of course there was the monumental decision of June 5, 1944 when his "Well, we'll go!" launched two million men into battle.

In addition to decision making, there were some clearly seen actions in which General Eisenhower displayed courage. He refused to wear a steel helmet. He would not ride in the heavily armored car which was furnished for his security. He made numerous flights to visit his various Army commanders and to the troops in weather which was extremely hazardous. On one occasion when Ike decided to fly the weather was so bad an RAF officer threatened that he would shoot Ike down if he tried to fly. Naturally he wasn't serious, but the British officer was most anxious to prevent Ike from endangering his life. Ike flew in spite of the danger because it was, in his opinion, vital that he visit the Army Command posts.

General Eisenhower, however, loved adventure. General Omar Bradley told a story about Ike which illustrates this love of adventure and indifference to danger:

I returned to the Army CP in the afternoon of July 4 (1944) after yanking the lanyard of a 155 to find that Eisenhower had squeezed into the back seat of Quesada's (Lieutenant General "Pete" Quesada of the Army Air Corps) P-51 for a fighter sweep over the Allied beachhead. They grinned like sheepish schoolboys caught in a watermelon patch. Quesada had been cautioned by Brereton to stick to the ground in France where he was worth more to us in a swivel chair than in the cockpit of a fighter.[40]

They swept back and forth across the fighting front, observing the action below them. Ike had fear, but not of being shot down. General Bradley said, "Eisenhower was frightened for fear word of his flight might leak back to newsmen," and said Ike, "General Marshall would give me hell."[41]

"In my days," General Eisenhower said, "a lieutenant didn't do anything but listen. He wasn't supposed to think and the senior officers were not very gentle in their methods of instruction." But he did speak up; "It never occurred to me to pull any punches when I was arguing with seniors. I've been slapped down all right, time and again, but I think that my friends, when they were recommending me to Marshall said there is an independent fellow who thinks for himself and who isn't interested in routine and ritual."[42] Marshall, as has already been discussed, was almost fanatical in his insistence that subordinates have the courage to speak their mind.

In time of peace such courage can jeopardize your career, and in Eisenhower's case it almost did. It was his outspokenness that resulted in a senior general attempting to stop Eisenhower's selection for the all-important career step of attending Command and Staff School at Leavenworth. Fortunately he was saved by Fox Conner.

Marshall

After Marshall's first session with President Roosevelt in 1939 the new Chief of Staff was unmoving in his opposition to one of the President's ideas. When he returned to his office he told a subordinate as he passed through his office, "Well, this is probably my last day as Chief of Staff." But he was not fired by the President because in a time of impending crisis one wants men of courage in the key leadership positions. Marshall was simply conducting himself in the same manner he had all his military career.

PREPARATION AND LUCK

The Role of Preparation

West Point, Virginia Military Institute, or any other military academy has never claimed that it produces finished officers. They do, however, produce wonderful material from which excellent officers can be made. A writer on World War II commented, "One miracle I could not explain is how the U.S., an unwarlike and unprepared country if ever there was one, was suddenly able to produce so large and so brilliant a group of military leaders . . . Where did they come from, and what had they been doing all those twenty years . . .?"

Service Schools

The answer to "What had they been doing all those twenty years" is a simple one; they were working and preparing. When the question was asked of over one hundred World War II officers who reached the rank of brigadier general or above the answers were all the same: our Army school system—the infantry and artillery schools, the Command and General Staff School at Leavenworth, the Army War College. At the branch school, for example the Infantry School at Ft. Benning, the men were taught how to shoot and handle all Army weapons. They were given experience in handling an infantry battalion, then a regiment, then a brigade. The next school up the line was Command and Staff School, where an officer learned more about leading a division and then moved up to the handling of a

division and an army corps. Finally, the most outstanding
officers went to the War College, where they studied the
command of armies, the organization and working of the War
Department, national policy, and war plans for the nation.
These were the most valuable years of training for an Army
officer. Only at these schools was the poorly manned and
equipped U.S. Army of the twenties and thirties able to gather
enough officers, men, and material to practice operations on
any scale approximating war. A military career was a life of
constant schooling and study. All the leaders who excelled in
World War II had spent hours in studying and digesting what
they learned at the outstanding schools conducted by the Army
during those years.

Cadets Marshall, Eisenhower, and Patton received only average grades at their respective "undergraduate" military schools.
Their performance in service schools after graduation and
commissioning was quite different. Second Lieutenant Marshall
in 1906 was assigned to the General Services and Staff School at
Ft. Leavenworth. There were fifty-four members in his class, all
of' them senior to Marshall in rank and experience. Much to
everyone's surprise, Marshall graduated number one in the class.
Then, because of his high standing, he remained at Leavenworth
for the Army Staff College. Again he was first in a graduating
class of officers senior to him in rank and experience.

Eisenhower did not have the opportunity to attend the
company grade school. He was assigned to the field grade
officers school in 1924 and, in a class of over two hundred,
graduated number one. Patton was an honor graduate of every
service school he attended. Douglas MacArthur was so brilliant
he did not attend any service schools as a student—he was
assigned as an instructor, even though he had never been
through the course.

Marshall

There was more to success as a military officer than attendance at service schools, however. As a child, Marshall was a

voracious reader of the books in his father's library. He
continued this habit at VMI, concentrating upon military
books. As an officer, he never wasted a precious moment during
his training years in preparing himself for the great tasks and
responsibilities that lay before him. Throughout his army
career, General Marshall had a passion for knowledge. As a
cadet at VMI, he went over the terrain of many of the battles of
the Civil War. In the Philippines, he visited every major
battlefield of the war against Spain; he also studied the postwar
campaigns against the recalcitrant Filipinos.

During maneuvers in the Philippines in January 1914 Lieutenant Marshall was named Chief of Staff of Detachment No. 1
to replace Captain Jens Bugge, who became ill with malaria, just
before the commencement of the operation. The commanding
general of the Philippines, General J. Franklin Bell, was quoted
as having stated a few days after the maneuvers were over that
Lieutenant Marshall was "the greatest potential wartime leader
in the Army."

In August 1916, Captain Marshall was assigned to Fort
Douglas as adjutant. He had the responsibility for training the
new recruits. Colonel Johnson Hagood wrote on Captain
Marshall's efficiency report in 1916, in answer to the question,
"Would you desire to have him under your immediate command in peace and in war?": "Yes, but I would prefer to serve
under his command . . . In my judgment there are not five
officers in the Army as well qualified as he to command a
division in the field . . . He should be made a brigadier general in
the Regular Army, and every day this is postponed is a loss to
the Army and the nation . . . He is a military genius and one of
those rare cases of wonderful military development during
peace . . . The Army and the nation sorely need such men in the
grade of general officers at this time, and if I had the power I
would nominate him to fill the next vacancy in grade of
brigadier general . . ." Colonel Hagood closed his evaluation of
Captain Marshall with the statement "He is my junior by over
eighteen hundred files."[1]

In his duties as an officer Marshall always tried to learn everything possible about the subject at hand. He had a wealth of general knowledge and was knowledgeable on specifics. He never spoke on any subject unless he felt he knew all there was to know about it. When the Army got a new weapon, he took it home with him, or to a warehouse if it was a large weapon, where he took it apart and reassembled it with painstaking care, with the manual in hand. Often he found the manual insufficient or incorrect and went about offering constructive suggestions for corrections. He found time to attend every school offered by the military which was pertinent to his career. Once, when he was in a mounted organization, he took a course in horseshoeing, so that he could better talk with the farrier who shod the horses![2]

Eisenhower

"I was not," General Eisenhower said, "a particularly good student at West Point. They had a course at West Point called Military History that was different from what it is now. One of the things we studied was the Battle of Gettysburg. The first thing we were required to do was memorize the name of every general officer or acting general officer. You had to know what he was commanding. Then they gave you the situation or the position of each of the commands at such and such an hour on such and such a day. I always hated memory tests, although I have a pretty good memory, but this wasn't the kind of thing that interested me; so I didn't pay any attention to military history and I almost got found [flunked] in the course. I despised it."

When he was injured in football he decided to resign several times, but classmates talked him out of it; so he stayed. Then, because of his injury, they were not sure they were going to commission him because it looked like he might be a burden on the government. After considerable discussion he was commissioned. "Then," said General Eisenhower, "I made up my mind that if I was going to have a military career I was going to have a good one. I don't mean to say I stopped having fun. I guess I was just as frolicking as anyone in my way. But when I put myself down to study I wasn't doing anything else. I was searching new plans, new ideas. I was very impatient about the idea of trench warfare and why we didn't break away from it. I read everything I could on trench warfare. I didn't get into that war at all; so I just accepted the training end of it because they said I had such special ability as a trainer. This was cold comfort to a young officer."

"There was no question that Fox Conner got me started in better methods of preparing myself. I was studying back in 1915, '16, '17, '18, '19, but I met him and I went with him in '21. He was the one that gave me a systematic plan of study. He had just been in the war as the operations officer of AEF. He was a smart, patient man, and he decided that I ought to amount to something; so he was going to see if I would."[3]

Fox Conner was an avid reader of military history. He gave then Major Eisenhower historical books to read and then asked him questions. He gave him a Civil War book, for example, and then asked, "How were the soldiers armed?"; "When did the revolving pistol come in?"; "When did the breech loading rifle come in?"; "What was the general character of the armaments in the South and North?"; "How did the South get them?".

He had Eisenhower set aside a room in his quarters in Panama that served as a study. Maps were placed on the wall for the study of world strategy. Conner had him teach classes to the post officers. The two were constant companions in the jungles in Panama where expeditions were sent out for exploration. Eisenhower wrote the field orders, letters, and accomplished all the other administrative matters.

It was a unique experience for a young man to receive the tutelage of one of the most brilliant and sage officers in the Army. Of all the training Eisenhower received, perhaps the most valuable was the result of Conner's vision in seeing that the key to the next World War, a fact he considered written into the Treaty of Versailles, would be Allied command. Twenty years before the event, Eisenhower began the study of allied unity; and this was, of course, where General Eisenhower performed his greatest service as Supreme Commander in World War II.

Patton

Once during World War II, General Patton was accused of making snap decisions. His immediate reply to this criticism was, "I've been studying the subject of war for forty-odd years. When a surgeon decides in the course of an operation to change its objective, to splice that artery or cut deeper and remove another organ which he finds infected, he is not making a snap decision but one based on knowledge, experience, and training. So am I."[4]

Patton devoted his life to preparing for becoming a great general. How did he prepare? In many ways. Other than General MacArthur, Patton personally owned the largest and most complete military library in the United States. MacArthur's library contained over 7000 volumes. Unfortunately it was destroyed by the Japanese during their occupation of the Philippines. Patton's library was only slightly smaller. Why was this important in Patton's development? This importance was made clear in the earlier quotation in Patton's letter to his son emphasizing the importance of history in military success: "To be a successful soldier, you must know history."

Patton, as did MacArthur, Eisenhower, and Marshall, studied the lives of the great captains—Alexander, Napoleon, Scipio, Marlborough, Cromwell, Lee, and Grant. Patton's favorite stories were not fairy tales, westerns, or Horatio Alger. He liked to hear of the exploits of King Arthur and the Knights of the Round Table, the battles of Frederick the Great, Genghis Khan, Napoleon and other great generals in history. He learned to appreciate very early in life that battles are won by men; and, therefore, one aspiring to high command should study the men fighting the battles. These generals undoubtedly helped to serve as guides and examples for Patton to follow, and they were a vital part of the final product.

When he was assigned to Fort Myer soon after graduation he and his wife did not get involved in the social affairs of Washington Society. He concentrated on his military duties, read military history in the evening, organized athletic events such as polo and horse shows, and started riding classes for the post dependents and enlisted soldiers. He was always working at improving himself.

After his performance in the Olympic Games of 1912 at Stockholm, in the Pentathelon event in which he was fourth out of over forty contestants, Patton concluded he needed additional instruction and practice in swordsmanship. In 1913 he took leave and went to Saumur, in France, and studied fencing at L'Ecole de Cavalerie. Based upon his studies in France, he designed a new cavalry saber. The Army authorities tested his new saber extensively and were so impressed with its superiority over the old U.S. Army design that it was adopted as the official Army saber. It continued as the standard Army sword until the saber was discontinued during World War I. To have redesigned the Army's saber was a significant achievement for such a junior lieutenant. This achievement was accomplished through study and hard work. Dedication was certainly another factor; he did it at his own expense while on his leave.

He was then sent to L'Ecole de Cavalerie on official status. His wife, who spoke very fluent French, accompanied him to the lectures, taking notes and translating the French works on swordsmanship for him. When Patton and his wife, Bea, were not attending classes or studying they would travel around the French countryside. Together they would study the terrain and re-fight the ancient battles he had read about in history books. He spent a great deal of time traveling the countryside of Breton and Normandy, which was to prove very beneficial to him in World War II during the invasion of France and the drive toward Berlin. One of his favorite pastimes was to practice mapping. He studied the art of map making so thoroughly that he developed the ability to see a flat map as three dimensional;

and he could, therefore, see ridges, valleys, rivers, and other topographical features almost as vividly as if he were physically located there.

During his many tours on the east coast, he studied the battles of the Civil War. He would follow the battles as closely as he could from start to finish, reenacting the events and moving the troops about in his imagination, based upon a most exhaustive study of the history of all the battles.

Patton's growth was enhanced considerably by the border clashes between the United States and Mexico in 1916, particularly through his association with then Brigadier General John J. Pershing, commanding officer of the Punitive Expedition. As has already been mentioned, Patton performed so outstandingly he was selected to be on Pershing's staff when Pershing was appointed to command the American Expeditionary Force in 1917. Through his World War I experiences, Patton became America's first tank expert. He studied tanks and their use intensely between the two wars. When World War II came, there was no living American soldier who knew as much as Patton about the mobility, mechanical features, fire-power and tactical use of tanks.

From the time of his graduation Patton was in on every significant event in which a soldier could be involved—the clash with Mexico, World War I, evicting the Bonus Marchers in the Battle of Anacostia of July 1929, and World War II. Patton was not in on all these events because of luck—when he wasn't selected for a significant event to gain further experience through practice he would fight for the opportunity, just as he did with Pershing in 1916 to get in on the Mexican dispute. There was no substitute for experience; Patton knew it and therefore got it. When he was needed he was ready because of his years of intensive preparation.

MacArthur

The story of Douglas MacArthur's preparation is easily told—preparation for high command was his life, he was dedicated to the study of his profession. He got an early start through his father's tutelage and reading the many biographies and military history books in his father's library. He did not marry until he was over forty; and during his bachelor days, he spent his evenings working and studying. This preparation was recognized in the fact, as previously stated, that MacArthur did not attend any service schools as a student—he was so brilliant that he was assigned as an instructor.

Continued Preparation

All of these generals were men who worked at their profession. They never stopped learning; they continued to grow throughout their careers. Some officers want to wait for the big challenge before they produce. Unfortunately they don't understand that the big challenge comes to the man who has been doing the seemingly little, insignificant jobs in an outstanding manner. General Simpson, for example, as a second lieutenant was assigned the task of digging a regimental latrine for 1200 men. "I decided," he said, "to build the best latrine the Army had ever seen." He did just that, and was then called upon to accomplish more significant tasks.

The story is the same for every officer who achieved top rank. They started as young officers to work hard, study, and give *every* job that extra-lick. Marshall, who during World War I handled hundreds of thousands of men, did not think he was too important to work with a squad during his China tour; MacArthur undertook the unpleasant task of military censor in 1916; Eisenhower was not too crazy about being a recruiting officer. But they did these jobs as well as the choice ones.

As a younger officer Omar Bradley used to get together with several other lieutenants once a week to discuss tactics. "All of us worked hard," he said. "We studied everything we could get our hands on. You start working hard right from the first. You can't say later on in life I will start studying. You have got to start in the beginning."

The beginning for Bradley went all the way back to his childhood. "My father was a country school teacher, "General Bradley reflected. "I was in school under him for several years and he drilled into me that I always had to know my lessons better than anybody else in the class. I had to uphold the family name, I suppose. I followed that rule the rest of my life and I always tried to do a better job than anybody ever expected me to do. I got a feeling of satisfaction out of it. I wasn't trying to get to be Chief of Staff. Work was a pleasure, and when it isn't you become a bore and get dissatisfied."[5]

When General Mark W. Clark was asked what was required for military success he commented: "I have thought a lot about this. If you went to the Command and Staff School back in the early thirties you were a pretty hot number. When we got the chance we realized that the grades and the reputation we made in school would determine our consideration for higher rank in an emergency. So everybody worked terrifically hard and the competition was great. When you graduated one of the factors in your rating was whether or not you were recommended for high command.

"The point I want to make is that I had worked hard, I had been a determined young officer, always trying to do the best I could. I was trained that way by my father. When the war came I had a good record, I was in the proper age group sitting there at the right time and I knew a lot of people who could help me. My association with General Marshall from 1936 to 1940 at Fort Lewis, Washington, was probably one of the greatest breaks I ever had . . .":[6]

Desire

And it was, of course, essential that a man *want* to achieve high position. "I always wanted to run the show," was the answer given by General Courtney Hodges. "Even when I was a kid I had that desire. During my military career I tried to prepare myself to be ready if ever I got a responsible job. I always tried to be the best lieutenant, the best captain, and in all various ranks I held I wanted to be the best."

"I was ambitious to be a successful officer. I was dedicated to the service, not to a good duty station. I took the bad stations along with the good."[7]

But desire did not mean that a man was working for the top position of Chief of Staff. General McNarney said of his career, "I don't know that I ever had any great desire to get to the top. I just took things as they came. I tried to do a good job. When I had one, I put a lot of effort into it. I had enough pride to want to do a good job. If you do, and people know you do, you just naturally gravitate to the top."[8]

General Spaatz said that "When I started to fly I decided I was going to be the best pilot there was."[9] General Haislip commented, "It is not the job that is important, it's how well the job at hand is done. An officer should always go looking for a hard job. He should never be afraid of sticking his neck out. I determined that if I was going to be successful as a leader I would have to do a job extra well. I tried to develop a policy that no matter what job I had I would try to give it that little extra lick—to do it just a little bit better than it had to be done. It wasn't a question of getting by. It was a question of doing something better than it had to be done."[10]

Some officers showed great promise in the junior grades during World War I, but flopped when given the opportunity for higher command in World War II. Why? Because during the period between the two wars they stagnated—they softened up; they stopped studying books and people. This was easy to do because of the small army the United States had in the twenties and thirties and the limited number of top slots available. The slowness of promotions was particularly discouraging. Such officers lost the desire or the will to accomplish a mission except in a routine manner.

On the other hand, many officers, such as Eisenhower, were bitterly disappointed because they did not see action in World War I; but they did not quit; they kept the urge to go on. They continued to work at grooming themselves for high command;

and when the second World War came they were ready, and they became the great leaders of the war.

The Role of Luck

General Eisenhower in a discussion of why men get to the top stated that "There's a lot of changes or little bends in the way and finally you come to a particular spot. Regardless of character, ability, dedication to the job, etc., there is still a lot of luck."[1][1]

General Collins also believed that "unquestionably luck had a lot to do with reaching the top. But I had worked hard. I had exceptional opportunities as a young officer. I took command of a battalion of 1000 men when I was barely 22 years old. I had to work terribly hard. I was under some wonderful people during those years, and of course one of the major ones was General Marshall down at Benning. We had a remarkable group of able people working together there then under Marshall's leadership. I happened to be lucky enough to be down there at that time."[1][2]

But luck was not all of it; there were hundreds of other officers there at the same time who never went above the rank of colonel. General Collins substantiated this fact, although it was not his purpose to do so, when he said later in the discussion, "General Marshall had thrown a lot of extra jobs to Charlie Bolte and me at Benning. We were both instructors (Bolte) and very dear friends during those days. We were put under pressure. We were given those extra responsibilities and you either made good on them or you did not make good."[1][3]

He did make good, and watching him perform like that were a fellow instructor in the Tactics Department, Major Omar N. Bradley; Courtney Hodges; and Collins' boss, Joe Stilwell.

When General Bradley was asked why some men reached the top positions and not others, he replied, "I would say luck plays an awfully large part in your success. You have to be able to perform when the opportunity occurs; however, the opportu-

nity doesn't occur for everyone. I was very lucky, being at the
right place at the right time to get a good job, and having a lot
of good people to help me do it. You have got to work hard,
you have got to know your job and there are certain characteristics of leadership you must always keep in mind. Then hope
that you are lucky."[14]

Luck in Battle

Luck is also important to the leader psychologically. When a
member of Napoleon's staff suggested the promotion of a
certain colonel to the rank of general, Napoleon asked, "What
are his qualifications?" The officer went on to cite that the
officer was courageous, a marvelous field leader, and that he
was brilliant; to all of this Napoleon replied, "I don't care if he
is brilliant—is he lucky?" Few commanders would deny the
importance of luck in determining his individual success or his
unit's success.

Patton

To Patton luck was particularly important. A member of
Patton's staff cited in his book on World War II, "Officially,
Third Army had a more discreet code-pseudonym than 'cocky
bastards'. It was LUCKY, Patton's own personal choice. Other
Headquarters had more sonorous designations: SHAEF—
LIBERTY; Twelfth Army Group—EAGLE; First Army—
MASTER. These were too high-flown for Patton. He selected
Lucky as epitomizing both the victorious career and the
ebullient character of his new and largest command (i.e. Third
Army)."[15]

The fact that you stay alive when others are being killed gives
one a reverent attitude towards God and luck. On the eve of
America's first action against the Germans, Patton wrote to his
brother-in-law:

"The job I am going on is about as desperate a venture
as has ever been undertaken by any force in the world's
history. We will have to meet and defeat superior numbers
on a coast where one can only land 60 percent of the time.
So my proverbial luck will have to be working all out.
However, I have a convinced belief that I will succeed."[1][6]

When the operation was successfully completed he said, "I'm
the Lord's favorite disciple...(The) Frenchmen have every
light burning when we sailed up to the coast. And the sea was as
flat as a hot cake."[1][7]
Patton lived through too many narrow escapes to mention all
of them. A few examples, however, should be cited to illustrate
the role of luck in Patton's career. In another letter he said of
the North African campaign:

"In this last show my car got hit while I was in it. A 155
shell hit the spot I had been sitting on two minutes after I
had left it, and another salvo threw mud all over me. An
Arab just missed me (who fired at him). I also forgot to
say that on two occasions, enemy planes pursued me down
the road, which is a form of sport I am not interested in.
Also, in going through a mine field, I got through all right,
but the next vehicle blew up. I was in the first vehicle."[1][8]

After the slapping incident in Sicily Patton became extremely
despondent. He had good reason to believe he would be
returned to the States, never to have a combat command again.
During his forced inactivity General Geoffrey Keyes, one of the
Corps commanders still in Italy, asked him if he would like to
visit the Italian front. General Patton accepted quite readily and
within twenty-four hours he was at the front. His aide described
the event most aptly:

General Patton, pleased as punch to be once again
within gunshot of an active front—any active front—lost no
time in climbing over the protecting sandbags and taking
pictures of the enemy emplacements on the opposite

slope. The German artillery responded with a deadly accurate salvo of 155's which set fire to the O.P. and almost buried the General in mud and dislodged rocks. From the number and proximity of the still-smoking shell splinters, steel-helmet dents, and a providential dud, the General was certainly justified in concluding as we descended from the O.O. that this was his closest call to date."[19]

After the event Patton said, "It proves that luck is still in—that I shall live to fight another day."[20]

But was all of Patton's success due to luck? Patton did not think so. When General Gerand of the French Army visited him in March 1945, Patton said, "I told him that I thought our success had been chiefly due to luck. He replied, 'no, to audacity,' and I believe he was right."[21]

The importance of luck to Patton can be summed up by quoting a conversation between General Eisenhower, when he was Supreme Commander, and Patton, when he was Third Army Commander. Ike had just approved the assignment to Third Army of another armored division, and Ike said to his fellow student of military history, "George, you are not only a good General, you are a lucky General, and, as you well remember, in a General, Napoleon prized luck above skill."[22]

Eisenhower

Ike was also fortunate enough to be blessed with luck. General Walter B. Smith said of Ike that "General Eisenhower was not only a great commander but a lucky one." Luck plays a role in your assignments, in working for influential man, in being in the right place at the right time. A military officer in addition to being lucky must believe in his own luck. It is a belief that keeps a general who is overwhelmed with momentous decisions from cracking under the strain.

General Eisenhower once said to Winston Churchill, "I am probably the most optimistic person in the world." He said to many others, "I am an incurable optimist." Optimism is part of luck. He insisted on an optimistic attitude from his staff—he almost forbid pessimism—he concluded we would succeed simply because we had to succeed. He always began his first conference with a new staff with a speech in which he said, "Defeatism and pessimism will not be tolerated in this Head-quarters! Anyone who cannot rise above the recognized obsta-cles and bitter prospects in store for us better ask for release. Those who do not will go anyway!" When reporters asked Ike what would have occurred if Anzio failed he answered, "I never considered failure because I do not let my mind think upon it that way."

MacArthur

When one considers the magnitude of responsibility and the overwhelming job faced by MacArthur, one might wonder how anyone could still find the strength to believe in luck or to have an optimistic attitude. But he did, and the importance of this quality was indicated by MacArthur's Air Chief, General George C. Kenney, "Optimism is axiomatic with leadership. And in those grave days and hours [late 1942], four words from MacArthur meant as much to me as a new squadron of airplanes. Those words were: 'George, we'll do it.' That atti-tude", said Kenney, "breeds victory and success."[2 3]

General MacArthur has had his optimism and belief in luck (or sense of destiny) branded as egotism. One admirer of MacArthur said of him, "In the abstract, would you say that it is wise to have a Supreme Commander who never had a single moment of pessimism in his entire life?" John Gunther's reaction to this statement was, "of course great egoists are almost always optimists."[2 4] MacArthur felt so strongly about luck as to refuse the offer of Lord Mountbatten's service in his command because the Britisher was unlucky.

THE PATTERN

Generals Eisenhower, MacArthur, Marshall, and Patton were self-appointed leaders. They were self-appointed because they had a characteristic possessed by very few men: the desire to be a commander and the willingness to work towards that goal. There are many officers who *think* they want command, but who are not willing, either consciously or subconsciously, to expend the effort required. There are some who get command and lose it. They lose it because they are incompetent and fail, or because they are unwilling after learning what it entails to undertake the responsibilities of command.

Command

This discussion raises a question which needs answering: What does command entail? To be a successful commander requires a willingness to devote twenty-four hours a day, seven days a week, to your command. This will often mean that your wife and family will have to take a secondary role to the mission. In addition, there must be a willingness for the commander and his family to live in a goldfish bowl, since their actions are closely observed by both subordinates and superiors. The commander must be willing to learn, teach, stress, and live with the basic and often elementary fundamentals necessary to develop his unit and still believe his talents for "bigger things" are not being wasted. He must like to be with young people and to live with their energy and the problems they create. The commander of large units must be able to delegate; and, when he does delegate, he must be willing to accept the responsibility for the failure of his subordinates. Command is complex, and the commander must be able to simultaneously handle training, maintenance, tests, administration, inspections, communications, messes, supply, athletics, discipline, job proficiency, awards, and public relations. He must be able to do all of these things concurrently.[1]

The top man must be able to take orders, for no leader is ever really in a position of not having to answer to someone or to some group. The commander must be willing to compete with other units in time of peace, without losing the spirit of cooperation and the fact that all the individual units together make up the whole team. Often he is expected to accomplish the impossible with inadequate means. If things go wrong the successful commander accepts the responsibility, even though the failure might rest with his staff, subordinates, or higher headquarters. He must be able to do the best he can with whatever he has, which on occasions might be very little. He must be able to produce the hard work and leadership to create a superior unit with average manpower. It is the commander's job to inspire them to put out the maximum and thereby build a superior unit.

The responsibility for the failure of a unit or mission rests with the commander. He must realize that failure generally results in his relief from command. Command requires a man who can physically and emotionally cope with the responsibility and strain without losing his effectiveness and his patience. Often, the compensation is only personal satisfaction; there is generally very little reward or glory, particularly in time of peace. And, the reward may go to a superior, rather than to the man most responsible for the performance of the unit or the accomplishment of the mission.

When one stops to consider the overwhelming tasks, the sacrifice, the pressure, the responsibility, the hard work, and the just and unjust criticism faced by the commander a second question arises: Why do men seek command? Here are the reasons given by some of our top World War II leaders.

"I think," said General Bradley, "it is because of a sense of accomplishment. I would emphasize to any young fellow going into the service to do his job and to be able to do it in such a way that he has a feeling of satisfaction and accomplishment. If you are in command of something and do a good job, you get a sense of accomplishment." General Collins said that command is "the great appeal to me about the Army—the handling of men. That to me has been the wonderful thing." General McAuliffe reflected, "I wanted command because in time of war that's the most important job, the most satisfying." "The men who seek command," in General Clark's opinion, "are those who are sparked by the desire to give everything their best. Nothing less than the best satisfies them."

The Pattern of Successful Military Leadership

This comparative study of American military leadership was begun with an inquiry as to whether our "leaders are born, not made" and, secondly, as to whether there is a pattern in the qualities necessary to successful military leadership. The leadership profiles of these four generals—Marshall, MacArthur, Eisenhower, and Patton—make it clear that these leaders were made, not born, and that there is a pattern of common leadership qualities which they shared.

This study shows clearly that a dedication to one's career—a willingness to work, study, and prepare—is an essential to success. MacArthur and Patton had an intense dedication to a successful military career early in their lives and were marked for success while still in West Point. Marshall's leadership qualities were evident at VMI, but the dedication to his career which made him outstanding was not shown until later. Eisenhower also showed some leadership qualities at West Point but, admittedly, did not take his military subjects very seriously. It was not until after he was commissioned that

Eisenhower decided that his military career would be a "a good one"; and with this dedication, his leadership ability rapidly became apparent. So this decision to devote one's life to a military career and the desire to be an outstanding leader are obviously necessary before an officer can make the most of other qualities.

While these leaders were not born to command, many of the qualities which were to make them great were evident in their early years as cadets. Three of them attained high cadet rank and the fourth, Eisenhower, was an acknowledged cadet leader. Their courage was revealed in Eisenhower's reactions to his football injuries and in Marshall's and MacArthur's reactions to their hazing. Each of them showed a high intelligence, and their academic achievements were in direct relation to their then dedication to their careers.

After these men were commissioned and each of them had decided upon a military career, their leadership profiles reveal the qualities which they had in common and which made them great—the pattern. Their character was of the highest; they shared the integrity, the humility, the selflessness, the concern for others, the reverence, and the showmanship which are present in most top military leaders. With the combination of this military character and their dedication, these men met the requirement of command with great success.

It would be impossible to succeed as a leader without the ability to make decisions quickly and well. As has been discussed, sound judgment in decision making and the feel or sixth sense which marks the great commander are largely the result of study and preparation. Marshall, MacArthur, Eisenhower, and Patton spent their entire military careers preparing for high command through study and through working as junior officers for the most outstanding generals—Marshall and Patton for John J. Pershing, Eisenhower under the tutelage of Fox Conner and Douglas MacArthur, and MacArthur through the most unique exposure of them all, his father, Arthur MacArthur. They had the desire for command; they craved responsibility. While others spent much time in social activities, this foursome worked war problems, held tactical and strategic discussions in their homes with talented contemporaries, taught classes, went over old battlefields, and reconstructed battles during leaves and travels; and they grew from studying the lives of other great captains. They digested the manuals on new weapons and bled foreign military representatives of all possible information of value. The epitome was Marshall's decision to take a course on horseshoeing.

And they were fighters—they asked to participate in every military action which took place during their careers. If a battle was going on, domestic or international, they wanted to be a part of it. This desire to be in the fight is too frequently mistaken by others as a desire to make war; rather, for these men, it was the ultimate opportunity to prepare themselves for top command. If we must fight wars, our finest junior officers must participate in them in order that they may be better prepared for those later wars in which they must lead.

At least as important as study is a basic love of and concern for people. A general can get his subordinates to carry out orders through fear, but never, under such conditions, will men give their all to a commander. The real leader is loved by his men because they can sense that the leader has a love for them. This is best portrayed in the leader's consideration for his staff, his commanders, his officers, his non-commissioned officers, and the lowest ranking private. This quality was a hallmark of the four generals in this study.

Marshall would not treat any officer haughtily; nor would he let any other officer do so with an enlisted man. He showed concern for the soldiers' families as well, even to the point of stretching regulations to feed them from the mess in difficult times. When his NCO's, Jigs and Kriz, gave so unselfishly to build the badly needed lecture halls at Fort Benning, he recognized them, and all enlisted men, by naming the halls in their honor. He quelled the Negro dissatisfaction by making it clear that he looked at all soldiers as individuals and judged them accordingly. His telephone calls to the wives of servicemen, his arranging for his staff to meet General Pershing were but a few of the many acts he performed out of consideration for his men.

Douglas MacArthur's concern for his subordinates was legendary. He personally undertook what was probably the most distasteful task ever assigned a peacetime leader, the eviction of the Bonus Marchers, rather than delegate it to a subordinate. His letters to the families of deceased soldiers in his command were wonderful gestures. The chocolate soda for General Eichelberger was a small matter, but both touching and amazing.

General Eisenhower showed a deep concern for his subordinates—the ceremony at the airport to pin on Mark Clark's third star, his attendance at his orderly's wedding, the introduction of General Walter B. Smith to the King of England, his protection of Leigh-Mallory when his recommendations were not followed, his visits to the troops—these are but a few of his memorable acts.

The rough, go-for-broke Patton was underneath a highly sensitive man, particularly when it concerned the men under his command. Tears came quickly when those close to him were killed, or when he visited the wounded in hospitals. His go-for-broke method of fighting was designed to save American lives; his outlook that it took eighteen years to make a soldier and only a few months to manufacture ammunition was typical of his attitude. His appreciation for the cooks, truck drivers, wire stringers, and others in non-combatant jobs developed a winning team, just as did his sharing "the booty" with the soldiers doing the fighting.

It was characteristic of each of these four generals that they gave full credit to their subordinates, playing down their own roles. They realized that no leader can do everything by himself; he must delegate his tremendous workload to others if he hopes to succeed and survive. Each of these generals spent considerable time and thought in selecting their staff officers and commanders. Then, when a task was delegated, they left their commanders alone to do their jobs. If a subordinate failed in war, they were unmerciful about firing or reassigning them.

Only MacArthur was an exception to this rule, and that was limited to his staff; he showed no such tolerance, however, with erring commanders.

Regardless of how able a leader may be, he will not achieve a position of top responsibility unless his ability is recognized by senior officers. This can be summed up in one word—sponsorship, a word that arouses many to ire; but it is a part of success, and it should not offend anyone when it is understood that it goes only to those who study, who prepare, and who produce: It reflects an awareness that when war occurs we must place our finest officers in the top command positions to protect and preserve our country and as many as possible of our fighting men.

Marshall quite probably would not have become Chief of Staff had it not been for General Pershing's active backing in the period between wars. General MacArthur was aided by the reputation of his famous father, and his tutelage from the great Arthur MacArthur was unique indeed. This relationship helped him to become aide to President Theodore Roosevelt during General J. Franklin Bell's tour as Chief of Staff, in 1914 when General Frederick Funston pulled him away from a desk job, and again by Chief of Staff Peyton March concurring with Secretary Baker's request that Douglas be an exception to the rule of reducing rank in 1920; There were many who furthered the career of General Eisenhower—General Walter Krueger, Mark Clark, Wade Haislip, Leonard Gerow, and most of all, Fox Conner. Stimson's knowledge of Patton's ability helped him get his second star, and aided him in some of the controversies that arose in 1943 and 1944. In each of these instances, however, the "sponsorship" was the result of knowledgeable, intelligent, top men recognizing the talent of a man who was to become a great military leader.

A leader must be able to communicate—with his men and, in a democracy such as ours, with the American people. Again, these generals each possessed this quality of leadership.

In World War II, the most important media for communicating with the American people was the press. Marshall's

technique with newsmen was to request each correspondent at a
press conference to rise and ask his questions at the outset.
When he then answered each question from memory, addressing
his reply to the newsman who asked the question, he made a
very favorable impression and established his brilliance with
these men. His honesty, frankness with, and confidence in the
newsmen also were involved in his rapport with a tough
profession. MacArthur seldom met with the press; but when he
did, he was eloquent and his words and speeches were truly
classic. He was a marvel at holding his audience in awe. He
recognized the value of good relations with the press, but this
relationship suffered from the actions of his staff members who
created bad feelings with the press in their well meaning and
intense loyalty to MacArthur. The key to Eisenhower's success
with newsmen was his honesty and trust in them, together with
the knowledge that he could be tough and that he understood
the importance of the news media. He neither censored, nor did
he permit his staff to censor, critical remarks about himself.
Informing the correspondents in advance of the Sicilian invasion
was unusual, but it added to a special style that was uniquely
Eisenhower's. Patton, because of his impetuousness, provided
the best copy of any American General in World War II; he was,
therefore, generally loved by the press.

These men were equally competent in communicating with
their men and for the same reasons—honesty, frankness, and
knowing how to reach soldiers. Their personal contacts with
soldiers radiated their warmth and their concern for the men
under their command. Patton's high pitched voice was no
handicap; and, in spite of his profanity, his speeches were
almost poetic.

Each practiced showmanship as a means of communication,
although the technique varied with each individual. The short
military jacket that General Eisenhower wore, commonly called
the "Ike" jacket, was a symbol that identified the Supreme
Commander. Nothing, however, in showmanship by anyone
could match the impact of General Eisenhower's smile; it
presented a warmth that won over anyone who saw it. The

corncob pipe, open-collar shirt unadorned with medals, the gold-crusted Field Marshall's hat that sat at a rakish angle, and the riding crop identified MacArthur. Then, there was the extreme showmanship of Patton with his tailored uniform and its rows of ribbons and decorations; his pink whipcord riding breeches; the high-topped cavalry boots, shined to a lustre; the pearl handled pistols; the riding crop; the gleaming stars on his helmet and collar; and his polished jeep with red upholstery, machine gun, siren and multiple tone French horn. No general was more colorful than Patton, and none was more successful in communicating with his men. Marshall's showmanship was that of simplicity. The objective of each was to reach down to his men; each accomplished this, in part, by showmanship.

But even if one is distinctive, he must be seen; this is his visual communication with his men. MacArthur was present for every landing in which his troops participated, walking to shore right after the first contingent of allied forces. He seldom visited or talked with the many men in his command, leaving that to his senior commanders; but he was always seen by his men where the action was heaviest. General Eisenhower, in spite of a horrendous schedule, always found time to visit his troops. Patton devoted much of his time to visiting the soldiers in his command and was almost fanatically insistent that his staff, corps and division commanders do the same. General Marshall, of course, was tied to Washington; but he made inspection trips overseas and to commands throughout the United States, in spite of a busy schedule, to judge for himself allied progress in fighting the war and to be seen by his soldiers.

The lives of Generals Marshall, MacArthur, Eisenhower, and Patton reveal a pattern for success which is available to every officer—indeed, to every person. Success, to the limits of one's innate abilities, is available to all those who dedicate themselves to their career, who are willing to work long and hard to prepare themselves, who recognize and develop that high character necessary to leadership, who love their fellow man and show their concern for his well being, and who can communicate with others in a manner that inspires confidence and devotion to duty.

FOOTNOTES

Chapter 1. THE EARLY YEARS

1. *Assembly*, January 1947, p. 8.

2. Letter from Colonel George R. Goethals, USA Ret, to Edgar F. Puryear, Jr. (hereafter EFP), November 5, 1962.

3. Letter from Colonel Robert H. Fletcher, USA Ret, to EFP, November 28, 1962.

4. Goethals Correspondence, *op. cit.*

5. Letter from Colonel Donald M. Berre, USA Ret, to EFP, November 12, 1962.

6. *Ibid.*

7. Fletcher Correspondence, *op. cit.*

8. Letter from Brigadier General Philip S. Gage, USA Ret, to EFP, October 14, 1962.

9. Fletcher Correspondence, *op. cit.*

10. Letter from Colonel Owen R. Meredith, USA Ret, to EFP, November 8, 1962.

11. Letter from Colonel Charles Hall, USA Ret, to EFP, November 13, 1962.

12. Letter from Lieutenant Colonel Fordyce L. Perego, USA Ret, to EFP, October 18, 1962.

13. Letter from Brigadier General Leo I. Ahern, USA Ret, to EFP, October 14, 1962.

14. Letter from Brigadier General Arnold N. Krogstad, USAF Ret, to EFP, October 25, 1962.

15. Letter from Mr. William H. Anderson, to EFP, October 17, 1962.

16. Letter from Major General George L. Van Deusen, USA Ret, to EFP, October 12, 1962.

17. Letter from Major General Wallace C. Philoon, USA Ret, to EFP, October 17, 1962.

18. Letter from Major General Thomas A. Terry, USA Ret, to EFP, November 11, 1962.

19. Personal interview with General William H. Simpson, USA Ret, September 1962.

20. Letter from Colonel Robert Sears, USA Ret, to EFP, October 9, 1962.

21. Gage Correspondence, *op. cit.*

22. Fletcher Correspondence, *op. cit.*

23. Gage Correspondence, *op. cit.*

24. Letter from Lieutenant Colonel Carleton G. Chapman, USA Ret, to EFP, October 14, 1962.

25. Letter from Brigadier General Clifford Bluemel, USA Ret, to EFP, November 8, 1962.

26. Meredith Correspondence, *op. cit.*

27. Letter from Colonel Harold W. James, USA Ret, to EFP, December 11, 1962.

28. "From Plebe to President," *Collier's,* June 10, 1955, p. 94.

29. *Collier's, op. cit.,* p. 92.

30. Letter from Major General Roscoe B. Woodruff, USA Ret, to EFP, December 13, 1962.

31. *Collier's, op. cit.,* p. 92.

32. *Ibid,* pp. 92-93.

33. Personal Interview with General of the Army Dwight D. Eisenhower, May 2, 1963.

34. *Collier's, op. cit.* p. 93.

35. Letter from Colonel Iverson B. Summers, USA Ret, to EFP, December 12, 1962.

36. Letter from Colonel Clifford R. Jones, USA Ret, to EFP, December 17, 1962.

37. *Collier's, op. cit.,* p. 92.

38. *Ibid,* p. 93.

39. *Ibid,* p. 94.

40. Letter from Colonel Richmond T. Gibson, USA Ret, to EFP, December 13, 1962.

41. Kenneth S. Davis, *Soldier of Democracy* (Garden City: Doubleday and Company, Inc., 1952) p. 138.

42. Letter from Mr. Edward B. Hyde to EFP, December 18, 1962.

43. Davis, *op. cit.,* p. 139.

44. Letter from Major Blackburn Hall, USA Ret, to EFP, December 29, 1962.

45. Letter from Colonel Charles C. Herrick, USA Ret, to EFP, December 28, 1962.

46. *Collier's, op. cit.*, p. 94.

47. Personal interview with General of the Army Dwight D. Eisenhower, May 2, 1963.

48. Letter from Colonel Joseph C. Haw, USA Ret, to EFP, January 2, 1963.

49. Gibson Correspondence, *op. cit.*

50. Letter from Colonel Raymond Marsh, USA Ret, to EFP, December 29, 1962.

51. Letter from Colonel Harold E. Small, USA Ret, to EFP, December 31, 1962.

52. *Collier's, op. cit.*, p. 94.

53. Letter from Colonel Hugh P. Avent, USA Ret, to EFP, January 7, 1963.

54. Letter from Brigadier General Carl C. Bank, USA Ret, to EFP, January 13, 1963.

55. Letter from Colonel John H. Cochran, USA Ret, to EFP, December 31, 1962.

56. Letter from Colonel Jacob W.S. Wuest, USAF Ret, to EFP, July 26, 1963.

57. Personal interview with Colonel Clark Lynn, USA Ret, February 16, 1963.

58. Personal interview with Major General Max C. Tyler, USA Ret, February 16, 1963.

59. Personal interview with Major General Julian L. Schley, USA Ret, February 16, 1963.

60. *Ibid.*

61. Letter from Major General U.S. Grant, 3rd, USA Ret, to EFP, August 12, 1963.

62. Wuest Correspondence, *op. cit.*

63. Frazier Hunt, *The Untold Story of Douglas MacArthur* (New York: The Deven-Adeur Company, 1954) pp. 31-32.

64. *Ibid*, p. 30.

65. Personal interview with Colonel George C. Cocheu, USA Ret, December 19, 1962.

66. Schley interview, *op. cit.*

67. Francis T. Miller, *General Douglas MacArthur* (Chicago: The John C. Winston Company, 1942) p. 55-56.

68. Interview between Dr. Forrest Pogue and Mr. Banks Hudson, December 11, 1958. Notes of interview were furnished to author by Dr. Pogue.

69. Forrest C. Pogue, *George C. Marshall: Education of a General* (New York: The Viking Press, 1963) p. 44.

70. Dr. Pogue's notes and personal interview between author and Dr. Pogue.

71. Statement by Johnson Hagood, cited in Robert Payne, *The Marshall Story* (New York: Prentice Hall, 1951) p. 17.

72. Pogue, *op. cit.*, p. 53.

73. William Frye, *Marshall, Citizen Soldier* (New York: Bobbs-Merrill, 1947) pp. 59-60.

74. Dr. Pogue—Mr. Banks Hudson interview, *op. cit.*

75. Pogue, *op. cit.*, p. 56.

76. Dr. Pogue's notes and personal interview.

77. Dr. Pogue interview with Erskine Miller.

78. *Pogue, op. cit.*, p. 55.

Chapter 2. ALTRUISM—PATIENCE—DEDICATION

General of the Army, George C. Marshall

1. Letter from Major General E.J. Dawley, USA Ret, to EFP, August 21, 1962.

2. Dawley Correspondence, *op. cit.*

3. Letter from Major General Paul L. Ransom, USA Ret, to EFP, September 4, 1962.

4. William Frye, *Marshall, Citizen Soldier* (New York: Bobbs-Merrill, 1947) pp. 145-146.

5. Frye, *op. cit.*, p. 189.

6. Letter from Brigadier General Thomas J. Betts, USA Ret, to EFP, August 16, 1962.

7. Letter from Colonel Frank B. Hayne, USA Ret, to EFP, March 7, 1963.

8. Hayne Correspondence, *op. cit.*

9. Letter from Brigadier General Arthur S. Champeny, USA Ret, to EFP, August 9, 1962.

10. Hayne Correspondence, *op. cit.*

11. Hayne Correspondence, *op. cit.*

12. Letter from Colonel O.Z. Tyler, Jr., USA Ret, to EFP, December 17, 1962.

13. Letter from Lieutenant General Frank E. Fraser, Arizona ARNG, Ret, to EFP, May 2, 1963.

14. General of the Army Omar N. Bradley, USA, *A Soldier's Story* (New York: Henry Holt and Company, 1951) p. 20.

15. Letter from Colonel Haydon Y. Grubbs, USA Ret, to EFP, December 11, 1962.

16.- Letter from Colonel Thomas F. Taylor, USA Ret, to EFP, February 5, 1963.

17. Forrest C. Pogue, *George C. Marshall: Education of a General* (New York: The Viking Press, 1963) p. 285.

18. The main source on General George C. Marshall's activities at Fort Screven was Colonel Frederick C. Matthews, USA Ret, (Letter to EFP, November 29, 1962).

19. Katherine T. Marshall, *Together* (New York: Tupper and Low, Inc., 1946) p. 18.

20. *Ibid*, p. 18.

21. Letter from Colonel Arthur Pickens, USA Ret, to EFP, May 27, 1963.

22. Letter from Colonel Walker S. Wood, USA Ret, to EFP, January 25, 1963.

23. Wood Correspondence, *op. cit.*

24. Letter from Major General Harry L. Bolen, USA Ret, to EFP, April 25, 1963.

25. Bolen Correspondence, *op. cit.*

26. Letter from Brigadier General Robert W. Davis, USA Ret, to EFP, April 29, 1963.

27. Letter from Major General Harry L. Bolen, USA Ret, to EFP, February 11, 1963.

28. Letter from Colonel William C. Moore, USA Ret, to EFP, November 28, 1962.

29. Letter from Colonel Herman O. Lane, USA Ret, to EFP, December 22, 1962. Colonel Lane was the investigating officer for the incident.

30. Letter from Colonel Edwin T. Bowden, USA Ret, to EFP, October 3, 1962.

31. Letter from Major General B.B. Talley, USA Ret, to EFP, September 9, 1962.

32. *New York Times*, February 27, 1938.

33. General of the Army Omar N. Bradley, USA, *A Soldier's Story* (New York: Henry Holt and Company, 1951) p. 21.

34. *Ibid*, p. 21.

35. Personal Interview with General of the Army Dwight D. Eisenhower, May 2, 1963.

36. *Ibid.*

37. Personal Interview with General J. Lawton Collins, USA Ret, September 10, 1962.

38. Personal Interview with General Mark W. Clark, USA Ret, December 17, 1962.

39. *Ibid.*

40. Letter from Major General Charles H. Corlett, USA Ret, to EFP, July 31, 1962.

41. *Stimson Diary*, December 11, 1940.

42. *Pearl Harbor Attack Hearings, Part 39, Joint Committee on the Investigation of the Pearl Harbor Attack, Congress of the U.S., Seventy-Ninth Congress* (Washington: U.S. Government Printing Office, 1946) p. 507.

43. *American Heritage*, February 1962, p. 80.

44. *Investigation of the Pearl Harbor Attack: Report of the Joint Committee on the Investigation of the Pearl Harbor Attack, 1943. American Heritage*, February 1962, p. 80. And *Investigation of the Pearl Harbor Attack: Report of the Joint Committee on the Investigation of the Pearl Harbor Attack, 79th Congress, 20 Session, Congress of the United States* (Washington: Government Printing Office, 1946) p. 252.

45. *Stimson Diary*, January 13, 1942.

46. *Stimson Diary*, January 14, 1942.

47. 48. Letter from Major General James R. Pierce, USA Ret, to EFP, August 24, 1962.

49. Letter from Brigadier General Charles H. Royce, USA Ret, to EFP, September 11, 1962.

50. *Stimson Diary*, September 8, 1942.

51. *Stimson Diary*, November 9, 1942.

52. Marshall, *op. cit.*, p. 110.

53. *Stimson Diary*, December 31, 1943.

54. General of the Army Dwight D. Eisenhower, *Crusade in Europe* (New York: Doubleday and Company, Inc., 1948) p. 317.

55. Personal Interview with General Eisenhower, May 2, 1963.

56. Harry C. Butcher, *My Three Years with Eisenhower* (New York: Simon and Schuster, 1946) P. 277.

57. *Ibid*, p. 464.

58. Robert E. Sherwood, *Roosevelt and Hopkins* (New York: Harper and Brothers, 1948) p. 689.

59. Letter from Colonel M.B. DePass, USA Ret, to EFP, November 20, 1962.

60. Betts Correspondence, *op. cit.*

61. *Ibid.*

62. Butcher, *op. cit.*, p. 92.

63. Eisenhower, *op. cit.*, p. 35.

64. Bradley, *op. cit.*, p. 20.

65. Letter from Major General Paul L. Ransom, USA Ret, to EFP, September 4, 1962.

66. Corlett Correspondence, *op. cit.*

67. Henry L. Stimson and McGeorge Bundy, *On Active Service in Peace and War* (New York: Harper, 1948) p. 330.

68. *Stimson Diary*, July 22, 1940.

69. *Stimson Diary*, March 20, 1941.

70. *Stimson Diary*, May 5, 1941.

71. *Stimson Diary*, November 27, 1941.

72. Stimson, *op. cit.*, p. 330.

73. *Stimson Diary*, December 11, 1941.

74. *Stimson Diary*, January 5, 1942.

75. *Stimson Diary*, May 25, 1943.

76. Butcher, *op. cit.*, p. 316.

77. *Stimson Diary*, May 13, 1942.

78. Letter from Major General Ward H. Maris, USA Ret, to EFP, September 10, 1962.

79. Marshall, *op. cit.*, p. 127.

80. *Stimson Diary*, September 15, 1941.

81. *Stimson Diary*, February 16, 1943.

82. Stimson Correspondence; Letter to President Roosevelt, February 16, 1943.

83. *Stimson Diary*, February 22, 1943.

84. *Stimson Diary*, February 15, 1943.

85. Mark W. Clark, *Calculated Risk* (New York: Harper and Brothers, 1950) pp. 335-336; and personal interview.

86. Maris Correspondence, *op. cit.*

87. Maris Correspondence, *op. cit.*

88. Maris Correspondence, *op. cit.*

89. Collins Interview, *op. cit.*

90. Personal Interview with Lieutenant General Willis D. Crittenberger.

91. General Lucian K. Truscott, *Command Missions* (New York: Dutton, 1954) p. 383.

92. Letter from Major General A.M. Jones, USA Ret, to EFP, August 10, 1962.

93. Letter from Colonel R.V. Murphy, USA Ret, to EFP, January 20, 1963.

94. Marshall, *op. cit.*, p. 176.

95. Letter from Brigadier General Guy Rowe, USA Ret, to EFP, May 5, 1963

96. Letter from Major General James R. Pierce, USA Ret, to EFP, August 24, 1962.

Chapter 3. DUTY—HONOR—COUNTRY

General of the Army Douglas MacArthur

1. "The Old Soldier Looks Back," *Life*, January 10, 1964, p. 50.

2. *Ibid*, p. 56A.

3. Frank Kelley and Cornelius Ryan, *MacArthur: Man of Action* (New York: Doubleday and Company, Inc., 1951) p. 63.

4. William A. Ganoe, *MacArthur Close-up* (New York: Vantage Press, 1962) p. 133.

5. *New York Times*, April 6, 1917.

6. Clarence H. Cramer, Newton D. Baker, *A Biography* (Cleveland: World Publishing Company, 1961) p. 129.

7. *New York Times*, March 16, 1918.

8. Letter from Colonel Albert Gilmore, USA Ret, to EFP.

9. Biographical Register of the Officers and Graduates of the U.S. Military Academy (Saginaw, Mich.: Seemand and Peters, Printers, 1920) pp. 1013-, 014.

10. *New York Times,* August 7, 1930.

11. Herbert C. Hoover, *Memoirs* (New York: Macmillan, 1951) p. 339.

12. *New York Times,* December 1, 1932.

13. *New York Times,* June 3, 1931-June 7, 1931.

14. *New York Times,* November 16, 1934.

15. Clark Lee and Richard Henschel, *Douglas MacArthur* (New York: Henry Holt and Company, 1932) p. 56.

16. *New York Times,* July 30, 1932.

17. Letter from General MacArthur to Captain Bonner Fellers, June 1, 1939.

18. Major General Charles A. Willoughby, *MacArthur 1941-1951* (New York: McGraw Hill, 1954) p. 91.

19. Major General Courtney Whitney, *MacArthur: His Rendezvous with Destiny* (New York: Knopf, 1956) pp. 24-25.

20. Personal Interview with Major General Courtney Whitney, USA Ret, December 20, 1962.

21. *Time,* February 19, 1945, p. 17.

22. Letter from Lieutenant General Samuel D. Sturgis, USA Ret, to EFP, September 4, 1963.

23. General of the Army Henry H. Arnold, *Global Mission* (New York: Harper, 1949) p. 292.

24. Lieutenant General Lewis H. Brereton, USA, *The Brereton Diaries* (New York: William Morrow and Company, 1946) pp.

25. Arnold, *op. cit.,* p. 272.

26. *Ibid,* p. 272.

27. Whitney, *op. cit.,* p. 11.

28. General George C. Kenney, *The MacArthur I Know* (New York: Duell, Sloan and Pearce, 1951) p. 40 and Personal Interview, February 16, 1963.

29. *Ibid,* p. 242.

30. Personal Interview with Lieutenant General Stephen J. Chamberlin, July 8, 1962.

31. Fleet Admiral William F. Halsey and Lieutenant Commander J. Bryan, III, *Admiral Halsey's Story* (New York: Whittlesey House, 1947) pp. 189-190.

32. Kenney, *op. cit.*, pp. 51-52.

33. *Ibid*, p. 114.

34. Personal Interview with Lieutenant General Stephen J. Chamberlin, USA Ret, July 8, 1962.

35. Willoughby, *op. cit.*, p. 8.

36. Ernest J. King and Walter Muir Whitehill, *Fleet Admiral King, A Naval Record* (New York: W.W. Norton and Company, Inc., 1952) p. 538.

37. Fleet Admiral William D. Leahy, *I Was There* (New York: McGraw-Hill Book Company, Inc., 1950) pp. 250-251.

38. Leahy, *op. cit.*, p. 254.

39. Halsey, *op. cit.*, pp. 154-155.

40. Letter from Brigadier General John F. Bird, USA Ret, to EFP, August 27, 1963.

41. Kenney, *op. cit.*, pp. 240-242.

42. *Ibid*, p. 57.

43. Brereton, *op. cit.*, p. 25.

44. Letter from General of the Army Douglas MacArthur to Captain Bonner Fellers, June 1, 1939.

45. Personal Interview with Major General Robert M. Danford, USA Ret, February 18, 1963.

46. General Robert L. Eichelberger, *Our Jungle Road to Tokyo* (New York: Viking Press, 1950) pp. 106-107.

47. Brereton, *op.cit.*, p. 18.

48. Kenney, *op. cit.*, pp. 63-64.

49. Personal Interview with Major General Courtney Whitney, USA Ret, December 20, 1962.

50. *Life, op. cit.*, p. 60. (Author's Italics)

51. *Ibid*, p. 62.

52. *Ibid*, p. 60.

Chapter 4. SOLDIER—STATESMAN—DIPLOMAT

General of the Army Dwight D. Eisenhower

1. Kevin McCann, *Man from Abilene* (New York: Doubleday and Company, Inc., 1952) p. 24.

2. *Ibid*, pp. 25-29.

3. Personal Interview with General of the Army Dwight D. Eisenhower, May 2, 1963.

4. *Ibid*.

5. General of the Army Dwight D. Eisenhower, *Crusade in Europe* (New York: Doubleday and Company, Inc., 1948) p. 14.

6. General Mark W. Clark, *Calculated Risk* (New York: Harper and Brothers, 1950) pp. 10-11; and Personal Interview.

7. *Ibid*, pp. 16-17; and Personal Interview.

7a. Forrest C. Pogue, General George C. Marshall, *Ordeal and Hope: 1939-1942* (New York: The Viking Press, 1966) pp. 162-163.

8. General Walter Krueger, *From Down Under to Nippon* (Washington, D.C.; Combat Forces Press, 1953) p. 4; Personal Interview, July 30, 1963.

9. Eisenhower Interview, *op cit*.

10. *Ibid*.

11. *Ibid*.

12. *Ibid*.

13. *Ibid*.

14. *Ibid*.

15. Eisenhower, *op. cit.*, p. 14.

16. *Ibid*, pp. 16-18.

17. *Ibid*, p. 22.

18. Harry C. Butcher, *My Three Years with Eisenhower* (New York: Simon and Schuster, 1946) pp. 247-248.

19. McCann, *op. cit.*, p. 51.

20. *Ibid*, p. 51.

414   Nineteen Stars

21. Kenneth S. Davis, *Soldier of Democracy* (New York: Doubleday, Doran and Company, Inc., 1945) p. 291.

22. General of the Army Henry H. Arnold, *Global Mission* (New York: Harper and Brothers, 1949) pp. 258-259.

23. Eisenhower Interview, *op. cit.*

24. *Ibid.*

25. Davis, *op. cit.*, pp. 196-197.

26. Eisenhower, *op. cit.*, pp. 18-19.

27. Personal Interview with General of the Army Omar N. Bradley.

28. Personal Interview with General Mark W. Clark,

29. Personal Interview with General Carl Spaatz,

30. Personal Interview with General Anthony McAuliffe,

31. Bernard Law, Viscount Montgomery of Alamein, *The Memoirs of the Field-Marshal the Viscount Montgomery of Alamein, K.G.* (Cleveland and New York: The World Publishing Company, 1958) p. 484 (Author's Italics).

32. Bryant, *Triumph in the West*, p. 139.

33. *Ibid*, p. 139.

34. Eisenhower, *op. cit.*, p. 4.

35. *Ibid*, p. 4.

36. *Ibid*, p. 451.

37. *Ibid*, p. 121.

38. Butcher, *op. cit.*, p. 639.

39. *Ibid*, p. 644.

40. Eisenhower, *op. cit.*, p. 446.

41. Eisenhower, *op. cit.*, pp. 29-30 (Author's Italics).

42. Butcher, *op. cit.*, p. 582.

43. Eisenhower, *op. cit.*, p. 151.

44. Letter from Major General Francis H. Lanahan, Jr., USA Ret, to EFP, August 2, 1963.

45. Eisenhower, *op. cit.*, p. 90.

46. General of the Army Omar N. Bradley, *A Soldier's Story* (New York: Henry Holt and Company, 1951) p. 353.

47. *Ibid*, p. 354.

48. *Ibid*, p. 354.

49. *Ibid*, pp. 477-78.

50. *Ibid*, pp. 487-88.

51. Eisenhower, *op. cit.*, p. 356.

52. Charles R. Codman, *Drive* (Boston: Little, Brown and Company, 1957) p. XVII.

53. Bradley, *op. cit.*, p. 399.

54. General George S. Patton, Jr., *War As I Knew It* (Boston: Houghton Mifflin and Company, 1947), p. 79.

55. *Ibid*, pp. 212-13.

56. Bradley, *op. cit.*, p. 422.

57. *Ibid*.

58. *Ibid*, p. 327-28.

59. Bradley, *op. cit.*, p. 138.

60. Eisenhower, *op. cit.*, p. 286.

61. Patton, *op. cit.*, pp. 381-382.

62. Butcher, *op. cit.*, p. 390.

63. Eisenhower, *op. cit.*, p. 181.

64. Letter from Lieutenant General Alvan C. Gillem, Jr., USA Ret, to EFP, August 19, 1963.

65. Eisenhower, *op. cit.*, p. 183.

66. Bradley, *op. cit.*, p. 357.

67. *Ibid*, p. 357.

68. Patton, *op. cit.*, p. 382.

69. *Ibid*, p. 393.

70. Butcher, *op. cit.*, p. 360.

71. *Ibid*, p. 480.

72. *Ibid*, p. 803.

73. Eisenhower, *op. cit.*, p. 224.

74. *Ibid*, p. 224.

75. *Ibid*, p. 225.

76. Bradley, *op. cit.*, p. 231.

77. Harry C. Butcher, *My Three Years with Eisenhower* (New York: Simon and Schuster, 1946) p. 165.

78. General of the Army Dwight D. Eisenhower, *Crusade in Europe* (New York: Doubleday and Company, Inc., 1948) p. 106.

79. *Stimson Diary*, November 20, 1943.

80. Eisenhower, *op. cit.*, pp. 61-62.

81. Winston S. Churchill, *The Grand Alliance* (Boston: Houghton Mifflin Company, 1950) p. 137.

82. Robert E. Sherwood, *Roosevelt and Hopkins* (New York: Harper and Brothers, 1948) p. 273.

83. Albert Norman, *Operation Overlord* (Harrisburg, Pa.: The Military Service Publishing Company, 1952) p. 8. See also Samuel Eliot Morison, *The Battle of the Atlantic*, Vol. I (Boston: Little, Brown and Company, 1947) p. 45-49; Churchill, *op. cit.*, pp. 137-138; Ray S. Cline, *Washington Command Post: The Operations Division* (Washington: Office of Military History, Department of the Army, 1951) pp. 58-60.

84. Gordon A. Harrison, *Cross-Channel Attack* (Washington: Office of the Chief of Military History, Department of the Army, 1951) pp. 6-12.

85. Winston S. Churchill, *The Grand Alliance* (Boston: Houghton Mifflin Company, 1950) p. 663.

86. Winston S. Churchill, *Hinge of Fate* (Boston: Houghton Mifflin Company, 1950) p. 384-85.

87. *Ibid*, pp. 432-33.

88. Mark W. Clark, *Calculated Risk* (New York: Harper and Brothers, 1950) pp. 27-28.

89. Butcher, *op. cit.*, p. 29.

90. Eisenhower, *op. cit.*, p. 194.

91. Winston S. Churchill, *Closing the Ring* (Boston: Houghton Mifflin Company, 1951) pp. 441-442.

92. Smith, *op. cit.*, p. 186.

93. Butcher, *op. cit.*, p. 35.

94. Robert E. Sherwood, *Roosevelt and Hopkins* (New York: Harper and Brothers, 1948) p. 651.

95. Eisenhower, *op. cit.*, p. 369.

96. *Ibid*, p. 51.

97. *Ibid*, p. 54.

98. *Ibid*, p. 56.

99. Clark, *op. cit.*, p. 122.

100. Butcher, *op. cit.*, p. 75.

101. Eisenhower, *op. cit.*, pp. 133-34.

102. Butcher, *op. cit.*, p. 151.

103. Smith, *op. cit.*, p. 200.

104. Letter from Colonel James Stack, USA Ret, to EFP, August 27, 1963.

105. Butcher, *op. cit.*, p. 189.

106. Butcher, *op. cit.*, p. 589.

107. Letter from Major General Lowell W. Rooks, USA Ret, to EFP, August 23, 1963. General Rooks was Chief of the Operations Section, General Staff, during the North African campaign.

108. Butcher, *op. cit.*, p. 7.

109. Eisenhower, *op. cit.*, p. 75. (Author's Italics).

110. Rooks Correspondence, *op. cit.*

111. Butcher, *op. cit.*, p. 116.

112. Eisenhower, *op. cit.*, p. 298.

113. *Ibid*, p. 170.

114. *Ibid*, p. 169.

115. Butcher, *op. cit.*, p. 333.

116. Eisenhower, *op. cit.*, pp. 58-59.

117. *Ibid*, pp. 298-299.

118. Butcher, *op. cit.*, p. 763.

119. Eisenhower, *op. cit.*, pp. 313-314.

120. *Ibid*, p. 389.

121. Letter from Lieutenant General Alvan C. Gillem, Jr., USA Ret, to EFP, August 19, 1963.

122. General of the Army Omar N. Bradley, *A Soldier's Story* (New York: Henry Holt and Company, 1951) p. 3.

123. Eisenhower, *op. cit.*, p. 254.

124. Eisenhower, *op. cit.*, pp. 213-214. (Author's Italics).

125. *Ibid*, p. 314.

126. Butcher, *op. cit.*, p. 723.

127. *Ibid*, p. 854.

128. Eisenhower, *op. cit.*, p. 455.

129. *Ibid*, p. 238.

130. *Ibid*, p. 455.

131. Letter from General Ben Lear, USA Ret, to EFP, August 17, 1963.

Chapter 5. BLOOD AND GUTS

General George S. Patton, Jr.

1. *The Medal of Honor of the United States Army* (Washington, D.C.: Government Printing Office, 1948) p. 235.

2. Herman Hagedorn, *Leonard Wood* (New York: Harper and Brothers, 1931) Vol. I, p. 145.

3. Alden Hatch, George Patton, *General in Spurs* (New York: Julian Messner, Inc., 1950) pp. 53-54; William B. Mellor, *Patton, Fighting Man* (New York: G. P. Putman's Sons, 1946) pp. 79-81.

4. *New York Times*, May 23, 1916.

5. Charles R. Codman, *Drive* (Boston: Little, Brown and Company, 1957) p. 145.

6. Hatch, *op. cit.*, p. 102.

7. General of the Army Dwight D. Eisenhower, *Crusade in Europe* (New York: Doubleday and Company, Inc., 1948) p. 102.

8. *Stimson Diary*, June 25, 1942.

9. *Stimson Diary*, March 26, 1941.

10. Stimson-Patton Correspondence.

11. Stimson-Patton Correspondence.

12. *Stimson Diary*, September 17, 1942.

13. *Stimson Diary*, August 26, 1942.

14. Letter from Major General Stanley E. Reinhart, USA Ret to EFP, October 24, 1962.

15. "War Letters," *Atlantic Monthly*, November 1947, p. 59.

16. Author's Italics.

17. Personal Interview with Brigadier General Don C. Faith, September 12, 1962.

18. The observer was Brigadier General John L. Whitelaw, Assistant Division Commander of the 17th Airborne Division.

19. Reinhart Correspondence, *op. cit.*

20. Letter from Major General Robert C. Macon, USA Ret, to EFP, October 8, 1962.

21. Mellor, *op. cit.*, pp. 103-104; Hatch, *op. cit.*, pp. 68-69.

22. General of the Army Omar N. Bradley, *A Soldier's Story* (New York: Henry Holt and Company, 1951) p. 44.

23. *Ibid.*

24. Mellor, *op. cit.*, p. 175.

25. *Ibid*, p. 175.

26. General George S. Patton, Jr., *War As I Knew It* (Boston: Houghton Mifflin Company, 1947) p. 290.

27. *Ibid*, pp. 335-336.

28. Patton, *op. cit.*, pp. 373-374 (Author's Italics).

29. *Ibid*, p. 350.

30. Mellor, *op. cit.*, p. 157.

31. "War Letters," *Atlantic Monthly*, November 1947, p. 60.

32. Patton, *op. cit.*, p. 187.

33. James H. Wellard, *General George S. Patton, Jr., Man under Mars* (New York: Dodd, Mead and Company, 1946) p. 154.

34. *Ibid*, p. 154.

35. "War Letters," *Atlantic Monthly*, December 1947, p. 35.

36. Patton, *op. cit.*, pp. 357.

37. Letter from Major General Leroy H. Watso , USA Ret, to EFP,

38. Patton, *op. cit.*, pp. 345-346.

39. Robert S. Allen, *Lucky Forward* (New York: Vanguard Press, 1947) p. 16 (Author's Italics).

40. Patton, *op. cit.*, p. 349.

41. Allen, *op. cit.*, pp. 128-129.

42. Patton, *op. cit.*, p. 349.

43. *Ibid*, p. 353.

44. "War Letters," *Atlantic Monthly*, December 1947, p. 37.

45. Letter of Instruction Number 1, dated March 6, 1944, Part IV, Paragraph 36.

46. Letter from Major General Lunsford E. Oliver, USA Ret, to EFP, October 9, 1962.

47. Patton, *op. cit.*, pp. 245-246.

48. Mellor, *op. cit.*, p. 214-215.

49. Patton, *op. cit.*, p. 355.

50. Letter from Major General John M. Devine, USA Ret, to EFP, November 11, 1962.

51. Letter from Major General Lunsford E. Oliver, USA Ret, to EFP, October 9, 1962.

52. Letter from Major General Robert C. Macon, USA Ret, to EFP, October 8, 1962.

53. General George S. Patton, Jr., *War As I Knew It* (Boston: Houghton Mifflin Company, 1947) pp. 329-330.

54. Robert S. Allen, *Lucky Forward* (New York: Vanguard Press, 1947) pp. 19-20.

55. Brigadier General Brenton G. Wallace, *Patton and His Third Army* (Harrisburg; Military Service Publishing Company, 1946) p. 17.

56. Patton, *op. cit.*, p. 361.

57. Wallace, *op. cit.*, p. 198.

58. General of the Army Omar N. Bradley, *A Soldier's Story* (New York: Henry Holt and Company, 1951) p. 473.

59. Carl von Clausewitz, *Principles of War* (Harrisburg: The Military Service Publishing Company, 1943) p. 14. (Author's Italics).

60. Patton, *op. cit.*, p. 239.

61. *Ibid*, p. 243.

62. James H. Wellard, *General George S. Patton, Jr., Man under Mars* (New York: Dodd, Mead and Company, 1946) p. 170.

63. Patton, *op. cit.*, p. 174.

64. *Ibid*, p. 120.

65. *Ibid*, p. 120.

66. *Ibid*, p. 120.

67. *Ibid*, p. 116. (Author's Italics)

68. *Ibid*, p. 354.

69. *Ibid*, p. 349.

70. Personal Interview with General Wade H. Haislip, USA Ret, September 1962.

71. Allen *op. cit.*, p. 117.

72. *Ibid*, p. 117.

73. "War Letters," *Atlantic Monthly*, January 1948, p. 54.

74. Allen, *op. cit.* p. 85.

75. "War Letters," *Atlantic Monthly*, December 1947, p. 36.

76. Patton, *op. cit.*, p. 388.

77. *Ibid*, p. 383.

78. "War Letters," *Atlantic Monthly*, January 1948, p. 53.

79. Patton, *op. cit.* p. 240.

80. Author's Italics.

81. Patton, *op. cit.*, p. 134.

82. *Ibid*, pp. 353, 386.

83. *Ibid*, p. 381.

84. *Ibid*, p. 355.

Chapter 6. THE MILITARY CHARACTER

1. Personal Interview with General of the Army Dwight D. Eisenhower, Mary 2, 1963.

2. Personal Interview with General of the Army Omar N. Bradley, February 15, 1963.

3. Personal Interview with General Mark W. Clark, USA Ret, December, 1962.

4. Personal Interview with General Lucian K. Truscott, USA Ret, September 11, 1962.

5. Personal Interview with General Carl Spaatz, USAF Ret,

6. Personal Interview with General J. Lawton Collins, USA Ret, September 20, 1962.

7. Personal Interview with General William H. Simpson, USA Ret, September 20, 1962.

8. Personal Interview with General Jacob Devers, USA Ret, September 12, 1962.

9. Personal Interview with General Albert Wedemeyer, USA Ret,

10. Personal Interview with General Anthony McAuliffe,

11. Forrest C. Pogue, *George C. Marshall: Education of a General* (New York: The Viking Press, 1963) pp. 129-130.

12. Kevin McCann, *Man from Abilene* (New York: Doubleday and Company, Inc., 1952) p.

13. Eisenhower Interview, *op. cit.*

14. *Ibid.*

15. Bradley Interview, *op. cit.*

16. Clark Interview, *op. cit.*

17. Collins Interview, *op. cit.*

18. Spaatz Interview, *op. cit.*

19. Robert Payne, *The Marshall Story* (New York: Prentice-Hall, 1951)

20. General Mark W. Clark, *Calculated Risk* (New York: Harper and Brothers, 1950) pp. 423-424.

21. *Stimson Diary,* March 20, 1942.

22. *Ibid,* March 20, 1942.

23. Pogue, *op. cit.,* p. 323.

24. Wedemeyer Interview, *op. cit.*

25. Wedemeyer Interview, *op. cit.*

26. Major General Courtney Whitney, USA Ret, *MacArthur: His Rendezvous with Destiny* (New York: Alfred A. Knopf, 1956) p. 88.

27. Personal Interview with General Joseph T. McNarney, USAF Ret,

28. General George C. Kenney, *The MacArthur I Know* (New York: Duell, Sloan and Pearce, 1951) pp. 114-115.

29. Personal Interview with Major General Courtney Whitney, USA Ret,

30. General George S. Patton, Jr., *War As I Knew It* (Boston: Houghton Mifflin Company, 1947) p. 88.

31. Charles R. Codman, *Drive* (Boston: Little and Brown, 1957) p. 235.

32. Robert S. Allen, *Lucky Forward* (New York: Vanguard Press, 1947) p. 280.

33. Clark, *op. cit.,* p. 149.

34. Harry C. Butcher, *My Three Years with Eisenhower* (New York: Simon and Schuster, 1946) p. 139.

35. *Ibid,* p. 41.

36. *Ibid,* p. 43.

37. General of the Army Dwight D. Eisenhower, *Crusade in Europe* (New York: Doubleday and Company, Inc., 1948) p. 75.

38. Colonel William A. Ganoe, *MacArthur Close-up* (New York: Vantage Press, 1962) pp. 143-, 44.

39. *Ibid,* p. 145.

40. Whitney, *op. cit.,* p. 155.

41. Kenney, *op. cit.,* p. 253.

42. Whitney, *op. cit.,* p. 159.

43. Letter from Brigadier General Philip S. Gage, USA Ret, to EFP, October 31, 1962.

44. William B. Mellor, Patton, *Fighting Man* (New York: G.P. Putnam's Sons, 1946) pp. 41-42.

45. *Ibid*, p. 54.

46. Clark Interview, *op. cit.*

47. Mellor, *op. cit.*, p. 144.

48. "War Letters," *Atlantic Monthly*, November, 1947, p. 61.

49. Patton, *op. cit.*, pp. 184-186.

50. Patton, *op. cit.*, p. 77.

51. Patton, *op. cit.*, p. 8.

52. "War Letters," *Atlantic Monthly*, November, 1947, p. 61.

53. Kenneth S. Davis, *Soldier of Democracy* (Garden City: Doubleday and Company, Inc., 1952) p. 453.

54. Butcher, *op. cit.*, p. 438.

55. Eisenhower, *op. cit.*, pp. 354-355.

56. Personal Interview with Major General William Arnold, USA Ret.

57. Robert E. Sherwood, *Roosevelt and Hopkins* (New York: Harper and Brothers, 1948) p. 915.

58. Personal Interview with General Carl Spaatz, USAF Ret,

59. Personal Interview with General William H. Simpson, USA Ret, September 20, 1962.

60. Personal Interview with General Lucian K. Truscott, USA Ret, September 1, 1962.

61. *U.S. News and World Report*, November 2, 1959, p. 52.

62. *Stimson Diary*, August 9, 1942.

63. *Stimson Diary*, September 28, 1942.

64. Robert S. Allen, *Lucky Forward* (New York: Vanguard Press, 1947) p. 249.

65. *Ibid*, p. 164.

66. Major General Courtney Whitney, USA Ret, *MacArthur: His Rendezvous with Destiny* (New York: Alfred A. Knopf, 1956) p. 154.

67. *Ibid*, p. 114.

68. General George C. Kenney, *The MacArthur I Know* (New York: Duell, Sloan and Pearce, 1951) pp. 97-98.

69. *Ibid*, p. 99.

70. Whitney, *op. cit.*, p. 187.

71. General Walter B. Smith, *Eisenhower's Six Great Decisions* (New York: Longmans, Green, 1956) p. 170.

72. General of the Army Dwight D. Eisenhower, *Crusade in Europe* (New York: Doubleday and Company, Inc., 1948) pp. 467-468.

73. *Ibid*, pp. 468-469.

74. *Ibid*, p. 470.

75. *Ibid*, p. 470.

76. Colonel William A. Ganoe, *MacArthur Close-up* (New York: Vantage Press, 1962) p. 135.

77. "War Letters," *Atlantic Monthly*, January 1948, p. 56.

78. *Ibid*, p. 56.

79. *Stimson Diary*, August 22, 1943.

80. Sherwood, *op. cit.*, p. 770.

81. *Stimson Diary*, September 15, 1943.

82. Sherwood, *op. cit.*, p. 759.

83. *Ibid*, p. 803.

84. *Stimson Diary*, December 17, 1943.

85. *Ibid*.

86. *Ibid*.

87. *Stimson Diary*, December 18, 1943.

88. *Stimson Diary*, September 28, 1943.

89. *Stimson Diary*, September 29, 1943.

90. *Stimson Diary*, November 11, 1943.

91. *Stimson Diary*, December 23, 1943.

92. Personal Interview with General of the Army Dwight D. Eisenhower, May 2, 1963.

Chapter 7. DECISION AND COURAGE

1. General Walter B. Smith, *Eisenhower's Six Great Decisions* (New York: Longmans, Green, 1956).

2. General of the Army Dwight D. Eisenhower, *Crusade in Europe* (New York: Doubleday and Company, Inc., 1948) pp. 246-247.

3. Harry C. Butcher, *My Three Years with Eisenhower* (New York: Simon and Schuster, 1946) p. 570.

4. Smith, *op. cit.*, pp. 19-20.

5. Eisenhower, *op. cit.*, p. 172.

6. *Ibid.*, p. 172.

7. *Ibid.*, p. 239.

8. *Ibid*, p. 240.

9. *Ibid*, p. 249.

10. Smith, *op. cit.*, pp. 53-55.

11. Eisenhower, *op. cit.*, p. 251.

12. *Ibid.*, p. 252.

13. General George C. Kenney, *The MacArthur I Know* (New York: Duell, Sloan and Pearce, 1951) p. 244.

14. Major General Courtney Whitney, *MacArthur: His Rendezvous with Destiny* (New York: Knopf, 1956) p.107..

15. *Ibid.*, p. 107.

16. Patton, *op. cit.*, p. 379.

17. *Ibid.*, p. 256.

18. *Ibid*, p. 8.

19. Charles R. Codman, *Drive* (Boston: Little, Brown and Company, 1957) p. 124.

20. Whitney, *op. cit.*, p. 39.

21. Major General Charles A. Willoughby, *MacArthur 1941-1951* (New York: McGraw-Hill, 1954) pp. 37-39.

22. Whitney, *op. cit.*, p. 25.

23. *Ibid*, p. 161.

24. *Ibid*, p. 197.

25. *Ibid*, p. 197 and Kenney, *op. cit.*, pp. 134-135.

26. Kenney, *op. cit.*, p. 106.

27. *Ibid*, p. 106.

28. Personal Interview with General Walter Krueger and General Walter Krueger, *From Down Under to Nipon*, (Washington: Combat Forces Press, 1953).

29. Whitney, *op. cit.*, p.

30. Kenney, *op. cit.*, p. 122.

31. "War Letter," *Atlantic Monthly*, November 1947, p. 60.

32. *Ibid*, p. 60.

33. Codman, *op. cit.*, p. 293.

34. General George S. Patton, Jr., *War As I Knew It* (Boston: Houghton Mifflin Company, 1947) pp. 305-306.

35. Codman, *op. cit.*, p. XII

36. Patton, *op. cit.*, pp. 107-108

37. *Ibid*, p. 157.

38. *Ibid*, p. 1, 2.

39. *Ibid*, p.

40. General of the Army Omar N. Bradley, *A Soldier's Story* (New York: Henry Holt and Company, 1951) p. 325.

41. *Ibid*, p. 325.

42. Personal interview with General of the Army Dwight D. Eisenhower, May 3, 1963.

Chapter 8. PREPARATION AND LUCK

1. William Frye, *Marshall, Citizen Soldier* (New York: Bobbs-Merrill, 1947) pp. 119-120.

2. Letter from Colonel Herman O. Lane, USA Ret. to EFP, December 22, 1962.

3. Personal interview with General of the Army Dwight D. Eisenhower, May 2, 1963.

4. Alden Hatch, *George Patton, General in Spurs* (New York: Julian Messner, Inc., 1950) p. 101.

5. Personal interview with General of the Army Omar N. Bradley, February 15, 1963.

6. Personal interview with General Mark W. Clark, December, 1962.

7. Personal interview with General Courtney Hodges.

8. Personal interview with General Joseph T. McNarney.

9. Personal interview with General Carl Spaatz.

10. Personal interview with General Wade Haislip.

11. Personal interview with General of the Army Dwight D. Eisenhower, May 3, 1963.

12. Personal interview with General J. Lawton Collins.

13. *Ibid.*

14. Personal interview with General of the Army Omar N. Bradley, February 15, 1963.

15. Robert S. Allen, *Lucky Forward,* (New York: Vanguard Press, 1947), p. 63.

16. "War Letters," *Ibid*, p. 57.

17. *Ibid,* p. 59.

18. Charles R. Codman, *Drive* (Boston: Little, Brown and Company, 1957) pp. 187-188.

19. *Ibid*, pp. 187-188.

20. "War Letters," p. 54.

21. Codman, *op. cit.*, p. 264.

22. General Walter B. Smith, *Eisenhower's Six Great Decisions.* (New York: Longmans, Green, 1956)

23. General George C. Kenney, *The MacArthur I Know* (New York: Duell, Sloan and Pearce, 1951) pp. 262-263.

24. John Gunther, *Riddle of MacArthur*

25. Personal interview with General George C. Kenney, February 16, 1963.

Chapter 9. THE PATTERN

1. This discussion is based upon an interview with General Bruce Clarke and his article, "So You Want Command?"

INDEX

A

Alanbrooke, Field Marshal
  Lord 171, 173
Alexander, Sir Harold R.L.G. 176, 307
Allen, Frank A. Jr. 220
Andrews, Frank, death of 167
Arnold, Henry H. 340
  Japanese attack on Philippines .. 127
Arnold, William 319
Athletics
  Eisenhower 16
  Marshall 38
  Patton 9
Avent, Hugh P. 18

B

Baker, Newton O. 109
Bataan 124
Battle of the Bulge 183, 246, 313
Bell, J. Franklin 44
  Appraisal of Marshall, 1914 379
  Marshall, aide to 292
  Service under Arthur MacArthur 107
Berlin, capture of 207
Betts, Thomas J. 82
Blesse, Fred 192
Bolen, Harry L. 64
Bonus March 118
Booz, Oscar L. 22
Bradley, Omar
  Accomplishment of command .. 395
  Assistant Secretary, General Staff 83
  Character 290
  Commandant, Infantry School .. 69
  Defensive action, Patton 283
  Eisenhower, appraisal of .. 170, 181

Fort Benning, instructor under
  Marshall 55, 58
Montgomery, Sir Bernard L.
  .... 181, 188, 189

Patton's intuition 362
Patton, slapping incident 195
Patton's staff 274
Relationship of American and British
  troops 189
Service career, appeal of 295
Brereton, Lewis H. 146
  Japanese attack on Philippines .. 128
Bullard, Robert L. 44
Butcher, Harry C. 212, 220

C

Cadet years
  Compared 39
  Eisenhower, Dwight D. 10
  MacArthur, Douglas 21
  Marshall, George C. 35
  Patton, George S., Jr. 1
Capehart, Homer 230
Chamberlin, Stephen J. 131
Character, see Military character
Churchill, Winston
  Attitude toward war 326
  Battle of the Bulge 184
  Choice of Supreme Commander 337
  Eisenhower, relationship with .. 175
  Eisenhower's political leadership 202
  European invasion decision 204
  Invasion of Southern France 175
  MacArthur's courage 371
  Marshall, relationship with 86

Meeting of Russian and American
   Armies 208
Military training 364
Clark, Mark W. 312
   Character 290
   Churchill 205
   Congressional briefing 93
   Desire to command 395
   Eisenhower, as Allied leader 170
   Eisenhower's career, effect upon 160
   Marshall, early service under 72
   Marshall's view of honors 298
   North African civil government . 201
   North African invasion 324
   Patton's commander 304
   Promotion to Lieutenant
     General 211
   Service career, appeal of 295
Cocheu, George 32, 34
Codman, Charles R. 287
Collins, J. Lawton
   Desire to command 395
   Fort Benning 57
   Intuition 363
   Luck 388
   Marshall
     relationship with 96
     staff duty under 71
   Service career, appeal of 296
Command, responsibilities of 393
Conner, Fox
   Appraisal of Marshall 80
   Candidate for Chief of Staff 121
   Eisenhower's career, effect
     upon 162, 167
   Preparing Eisenhower for
     command 381
Corlett, Charles H. 73, 84
Corregidor 126, 368
Courage
   Eisenhower 375
   MacArthur 367

   Marshall 376
   Patton 372
Cota, Norman D. 268
Crittenberger, Willis D. 97
Cunningham, Frederick H. 21, 24
Curtin, Prime Minister John 145
Craig, Malin 45
   Marshall's duty under 68

D

D-Day decision 354
Darlan, Jean Francois 200
Davis, Robert W. 64
Davis, Thomas J. 192
Dawley, E. J. 45
Decision making
   Generally 351
   Eisenhower 352
     airborne landings 352
     D-Day 354
     Sicilian invasion 355
   Feel or sixth sense 361
   MacArthur 358
   Patton 360, 374
     sixth sense 362
   Preparation for 362
De Gaulle, Charles 199
Desire to command 386, 395
Devers, Jacob 291
Devine, John M. 269
Discipline, Patton 254
Douglas, Lewis 303
Drum, Hugh 77

E

Early, Steve 224
Eddy, Manton S. 280, 284

Eichelberger, Robert L.
.... 125,133,143,148
Eisenhower, Dwight D.
Aides 212
Air Force, relationship with 211
Allied leader 170
Athletics 16
Berlin, capture of 207
Bonus March 120
Cadet years 10
Character 289
Childhood 10
Command and General Staff
School 161
Command responsibility, view of 210
Commanders, relationship with . 179
Conner, Fox, effect upon career
.... 80, 121, 162, 167, 381
Coordination of forces 210
Courage 375
Criticized as pro-British 177
Decision making 352
Desire to command 386
Early career 153
ETO command, appointment ...166
European invasion decision 203
French civil government 220
Humility 305
Invasion of Southern France 175
Luck 388,391
MacArthur's self confidence 301
MacArthur, service under 158
Marriage 154
Marshall, relationship with 79
Montgomery and Bradley as equal
commanders 223
Montgomery, Sir Bernard L., rela-
tionship with 179
Navy, relationship with 210
North African civil government . 199
Offers to leave service 293
Optimism 392

Patton, early duty with 162
Patton, friendship with 239
Patton, relationship with 191
Philippine service 159
Political philosophy of command
.... 209, 321
Political problems of allied command
............................198
North Africa 199
Preparation for command 380
Press relations 218
Press releases 305
Religious views 317
Selection of bombing targets ...209
Service schools 378
Sicilian invasion revealed to press 221
Staff duty under Marshall 70
Staff, relationship with 212
Stark, Harold, relationship with . 211
Supplies, sharing with British ...187
Temper 216
Visits to troops 224
War Plans Division, appointment
to 153, 164
Emery, Frank E., Jr. 13

F

Fellers, Bonner 125, 126, 140
Fletcher, Robert H. 6
Fraser, Frank E. 54
Funston, Frederick 107

G

Gage, Philip S. 7, 312
Ganoe, William A. 148, 309
Gerow, Leonard T. 154, 165
Gillem, Alvan C., Jr. 193, 226
Gilmore, Albert 111

Girard, Henri H. 199
Goethals, George 3, 4
Grant, Ulysses S., III 30
Grow, R.W. 249

H

Hagood, Johnson, early appraisal
　of Marshall 379
Haislip, Wade H.
　Intuition 363
　Patton's drive 280
　Pride in performance 387
Halsey, William F. 131
　Relationship with MacArthur ... 138
Hargrave, Pearlie 214
Haskell, William H. 77
Hayne, Frank B. 51, 53
Hazing
　MacArthur 21
　Marshall 35
Hazlett, "Swede" 10
Haw, Joseph C. 18
Herrick, Charles C. 12
Hodges, Courtney 286
　Desire to command 386
Hoover, President Herbert
　Appointment of MacArthur as
　　Chief of Staff 112
　Bonus March 119
Hopkins, Harry 299
Hudson, Banks 38
Humility
　Eisenhower 304
　MacArthur 300
　Marshall 297
　Patton 303
Hurley, Patrick J. 119

J

James, Harold W. 11
Jones, Clifford R. 12, 14

K

Keehn, Roy D. 60
Kenney, George C.　130, 133, 139, 142
　　　　　　　　144, 145, 149, 302
　Aerial attack on Philippines 330
　MacArthur's courage 370
　MacArthur's decisions 359
King, Ernest J. 210, 269, 340
Krueger, Walter 133
　Eisenhower's career 161

L

Leahy, William D. 136, 299, 340
Lear, Ben 232
Lee, Clark 318
Lee, Ernest R. 213
Leigh-Mallory, airborne landings in
　Cherbourg 353
Luck
　Bradley 388
　Collins 388
　Eisenhower 388, 391
　Luck in battle 389
　MacArthur 392
　Patton 389
Lynn, Clark 29

M

MacArthur, Arthur 21, 33
　Career 104
　Medal of Honor 105
　Philippine duty 150
MacArthur, Douglas
　Air Force, relationship with 129
　Air Force, separate 302
　Bonus March 118
　Cadet years 21

Chief of Staff 112
    depression years 115
Courage 367
Death of 103
Divorce 294
Early career 107
Eisenhower's service under 158
Father's career 104
Hazing at West Point 21
Humility 300
Island-hopping strategy 134
Japanese attack on Philippines .. 127
Japanese surrender 142
Luck 392
Navy, relationship with 134
New Guinea campaign 139
Medal of Honor 302, 368
Optimism 392
Oratory 144
Philippine Army career 123
Political philosophy 320
Preparedness for war 335
Press relations 143
Rainbow division 109, 118
Religious views 309
Service schools 378
Showmanship of 141
Staff and commanders 127
Study of history 365
Subordinates, relationship with . 147
Visiting combat areas 139
West Point, feelings about 41
World War I career 109
World War II career 124
Macon, Robert C. 252, 271
Maitland-Wilson, Sir Henry 187
March, Peyton C.
    Service under Arthur MacArthur 107
    Relationship with Douglas
        MacArthur 112
Marshall, George C.
    Aide to J. Franklin Bell 292

Air Force build-up 299
Appointment of Eisenhower to
    General Staff 160, 164
Army War College, instructor 52
Athletics 38
Career generally 43
Chief of Staff, appointment 69
China duty 48
Choice of European Supreme Com-
    mander 337
Churchill, relationship with 86
Civilian Conservation Corps 59
Command responsibility, view of 210
Congress, relationship with 90
D-Day Commander, rumored ap-
    pointment as 92
Death of wife 52
Discouragement with service career
    293
Eisenhower, relationship with ... 79
Eisenhower, staff duty 70
European invasion decision 203
Fort Benning duty 53
Fort Benning, future WWII com-
    manders 58
Fort Screven duty 58
Humility 297
Illinois National Guard instructor 59
Inspection trips 99
Intuition or imagination 364
Joint Chief, creation of 299
North African invasion 324
Patton, slapping incident 194
Pearl Harbor 74
Personnel selection, WWII 77
Political philosophy . 321, 323, 324
Preparation for command 378
Press relations 94
Promotion to First Lieutenant .. 292
Relationship with subordi-
    nates 81, 96
Religious views 319

Roosevelt, relationship with 89
Second marriage 56
Selflessness 336
Service schools 378
Stimson, relationship with 84
Vancouver Barracks duty 66
VMI cadet years 35
     feeling about VMI 41
Washington, D.C. staff duty 68
World War I career 44
McAdams, Emory S. 60

McAuliff, Anthony "Nuts"
     Character 291
     Desire to command 395
     Eisenhower as Allied leader 170
     Handling of men 364
McClure, Robert A. 221
McKeogh, Michael 213

McNarney, Joseph T. 301
     Pride in performance 387
Mercer, Hugh 2
Mickelson, Stanley 82

Middleton, Troy 282
Military attitude toward war
     Eisenhower 332
     Generally 325
     MacArthur 329
     Patton 326

Military character
     Attitude toward war 325
     Courage 367
     Decision making 351
     Definitions of 289, 346
     Desire to command 386
     Generally 289
     Humility 297
     Luck 388
     Political philosophy 320
     Religion 308
     Role of character in military
         career 345

Selflessness 336
West Point 349
Montgomery, Sir Bernard L.
     Appraisal of Eisenhower 170
     Battle of the Bulge 183
     D-Day decision 357
     Eisenhower, relationship with .. 179

N

Napoleon
     Coalitions of enemies 172
     Decorations for troops 267
     Luck 389
     Religious views 310
Naylor, William K. 49
Nimitz, Chester W. 135
Nichols, Edward W. 292
Nicholson, Leonard K. 37

O

Oliver, Lunsford E. 269
O'Neill, James H. 313
Optimism 392

P

Patch, Alexander 286
Patterson, Robert P. 279
Pattern of leadership
     Cadet careers 396
     Character 396
     Concern for others 397
     Decision making 396
     Dedication to career 395
     Delegation of responsibility 398
     Desire for command 396

Generally 395
Sponsorship 399
Patton, George S., Jr.
Aerial bombing support 327
Aide to Stimson 235
Athletics 9
Attire 249
Attitude toward war 326
Battle of the Bulge ... 184, 186, 246
Bonus March 121
Booty, sharing of 265
Cadet years 1
Casualties, prevention of 326
Childhood 1
Combat theory 274
    defensive action 283
    flanks 280
    planning 279
    retreat 282
Communications to troops 243, 399
Courage 372
Decorations for troops 267
Discipline 254
Early career 234
Early duty with Eisenhower 162
Eisenhower, friendship with 239
Eisenhower, relationship with .. 191
Family 2
Gasoline shortage 277, 278
Grandfather 2
Humility 303
Insignia, wearing of by officers .. 257
Luck 389
Montgomery, relationship with
    .... 186, 188
Normandy landing 244
North African campaign .. 242, 254
Personal leadership 259, 286
Pershing's aide 236
Political philosophy 321
Preparation for command . 382, 396
Preparedness for war 335
Profanity 248

Public speeches during war 196, 198
Red Ball Express 277
Religious views 311
    the "dry weather" prayer 313
Service schools 378
Showmanship of 249, 400
Sicily campaign 186
Slapping incident 191
Soldier's appearance 254
Stimson, effect upon career
    .... 194, 235, 238, 240
Study of history 367
Subordinates, relationship with . 269
Tanks, World War I 238
Training of troops 253
Transporting of troops 265
VMI year 3
War with Mexico 236
Welfare of his troops 263
World War I career 238
World War II career 243
Peabody, Hume 15
Pearl Harbor, Marshall's role 74
Pershing, John J.
Allied command 174
Appraisal of MacArthur 121
Best man at Marshall's wedding .. 56
Choice of European Supreme Com-
    mander 340
Marshall, aide-de-camp 48
Mexican War 236
Patton's career 236, 238
Relationship with Peyton March . 79
World War I 238
Peyton, Philip B. 37, 47
Pickens, Arthur 60
Pogue, Forrest 37
Political philosophy
Eisenhower 321
MacArthur 320
Marshall 321
Patton 321
Simpson 322

Spaatz 321
Truscott 322
Preparation for command
　Bradley 385
　Clark 386
　Eisenhower 380
　MacArthur 384
　Marshall 378
　Patton 382
　Service schools 377

Q

Quesada, Pete 375

R

Rainbow Division 109, 118, 368
Ransom, Paul L. 46
Reinhart, Stanley E. 245, 252
Religion
　Definitions of 308
　Eisenhower 317
　MacArthur 309
　Marshall 319
　Patton 311
Roosevelt, President Franklin D.
　Air Force build-up 299
　Choice of European Supreme Commander 337
　Extension of MacArthur's term as Chief of Staff 118
　Marshall, relationship with 89
　North Africa, civil government .. 200
　Pacific strategy 136
Roosevelt, Theodore—Rough
　Riders 235
Root, Elihu 33, 150

S

Schley, Julian L. 30
Schmidt, W. R. 262

Scott, Hugh L. 238
Sears, Robert 7
Selflessness
　Command quality 71
　Eisenhower 336
　Marshall 336
Service career
　Appeal of 295
　Financial reward, lack of 292
Short, Walter C. 75
Sibert, William L. 44
Simpson, William H. 7, 286
　Character 291
　Intuition 363
　Political philosophy 322
Smith, Walter Bedell 214
　Airborne landings in Cherbourg . 352
　D-Day decision 357
　Eisenhower, appraisal of 212
　Secretary to Marshall 82
Spaatz, Carl "Tooey"
　Character 290
　Desire to command 387
　Eisenhower as Allied leader 170
　Eisenhower, relationship with .. 211
　Political philosophy 321
　Service career, appeal of 296
Spellman, Cardinal 150
Sponsorship 399
Stark, Harold R. 203
　Eisenhower, relationship with .. 211
Stimson, Henry L.
　Choice of European Supreme Commander 338
　European invasion decision 206
　Joint Chief, creation of 299
　Marshall, relationship with 84
　Military leaders' political philosophy 324
　Patton's career .. 194, 235, 238, 240
　Personnel selections with Marshall 77
Sutherland, Richard 125

T

Taft, President Howard 33
Tedder, Air Marshal—D-Day deci-
   sion 357
Terry, Thomas A. 7
Truscott, Lucian 97, 285
   Character 290
   Intuition 363
   Political philosophy 322

V

Van Fleet, James A. 14
Virginia Military Institute
   Marshall, George C. 35
      feelings about 41
   Patton 3

W

Ward, Orlando 249

Watson, Leroy H. 263
Wedemeyer, Albert C.
   Character 291
   MacArthur's reported vanity ... 300
West Point
   Effect upon graduates 40
   Eisenhower's cadet career 10
   MacArthur's cadet career 21
   Military character 349
   Patton's cadet career 3
   Training in discipline 259
Whitney, Courtney 125, 331
   MacArthur's courage 371
   MacArthur's reported egotism .. 302
Williams, Robert L. 18
Wood, Leonard 234
Wood, Walter S. 63
Wuest, Jacob W.S. 31

Z

Zhukov, Marshal 251
   Casualties, attitude toward 333
   Prisoners of war 334